fourth edition

Understanding and Sharing

An Introduction to Speech Communication

fourth edition

Understanding and Sharing

An Introduction to Speech Communication

Judy Cornelia Pearson
Ohio University at Athens

Paul Edward Nelson
Ohio University at Athens

wcb
Wm. C. Brown Publishers
Dubuque, Iowa

Book Team

Editor *Stan Stoga*
Designer *David C. Lansdon*
Production Editor *Harry Halloran*
Photo Research Editor *Carol M. Smith*
Permissions Editor *Vicki Krug*
Visuals Processor *Joseph P. O'Connell*

wcb group

Chairman of the Board *Wm. C. Brown*
President and Chief Executive Officer *Mark C. Falb*

wcb

Wm. C. Brown Publishers, College Division

President *G. Franklin Lewis*
Vice President, Editor-in-Chief *George Wm. Bergquist*
Vice President, Director of Production *Beverly Kolz*
National Sales Manager *Bob McLaughlin*
Director of Marketing *Thomas E. Doran*
Marketing Information Systems Manager *Craig S. Marty*
Marketing Manager *Kathy Law Laube*
Executive Editor *John Woods*
Manager of Visuals and Design *Faye M. Schilling*
Manager of Design *Marilyn A. Phelps*
Production Editorial Manager *Colleen A. Yonda*

Cover Collage by Jeanne Marie Regan

The credits section for this book begins on page 411, and is considered an extension of the copyright page.

Library of Congress Catalog Card Number: 87–71281

ISBN 0–697–04377–0

Printed in the United States of America by Wm. C. Brown Publishers 2460 Kerper Boulevard, Dubuque, IA 52001

10   9   8   7   6   5   4   3   2   1

Dedicated to our parents:
Sophia and J. D.
Ferne and H. B.

brief contents

part 3

Public Communication   223

contents

part 2

Interpersonal Communication 117

p a r t   3

Public Communication   223

chapter activities

p r e f a c e

The fourth edition of *Understanding and Sharing* reflects not only our experiences as instructors but also the use that we and our colleagues and students have made of the text since it was published in the first three editions. A textbook must fit the goals of the course, the background and experience of the teacher, and the abilities of the students. *Understanding and Sharing* is an appropriate text for a beginning course in speech communication that emphasizes both interpersonal communication and public speaking.

The Fourth Edition

This edition will be familiar to previous users of the text. The book is not a drastic revision. The theme, approach, and organization of the third edition remain basically the same as the first two editions. Nonetheless some changes were necessary to make the book more useful and appropriate. Chapter 1 has been reworked to function as a more effective introduction to the study of communication, and some of the contemporary settings in which communication occurs, such as the family, the organization, and the health setting have been added. Chapter 2 in the third edition, which considered both perception and the role of self in communication, has been split into two chapters in this edition. Chapter 2 considers perception and chapter 3 focuses on self-awareness and self-concept. Listening is now considered in chapter 4. In the area of interpersonal communication, this edition presents a new chapter (8) which focuses on communication with friends and family. Additional information has been added on leadership in chapter 11. The user will also notice a careful update of research, content, and illustrations throughout the text.

Understanding and Sharing takes a skills approach to help students learn effective communication behavior in interpersonal and public situations. The book attempts to combine speech heritage with the results of recent experimental studies, pedagogy, and classroom experience. *Understanding and Sharing* can help a student discover the kinds of questions to ask in an interview, the characteristics of the leader in a small group, and the functions of an introduction, body, and conclusion in a public speech. However, it is the instructor who can help students apply on a practical level the skills that are described here. The book, the instructor, and the students become partners in a creative transaction that results in learning communication skills through practical application.

Audience

Understanding and Sharing is for both the experienced instructor, who can richly supplement any textbook with personal knowledge, and the graduate teaching assistant, who is in the classroom for the first time.

It is intended for students in their first speech course at a community college, technical school, four-year liberal arts college, or university; and it was designed to appeal to their interests and written on their own vocabulary level. We have tried to make speech communication concepts clear by defining them when they are introduced, by listing key terms at the beginning of each chapter, and by assembling concepts and terms alphabetically in the glossary.

Organization

Understanding and Sharing is divided into three major parts, each of which focuses on communication skills.

Part 1, "Elements of the Communication Process," begins with a chapter on the nature of communication, in which communication is defined and related to the self. Perception is related to communication in chapter 2. Chapter 3 focuses on self-awareness and self-concept. The importance of listening is considered in chapter 4. Chapters 5 and 6 deal with nonverbal and verbal codes, respectively.

Part 2, "Interpersonal Communication," opens with a chapter on interpersonal relationships and considers self-disclosure and conflict. Communication with friends and family are emphasized in chapter 8. Chapter 9 provides specific information on the practical, applied area of interviewing and chapter 10 includes the same kind of information about the small group setting. Chapter 11 presents information on leadership in the small group.

Part 3 of the text focuses on "Public Communication." This section begins with a consideration of topic selection and audience analysis in chapter 12. Speaker credibility is examined in chapter 13. Chapter 14 provides new information on finding information for the public speech. Organizing the public speech is the topic of chapter 15. Delivery and visual aids are discussed in chapter 16. The last two chapters of the text are devoted to practical applications that examine in detail the two most common types of speeches in the basic course: the informative speech and the persuasive speech.

All of the chapters emphasize application of speech concepts; all of them concentrate on skills that can be immediately employed in interpersonal and public communication.

Special Features

Each chapter begins with objectives that state specifically what students should be able to do when they have completed the chapter. Educational research indicates that students learn better if they know specifically what is expected of them. The chapter is previewed in the introduction, and throughout the chapter application exercises are strategically placed so students can test ideas for themselves immediately after learning about them. Contemporary cartoons, photos, and line drawings illustrate concepts effectively for those students who learn best through visual means. Chapter 9 on the interview, chapters 10 and 11 on small groups and leadership, chapter 17 on the informative speech, and chapter 18 on the persuasive speech are especially helpful to students in implementing their knowledge through practical applications. Subject matter is summarized at the end of each chapter.

Instructor's Resource Manual

Understanding and Sharing and the Instructor's Resource Manual that accompanies it are our answer to the text selection problems that we have encountered over the years. Because many textbooks were too theoretical for our pragmatic students, we wrote a skills-oriented book with ideas for everyday application. Because some books were good for public speaking and others were good in interpersonal communication but few were good in both areas, we tried to write an effective book in both areas of speech communication. Because we found the development of useful classroom activities to be lacking, we have provided a resource manual filled with them. Finally, because we found exam questions difficult to develop and resource materials time consuming to find, the Instructor's Resource Manual provides them for every chapter.

Each chapter of the Instructor's Resource Manual includes true–false, multiple-choice, and essay questions which are available on TestPak. TestPak is a free, computerized testing program available to adopters of *Understanding and Sharing,* which offers you convenience and efficiency in composing your multiple-choice and true–false tests.

Beginning instructors will find the manual's quarter and semester schedules for a course based on *Understanding and Sharing* especially helpful. All instructors will be helped by the manual's resource material and activities, from which instructors can select those items that best fit their own teaching style and the objectives of their course. These classroom-tested exercises include explanations of what usually occurs when students do the exercises, what the students are to learn, and what implications of the exercise the instructor should emphasize.

The Authors

Because the textbook is an impersonal entity—the reader does not see the writer and, even worse, the writer cannot see the reader—we self-disclose to reduce the distance between us and the persons who read *Understanding and Sharing:*

Judy Cornelia Pearson is first and foremost a teacher. She earned her doctorate at Indiana University and served as basic course director at Bradley University, Indiana University–Purdue University at Fort Wayne, Iowa State University, and at Ohio University. She is currently a Professor of Interpersonal Communication at Ohio University.

Paul Edward Nelson earned his Ph.D. at the University of Minnesota and was the basic course director at the University of Missouri, chair of the Speech Department at Iowa State University, and is currently the Dean of the College of Communication at Ohio University.

We have taught speech fundamentals most of our professional lives. More importantly, fundamentals is what we like best. We both were honored to win the Central States Speech Association's Outstanding Young Teacher Award, and both of us attribute much of our abiding interest in fundamentals to the enthusiastic support of our colleagues in the Midwest Basic Speech Director's Conference.

Jeff Ringer is particularly well qualified as coauthor of the Instructor's Resource Manual because he is a sensitive and energetic teacher who knows firsthand the needs of a beginning teacher. He received his Ph.D. at Ohio University under the directorship of Judy Pearson, and he currently teaches at St. Cloud State University. Jeff updated the materials in the Instructor's Resource Manual for the fourth edition of *Understanding and Sharing*.

Acknowledgments

Understanding and Sharing is a cumulative effort by publishers, editors, critic-evaluators, students, fellow teachers, and the authors. We have been fortunate to have supportive colleagues and administrators who support research and writing activities. We have also supported each other both personally and professionally—because we are husband and wife, as well as professional colleagues.

Our graduate professors at Indiana University and the University of Minnesota, our colleagues at many colleges and universities who share our affection for speech fundamentals, and our six children, who can blame us in later years for ignoring them to write a book, deserve our special thanks. The people at Wm. C. Brown Publishers have earned our grateful appreciation. We are also grateful for the helpful suggestions from college and university faculty members who evaluated the previous editions of *Understanding and Sharing:* Martin H. Brodey, Montgomery College; Jerry D. Feezel, Kent State University; Judith Friedman, Bergen Community College; Marilyn Kelly, McLennan Community College; Edward J. Harris, Jr., Suffolk University; Harry Hazel, Gonzaga University; Larry D. Miller, Indiana University, Bloomington; Michael B. Minchew, Mississippi University for Women; David E. Mrizek, San Antonio College; William J. Seiler, University of Nebraska, Lincoln; Curt Siemers, Winona State University; Chris Gwaltney Pearson, Vincennes University; John J. Gibbons, DeVry Institute of Technology; Richard D. Britton, Suffolk County Community College; William C. Shrier, Illinois Central College; Sandra Manheimer, Bradley University; Dennis R. Smith, San Francisco State University; William L. Robinson, Purdue University Calumet; Douglas M. Trank, The University of Iowa; William A. Hahn Jr., Illinois Central College; Ann E. Busse, Northern Illinois University; Walt Terris, San Francisco State University; Raymond L. Lambert, Edison Community College; and Judith Willner, Coppin State College. We would also like to thank those who evaluated the fourth edition at several stages of development: Arthur Grachek, St. Cloud State University; Jerry Feezel, Kent State University; Violet Asmuth, Edison Community College; David Mrizek, San Antonio College; Ruth Aurelius, Des Moines Area Community College; Lars Hafner, St. Petersburg Junior College; Edward Lee Lamoureaux, Bradley University; Nancy Moore, Green River Community College; Rudolph Busby, San Francisco State University; Richard Salamon, St. Louis Community College at Forest Park; Kathy Spanton, Broward Community College North; Armeda Reitzel, Humboldt State University; Judith Willner, Coppin State College; and Chris Pearson, Vincennes University.

Judy C. Pearson
Paul E. Nelson

fourth edition

Understanding and Sharing

An Introduction to Speech Communication

part 1

Elements of the Communication Process

Communication is the process of understanding and sharing meaning. In this first section of the text, the elements of the communication process are considered. Among the topics discussed are perception, self-concept, listening, nonverbal codes, and verbal codes.

In chapter 1, "The Nature of Communication," we look at a definition of communication, and the contexts and settings in which communication occurs. Chapter 2, "Perception: The Process of Understanding," explains the role of perception in the communication process, why differences occur in perception, and the activities involved in perception. Chapter 3, "Self-Awareness and Self-Concept: Understanding Yourself," focuses on the importance of self-awareness and self-concept in communication. In chapter 4, "Listening: Understanding Another," we turn our focus to the other person in communication. Listening is defined and discussed. Chapter 5, "Nonverbal Codes: Sharing with Others," discusses various nonverbal codes, such as bodily movement and facial expression, space, touching, vocal cues, and clothing and other artifacts. In chapter 6, "Verbal Codes: Sharing with Others," we examine how words create a major obstacle to communication and how verbal skills can be improved.

The Nature of Communication

S *peech is civilization itself. The word,*
even the most contradictory word,
preserves contact—it is silence which
isolates.

Thomas Mann

E *ffective loving calls for knowledge of the*
object. . . . How can I love a person
whom I do not know? How can the other
person love me if he [she] does not know me?

Sidney M. Jourard

A *mericans report that their greatest fear*
is the fear of speaking in front of a
group.

Bruskin Report

Objectives

1. Define communication and the relationship between understanding and sharing.
2. Explain the role of self and others in communication.
3. Identify the components involved in the communication process and the relationships among those components.
4. Differentiate among these contexts: intrapersonal, interpersonal, and public communication.
5. Distinguish among these settings: family communication, organizational communication, and health communication.

Key Terms

communication	decoding
process	noise
understanding	intrapersonal
sharing	communication
meaning	interpersonal
message	communication
thought	dyadic
action	communication
interaction	small group
transactional view	communication
source	public
receiver	communication
channel	family
feedback	communication
code	organizational
verbal codes	communication
nonverbal codes	health
encoding	communication

Communication pervades all aspects of our lives. We spend more time in verbal communication than in any other single activity.[1] Many of us recognize the increasing importance of communication skills in business and industry as well as in personal relationships.[2] A growing number of people seem to realize they do not communicate as well as they could. As one of the preceding quotations suggests, many Americans report they fear public speaking. Finally, we appear to believe we can improve our communication skills. The large number of courses that deal with speech communication, the best-selling self-help books, and the popularity of information on communication all confirm the notion that communication skills can be taught.

This text will help you to improve your ability to communicate with other people. You will learn to understand others and to be understood by them. You will learn to establish shared meanings with others. Your social needs and your task-related needs—to get a job, to solve a problem, or to persuade others—will be more easily accomplished as you improve your ability to communicate with others. As you read this text and as you participate in the suggested activities and exercises, your confidence as a communicator will increase, and you will become more competent in achieving your personal and professional goals.

In this chapter we will introduce you to the topic of the text. In order to understand the nature of communication, you will be provided with a definition and an explanation of communication. The components of communication will be identified. The contexts of communication will be explained and some of the settings of communication will be named. We will begin with a definition and an explanation of communication.

A Definition of Communication

Communication: The Process of Understanding and Sharing Meaning

The word *communication* is used in a variety of ways. Before we use the term any further, we should establish a common understanding of its definition. *Communicate* comes from the Latin *communicare,* which means "to make common." This original definition of the word is consistent with the definition of communication used in this text.

In this text, **communication** is defined as the process of understanding and sharing meaning. Communication is considered a **process** because it is an activity, exchange, or set of behaviors—not an unchanging, static product. Communication is not an object we can hold in our hand—it is an activity in which we participate. David Berlo, a well-known communication scholar, probably provides the clearest statement about communication as a process. Berlo writes:

> If we accept the concept of process, we view events and relationships as dynamic, ongoing, ever-changing, continuous. When we label something as a process, we also mean that it does not have a beginning, an end, a fixed sequence of events. It is not static, at rest. It is moving. The ingredients within a process interact; each affects all of the others.[3]

Communication is an activity in which we participate.

How does the notion of process translate into examples of communication? When we talk about the communication that occurs when someone gives a speech, we are considering the speaker's words, gestures, movement, clothing, volume, tone, enunciation, and pitch; the audience's response to the speech; the environment in which the speech occurs; and all other factors that affect the event. A speech is not simply the written transcript, or text, of the speech. Similarly, the communication that occurs between two individuals is not adequately represented by a tape recording of the words the two communicators used. The communication between them includes any previous relationship that exists between them; their feelings, motivations, and intents; the non-verbal elements of the exchange, such as how closely they sit, the amount of eye contact, the gestures employed, and the facial expressions; the purpose of the conversation; and how these variables affect each other.

The process nature of communication is especially relevant in our culture today. Our society has grown in scope and size, relationships have increased in complexity in our culture, and changes occur with even greater rapidity than in the past. The media affect our view of reality more today than they did ten or twenty years ago; family structures are being altered so that the traditional "nuclear" family is no longer the norm; there are more older people in the 1980s than in the 1960s or 1970s; individuals in our culture are increasingly mobile and frequently move across the country for job advancement; and the labor force evidences unemployment and misemployment—people with little training or interest in their current jobs.

How do these changes affect the communication process? The complexity of our relationships requires us to be more flexible. We may play several roles each day—student, parent, friend, and co-worker, for example. Others must play several roles, too, and we must be responsive or sensitive to their behavior. Changes in the family structure do not allow us to draw obvious conclusions about other people. For instance, a woman who is a mother may have "biological children," "adopted children," or "stepchildren." She may have a husband who lives in the family home, she may be separated or divorced, or she may never have been married. Our increased mobility requires us to initiate relationships with others more quickly and to terminate them more frequently. Obviously, all of the changes in our society affect our communicative behavior.

Communication requires **understanding.** People involved in communication must understand what they are saying and hearing. All of us have been in situations in which we could repeat another person's message but could not understand it. For instance, you may have taken a course in which you studied a technical or specialized vocabulary. You may have found yourself writing or even saying words you did not fully understand. Your ability to parrot a sound is not sufficient evidence that you understand the meaning of what you are saying. Communication does not occur unless understanding exists, no matter how rudimentary it is.

Understanding, in a basic sense, suggests that we have common meanings for words, phrases, or nonverbal symbols. Understanding, in a larger sense, means that we are able to grasp a person's meaning. The importance of this kind of understanding was emphasized by Carl Rogers in his book *On Becoming a Person* when he wrote, "I have found it of enormous value when I can *permit* myself to understand another person."[4] We will find that, to the extent that we begin to understand the verbal and nonverbal communication that others use, we will become more competent in understanding other people.

In addition to understanding, communication involves **sharing.** Consider the popular use of the word *sharing.* We share a meal, we share an event, we share a sunset. Sharing is a gift that people exchange. We can also share with ourselves—when we allow ourselves time to relax and daydream, time to consider who we really are, and what our goals truly are. We share with others when we talk to them alone or in larger groups. Regardless of the context, communication involves sharing.

The sharing that occurs in communication is not necessarily a totally positive experience. We must remember that it can also be neutral and even negative. For example, when you softly touch someone you love, you share an understanding of the meaning of the caress, and the shared message is most likely positive. When you offer directions to a stranger, the two of you must share an understanding of the meaning of such words as "third stop sign," "large church," "left," and "right," but the shared message is neutral. Finally, when you are told that your job has been eliminated and that your services are no longer needed, you and your employer may share a common understanding of the situation, but the shared understanding is probably a negative experience for you.

Human communication involves
understanding and sharing among people.

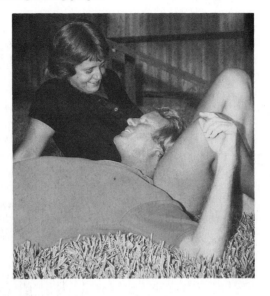

In the process of communication, the object of our understanding and sharing is **meaning.** Earlier definitions of communication have identified *messages* or *thoughts* as the objects of sharing. Neither of these terms is as accurate as *meaning,* however. The term **message** is not sufficient because it does not imply any level of understanding. If you repeat a Portuguese phrase to a student from Brazil, this only shows that you have heard the phrase and can repeat it. No communication has occurred, even though you have shared a particular message. **Thought** is also a troublesome term. It is very difficult to define thoughts and even more difficult to determine when our thoughts are the same as another person's. The term *meaning* refers to that which is felt to be the significance of something and is a more accurate and useful descriptor of the object of communication.

The examples of sharing that we presented in a preceding paragraph can also illustrate the difference among messages, thoughts, and meaning. When we reach out to touch a loved one, we may be thinking about a past experience that was particularly touching or made us feel especially close to that person, and our message may be that we want to repeat that experience; however, the meaning of the nonverbal communication exchange arises from the definition that the two people attach to it. When someone asks for directions to a large classroom building, we might think about a class we had in the building last term and send a message about our negative experience, but the meaning is the shared understanding of how to proceed to the building from our current location. Thoughts about our employer firing us may be complicated, even if the message on the "pink slip" is euphemistic and brief; but the meaning of the event will have long-range implications.

Figure 1.1
Barnlund's "six people" involved in every two-person communication.

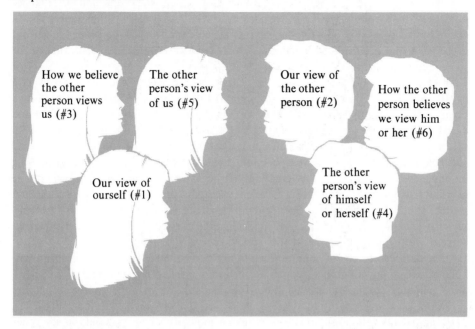

Communication Within, Between, and Among People

The term *communication* may be used broadly to refer to the understanding and sharing that occur among animals other than humans.[5] In this text, we limit our discussion to human communication, the communication that occurs within, between, and among human people. As such, we observe that communication involves the self and others.

Communication Begins with the Self

Communication begins with the self. As Carl Rogers wrote, "Every individual exists in a continually changing world of experience of which he [or she] is the center."[6] All of our communication is viewed from the perspective of self. Chapter 2 discusses the role of perception in communication and the difficulties that occur because each of us has separate perceptions of reality. Chapter 3 considers the central role of self in communication and stresses the importance of self-awareness and self-concept in the communication process. Sharing ourselves with others in the interpersonal and public communication settings is discussed in chapters 7, 8, and 13.

Dean Barnlund, a communication scholar, introduced the notion that communication is viewed from one's own perspective in his discussion of the "six persons" involved in every two-person communication situation (figure 1.1).[7] These six persons emerge from first, the way in which you view yourself; second, the way in which you view the other person; third, how you believe the other person views you; fourth, how the other person views himself or herself; fifth, how the other person views you; and sixth, how the other person believes you view him or her. Barnlund believes that we "construct" ourselves, as well as other persons, through the relationships that we have, wish to have, or perceive ourselves as having. He encourages us to consider the various perspectives that are involved in communication and to recognize the centrality of the self in communication.

An example may clarify Barnlund's "six people." Suppose you see yourself as a slightly overweight, intelligent college junior (1). You perceive your roommate as a very attractive, slightly "spacey" college sophomore (2). She views you as an older and wiser friend (5), and sees herself as very bright but in need of a good diet (4). Nonetheless, you treat her as though she has no weight problem, while you do; and you tend to discount her opinions because you think that she doesn't have much insight. As a consequence, she seldom talks to you about her negative feelings about her body image and rarely shares her ideas (6). In addition, she does not view you as overweight, but she does think that you are experienced and bright. Therefore, you tend to "mother" her with your advice and guidance, and you talk a great deal about your "weight problem" to try to convince her of the seriousness of your feelings (3).

All of our perceptions of communication are tied to ourselves. In our descriptions, explanations, and evaluations of communication, we reflect a great deal of ourselves. As participants in communication, we are limited by our own view of the situation. For example, a woman might describe a heated conversation with her spouse as, "Nothing at all. He made a mountain out of a molehill." The husband, on the other hand, might conclude that, "She never really has understood me."

Communication Involves Other People

Even when we "talk to ourselves," communication involves other people. We view communication from our own perspective and with our unique perceptual processes; however, the self we know is largely learned from others. George Herbert Mead explains that self originates in communication. The child, through verbal and nonverbal symbols, learns to accept roles in response to the expectations of others.[8] We establish our self-image, the sort of person we believe we are, by the ways in which other people categorize us. The positive, negative, and neutral messages that others offer us enable us to determine who we are. Our self-definition, then, arises through our interactions with others.

Communication also involves others in the sense that the effective communicator considers the other person's needs and expectations as he or she selects appropriate messages to share. The effective communicator understands that a large number of messages can be shared at any time, but that sensitivity and responsiveness to the other communicator are essential. Thus, we observe that communication begins with the self, as defined largely by others, and involves others, as defined largely by the self.

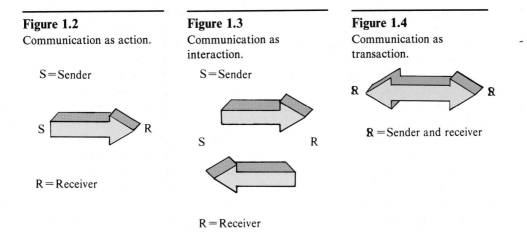

Figure 1.2
Communication as action.

S = Sender

S [ ] R

R = Receiver

Figure 1.3
Communication as interaction.

S = Sender

S   R

R = Receiver

Figure 1.4
Communication as transaction.

R   R

R = Sender and receiver

Communication Is Transactional

In the past, people believed that communication could be viewed as **action,** that is, one person sends a message and another person receives it. This view is depicted in figure 1.2. This view can be compared to the situation in which one person holds a basketball and throws it to another. The second person does not return the ball, she only catches it or fumbles it.

A second view evolved. Communication is viewed as **interaction:** one person sends a message to a second person who receives it and, in turn, responds with another message. The communicators take turns sending and receiving messages. This point of view is pictured in figure 1.3. To continue with our basketball analogy, this perspective would be similar to a game of catch. Each person catches (or drops) the ball and each person throws the ball. However, the ball cannot be thrown until it is caught.

The **transactional view** of communication may have originated with Oliver Wendell Holmes who explained problems in communication by considering the role of differing perceptions, constructs, and ideas that two people might have regarding the people involved in communication.[9] Although this view of communication may have germinated with Holmes in the mid-nineteenth century, it has been only recently discussed by communication scholars. John Stewart suggests that transactional communication may be called relationship communication, because meanings are largely born out of the perceptions that we create or hold about others while we are actively engaged in communicating with them.[10] As a result, we construct and display our selves, as well as our social world, through communication transactions. We become who we are through our communication with others.

Viewing communication as a transaction means we believe that communicators simultaneously send and receive messages (fig. 1.4). Rather than identifying people as senders or receivers, we suggest people serve as senders and receivers of messages at the same time. Thus, speaking and listening are not separate activities, nor do they occur one at a time. According to the transactional view, people are continually sending and receiving messages. They cannot avoid communication. This most recent view of communication is accepted in this text. We view communication as a confusing ball-game in which a person catches and throws an unlimited number of balls at any time, in any direction, to any other person. An individual's throwing a ball is not dependent upon his ability to catch one first. He or she does not always "take turns" in this game. The game has some rules and some predictability, but from time to time, balls fly through the air without preplanning or preparation.

In some settings, one person may serve as the primary transmitter of messages while another person or persons serve primarily as receivers of messages. For example, in public speaking, we can identify a speaker and an audience of listeners. In interpersonal communication, such a distinction frequently cannot be made. In those situations in which one person is perceived as the initiator of messages, or as the speaker, we refer to the listeners' transmission of verbal and nonverbal messages as feedback, which will be defined more fully later in this chapter.

Components of Communication

We have defined communication as the process of understanding and sharing meaning. We now examine some of the components that are integral to the process, including people, messages, channels, feedback, codes, encoding and decoding, and noise.

People

People are involved in the human communication process in two ways. They serve as the *sources* and the *receivers* of messages. The **source** is the component that initiates a message. The **receiver** is the component that absorbs or takes in the message. Individuals do not perform in these two roles independently. Instead, they are the source and the receiver of messages simultaneously and continually.

As you know, people are not like programmed computers or machines. They do not respond in a uniform way to all messages nor do they provide the same messages in exactly the same way. Individual characteristics of people, including their race, gender, age, culture, values, and attitudes affect both their sending and receiving qualities. Intercultural communication and gender and communication have both become increasingly important topics during the past three decades. Throughout this text you will find examples that illustrate that an individual's membership in a culture or subculture affects his or her communication behavior.

Message

The **message** is the verbal and nonverbal form of the idea, thought, or feeling that one person (the source) wishes to communicate to another person or group of people (the receivers). It is the content of the interaction. The message includes the words and phrases that we use to communicate our ideas as well as our facial expressions, bodily movements, gestures, touch, tone of voice, and other nonverbal codes. The message may be relatively brief and easy to understand, or it may be long and complex. Some messages are intentional, while others are accidental.

Channel

The **channel** provides the mode by which a message moves from the source of the message to the receiver of the message. Both light waves and sound waves are major channels when we interact with another person and we can see and hear him or her. Similarly, if we are watching television or a movie, we rely on both light waves and sound waves. Some forms of communication require only one channel. For instance, we rely on sound waves alone when we listen to the radio or are plugged into an "audio-only" conference call. We rely exclusively on light waves when we read a book or when we read the print on a computer monitor.

Feedback

In some settings, one person may serve as the primary source of messages while another person or persons serve primarily as receivers of messages. In those situations in which one person is perceived as the source of messages, or as the speaker, we refer to the listeners' transmission of verbal and nonverbal messages as feedback. **Feedback** is the receivers' verbal and nonverbal responses to the source's messages. The responses must be received and understood by the source. Feedback provides important information to the source concerning the need to alter, embellish, correct, or reinforce the messages that he or she is sending. The role of feedback is discussed in more detail in chapter 4.

Codes

People have ideas or thoughts they wish to express, and they do so in the form of messages. How do our thoughts become messages? We use codes to share our ideas with others. We typically use the word *code* to describe the secret language that children use or to refer to specialized, stylized, or shortened languages, such as Morse code. For our purposes, however, a **code** is any systematic arrangement or comprehensive collection of symbols, letters, or words that has an arbitrary meaning and is used for communication.

Two major types of codes are used in communication: verbal codes and nonverbal codes. **Verbal codes** consist of words and their grammatical arrangement. It is easier to think of the German or French language as a code than it is to realize that our own language is a code. All languages are codes. The English symbols, letters, and words we use are arbitrary. We have no more reason to call a heavy outer garment by the word *overcoat* than a German does to call it *der mantel*. Nature does not provide a rationale for any particular language. Chapter 6 discusses the importance and role of verbal codes in communication.

Nonverbal codes consist of all symbols that are not words, including our bodily movements, our use of space and time, our clothing and other adornments, and sounds other than words. Nonverbal codes should not be confused with nonoral codes. All nonoral codes—such as bodily movement—are nonverbal codes, but nonverbal codes also include oral codes, such as pitch, duration, and rate of speech, as well as sounds like *eh* and *ah*. Nonverbal codes refer to *all* codes that do not consist of words. Chapter 5 discusses the nature and role of nonverbal codes in communication.

Encoding and Decoding

If communication involves the use of codes, the process of communicating can be viewed as one of encoding and decoding. **Encoding** is defined as the act of putting an idea or thought into a code. **Decoding** is assigning meaning to that idea or thought. For example, suppose you are interested in owning a St. Bernard, and you are trying to describe this breed of dog to a relative who wants to help you find such an animal. In your own mind, you visualize a friend's St. Bernard who lived in your neighborhood when you were a child. You picture the dog's frisky gallop, his silky hair, his mischievous ways, and his big brown eyes. When you put your vision into words, you might say that a St. Bernard is a large brown and white dog with long hair. You encode your memories and perceptions of a particular dog into words that describe the breed. When your relative hears this definition, she decodes the words and creates a picture of her own. Her own experience with smaller dogs affects her decoding. The picture that she gains from your definition is of a German shepherd. As we can see, misunderstanding often occurs because of the limitations of our language and the inadequacy of our descriptions. Nonetheless, encoding and decoding are essential in sharing our thoughts, ideas, and feelings with other people.

Noise

Any factor that intervenes between encoding and decoding is known as **noise**. Noise is generally thought of as static—stimuli that are external to the person or persons engaged in communication. But it also includes interference that is internal to one or both of the communicators. External noise includes loud banging, confusing lights, strong and unpleasant odors, and so forth. Internal noise may result from worries, daydreams, or a negative reaction to a particular word.

Contexts of Communication

Communication does not occur in a vacuum. Communication occurs in a *context,* a set of circumstances or a situation. The importance of the context may alter such that the context is less obtrusive in some situations and of greater importance in other situations. The number of people involved in communication affects the kind of communication that occurs. We may communicate with ourselves, with another person, or with a large number of others. The differences between these situations affect our choices of the verbal and nonverbal codes we will most appropriately use.

This text is organized around the contexts of communication. These contexts are defined in terms of our definition of communication as the process of understanding and sharing meaning. Let us preview the contexts covered in the text. Each is examined in more detail in upcoming chapters.

Intrapersonal Communication

Intrapersonal communication is the process of understanding and sharing meaning within the self. Why would we need to communicate with ourselves? Imagine that you have a close friend with whom you agree on nearly everything. You feel the same way about premarital sex, about attending church or synagogue, about the relationship between women and men in our culture, about studying for classes, and about interesting potential careers. However, one day you learn that your friend is dating someone whom you abhor. This individual, in your opinion, is not attractive, not bright, not interesting, and has a limited future. When you begin to share your feelings with your friend, your friend becomes angry with you and replies it is just one more example of your narrow-mindedness. You probably feel a certain amount of psychological discomfort. What is likely to occur? You could simply dismiss your friend's remark and the new relationship as irrelevant and act as though nothing has happened to alter your friendship. You could immediately dismiss your friend from any future interactions with you. You could decide you were wrong to prejudge your friend's new relationship and that she or he is right in pointing it out to you. None of these outcomes is immediately likely, however. Instead, you are more apt to consider these alternatives—and others—as you try to understand what has occurred. In a sense, you are examining alternative explanations for what has happened and attempting to gain some consistency or coherence among the events and beliefs that you have held. You are engaged in communication within yourself.

Intrapersonal communication occurs, as this example suggests, when we evaluate or examine the interaction that occurs between ourselves and others. Intrapersonal communication is not limited to such times, however. This form of communication occurs prior to, and during, other forms of communication as well.

Intrapersonal communication is far more complex than it may appear. Involved in intrapersonal communication is how our central nervous system operates, the functioning of the left and right hemispheres of our brains, our facility to think, and other physiological properties. One communication expert states that intrapersonal communication involves the gathering, storing, and retrieving of information, and is surrounded by three components: (1) the cognitive component, which includes meanings and language; (2) the affective component, which contains attitudes and self-concept; and (3) the operational component, which includes listening and speaking.[11]

Intrapersonal communication is not restricted to "talking to ourselves"; it also includes such activities as internal problem solving, resolution of internal conflict, planning for the future, emotional catharsis, evaluations of ourselves and others, and the relationships between ourselves and others. Intrapersonal communication involves only the self, and it must be clearly understood by the self because it constitutes the basis for all other communication.

Intrapersonal communication is the process
of understanding and sharing meaning
within the self.

We are engaged in intrapersonal communication almost continually. We might become more easily absorbed in "talking to ourselves" when we are alone—walking to class, driving to work, taking a shower—but most of us are involved in this form of communication in the most crowded circumstances as well—during a lecture, at a party, or when visiting friends. Think about the last time you looked at yourself in a mirror. What were your thoughts? Intrapersonal communication is almost continuous, and yet we seldom focus on our communication with ourselves.

Interpersonal Communication

Interpersonal communication is the process of understanding and sharing meaning between ourselves and at least one other person when relatively mutual opportunities for speaking and listening occur. Interpersonal, like intrapersonal, communication occurs for a variety of reasons: to solve problems, to resolve conflicts, to share information, to improve our perception of ourselves, or to fulfill such social needs as the need to belong or to be loved. Through our interpersonal communication, we are able to establish relationships with others that include friendships and romantic relationships. In chapters 7 and 8 interpersonal relationships and our relationships with friends and family members will be considered.

The Case of Sharon Black

Sharon Black, a sophomore at an extension university, worked thirty hours a week at a local department store—a very busy schedule. Sharon wanted to spend more time with her coworkers, but her college work interfered. The other workers usually ate lunch together, but Sharon had a class that started at 12:30 P.M. four days a week. She usually couldn't attend parties because she had homework to do.

Sharon became increasingly quiet at work and felt more alienated as time passed. Her coworkers began to suspect that "the college girl" was avoiding them because she felt superior. They began to plan activities that excluded Sharon.

Sharon's work was exemplary, and she became eligible for promotion to supervisor. Her boss told her that a lot depended on whether the other workers would accept her leadership and cooperate with her. But Sharon's coworkers were resentful of the possible promotion of a person who had so little experience at the store. They also felt that she was being "pushed ahead" because she was a college student. At lunch that day, they decided that Sharon would not get the promotion if they had anything to say about it. One of the women offered to tell the boss how they felt.

Sharon was called into the office two days later. Her boss explained that she wasn't going to be promoted because she didn't seem to be getting along well with the others, and it did not look as if they would cooperate with her. Sharon broke into tears and ran from the office.

1. What made Sharon's coworkers feel that Sharon thought she was superior to them?
2. Explain the intrapersonal communication that may have occurred for Sharon. What kinds of internal conflicts was she likely to have been experiencing?
3. Why did the misunderstanding between Sharon and the others grow to this level? Why did they not discuss their differences?
4. Write a dialogue in which Sharon and her coworkers discuss their perceptions.
5. Is Sharon's situation realistic? Identify a similar experience in which you had a misunderstanding with another person or with other people. How did you resolve it?
6. What conclusions can you draw about communication problems with others?

Dyadic communication, a subset of interpersonal communication, simply refers to two-person communication and includes interviews with an employer or teacher; talks with a parent, spouse, or child; and interactions among strangers, acquaintances, and friends. **Small group communication,** another subset of interpersonal communication, refers to communication involving three or more people. Small group communication occurs in social organizations, such as clubs, civic groups, and church groups, and in business settings for the purpose of problem solving or decision making.

The addition of another person complicates communication greatly. Although each of us holds conflicting perceptions, beliefs, values, and attitudes (indeed, a great deal of our intrapersonal communication concerns these conflicts), the differences between two people are generally far greater than those within an individual. In addition, we all have different ways of expressing what we feel. Consequently, the possibility of successful communication decreases.

Next to intrapersonal communication, interpersonal communication is generally considered the most influential form of communication and the most satisfying to the individuals involved in it. Interpersonal communication typically occurs in an informal setting and involves face-to-face verbal and nonverbal exchanges and a sharing of the roles of source (speaker) and receiver (listener).

Public Communication

Public communication is the process of understanding and sharing meaning with a number of other people when one person is generally identified as the source, or speaker, and others are recognized as receivers, or listeners. The speaker adapts his or her message to the audience in an attempt to gain maximum understanding. Sometimes, virtually everyone in the audience understands the speaker's message; at other times, many people fail to understand the speaker. A variety of factors contribute to the level of understanding that the speaker achieves. We discuss these factors in part 3 of this text.

Public communication, or public speaking, is recognized by its formality, structure, and planning. We are frequently the listeners in public communication: in lecture classes, at convocations, and in church. Sometimes, we are speakers: when we speak before a group, when we try to convince other voters of the merits of a particular candidate for office, or when we introduce a guest speaker to a large audience. Public communication most often has the purpose of informing or persuading, but it can also have the intent of entertaining, introducing, announcing, welcoming, or paying tribute. We will consider public communication in chapters 12 through 18.

The various contexts—intrapersonal, interpersonal, and public—in which communication can occur can be categorized on the basis of the number of people involved, the degree of formality or intimacy, the opportunities for feedback, the need for prestructuring messages, and the degree of stability of the roles of speaker and listener. Table 1.1 summarizes the differences among the communication contexts considered in this text. Table 1.1 indicates that, as more and more people are added to the communicative context, the degree of formality increases, the degree of intimacy decreases, the opportunities for feedback decrease, the need for prestructuring messages increases, and the roles of speaker and listener become increasingly stable.

This text proceeds from the most basic context in which communication occurs—intrapersonal communication—moves to interpersonal communication, and concludes with public communication. In each context, we examine the roles of self and others and how individuals attempt to establish understanding and sharing.

Settings of Communication

Communication occurs in various contexts, as we observed in the last section. The setting, or place, in which communication occurs is another important consideration. Settings that are widely studied today include the family, the organization, and the

Table 1.1 Differences in Communication Contexts.

	Intrapersonal Communication	Interpersonal Communication		Public Communication
		Dyadic Communication	Small Group Communication	
The number of people involved	One	Two	Usually three to ten; may be more	Usually more than ten
The degree of formality or intimacy	Most intimate	Generally intimate; interview would be formal	Intimate or formal	Generally formal
The opportunities for feedback	Complete feedback	A great deal of feedback	Less than in intrapersonal communication, but more than in public communication	Less than in small group communication, but more than in mass communication
The need for prestructuring messages	None	Some	Some	A great deal
The degree of stability of the roles of speaker and listener	The individual serves as both speaker and listener	Speaker and listener alternate; unstable	Speakers and listeners alternate; unstable	Highly stable; one speaker with many listeners

health setting. Because of the importance of these three settings, we will pay special attention to them in this chapter and throughout the book research results and examples are provided.

Family Communication

Communication occurs within families, as you well know. Within recent times, we have begun to study this phenomenon. Even as we have studied communication within the family, the nature of the family has changed. Pearson defines a family as "an organized, relational transactional group, usually occupying a common living space over an extended time period, and possessing a confluence of interpersonal images which evolve through the exchange of meaning over time."[12] This definition, which will be examined in more detail in chapter 8, reflects the contemporary American family which includes unmarried couples, couples with no children, single-parent families, blended families, dual-worker families, and extended families, as well as traditional nuclear families.

Communication is vital among family members.

Communication within the family is vital. As Bochner notes, "The most fundamental aspect of family process is communication."[13] **Family communication** is important for two reasons. First, families teach their members how to interact with each other and with others. Second, communication is essential to family life because through it, family units are either successful or unsuccessful. Let us consider these two features in more detail.

First, family members teach each other about appropriate and effective ways to communicate with each other. Parents teach children when to talk, how to talk, which topics are appropriate, and generally how to feel about communication. Some families develop highly idiosyncratic communication patterns and continue to teach their offspring the same patterns. Others develop communication patterns that are highly similar to many other families.

Second, family units survive or fail to survive through their communication. Family relationships, just like other human relationships, go through periods of development, stability, and deterioration. The family is not an entity that will survive regardless of the pressures placed upon it. Effective communication among family members is essential for the family to cope with the everyday stress and strain of living.

Many of the communication skills that are important to family members are considered within interpersonal communication. For instance, family researchers find that such topics as listening, empathy, self-disclosure, self-assertion, decision making, conflict management, power, nonverbal communication, self-concept, and role development are essential to understanding communication within the family. We will cover these topics in chapters 3 through 8. At the same time, these topics sometimes take on unique meaning when they are considered within the family setting. Throughout the text we will try to supply examples from family life, and we will specifically focus on this setting in chapter 8.

Organizational Communication

Organizational communication is communication that occurs in an organization. What is an organization? All of us can immediately name organizations such as General Motors, General Foods, McDonald's, IBM, RCA, Xerox, and Proctor & Gamble. These large profit-making corporations are clearly organizations. When you think of the word "organizations," you may think about groups to which you or others belong, such as religious groups, social clubs, civic organizations, self-help groups, or neighborhood groups. These, too, are organizations.

Adler defines an organization as "a structured, coordinated, hierarchical body existing for the purpose of achieving one or more goals, made up of replaceable individuals who have specialized roles."[14] Organizations may be large or small. They may have a variety of different purposes including making a profit, creating recreational opportunities, or serving some humanitarian goals. They may be structured differently with a clear superior-subordinate arrangement or they may be less rigidly structured. People may be relatively fluid in organizations; that is, they may join and quit frequently. On the other hand, the membership of the group may be fairly stable with few new members being admitted or expelled.

The common element of all organizations is communication. Weight Watchers, Walt Disney World, the Republican Party, Alcoholics Anonymous, Civitan, the Elks, Chrysler, CBS, and General Mills all depend upon effective communication in order for their organizations to meet their goals. Individuals within these organizations depend upon intrapersonal, interpersonal, and public communication.

People who study organizational communication often focus on the organizational structure, including networks, information flow, and the physical environment. They discuss the communication climate within organizations and how conflict can be effectively managed. Interviews and small group work, which we will cover in chapters 9 through 11, are very important in the organization. In addition, many organizational members must make formal presentations or public speeches, covered in chapters 12 through 18 of this text.

Health Communication

Health communication is a more recent research topic than is organizational communication. **Health communication,** according to Kreps and Thornton, is "an area of study concerned with human interaction in the health care process."[15] Researchers on health communication have studied such topics as the doctor-patient relationship, nurse-patient relationship, communication within the medical profession, communication with the elderly, health information acquisition and health campaigns, consumer health information needs, and communication concerns of social workers and family counselors.[16]

Communication is essential in the health care setting.

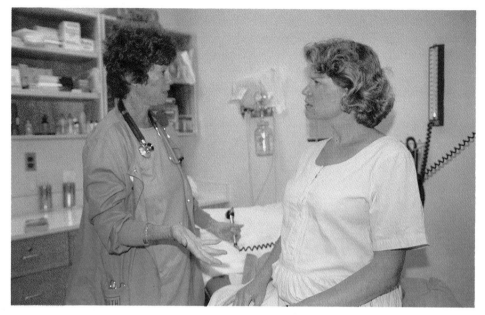

Health communication is an important setting to study because accurate and appropriate communication can literally be a life or death matter. Health care providers and users both must be able to interact in the interpersonal context. As the research in this area continues, we will probably be able to better answer questions about the impact of communication on important health outcomes. We also may learn how this setting affects our communication behaviors.

The importance of health communication will be addressed in this text through the examples and research in the appropriate sections. In addition, you should observe the information on perception, self, listening, nonverbal and verbal communication (covered in chapters 2 through 6), interpersonal communication (chapters 7 and 8), and the interview (chapter 9) are all generally applicable to this newly emerging communication setting.

Summary

Speech communication is a relevant topic for the contemporary college student. In this chapter you were introduced to the basic terminology and some of the essential concepts that will guide your understanding in the rest of the text. You learned that communication is the process of understanding and sharing meaning. In this book, we limit our discussion to human communication. Human communication begins with the self and involves others. Communication involves people, messages, channels, feedback, codes, encoding and decoding, and noise. People serve as the sources and receivers of messages. Messages include ideas, thoughts, and feelings that one individual wishes to communicate to another person or group of people. Channels are the modes by which messages move from the source of the message to the receiver of the message. Feedback includes the verbal and nonverbal responses provided by the receiver to the source. Codes are systematic arrangements of symbols, letters, and words that have an arbitrary meaning and are used for communication. Encoding occurs when we put a thought or idea into a code. Decoding occurs when we assign meaning to that thought or idea. Any factor that intervenes between encoding and decoding is known as noise.

Communication occurs in differing contexts, including the intrapersonal, interpersonal, and public. The number of people involved, the degree of formality or intimacy, the opportunities for feedback, the need for prestructuring messages, and the degree of stability of the roles of speaker and listener all vary as a result of the communication context. This text is organized on a contextual basis with a consideration of self and others in each context. Communication also occurs in settings. Three contemporary relevant settings are the family, the organization, and the health setting.

While you may spend a great deal of your time engaged in communication, you may find that you do not communicate as successfully as you might wish. This text will assist you in improving your ability to communicate with other people.

Perception: The Process of Understanding

A *t 8:07* P.M. *on March 7, 1987, a late-model blue sedan was involved in a collision with a lightweight ten-speed bicycle at 2200 College Drive. No one was injured, but the bicycle was damaged.*

Police report

D *id you hear what happened last night? I didn't get all the details, but some instructor ran into a student on a bicycle. It's bad enough that those guys have to flunk us—now they're running over us!*

College student

I *am sorry to report that an unfortunate accident occurred last evening. As a result of our inadequate street lighting, an automobile driven by a student was hit in the rear bumper by a faculty member on a bicycle. Luckily, no one was injured, but the front fender on the bicycle was bent.*

Dean of the college

Objectives

1. State the differences between the view of perception as passive and the view of perception as active; describe a situation that illustrates creative meaning as opposed to inherent meaning.
2. Discuss the processes of selection, organization, and interpretation as they apply to the perception of others.
3. Describe an experience in which you and another person had different perceptions of the same stimuli and discuss the reasons for those differences.
4. Explain how your roles, culture, and subculture affect your perceptions.
5. Give examples that illustrate the processes of organization: figure and ground, proximity, closure, similarity, and perceptual constancy.

Key Terms

perception	selection
passive perception	organization
objective	interpretation
perception	selective attention
inherent meaning	selective retention
subjective	stereotyping
active	figure and ground
creative	closure
interpretive	proximity
perceptual	similarity
constancy	context
	compare

These are three descriptions of the same accident. They can be recognized as descriptions of a similar event, but they vary in all other details. The first description, from the police report, is descriptive, disinterested, and dry. The second, from a student, is embellished and more interesting. The dean offers an explanation for the accident and gives more details.

In none of the descriptions does the speaker claim to have witnessed the accident. But eyewitness accounts also vary greatly. Accident reports are filled with conflicting evidence. People who have seen an automobile accident, for example, will disagree about who was at fault; the number of people involved; the year, the make, and even the color of the vehicles.

Differences in perception, in the way people see, hear, smell, taste, or feel a specific stimulus, are common. Whether we are describing an event (say, an automobile accident), an idea (how communication occurs), or something about ourselves (how we feel about our own bodies), we encounter differences in perception. Individual experiences are not identical. Neither are individual perceptions, even of the same event. Perceptions are personal constructs of the perceiver.

How Does Communication
Involve Perception?

Perception is the process by which we come to understand ourselves and others. Understanding is necessary to communication. In order to make the connection more concrete, let us delineate two specific ways in which perception is related to communication.

Our perceptions of ourselves affect our communication. If we believe ourselves to be shy, we may tend to avoid communicating. If we believe that we are aggressive, we may tend to dominate conversations and to be loud and boisterous. We sometimes draw inferences about other people's self-concepts from the way they speak. In chapter 3, we explore further the role of self in communication.

Perception is also important because it is the process by which we come to understand others. We make judgments and draw conclusions about other people within a few seconds of meeting them.[1] We use the nonverbal cues available, including the person's facial expressions, vocal patterns, bodily language, clothes, and jewelry, as well as what the person says. Our perception of the other person, including the way the person looks, sounds, and smells, provides immediate information.

The perceptions we have of others affect our communication with them. A number of minority group people—blacks, Mexican-Americans, and handicapped persons, for example—have related their experiences with others. Frequently, the early portion of a conversation focuses on their uniqueness—their race, their nationality, or their particular handicap. People who talk with them tend to be limited in their early perceptions. Often, the topic of conversation does not shift until these persons have known each other for some time. We will examine in more detail how we understand others in chapter 4.

Our perceptions of ourselves affect our interactions with others.

What Is Perception?

In the past, people believed that perception was nothing more than sensing objects in the environment: people were merely tape recorders that recorded the events that occurred around them—**passive perception.** Sights, sounds, smells, and other stimuli were sent to them. A second implication was that people were objective. In other words, no one added or subtracted from the stimuli—**objective perception.** This point of view also implied **inherent meaning** in the object being perceived. No room for interpretation existed because the stimulus supposedly contained all of the meaning.

What occurs in perception is that our sensory receptors (eyes, ears, noses, tongues, and bodies) are stimulated by objects in our environment. The stimulus may be a spoken word, an unusual smell, a brush against our arm, the written word, or some unique taste. The sensory receptors capture the particular stimulus, and nerves transmit the sensation to the brain. The brain interprets the sensation and assigns meanings to it in order for us to gain an understanding of the stimulus. This cycle is depicted in figure 2.1. We will consider the processes that occur in perception later in this chapter. At this point, we simply note that perception is far more complex than merely sensing stimuli.

The contemporary view of perception is that it is **subjective, active, creative,** and **interpretive.** People add to and subtract from the stimuli to which they are exposed.

Figure 2.1

Perception is far more complex than merely
sensing stimuli.

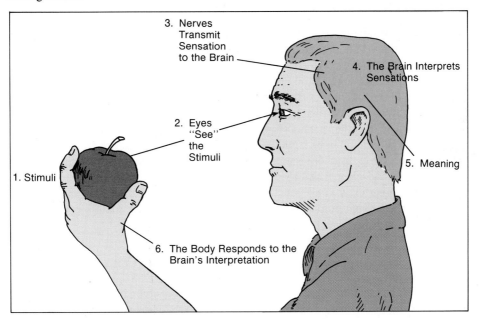

They blend the external stimuli and their internal states. Recent research on the human brain demonstrates that individual brain development is highly variable. In addition, as we shall discover in the next section, factors other than physiological differences between people account for differences in perception.

Consider the last time you were driving in the country. As you drove between the fields on the two-lane highway, your attention shifted from one stimulus to another. You did not passively absorb all of the stimuli in the environment, but you actively chose to focus on the sports car that zoomed past you and to ignore the family sedan you followed for a number of miles. When a large van came into view in your rearview mirror, you did not objectively perceive the vehicle, but instead you began to think about your truck-driver friend, and you subjectively thought about the truck as a means of income. When you looked at the fields planted with corn and barley, you did not identify an inherent meaning in the plants that others would easily share, but you recognized, in your creative way, that the plants were different from those with which you were familiar.

To understand how the contemporary view of perception affects communication, try to remember the last week of final exams. Perhaps, as you were rushing to an exam, you noticed one of your friends coming toward you. You singled out your friend from a number of other people on the sidewalk. When you noticed him, you did not drop your glance, but you maintained eye contact to signal you wanted to talk for a moment or two. As you began the conversation, you noticed it was beginning to rain and the rain was very cold. You began to feel uncomfortable and wondered why your friend continued to talk. Your thoughts shifted back to the exam. Your friend remarked that you seemed touchy. As he walked away, your friend told himself, "That's what happens when you lend people money—they try to ignore you!"

If you assumed that the older view of perception was accurate, this conversation would be difficult to interpret and understand. If you take into consideration that perception is active, subjective, and creative, your friend's misunderstanding can be explained. Recall the diagram of Barnlund's "six people" in chapter 1. Instead of holding a single objective view of this encounter, we recognize at least two perspectives are possible: the way the other person views the situation and the way you view it. Further, each of you had unique views of yourselves, each other, and the way you believe you were perceived. True, you both reacted to the same external stimuli—the sight of each other, the extended glance, and the cold rain. But your inner state, including anxiety over the upcoming exam, and your friend's inner state, including his concern about money he had lent you, produced a unique communication that could be viewed from a variety of perspectives.

Why Do Differences in Perception Occur?

We have just demonstrated a common phenomenon—different people perceiving the same event in different ways. Moreover, perception is subjective, active, and creative. Differences occur in perception because of physiological factors, different past experiences, and differences in present feelings and circumstances.

Physiological Factors

None of us is physiologically identical to anyone else. We vary in height, weight, body type, sex, and in our senses. People can be tall or short, have less than perfect vision, or suffer from impaired hearing. They can be particularly sensitive to smells or odors. Sensitivity to temperature similarly varies from one individual to another.

Biological sex may be an important physiological difference to be considered in perception. Some authors have suggested that hemispheric differences in the cerebral cortex of the brain are sex-linked. These differences are said to account for females' language facility and fine hand control and males' spatial and mathematical abilities, as well as their increased likelihood of suffering with dyslexia, stuttering, delayed speech, autism, and hyperactivity.[2] However, conclusive evidence has not been established for an anatomic difference between the brain structures of human females and males.

Past Experience

Just as our physiological features affect our perceptions, our past experiences similarly alter what we see or hear. Our past experiences lead us to expectations about the future. For instance, suppose you were given a reading assignment in one of your courses and, on the day your assigned reading was to have been completed, your instructor asked you to put away your books and to number from one to twenty-five on a sheet of paper. What would you assume? Most likely you would predict that you were about to have a quiz or exam on the required reading. This assumption about the current situation is based on your past experiences.

The idea that our past experiences create expectations about the future is basic to the theory of **perceptual constancy.** According to perceptual constancy, we rarely change our perceptions of something once we have established a particular image of it. We are able to "see" the objects in our bedroom, even when the light bulb burns out and the room is dark. If we move some items from a counter on which they have rested for a long time, we may still "see" the objects there even after they are gone. Similarly, amputees often report they still experience some "feeling" in the location of their missing appendage. All of us have a tendency to view things as stable and unchanging after we have formed our opinion.

Perceptual constancy operates on other levels as well. We frequently come to hold an attitude and then refuse to alter that attitude, even when we are provided with contrary evidence. This phenomenon is called an attitude-set or mind-set. The harmful effects of tobacco, caffeine, and alcohol have been revealed in the past few years. Many people held a previous attitude that these drugs were not hazardous to their health. Their past experience with these drugs and their mind-set do not allow them to perceive the new data as important or meaningful to them.

Differences in perception based on past experiences also occur because of the roles we play, the culture with which we are familiar, and the subculture of which we are a part. Our roles, for example, may include being a student, a worker, a son, or a daughter. These roles affect our perceptions of the events around us. We may play specific roles in particular communication contexts. For instance, you may always perceive yourself as a supportive conversationalist when you are talking to another person. To fulfill this role, you may listen carefully and provide many verbal and nonverbal responses to the other communicator. If you perceive yourself as a "clown" or "tension-releaser" in a small group setting, you might perceive any slip of the tongue as an opportunity for creating humor.

How does growing up in different cultures affect our perceptions? We learn how to perceive the people and events around us based on cultural values, attitudes, and beliefs. In chapter 6, we will observe that people's culture affects their language. At this point, we recognize our culture affects our perceptions. Singer, an intercultural communication researcher, maintains that what we see, hear, taste, touch, and smell are conditioned by our cultures. He postulates that our perceptions are largely learned. Further, he observes that the greater the experiential differences among people, the greater the disparity in their perceptions. On the other hand, the more similar their experiential backgrounds, the more similarly they will perceive the world.[3]

Some examples may clarify the relationship of culture to perceptions. In Malaysia, exchanging gifts when you visit someone's home is expected behavior; in Canada, it would be viewed as unusual. In the Philippines, women and men are treated more equally than in India. The relative importance of communication and of silence changes,

Our cultural background affects our perceptions and our interactions with others.

too, as we move from one culture to another. Americans generally hold a strong, positive feeling toward oral communication, but some other cultures do not share this perception. In many parts of the world, silence, rather than talk, is the preferred mode of behavior.

The attitudes, values, and beliefs of our culture affect our perception of ourselves as well as our perceptions of other people. For instance, if you grew up in a culture that treated children as unique and capable individuals, you might feel far differently about yourself than if you grew up in a culture that viewed children as property or that viewed children as an interference in achieving "the good life." Similarly, women who are taught to perceive their role as secondary to men are apt to perceive assertive women as impolite, improper, or inappropriately socialized.

Growing up in different subcultures encourages differences in perception, too. The crowding that occurs on a street in a large city is upsetting to a rural person. Similarly, country children are more likely to become apprehensive about communicating than are urban children.[4] Women and men learn to perceive the world around them in vastly different ways, which results in different modes of communicating. *Gender and Communication,* a recent textbook, cites hundreds of sources that demonstrate the specific and unique ways that women and men perceive the world and communicate about it.[5] Similarly, individuals in the black community learn to perceive the world differently than do Americans of Mexican heritage.

Subcultural differences, including differences in age, affect our perceptions and communication.

One subcultural difference with which you are probably familiar is the so-called generation gap. The difference in age between yourself and your parents, instructors, or classmates may significantly affect your perception of them and, consequently, your communication with them. A difference in age can affect how you respond to music and perceive events, what you say about them, and the meanings that are evoked when they are mentioned in a conversation. Subcultural differences affect our perception and, thereby, our communication.

Present Feelings and Circumstances

Differences in perception also arise from different feelings and circumstances. A headache, backache, or toothache can cause you to perceive a critical comment when a friendly one is being offered. You sometimes may not see a stop sign if your thoughts are elsewhere. Your health may affect your ability to perceive sensory stimuli. Similarly, if you are tired, you may perceive stimuli differently than when you are well-rested. Other physiological needs like hunger or thirst may affect your perceptive skills.

Your daily, monthly, or yearly cycle may affect how you perceive stimuli. If you are an "evening person" you might not be able to discriminate among multiple choice answers on an exam at 8 A.M. as well as you could later in the day. If you are having a bad week, you might be offended by the humor of one of your friends; later in the month, you might find the same remark very humorous. Accordingly, you might perceive stimuli more acutely in the cooler months of winter than you do in the warmer summer months.

If you have ever spent a night alone in a large house, a deserted dormitory, or an unfamiliar residence, you probably understand that perceptions are altered by circumstances. Most people experience a remarkable change in their hearing at night when they are alone. Creaking, whining, scraping, cracking sounds are heard, although none was heard in the daytime. The lack of other stimuli—including light, other sounds, and other people with whom to talk—coupled with a slight feeling of anxiety, provide the circumstances that result in more acute hearing.

Similar circumstances may account, in part, for the mirages seen by lonely travelers. Commander Robert Peary encountered massive snowy pinnacles that appeared to rise thousands of feet above the plain of solid ice deep inside the Arctic Circle in 1906. Seven years later, Donald MacMillan, another explorer, verified his discovery. However, when MacMillan asked his Eskimo guide to choose a course toward the peaks, the guide explained that the spectacle was only *poo-jok* (mist). Meteorologists have explained the existence of such mirages but have hastened to add that they are "reported infrequently because people aren't looking for them."[6] The variance in the feelings and circumstances of the many explorers may account for the differences in sighting or not sighting specific illusions.

What Occurs in Perception?

According to the most recent information, people engage in three separate activities during perception. None of us is aware of these separate processes because they occur quickly and almost simultaneously. Nonetheless, each activity is involved in our perceptions. The three activities include **selection** (we neglect some of the stimuli in our environment and focus on a few), **organization** (we group the stimuli in our environment into units or wholes), and **interpretation** (we give particular meanings to stimuli).

Selection

None of us perceives all the stimuli in our environment. For example, if you drove to school today, you were bombarded with sights, sounds, smells, and other sensations during your ride. At the time, you elected to perceive some of the stimuli, and you chose to disregard others. Now, you can recall some of the stimuli you perceived, but you have forgotten others. In the future, you will also expose yourself to some sensations and ignore others.

Our selectivity is of at least two types. First, we are selective in the stimuli to which we attend. **Selective attention** means we focus on certain cues and ignore others. On our way to school, we check our timing with the bank clock, but we fail to notice the couple walking in front of the bank. We may overhear someone gossiping about us in the next room but not hear what one of our parents is saying in the same room.

Second, we select the stimuli we will recall or remember. **Selective retention** means we categorize, store, and retrieve certain information, but discard other information. If you played the car radio on your way to school, try to remember one of the songs you heard, or one of the commercials, or one of the public-service announcements. Although your attention may have been drawn to a particular song or message this morning, you may find that you cannot remember anything you heard. Your mind has discarded the sounds you heard from your radio. You may recall a criticism your date offered last night but have forgotten your mother made a similar comment two days ago.

The relationship between selection and communication can be clarified by the concept of stereotyping. **Stereotyping** is the process of placing people and things into established categories, or of basing judgments about people or things upon the categories into which they fit, rather than on their individual characteristics. Stereotyping has a negative connotation because we sometimes exhibit "hardening of the categories," placing items in inappropriate categories, or else we do not recognize that others categorize differently than we do. All of us stereotype to a certain extent, but particular stereotypes vary from person to person. Stereotyping involves selective attention and selective retention.

A specific example will illustrate the relationship among these concepts. Suppose you perceive women to be emotional and men to be logical. To maintain this stereotype, you selectively attend to women who behave emotionally and ignore those who are unemotional. Similarly, you selectively attend to men who are logical, rather than to those who seem unpredictable. When you try to recall the significant men and women in your life, you find the women were either moderately or extremely emotional and the men were fairly rational. You have selectively retained the memory of those who fit your stereotype. Selectivity in perception affects stereotyping, and stereotyping is a process by which we categorize so we can communicate with others. We examine the processes of stereotyping, abstracting, and categorizing further in chapter 6, when we consider verbal codes and words we have developed and used.

Organization

All of us have a tendency to organize the stimuli in our environment. The unorganized figure 2.2 is difficult to describe if we only glance at it for a minute. When we attempt to describe it, we do so by organizing the lines we see. We might say it consists of straight and squiggly lines, or it has a rectangle, a triangle, and a square, or we may

Figure 2.2
The unorganized figure.

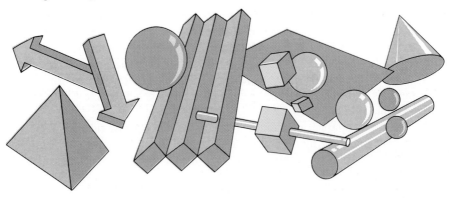

Figure 2.3

An example of figure and ground: A vase or twins?

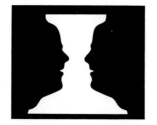

Figure 2.4

An example of figure and ground: Ink blobs or a bearded man?

categorize the stimuli in some other way. The important point is we attempt to organize the figure as we describe it.

We organize stimuli in a number of ways. One method of organizing is to distinguish between **figure and ground.** In figure 2.3, some people perceive a vase or a candlestick, while others perceive twins facing each other. People who see a vase identify the center of the drawing as the figure and the area on the right and left as the ground, or background. Conversely, people who see twins facing each other see the center as the background and the area on the right and left as the figure.

Figure 2.4 is another illustration of the principle of figure and ground. As we first glance at the drawing, we perceive nothing but ink blobs—nothing is clearly distinguishable as either the figure or the background. If we continue to look at the drawing, however, we perceive the face of Christ or of a bearded man at the top center of the picture. When we see the face, it becomes the figure; the rest of the drawing becomes the ground.

Just as we use figure and ground to organize visual stimuli, we also use it to organize the messages that people offer us. For example, traditional values in the American culture placed the husband as the head of the household while the wife was viewed as less important. Symbolically, wives, rather than husbands, have changed their names to become part of a newly established family. Recently, a grandmother was curious about her granddaughter's reluctance to change her last name to her spouse's name upon marriage. Speaking to the couple, but focusing on the granddaughter, the grandmother asked, "And why didn't you change your name?" The husband replied, "I already had my career established and I thought it would confuse my clients."

The actress Ina Claire, who was an early star in "talking pictures," married John Gilbert, who was a romantic hero of silent movies. Shortly after their marriage took place, a reporter asked her how it felt being married to a celebrity. Ina Claire replied, "Why don't you ask my husband?"[7]

In both of these examples, the humor or surprise occurs because the communicators have a different notion of figure and ground. In the first example, the grandmother perceives the husband as the figure and the wife as the ground while the husband articulates the opposite assumption. In the second case, the actress suggests to the reporter that she, rather than her husband, is the celebrity.

Figure 2.5
An example of closure: Ink blobs or a cat?

Figure 2.6
An example of closure: A triangle or straight lines?

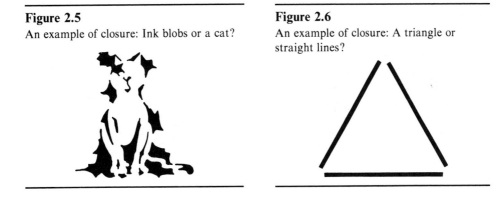

Figure 2.7
An example of closure: A circle or straight lines?

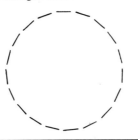

Another way of organizing stimuli is described as **closure.** We engage in closure every time we fill in things that do not exist. If someone showed us figure 2.5 and asked us what we perceived, we would probably say that it was a picture of a cat. But, as we can clearly see, the figure is incomplete. We can see a cat only if we are willing to fill in the blank areas. Additional examples of closure are given in figures 2.6 and 2.7. Most of us would identify figure 2.6 as a triangle and figure 2.7 as a circle, rather than claiming that both are simply short lines.

Closure is used in our interactions with others. When we fill in a word or a phrase for another person, we are using closure. When we have a long-term relationship with another person, we can frequently communicate with them without speaking at all. Alfred Hitchcock, the producer of such movies as "Psycho" and "The Birds," was able to create such thrillers without the advantage of having an audience observe the work as it was being created. In fact, Hitchcock never sat among his audiences when they viewed his completed films. A reporter asked him if he missed hearing them scream. "No," he replied, "I can hear them when I'm making the picture."[8] His successful film career may have occurred, in part, because he was able to "fill in" the audience response to his work.

Perception: The Process of Understanding   35

We also organize stimuli according to their **proximity.** The principle of proximity or nearness operates whenever we group two or more things that simply happen to be close to each other. When we group according to proximity, our assumption is "birds of a feather flock together," even though we know this is not always true. In figure 2.8 we tend to perceive three groups of lines with three lines in each group, rather than nine separate lines, because of the principle of proximity or nearness.

We use proximity in our interactions with others as well. For example, we use people's occupations to make assessments of their behaviors. We may assume that if a person is a writer, he or she would be fluent with language, or if a person is a mathematician, he or she would be able to consider the symbolic nature of things. A politician used such an assessment boldly. At an embassy reception, he approached Ann Landers, newspaper columnist, and drawled, "So you're Ann Landers. Why don't you say something funny?" Without missing a beat, Landers replied, "Well, you're a politician. Tell me a lie."[9]

Similarity also helps us to organize stimuli. We sometimes group elements together because they resemble each other in size, color, shape, or other attributes. For example, we tend to believe that people who like the music we do also enjoy the same movies we do. We assume that a suit that looks like one of our own is probably within the same price range. In figure 2.9, we perceive squares and circles, rather than a group of geometric shapes, because of the principle of similarity.

Figure 2.8

An example of proximity: Three groups of lines or nine separate lines?

Figure 2.9

An example of similarity: Squares and circles or a group of geometric figures?

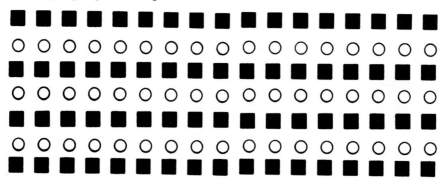

Elements of the Communication Process

Similarity is useful as we organize messages others send to us. Reporters frequently asked former President Jimmy Carter about his stance on moral issues since he was a devout Southern Baptist. They probably reasoned that since he had a strong religious background, he would similarly hold clear moral values. Carter was able to use this situation to a humorous advantage on one occasion. A reporter asked him, "Mr. President, how would you feel if you were told that your daughter was having an affair?" "Shocked and overwhelmed," replied Carter, adding, "but then, she's only seven years old."[10] The reporter may have expected Carter's initial response, on the basis of similarity, but was surprised by the rationale offered in the second part of the answer.

To understand the relationship between the organizing of stimuli and communication, let us consider a typical party. When you arrive at a party, you immediately begin to organize the stimuli—the people there—into groups. You focus first on your friends and acquaintances, who serve as *figure,* and largely ignore the strangers present, who serve as *ground.* Those friends who are standing closest to you will talk with you first because of their *proximity.* The people with whom you will spend the most time are those who you perceive to be *similar* to you. Finally, you notice two married friends, separated for a number of months and considering divorce, arrive together. As the evening progresses, they tend to stand together and to talk in an intimate way. You achieve *closure* by assuming they have reconciled their differences. When you approach them, your mood is light and your conversation is spirited. This example illustrates how organizing stimuli—one activity of perception—affects communication. It helps to determine with whom we speak, how we speak, what we speak about, how long we speak, and the tone of voice we use.

Interpretation

Each of us interprets the stimuli we perceive. The more ambiguous the stimuli, the more room we have for interpretation. The basis for the well-known inkblot test lies in the principle of interpretation of stimuli. Figure 2.10 shows three inkblots a psychologist might ask you to interpret. The ambiguity of the figures is typical.

Figure 2.10
An example of interpretation: The inkblot.

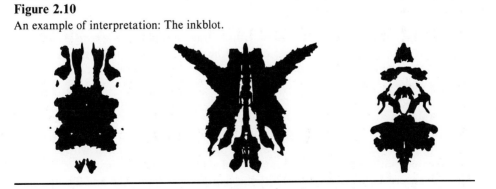

Figure 2.11

An example of the usefulness of context in the interpretation of stimuli.

Figure 2.12

An example of interpretation: Which line is longer?

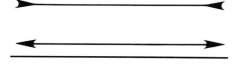

Figure 2.13

An example of interpretation: Is the width of the holder the same length as the candle?

In our interpretation of stimuli, we frequently rely on the **context** in which we perceive the stimuli, or we **compare** the stimuli to others. Sometimes, there are helpful clues. For example, in figure 2.11, the letters and numbers are useful to us as we attempt to interpret the middle figure. The contexts indicate that, in the top diagram, the middle figure is two number ones with a dash between them, while in the bottom diagram, the middle figure is an H.

Nonetheless, comparisons and the use of context can be confusing. All of us are familiar with figures like 2.12 and 2.13. In these figures, we perceive differences in the lengths of the lines, and in the height of the candle and the width of the candle holder, although no differences exist.

John Gilbert, an early film actor, provides a humorous example of failing to use the context in interpreting a verbal response. Gilbert was especially anxious to speak with a particular actress at rehearsals one day and he asked a stagehand where she was. The stagehand replied, "She's round behind." Gilbert quickly replied, "Yes, I know that, but where is she?"[11]

The relationship between the interpretation of stimuli and communication can be demonstrated in a situation that may be familiar to you. Women who work in large businesses or corporations more frequently serve in secretarial or clerical positions than in executive or managerial jobs. As a result, a person who is unfamiliar with a particular office may mistakenly request a cup of coffee from the lawyer instead of her secretary. The stereotype leads the visitor to an inaccurate assumption and an incorrect interpretation, which, in turn, leads to difficulty in communication.

Differences in Perception

Jack can see he sees
what he can see Jill can't see,
and he can see
that Jill can't see that she can't see,
but he can't see WHY
Jill can't see that Jill can't see. . . .
Jill can see Jack can't see
and can't see he can't see.
Jill can see WHY
Jack can't see,
but Jill cannot see WHY
Jack can't see he can't see. . . .
Jack can't see he can't see
and can't see
Jill can't see Jill can't see it,
and vice versa.[12]

Differences in perception can be overcome in our interaction with others.

R. D. Laing includes this poem in his collection *Knots*. The poem captures the complexity of perception and the difficulty of establishing common perceptions.

Discuss an experience in which you and another person attempted to reach an agreement but could not. Identify the differences in perception, suggest reasons for those differences, and enumerate the methods you attempted to use to validate your perceptions.

Interpretation is important in our interactions with others. Sigmund Freud, the founder of modern psychoanalysis, relied upon interpretation in his analytic work. Freud is remembered for a number of theories, many of which remain controversial. He is also remembered through anecdotes. Perhaps one of the most well known concerns cigar smoking. Freud was a habitual cigar smoker and on one occasion, as he was puffing on a long cigar, one of his students asked him about the habit. The student noted that cigar smoking is often thought of as a symbolic activity and that the cigar is frequently interpreted as a phallic symbol or as an emblem of masculinity. The student asked Freud if cigar smoking carried any particular symbolic weight for him. Freud puffed reflectively for a few moments, and then replied, "Sometimes a cigar is just a cigar."[13] The humor is derived from Freud's unwillingness to interpret the act.

Summary

In this chapter we examined the role of perception. Perception is the process by which we come to understand ourselves and others, and understanding is an activity basic to communication. The older view of perception suggested it was passive and objective, and that meaning was inherent in the stimuli perceived. The contemporary view of perception is that it is a subjective, active, and creative process.

Differences in perceptions arise among people. Physiological features of the individual, including height, weight, body type, gender, and differences in our senses, contribute toward those differences in perceptions. Past experiences, including those dependent on our cultures and subcultures, affect our perceptions also. Finally, our current circumstances and our present feelings affect our perceptions.

What occurs in perception? While we are unaware of the separate processes that occur, we engage in selection, organization, and interpretation. Each of these was examined in detail in this chapter. In the next chapter we will consider a related topic, understanding oneself.

Self-Awareness and Self-Concept: Understanding Yourself

I have to live with myself, and so
I want to be fit for myself to know;
I want to be able as days go by,
Always to look myself straight in the eye.

> Edgar A. Guest,
> Myself

Know thyself

> attributed to Thales

To love oneself is the beginning of a life-
long romance

> Oscar Wilde, An
> Ideal Husband, III

Objectives

1. Discuss why self-awareness is important; suggest some of the barriers to self-awareness.
2. Identify the factors that inhibit change of self-concept; give an example of how your self-concept has changed in the last few years.
3. Define your self-image and self-esteem.
4. Show that self-concept is a process by describing how your self-concept differs in different situations and at different times.
5. Explain the relationship between the self-fulfilling prophecy and the formation of self-concept.
6. Identify some ways in which gender affects self-concept.

Key Terms

self-awareness
Maslow's
  hierarchy of
  needs
self-concept
symbolic
  interactionism
prepatory phase
play stage
game stage
Johari Window
open self
blind self

hidden self
unknown self
confirmation
rejection
disconfirmation
self-image
self-esteem
self-consciousness
self-fulfilling
  prophecy
locus of control
androgynous

These quotations confirm the importance of knowing and accepting ourselves. In chapter 1, we stated that communication begins with oneself. In chapter 2, we detailed the importance of perception in the communication process. In this chapter we combine the two notions to consider perception of oneself, or self-awareness and self-concept.

Self-Awareness

How we perceive ourselves plays a central role in communication, regardless of whether the communication is in a daydream, a journal, a small group, or at a podium. The first step in the improvement of our communication skills, consequently, is to become aware of our perceptions of ourselves—**self-awareness.** Unfortunately, most of us have been taught to disregard or to minimize our feelings and emotions. As children, we were told, "Be quiet," "Don't cry," or "Try to act like a man (or a lady)."

If we are sensitive to children, we recognize they have two universal characteristics: their spontaneity and the completeness of their responses. They respond immediately and completely to their world. Small children laugh easily and with their whole body. Frustrated youngsters respond with their entire being.

Through conditioning, children learn that many responses are inappropriate. Giggling in church is not socially approved; screaming at parents is not condoned; loud crying in public places is not rewarded. Through training and conditioning, children learn to think before they react.

Teaching children to think before they react may be essential as a society, but we pay a high price as individuals. By analyzing the situation first and then responding appropriately, we lose touch with our emotions. We learn to intellectualize our feelings away. Many of us become so successful at this we are unable, as adults, to describe or even to understand our own emotions.

Rediscovering ourselves is essential to our mental health and, in turn, to our ability to communicate. Abraham H. Maslow, a well-known psychologist, was one of the first to stress the importance of self-awareness or self-study. Maslow felt people must become what they can become. In **Maslow's hierarchy of needs** in figure 3.1, the most basic needs are physical, followed by the needs for safety and security, social acceptance, esteem, and self-actualization.[1] Physical needs include our needs for food, sleep, sex, and water. Safety and security needs include our needs for stability, order, predictability, and freedom from fear, harm, injury, and chaos. Among our social needs are our needs to belong, to feel a part of social groups, and to feel acceptance, approval, and affection. Our esteem needs are based on our need to feel competent, confident, and to receive the recognition others can give to us. Finally, our self-actualization needs include our desires to live up to our unique potentialities and our needs for self-fulfillment.

Other psychologists have also discussed the importance of self-actualization. Carl Rogers labeled the self-actualized person as "the fully functioning person"; Sidney Jourard discussed the "disclosed self"; Marie Johoda spoke of the "mentally healthy";

Figure 3.1

Maslow's hierarchy of needs.

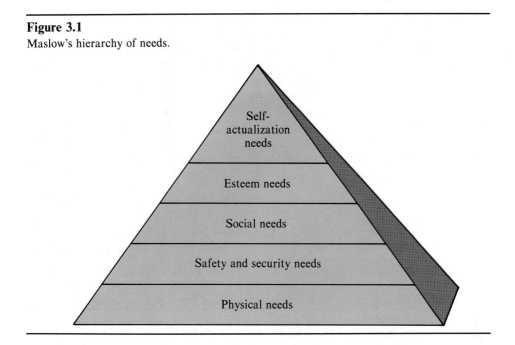

Charles Morris identified the "open self"; and Theodore Landman wrote about the "beautiful and noble person." All of these psychologists held an optimistic, empirically based view that recognized increased self-awareness leads to self-actualization.

Will Schutz echoed this point of view and agreed about the importance of self-awareness. In *Here Comes Everybody,* Schutz considered the relationship between self-discovery and self-actualization:

> Every thought, gesture, muscle tension, feeling, stomach gurgle, nose scratch, fart, hummed tune, slip of the tongue, illness—everything is significant and meaningful and related to the now. It is possible to know and understand oneself on all these levels, and the more one knows the more he is free to determine his own life.
>
> If I know what my body tells me, I know my deepest feelings and I can choose what to do. . . . Given a complete knowledge of myself, I can determine my life; lacking that mastery, I am controlled in ways that are often undesirable, unproductive, worrisome, and confusing.[2]

When we become aware of ourselves, our controlling agent becomes, not an outside force, but ourselves. Our self-awareness can be seen and heard in our communicative behavior. People who are aware of themselves express emotions both verbally and nonverbally. They cry, they laugh, they speak in expressive tones. Their bodies communicate their fear, disappointment, joy, and pleasure.

Increasingly, people are becoming aware of the importance of self-awareness. As early as 1972, football star Rosey Grier sang "It's All Right to Cry" on the album *Free to Be . . . You and Me.* The song spoke of the importance of responding honestly and spontaneously to one's emotions. It suggested we should not allow ourselves to rationalize our problems and that, instead, we should work to keep in close touch with our emotions. The price of losing close touch with our emotions is high.

Rosey Grier, pictured on the next page, is unusual. Many people have difficulty expressing their feelings. Sorrow, fear, anxiety, and loneliness appear to be particularly difficult for us to express. But communicating these feelings to others is psychologically healthy. Our interpersonal relationships can be enhanced by a fuller and more complete expression of our feelings.

Many adults who have learned to deny their feelings are making attempts to rediscover them. Warren Doyle, a Ph.D. from the University of Connecticut, approached self-discovery by backpacking alone. Doyle set two records for hiking the 2,040-mile Appalachian Trail. He reported:

> There's a theory that most people have high self-concepts that crumble in situations of crisis or adversity. Many of us never have a chance to find out who we really are. . . . I was alone for sixty-six days. I lost my physical fat and my emotional fat as well. I saw myself as I really was.[3]

We may not be able to go hiking alone, but we can all make some moves to increase our self-awareness. We can focus on our bodies, our feelings, our emotions, and the present. We can concentrate on how we feel about something, rather than on the way we think we are expected to feel. We can look to ourselves, rather than to others, for solutions to problems. We can take responsibility for our own point of view, as well as our own behavior. We can try to identify what we want to do and then work hard to do it well.

Self-awareness is essential to successful communication, but sometimes people stress self-control more than self-expression. Too much self-control can result in an avoidance of communication, on the one hand, or aggressive communication, on the other. Overly self-controlled people avoid being expressive and stating their own feelings, emotions, and opinions. Or, they may rebel and behave aggressively, trying to control and manipulate others through communication.

Consider Jim, an unassertive speaker. Jim was bright, the oldest of four children. His parents reminded him and others that "Jim always does what's right." When he was small, Jim was praised for "not being lippy" and for "not talking back." When he became a man, people complimented him for "being such a good listener." Jim learned self-control. Now he complains, "No one knows who I am—not even me."

Marcia was taught to be "seen and not heard." She expressed herself when she was a child, but she soon learned the power of disapproval. Her parents, who tried to control her, succeeded only in making Marcia attempt to control her younger brother. Marcia monitored her brother's every expression. Now, Marcia is viewed as very domineering and unpleasant. She writes, "I know people don't like me, and I don't blame them. I don't like myself."

Self-awareness is essential to communication, but too much self-control can result in avoidance of communication.

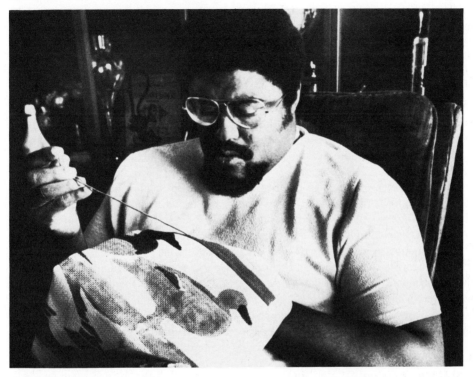

Kampf Um Dein Leben

Kampf um dein leben is German for "fight for your life." e. e. cummings expressed the importance of this sentiment when he wrote, "To be nobody—but—yourself in a world which is doing its best, night and day, to make you everybody else means to fight, and never stop fighting."

Explain the significance of cummings's statement. Apply his observation to your own life. At which points in your life have you had to fight to become the person you perceived yourself to be? Each of us feels conflicting tugs to be unique and individualistic and at the same time to be normative or similar to others. We may wish to behave both as others do and differently from them. Can you identify some specific behaviors in which you engage that make you different from most others? Can you identify behaviors in which you conform to others? Why do you conform in some cases but behave differently in others? Do you consciously choose when you will be "yourself," regardless of the consequences, and when you will do what others wish you to do, again, regardless of the outcome? In the struggle between behaving the way you wish to behave and the way others wish you to behave, which force dominates? In what ways does this affect your communication with others? How does it affect others' communication with you?

To function more fully and to communicate more effectively, we need to learn how to gain more awareness of ourselves. Self-control, like control by others, can result in a lack of self-expression. As a result, we may find that we are not sensitive to others with whom we would like to talk. We may not even be aware of the topics about which we would enjoy speaking and the situations in which we would find communication pleasant. Or, we may find we are reticent or aggressive toward others.

Self-Concept

Self-concept is each person's consciousness of his or her total, essential, and particular being. Included in self-concept are all of our physical, social, and psychological perceptions about ourselves. These perceptions are a result of our past, present, and projected experiences and interactions with our environment—including the people in our environment.

The importance of others in determining self-concept cannot be overemphasized. We do not move from the spontaneous beings we are as children to complex adults without the intervention of countless other people. Our self originates in interactions with others. Our communicative exchanges tell us what our roles are and encourage or discourage us from internalizing specific predispositions.

Early theorists contributed to a theory that George Herbert Mead originated.[4] That theory—**symbolic interactionism**—has important implications for us. Mead felt that people were actors, not reactors. He suggested that people develop through three stages. The **preparatory phase** includes the stage in which infants imitate others by mirroring. The baby may wash off a surface, put on mommy's or daddy's shoes, or pat the dog, but the child does not necessarily understand the imitated acts.

In the **play stage,** the child actually plays the roles of others. She may pretend to be mommy, daddy, the postal carrier, a nurse, or a doctor. Each role is played independently; the behaviors are not integrated into a single set of role behaviors. In other words, the child does not play a Superwoman who is a mother, a wife, a runner, an airplane pilot, a writer, and a teacher.

In the **game stage,** the child responds simultaneously in a generalized way to several others. The child determines a composite role by considering all others' definitions of self. The person thus develops a unified role from which to see the self. This perception is the overall way that other people see the individual. People unify their self-concepts by internalizing this composite view. This self-picture emerges from years of symbolically interacting, or communicating, with others. Your integrated self will tend toward the behaviors others encourage you to perform and will tend away from behaviors others discourage you from performing. Later in this chapter we will discuss the self-fulfilling prophecy which is consistent with symbolic interactionism.

One way to understand the influence of others on our self-concept is through the **Johari Window,** depicted in figure 3.2.[5] The Johari Window is a square that is divided into four areas. Each of these areas, or quadrants, contains a different picture of self.

The **open self** in the first quadrant represents information about yourself known to you and known to others. Included in this quadrant might be your name, nickname, gender, age, and religious affiliation or membership.

Figure 3.2
The Johari Window.

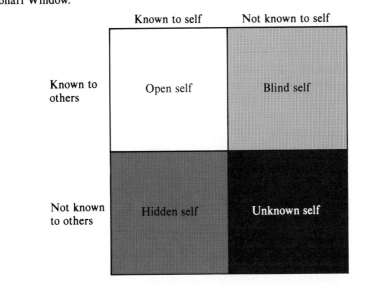

The second quadrant, the **blind self,** consists of information not known to you but known to others. Included here would be behaviors in which you engage of which you are unaware, such as blinking frequently when you feel threatened, interrupting others when they talk to you, or bragging about your grade point average. Also included in this quadrant are occurrences no one has told you about—you were adopted, you nearly died in infancy, or your grandfather was a thief.

The third quadrant, the **hidden self,** includes information you are aware of about yourself but you have not shared with others. You might have done something about which you are embarrassed or ashamed—stolen merchandise from a department store, had an abortion, or cheated on a test—or about which you are proud—made the Dean's list, received a scholarship, or were chosen for an important award.

The **unknown self** in the fourth quadrant includes information that no one—not you or anyone else— knows. For whatever reason, people submerge parts of themselves and let no one, including themselves, know about these parts. Consider those persons who join Alcoholics Anonymous, who announce they are gay, or who are able to identify a part of their personality after years of therapy. An individual does not "become" an alcoholic when he or she announces it, people do not endorse homosexual behavior for themselves without any previous history of homosexual behavior, and the part of the personality that emerges after years of therapy has been part of the self for some time. Sometimes, hypnosis, therapy, or other mind-altering experiences allow a person to glimpse the unknown self.

This examination of the Johari Window allows us to see why others may respond to us differently than we expect. For instance, others may respond to information in the blind area of your self. Someone may see you as highly knowledgeable about interpersonal relationships and frequently seek your advice. You may not perceive yourself as very knowledgeable in this area and question the person's interest in your ideas. Or, your parents may treat you very protectively because you nearly drowned in a friend's swimming pool when you were a toddler. You may find your parents' behavior strange since you have never been told of the swimming pool incident.

Watzlawick, Beavin, and Jackson have suggested other people respond to us in three distinct ways.[6] These responses include confirmation, rejection, and disconfirmation. **Confirmation** occurs when others treat us in the manner consistent with our own notion of who we are. For instance, if we see ourselves as athletic and knowledgeable about physical fitness, we are confirmed when others ask our advice about jogging, working out, and staying in good physical shape. Confirmation is not only satisfying, it strengthens our established self-concept.

Rejection occurs when others treat us in a manner inconsistent with our self-definition. Consider people who mistakenly believe they have unusual insight in solving problems. These individuals believe their ideas are generally excellent and that others can benefit from them. In group meetings, these people offer their ideas freely, but they observe that no one seems to respond positively to their ideas. Their ideas are ignored and are discarded as unworkable. The result is that individuals' definitions of self are rejected. These people's self-concepts may be altered over time if they continue to receive messages that reject the previously established perception of self.

Disconfirmation occurs when others fail to respond to our notion of self or when others respond in a neutral way. Neutrality may not sound disconfirming, but consider small children who make continual attempts to gain responses to their notions of self from their parents. Consider marital partners who have spouses who rarely offer personal comments. Think about grandparents who are the recipients of little conversation, and almost no conversation about how they are seen by others. These individuals are disconfirmed, and their self-concept may be altered as a result of such interactions. Disconfirmation suggests to people they do not exist or they are irrelevant to others. People who are disconfirmed may experience loneliness and alienation.

Two Components of Self-Concept

Self-Image

Self-concept is composed of two parts. *Self-image* is the descriptive part of self, while *self-esteem* is the evaluative part of self. Your **self-image** is the picture you have of yourself, the sort of person you believe you are. Included in your self-image are the categories in which you place yourself, the roles you play, and other similar descriptors all of us use to identify ourselves. If you tell an instructor you are a married woman with three children and "only" a part-time student, you are calling attention to several aspects of your self-image—the roles of wife, mother, and part-time student.

Consider what you say about your academic status. Do you tell people you are a "part-time student," a "commuter student," a "community college student," a "dormie," a "college student," a "university student," or simply "a student"? The label you use to identify yourself indicates your self-image and, to some extent, affects your communication.

Our self-image is originally based on categorization by others. Other people categorize us by role: husband, mother, boss. Others categorize us by personality traits—intelligent, enthusiastic, neurotic, superstitious—or by physical characteristics—tall, beautiful, wiry. Family roles are used most often in the categorization of other people, followed by occupation, marital status, and religious affiliation.[7]

The roles we play directly influence the way we communicate. The role of parent calls for a kind of communication that is different from a student's. What you say, how you say it, to whom you speak, and how frequently you speak are largely determined by the roles you play.

Self-Esteem

Our self-image is *descriptive,* while our self-esteem includes *evaluative feelings* that bear some relationship to our self-image. **Self-esteem** is how we feel about ourselves, how well we like ourselves. A professional woman shares her self-esteem when she explains she really enjoys being both a mother and a college professor and seldom feels any conflict between the two roles. You share your self-esteem when you say how excited you are about the prospect of a career in retail sales or industrial management and how eager you are to begin your work.

Self-esteem is usually based on perceptions of our own successes or failures. If you have a favorable attitude toward yourself, you are said to have high self-esteem; if you have unfavorable or negative attitudes toward yourself, you have low self-esteem. Self-esteem—whether high or low—is easily observed when we communicate with other people. The way they communicate to us, in turn, affects our self-esteem.

Excessive concern over self-esteem, however, is often associated with **self-consciousness**. People who are self-conscious are usually shy, easily embarrassed, and anxious in the presence of other people. Most of us are sometimes shy, embarrassed, or anxious. Nearly all public speakers experience stage fright from time to time. A self-conscious person, however, suffers stage fright in all situations, to the point of being unwilling to even try to speak before any group. Self-conscious people experience shyness, embarrassment, and anxiety regularly.

Self-Concept in Process

If someone asks you who you are, you might respond in a variety of ways—depending upon the situation, the other person, and the way you feel at the moment. If you are applying for a job and the person requesting information is the prospective employer, you might identify yourself in terms of specific work experience or educational background. If the situation involves an intimate friend or spouse, you would probably respond with far different information—perhaps with more emphasis on your feelings than on your specific experiences.

When we say our self-concept is *in process,* we mean our self-concept is not the same in all situations, with all people, and at all times. Indeed, the situations, people, and times directly impact upon how we see ourselves. We selectively attend to some parts of who we are, and we ignore other parts. As was observed earlier, the importance of others and events outside of ourselves in determining our self-concept cannot be overemphasized. Since our self originates in interactions with others, the view of ourself we share in class is different from the view of ourself we share at a party. The verbal and nonverbal symbols offered by others encourage us to play different roles for our employer and for our family. By placing ourselves in the positions of others and attempting to view ourselves as we imagine others see us, we change from stumbling adolescents into competent young adults.

In considering the notion that self-concept changes, we should also consider how self-concept was originally formed. In essence, our self-concept is determined by the treatment we receive from others and the relationships we have with them. Our self-image, as we have stated, occurs as a result of our being categorized by others. Our self-esteem depends on whether we have been rewarded or punished by them.

From the moment we are born, and some scholars believe even earlier, the treatment we receive from others influences who we believe we are. As babies, we respond to the nonverbal messages of hugging, kissing, cuddling, and touching. As we begin to understand language, we respond to verbal messages as well. Early verbal messages—"Big boys don't cry," "Little ladies don't make messes," and "Daddy thinks you're the best baby in the whole world"—influence our self-concept, as well as shape our self-control and self-expression.

Small children are trusting, and they have little experience on which to draw; consequently, they believe what other people tell them. Parental evaluation—verbal and nonverbal—has a particularly strong effect on the development of the child's self-concept. And what the parents believe about the child has a tendency to become a self-fulfilling prophecy.

The **self-fulfilling prophecy** is the tendency to become what people expect you to become. In the book *Pygmalion in the Classroom: Teacher Expectation and Pupils' Intellectual Development,* Rosenthal and Jacobson speak of the importance of the self-fulfilling prophecy. These two researchers summarize a number of studies of academic performance that show that students who are expected to do well actually do perform better. Rosenthal and Jacobson conclude:

> To a great extent, our expectations for another person's behavior are accurate because we know his [or her] past behavior. But there is now good reason to believe that another factor increased our accuracy of interpersonal predictions or prophecies. Our prediction or prophecy may in itself be a factor in determining the behavior of other people.[8]

Our self-concepts originate in our
interactions with significant others.

The self-fulfilling prophecy is relevant to self-concept. Our concept of ourselves originated in the responses we received when we were young, and, to some extent, self-fulfilling prophecies help to maintain our self-concept. In many ways, we attempt to behave consistently with other people's expectations, regardless of whether those expectations are positive or negative. Suppose a small girl is complimented by her family for being quiet, praised by her elementary school teachers for her lack of assertiveness, and encouraged by cultural constraints not to speak up. The result can be a reticent young woman who is afraid to make a speech. On the other hand, suppose a child is praised for talking, is encouraged to put her ideas into words, and is congratulated for winning debates. The result might be a young woman who truly enjoys talking. The self-fulfilling prophecy affects our self-concept, which, in turn, affects our communication with others.

The self-fullfilling prophecy is not quite so simple. We do not simply and routinely behave in the ways other people expect. A transaction occurs between other people's expectations and our expectations for ourselves. For some people, other people's expectations play a more important role than their own expectations. For others, their own expectations are more relevant than are the messages they receive through interaction. This caveat helps us to understand why Rosenthal and Jacobson's study has been questioned in more recent investigations.

In his insightful, though somewhat depressing, book titled *Lost in the Cosmos: The Last Self-Help Book,* Walker Percy discusses the idea that we continue to gain more and more information about a number of things, including the cosmos, but that we know increasingly less about ourselves. Percy identifies some of the unique features of the self that appear to apply to most people in our culture.

One of the characteristics of the self Percy identifies is particularly relevant here is how the self feels misplaced. Percy describes our situation of attempting to be the person we believe others want us to be, while encouraging others to be the self that they believe we want them to be. He provides an example:

> Imagine you are walking down Madison Avenue behind Al Pacino, whom you have seen frequently in the movies but never in the flesh. He is shorter than you thought. His raincoat is thrown over his shoulder. Hands in pockets, he stops to look in the window of Abercrombie & Fitch. His face takes on a characteristic expression, jaws clenched, eyes dark and luminous, like young Corleone in *The Godfather*. The sight of Pacino in the flesh acting like Pacino on the screen gives you a peculiar pleasure. Then you become aware that, though Pacino is looking at the articles in the window display, he is also checking his own reflection in the glass. This, too, gives you pleasure, though of a different sort. Explain the difference. (Hint: The aesthetic pleasure of seeing an instance of a symbol, Pacino in the flesh at Abercrombie's, measure up and conform to the symbol itself, Pacino on the screen, and the different pleasure of seeing the instance, Pacino, rescued from the symbol and restored to human creatureliness, the self in all its vagary, individuality, and folly. The first case: Ah, there is Pacino acting just like Corleone! The second case: Ah, there is Pacino acting like me!)[9]

As Percy illustrates in his book, the complicated, multifaceted individuals we become are not only a result of other people's responses and reactions to us, but also our perception of the meaningfulness of those responses and reactions. Each of us receives unique and individual responses from others; moreover, we react to the responses in specialized and individualistic ways. Percy illustrates Barnlund's "six people" presented in chapter 1.

Gender Differences in Self-Concept

We also observed in chapter 1 that gender differences in communicative behavior have been widely studied in the past three decades, and our discussion of self-concept is incomplete without our consideration of gender. In this section we will share some of the important findings relative to gender and self-concept.

Earlier in this chapter we noted one's integrated self tends toward the behaviors others encouraged and tends away from behaviors others discouraged. From the time we are born, we are treated differently because of our biological sex. We dress male and female babies in different kinds and colors of clothing. Parents respond differently to male and female infants.[10] We describe male and female babies with different adjectives: boys are strong, solid, and independent, while girls are loving, cute, and sweet. People describe identical behavior on the part of infants differently if they are told the infant is a "boy" or a "girl."[11] Preschool children observe commercials and cartoons

Table 3.1 Masculine and feminine scale items

Masculine Items		Feminine Items	
Aggressive	Hard-headed	Appreciative	Jolly
Arrogant	Industrious	Considerate	Modest
Assertive	Ingenious	Contented	Praising
Autocratic	Inventive	Cooperative	Sensitive
Conceited	Masculine	Dependent	Sentimental
Confident	Opportunistic	Emotional	Sincere
Cynical	Outspoken	Excitable	Submissive
Deliberate	Self-confident	Fearful	Sympathetic
Dominant	Sharp-witted	Feminine	Talkative
Enterprising	Shrewd	Fickle	Timid
Forceful	Stern	Forgiving	Warm
Foresighted	Strong	Friendly	Worrying
Frank	Tough	Frivolous	
Handsome	Vindictive	Helpful	

on television, are read books, and play with toys in which "appropriate" sex roles are depicted. In many ways, people are treated differently because of their biological sex.

Since the messages about sex roles are abundant, we may be surprised children do not develop specific sex role conceptions earlier than they currently do. Before the age of three, children have little notion of their sex role, but between the ages of three and five, sex roles develop.[12] Between the ages of five and seven, gender constancy, or the tendency to see oneself consistently as a male or female, develops in most people.[13] Role models, educational institutions, games and toys, and children's literature all reinforce different male/female roles.

Females are encouraged to behave in a feminine manner and males are encouraged to behave in a masculine way. How are femininity and masculinity expressed in our culture? Table 3.1 depicts the personality characteristics that have been validated in a well-known masculinity-femininity measure.[14] Although recent evidence demonstrates that all women are not feminine and all men are not masculine, a strong relationship exists between being a man and being masculine and being a woman and being feminine.[15]

Our culture tends to be masculinist, that is, masculine attitudes, predispositions, and characteristics are more highly valued than are those associated with femininity. For example, our dominant culture is more likely to reward people who are independent, assertive, confident, dominant, forceful, industrious, inventive, shrewd, strong, and tough than it is to reward people who are considerate, contented, cooperative, dependent, emotional, forgiving, friendly, helpful, modest, sensitive, sentimental, sincere, submissive, sympathetic, timid, and warm. Since men are more likely to possess masculine characteristics and women are more likely to possess feminine characteristics, we should not be surprised that men rise to leadership positions in both government and industry. Even feminine occupations such as elementary teaching often have men at their heads in the form of principals or superintendents.

The tendency of women to act in a feminine manner within our culture, which many perceive as being biased toward men, often causes women to report lower self-esteem than men do. Although some studies have not reported differences between women and men,[16] most research provides evidence of lower self-esteem in women than in men.[17]

Other specific factors alter the relationship between one's biological sex and one's self-concept. For instance, a woman's sense of being home- or career-oriented makes some difference in how she defines her self-esteem. Women who are home-oriented base their self-esteem more on friendships and social abilities and less on intellectual and technical abilities, while career-oriented women tend to base their self-esteem on intellectual and technical abilities rather than on friendships and social abilities.[18]

Single women also tend to be higher in self-esteem than married women. Single women value personal growth and achievement, stating they are self-determined, while married women value personal relationships and describe themselves with associated characteristics, kinship roles, and household activities.[19]

Although this information on gender differences in self-esteem may be depressing, particularly if you are a woman, you should keep in mind that the self-concept is not an unchanging commodity. In the next section we will consider how the self-concept is in process, and we will offer some specific information on the changing self-concepts of women and men.

Improving Self-Concept

Numerous people have made dramatic changes in their life-style, behavior, and, in turn, their self-concept. Our news is filled with stories of ex-cons who become responsible members of the community, alcoholics who are able to abstain from drinking, and highly-paid television, movie, and rock stars who are able to overcome their fame and have fairly normal family lives. Dramatic changes occur in people. While we might not choose to follow the paths of those in the news, they do provide evidence that people can change.

Barriers to Improving Self-Concept

Altering our self-concept is not a simple matter, however. One of the factors that makes change difficult is that people who know us expect us to behave in a certain way. In fact, they helped to create and maintain the self-concept we have. These people will continue to insist we maintain a particular self-concept, even when we are attempting to change. For example, you may find that ridding yourself of sarcastic remarks is not an easy task, since others have learned to expect them from you and may interpret any remark you make as a sarcastic response.

Sometimes, we find ourselves working against ourselves when we try to change our self-concept. For instance, you may see yourself as a procrastinator. Even when you set out to do things on time, you may find that you never quite finish them until it is almost too late. You may be behaving this way because it fits in with another element of your self-concept: "responds to pressure," "does magic overnight," or "never lets his friends or family down." We can alter one aspect of our self-concept only to the extent it does not contradict other aspects. If your nonassertiveness fits with your self-concept of being warm and supportive of others, you may find it difficult to become more assertive unless you are also willing to be less supportive on some occasions.

Another problem in altering our self-concept occurs even when we have changed and others recognize we have changed. Sometimes, we hamper the development of our self-concept. For example, if you were shy as a youngster but have become more outgoing, you may properly think you are communicative. Others agree. And still, you may continue to worry about being viewed as reticent.

Steps to Improving Self-Concept

If we wish to change our self-concept to improve our ability to communicate with others, at least two steps are essential. First, we need to *become aware* of ourselves; then we need to establish a positive attitude toward ourselves and toward others. The first step is not an automatic, natural process. We are conditioned to be out of touch with ourselves. We need to develop sensitivity to our own feelings and our own thoughts.

It is essential we acknowledge *all* of our feelings. We are all more familiar with certain aspects of ourselves than others. If we have low self-esteem, we probably focus on those aspects of ourselves that we see as problems or deficiencies. If we have high self-esteem, we probably ignore our liabilities and focus on our assets. All of us have negative as well as positive characteristics, and it is important we recognize both of these aspects of ourselves.

Take the study of communication as an example. Some people feel that studying communication is a waste of time because they are experienced public speakers, or because they have been successful in small group discussions, or because they can successfully communicate with one other person at a time. On the other hand, other people feel the study of communication is useless to them because they suffer from communication apprehension. They feel they simply cannot give a speech, or they cannot talk to a member of the opposite sex and never will, or that communication is just frustrating to them, regardless of the communication situation.

The second group, people who suffer from low self-esteem, generalize from one type of communication situation, in which they feel they fail, to all other communication situations. The first group, people who enjoy high self-esteem, generalize from specific communication successes to all other communication situations. It is essential to our understanding of ourselves that we acknowledge all of our abilities and failings and not make the error of generalizing from one or two specific cases. Few people are competent in every communication situation; fewer still are incompetent in all communication situations.

To become more aware of ourselves, it is also necessary that we *focus* on ourselves, rather than on others. Instead of using your parents' perception of you, try to establish your own view. Rather than deciding "who you are" on the basis of cultural standards and norms, attempt to make your assessment on the basis of your own standards and norms. No one else knows you as well as you do—it is important you use yourself, the best source available to you.

One woman, Alice, can illustrate the importance of focusing on ourselves instead of on others. She attended an assertiveness training workshop because she was unable to talk to her husband about family finances. She was sure her husband felt that he should be the family financial expert; yet, during their ten years of marriage, Alice had witnessed countless near-crises of a financial nature. Every time she tried to talk to her husband, he acted sullen and withdrawn. His responses encouraged her to keep her ideas about finances to herself. Alice found herself in a vicious circle. She believed he was not competent to handle money, and she was unassertive in talking about it.

As Alice worked through her communication problem, she made a number of discoveries. Confronting her husband with the situation, Alice found he did not really want to handle the money and preferred she handle the finances. He had only seemed sullen and withdrawn because he was embarrassed by his ineptitude in economics and simple math. Alice also found she was more capable of balancing the checkbook, budgeting the family resources, and investigating investments. She finally realized she had been taking her cues from her husband, rather than from herself. Focusing on ourselves, rather than on others, is essential to become aware of who we are.

The second step in changing our self-concept—*establishing a positive attitude* toward ourselves and others—is more difficult than increasing self-awareness. If we are to alter our self-concept, we must strive for the situation in which we believe that we, and other people also, are worthy of liking and acceptance. We need to reject highly critical attitudes about both ourselves and others. We need to develop the belief that we, and others, have potentialities worthy of respect. We need to free ourselves of anxiety, insecurity, cynicism, defensiveness, and the tendency to be highly evaluative. Our goal should be to free ourselves so we can establish meaningful relationships with ourselves and with others.

It was very important that Alice did not verbally attack her husband for his nonverbal behavior. When she approached him about the problem, she did so in a clear and straightforward way. She did not criticize his inability to handle the finances or his inability to talk to her about his problem. Instead, she tried to communicate her respect for him, while, at the same time, she discussed a problem. She showed her concern about their family's problem while maintaining her love for her husband.

Alice exemplifies the kind of respect we should feel for everyone. We may not accept another person's behavior, but we need to maintain an appreciation for his or her potentialities that goes beyond the immediate situation. This kind of respect or appreciation of other people allows us to become the kind of person we truly wish to become.

In the album notes for *Sharepickers,* Mason Williams wrote the following:

Here I Am Again

One night after a concert with a symphony orchestra, I was sitting by myself in my room, wondering what a super-duper love star like me is doing all alone, and I began to feel sorry for myself. I started thinking about where I was and how I had got here. I felt like I was going to cry, so naturally I grabbed my guitar to catch the tears and wrote this song, which is about living a way of life and writing songs off to it beyond the need to.

I realized I was just another blues singer with nothing to be blue about except being stuck having to sing the blues, trapped by the truth—it's not what you don't do that holds you back, it's what you do well that gets you. It seems like if you're successful at something and it comes easy, you always try to free ride it past the right point. I've met a lot of people who are stuck in spiritual ruts because they'd latched onto a magic and tried to ride it too far. Good luck turns bad on you after awhile; you have to learn where to get off. I realized I'd missed my stop. Here I was alone again writing another lonely song about being alone again, instead of really being with a friend. I had used music, God bless it, just to get to the top. It was only a ticket, and here I was fondling my ticket in a hotel room in Hartford, Connecticut, way off the track.

I realized that all my life I'd been afraid—afraid to ask for what I wanted—because of what I wanted. I realized that I had become rich and famous, a star, just so everything would come to me—even more than I could use—and I could take my pick from it without risking rejection. Suddenly it struck me that that's probably why most successful people are unhappy. They get themselves into a position where they don't have to ask for things, without realizing that if they don't practice asking for what they want from others, they're not good at asking for what they want from themselves—which means they don't know what they want. And you know, you never can satisfy somebody who doesn't know what he wants.

You have to practice asking to be a good asker. What's more, you have to practice *true* asking. You've got to ask for what you really want and not what somebody else wants you to ask for or what you think is right to want. Practice doesn't make perfect unless you practice perfectly.

That's what praying is all about, my friends. To pray is to practice asking, and if you're not really asking, you're not really practicing. A person could spend the rest of his life afraid to ask for what he wants, because of what he wants, whether he really wants it or not.[20]

Williams lends support to the idea that it is essential to know ourselves and our needs to be satisfied. Suggest needs of your own that must be fulfilled for you to be satisfied. Is it necessary for you to alter your behavior to meet these needs? Have you been avoiding this? Do you need to enlist the help of others? Write down one or two needs you have not been meeting. Resolve to change your behavior and enlist any necessary help from others to meet your needs. If you feel comfortable doing so, report the results to your classmates. You may be able to help others find the courage to make changes, too.

Is it necessary for you to alter your self-concept to meet your needs? For instance, if you feel you need a full-time career in teaching to satisfy your desire to serve others, you might have to change your view of yourself as someone who is too busy with a family to pursue a career. If you need a certain amount of time alone each day, you may have to alter your view of yourself as a person who always has time for everybody.

Gender Differences in Improving Self-Concept

Earlier we noted women and men do not develop similar self-concepts. We explained that because men are viewed more positively in our culture than are women, they develop a more positive self-concept. Here we will observe that other factors interact with gender and they suggest some ways for improving one's self-concept.

One's locus of control affects self-concept. The placement of locus of control allow women to perceive themselves as favorably as men. Sixth grade girls who had high internal **locus of control** (they perceived themselves, rather than outside forces, to be responsible for the events in their lives) viewed themselves as favorably as did sixth grade boys. Sixth grade females with a strong external locus of control (they perceived people and events outside of themselves controlling their lives) viewed themselves significantly lower on measures of self-esteem.[21] Girls who have an external locus of control may be more susceptible to the debilitating effects of the sex-biased culture than are girls who look within for control of the events of their lives.

The results of a national study of successful female professors lends support to this conclusion. Women who were successful in gaining promotion and tenure in the field of speech communication were asked to offer their advice on success to others. These women suggested that others should 1) exhibit **androgynous** (a combination of traditional masculine and traditional feminine) and flexible behavior, 2) do their jobs well, 3) develop internal locus of control, and 4) gain the support of others. The third point is particularly relevant to the importance of developing one's own standards rather than relying upon the perceptions of others.[22]

Although women may have some unique problems in establishing positive self-esteem, they can do so. The female sex role may encourage low self-esteem and depression insofar it teaches women they are weak and not in control of their own fate. However, women can alter their self-perception by participating in self-help groups. Women who participated in such groups tended to overcome low self-esteem, reduced depression in their lives, decreased their tendency to blame others, and felt that they were more in control of their own lives.[23]

Both women and men can change their self-concepts. We are not saddled with an unchanging sense of self that will limit our opportunities or negatively affect our communicative opportunities with others. The available research suggests means by which we can more positively view ourselves, and in turn, those with whom we interact.

Summary

In this chapter we examined how we come to understand ourselves. Self-awareness plays a central role in communication. Parental and social conditioning reinforces our lack of self-awareness. Self-awareness is essential to our mental health and to our ability to communicate competently.

Self-concept is each person's consciousness of his or her total, essential, and particular being. Our self-concept is affected by our interactions with others. Other people may confirm, reject, or disconfirm our self-concept.

Self-concept consists of self-image and self-esteem. Our self-image is the picture we have of ourselves, the sort of person we believe we are. Included in our self-image are the categories in which we place ourselves, the roles we play, and the other ways in which we identify ourselves.

Self-esteem is how we feel about ourselves, how well we like ourselves. To have high self-esteem is to have a favorable attitude toward yourself; to have low self-esteem is to have an unfavorable attitude toward yourself. Self-consciousness is excessive concern about self-esteem; it is characterized by shyness, embarrassment, and anxiety in the presence of others.

Self-concept is in process. Our self-concepts change with the situation, the other person or people involved, and our own moods. Our self-concept is originally formed by the treatment we receive from others and our relationships with others. It is maintained largely through our interactions with others.

Gender differences affect self-concept. People are treated differently from the time they are born on the basis of their biological sex. Furthermore, the culture tends to be masculinist. As a result, women tend to have lower self-esteem than do men. These findings are consistent with studies that have shown members of minority groups often suffer from negative self-esteem because they have responded to the evaluations of the dominant culture.

Self-concept can be improved, but the process is not a simple matter. The two essential steps in changing self-concept are becoming aware of ourselves and establishing a positive attitude toward ourselves and others. Both women and men can improve their self-concepts.

Listening: Understanding Another

*I*t is the province of knowledge to speak and it is the privilege of wisdom to listen.

Oliver Wendell
Holmes

I like to listen. I have learned a great deal from listening. Most people never listen.

Ernest Hemingway

I know that you believe you understand what you think I said, but I am not sure you realize that what you heard is not what I meant.

Anonymous

Objectives

1. Distinguish between listening and hearing.
2. Explain two kinds of listening.
3. Give examples of four kinds of external distractions that interfere with listening and empathy.
4. Give examples of the internal factors that interfere with listening.
5. Discuss the ways in which we can overcome the barriers to effective listening and improve our ability to understand other people.

Key Terms

listening
hearing
active listening
feedback
defensiveness
interpretive
 listening
factual
 distractions
semantic
 distractions

mental
 distractions
physical
 distractions
self-focus
defensiveness
experiential
 superiority
egocentrism
status
stereotypes

In chapters 2 and 3, we discussed the importance of understanding our world and understanding ourselves as we considered the relevance of perception and self-awareness to communication. In this chapter we extend our discussion of understanding to understanding another person. In communication, the basic method of understanding others comes through listening. Listening is an essential skill that must be practiced if our goal is to understand another person.

When we think about communication, we usually focus on the speaking, or sending, aspect. If someone says she is enrolled in a speech class, we ask how many speeches she has to make. If someone says he had a talk with his family, we ask him what he said. The other activity involved in communication—listening—should be given equal consideration. **Listening** is the process of receiving and interpreting aural stimuli.

Listening is a complex activity and involves far more than simply hearing a sound. **Hearing** is a natural, physiological function we have unless we suffer a physiological loss. Listening is a selective activity that involves both the reception and the interpretation of aural stimuli. Current investigators are attempting to determine the specific skills involved in listening.[1] You may recognize the complexity of listening if you consider your own experiences. For example, you may have heard a popular song a dozen times but never have listened to the words. You may hear what another person has to say but not listen to the content or intent of his or her message.

Most of us have been in situations in which another person assumed listening and hearing were the same. We can all recall reprimands from our parents like, "What do you mean you didn't clean your room? I came into the living room, where you were watching TV, and told you to do it. I know you heard me." An instructor might have said to you, "I just asked you a question. Everyone else in the room heard it. Why didn't you?" Many people incorrectly assume listening and hearing are the same.

Similarly, many people incorrectly believe they listen well. Most of the evidence, however, is in the other direction. In general, when tested immediately after a message, people recall about one-half of what they have heard, even when they have been informed they will be tested on the information. When they are tested two months later, they recall only about one quarter of the information.[2]

No matter how well or poorly we listen, listening is an essential communicative activity. Listening is a fundamental component of communication, and we spend a great deal of time engaged in the activity. A classic study stated we spend more than 40 percent of our time engaged in listening.[3] Similarly, contemporary studies demonstrate we listen to a greater extent than we engage in any other form of verbal communication. Weinrauch and Swanda found that business personnel, including those with and without managerial responsibilities, spent nearly 33 percent of their time listening, almost 26 percent of their time speaking, nearly 23 percent of their time writing, and almost 19 percent of their time reading.[4] When Werner investigated the communication activities of high school and college students, homemakers, and employees in a variety of other occupations, he determined they spent 55 percent of their time listening, 13 percent reading, and 8 percent writing.[5] Many other studies have documented the great amount of time people spend listening.[6]

We listen more than we talk, write, or read.

If these investigations were to be repeated in the 1980s, perhaps an even larger percentage of our time would be shown to be devoted to listening. Today, as in the past, we spend time listening to people in social situations, in the classroom and at work. The developments in mass communication and technological advancements, however, have encouraged additional modes of listening. Today, we listen to radio, television, records, cassette tapes, movies, cable programs, word synthesizers, and people brought to us by teleconference calls.

Two Properties of Effective Listening

We engage in listening for a variety of reasons—for appreciation, discrimination, comprehension, evaluation, empathy, and therapy.[7] Listening can be distinguished in terms of purpose, behavior of the listener, nature of the information under discussion, communication setting, and many other categories. Nonetheless, effective listening has two aspects: it is active and it is interpretive. Let us consider each of these two essential qualities.

Active Listening

Active listening has been defined as "involved listening with a purpose."[8] Over twenty-five years ago, active listening was distinguished from passive listening:

> In the former, the individual listens with more or less his total self—including his special senses, attitudes, beliefs, feelings, and intuitions. In the latter, the listener becomes mainly an organ for the passive reception of sound, with little self-perception, personal involvement, . . . or alive curiosity.[9]

Active listening is generally desirable in interpersonal communication situations, but it may also be used effectively in the public speaking setting. Active listening requires activity on the part of the listener. The listener does not lethargically sit or stand while another speaks; instead, active listening is characterized by movement, change, and responsiveness on the part of the listener.

Active listening implies **feedback** is offered to the speaker. Feedback was defined in chapter 1 as the listener's verbal and nonverbal responses to the speaker's messages. The responses must be received and understood by the speaker. Feedback allows us to monitor our communication with others and to avoid many misunderstandings. For example, speakers can alter, correct, or enforce their original messages as they observe and interpret the feedback offered to them. They may add additional examples or speak more concretely if the listener does not appear to understand the point being made. They may retract what they have said or apologize for their position if they believe the listener is disagreeing with them. Finally, they may embellish their message and even take a more radical stand if they recognize agreement coming from the listener.

Feedback can be distinguished along a number of lines, but the discussion in this chapter is limited to the difference between positive and negative feedback. Positive feedback includes such nonverbal behaviors as positive facial expression, smiling, laughing, a forward body lean, increased touching, and movement toward the other person. Verbal examples of positive feedback are statements like, "I understand," "Yes," "I agree," and "Why don't you tell me more?" Positive feedback results in speakers increasing the length of their messages, decreasing linguistic errors and nonfluencies, and decreasing feelings of **defensiveness** (the tendency to protect ourselves against danger or intimacy).

Negative feedback is characterized by frowns and other negative facial expressions, movement away from the speaker, decreased touching, a focus on people other than the communicator, decreased eye contact, and general nonresponsiveness. Statements like, "I don't know what you're talking about," "I don't agree with you," "Who cares?" and "I don't want to hear any more," are extreme examples of negative verbal feedback. Negative feedback results in a message of decreasing length, an increasing number of linguistic errors and nonfluencies, and increasing feelings of defensiveness on the part of the speaker.

You may have observed that not all feedback is clear; nor is all feedback useful. For feedback to be effective, the speaker needs to be able to understand a listener's response, the speaker must be able and willing to accept the information, and the speaker must be able to act on the information.

If you are a listener and want to provide effective feedback, you must first carefully choose any words you intend to use so the other communicator will understand what you mean. Is the other person likely to understand the language you have chosen? Will the other person be aware of what you are describing? Can you place your feedback in a context in which the meaning will be more easily understood? Should you preface your feedback with explanations, observations, or other information?

Second, to help the other communicator accept the information you are providing, you need to consider his or her feelings, attitudes, and values. Avoid "loaded" terms that might produce emotional reactions. Attempt to be descriptive, rather than evaluative. For example, instead of saying, "I don't know why you expect others to help you!" or "You are too upset to be reasonable!" or "No one would want to listen to you!" you might offer, "I understand you want someone to help you," or "I see you're upset," or "Do you simply want someone to listen to you?" State your perceptions as opinions and reactions, rather than as absolute and indisputable facts. Refer to specific, observable behavior, rather than general or global issues. Discuss the relevant behavior, rather than the person. Communicate acceptance of the other person and his or her right to view the world in a manner different from your own.

Third, to help the other communicator act on your feedback, you may need to examine the content of your response. Do not provide feedback to individuals about things over which they have no control. Consider how improvement may occur once the other individual has received your feedback. Suggest specific outcomes, rather than leaving the person bombarded with general information. Provide possible means of altering behavior.

An example may clarify these suggestions. Suppose you are talking about the possibility of your university changing from its current calendar to an alternative one. For instance, if you are currently on a quarter system, you might be discussing the possibility of changing to a semester system. Your friend is in favor of such a change and explains all of his or her reasons for this position. After you have listened carefully to your friend's message, you might respond, "I understand you want to change from a quarter system to a semester system because, under the quarter system, the courses are too superficial and do not have enough depth, and because you do not get to know your instructors well enough. I think your point of view is clear and you have carefully thought about this issue. I am not in favor of the change, and I would like you to consider some of the arguments on the other side. Would you be willing to listen to some of them?"

This example illustrates clear and useful feedback. In your feedback, you have used clear language so your partner should understand what you are stating. You have helped your friend to accept the information by first considering his or her feelings and attitudes before stating your own. You have not used evaluative language, but you have remained highly descriptive. You have stated the two positions as though reasonable individuals could hold either point of view. You have relied upon the other individual's words, rather than on issues or matters that go far beyond the current discussion. Finally, you have helped the other person to act upon your feedback. You have clearly stated you would appreciate having your friend listen to arguments on the other side of the issue as well. You did not provide feedback over an issue about which he or she has no control, and you suggested a specific behavior the person could exhibit.

Do not be discouraged if you find it is easier to read about effective feedback than it is to provide it. Providing appropriate feedback is particularly difficult when the topic is one about which the two communicators have strongly divergent opinions. With practice, however, you can improve your ability to offer feedback that is clear and useful to others with whom you communicate.

The example provided illustrates feedback about verbal message content. We also provide feedback about message delivery and/or the relational aspects of the communication. For instance, suppose that a teacher tells you in a sarcastic tone, "One more perfect speech and you're going to graduate in less than one year of college!" You know your instructor's purpose is to offer you positive support for the fine speech you have given and you actually cannot graduate in less than one academic year of college. To demonstrate your understanding, you might offer the feedback, "Can I get a Ph.D. in two years?" This example also illustrates that feedback can be responsive to nonverbal, as well as verbal, elements.

Interpretive Listening

Interpretive listening has understanding as its basic goal. When someone attempts to engage in interpretive listening, he or she admits meaning is created through the give-and-take of interaction. Communication as action is displaced with communication as transaction as we discussed in chapter 1. Individuals mutually interpret each other's remarks until a shared meaning arises.

Interpretive listening is identified by a number of basic qualities including openness, play, and the fusion of horizons.[10] *Openness* refers to the idea that meanings are not totally determined when two people begin an interaction. This quality means far more than simply saying that the communicators are open to each other. They are also open to the creation of the development of meaning between themselves. Meanings are not completely predetermined and brought to the interaction; instead, they are a by-product of it. The conversation is thus fluid and based on the several variations within the context.

A humorous example of the openness that can be involved in interpretive listening is provided by Mel Brooks, the film director of such movies as *Blazing Saddles* and *Young Frankenstein*.

> Asked what he thought of critics, Brooks replied, "They're very noisy at night. You can't sleep in the country because of them." His interviewer politely corrected him: "I said *critics,* not crickets."
> "Oh, critics! What good are they? They can't make music with their hind legs."[11]

Brooks' openness with words and the fluid meanings he supplies account for a great deal of his humor.

The term *play* is used both metaphorically and to describe the conversations in which we engage. You will recall that in distinguishing communication as action, interaction, and transaction, we used the comparison of throwing a ball back and forth. In the same way, when we view listening as interpretive, we are suggesting that people engage in an activity that has a to-and-fro movement. Turn-taking, or questioning and answering, marks our interaction with others.

The play involved in interpretive listening is obvious in a great deal of humor that occurs in everyday conversation, including the story about Mel Brooks. The term "wordplay" itself attests to the playfulness that is involved. Intimate couples often develop their own language to refer to the parts of their anatomy as well as their sexual intimacy, demonstrating another level of playfulness in interpretive understanding.

A *fusion of horizons* suggests that each person possesses a perspective that can be joined to another's point of view. One writer defines a horizon as "the range of vision that includes everything that can be seen from a particular vantage point."[12] An individual's horizon changes as he or she changes and moves as he or she moves. Nonetheless, it constitutes his or her unique view and of course, embodies one's prejudices, values, attitudes, and beliefs.

When we are able to fuse our horizons with another person, we do not devalue our own perspective nor do we disregard that which we have come to believe. Instead, we achieve understanding by attaining "a higher universality that overcomes, not only our own particularity, but also that of the other."[13] The two views become one at a more abstract, or higher, level. Just as Hegel suggested we move from thesis to antithesis to synthesis, the two communicators each offer their unique point of view which is subsumed under a synthesis that combines both.

When two individuals are able to achieve this fusion of horizons, they do not dismiss all differences or fail to recognize that distinctive points of view still remain. Instead, they learn to appreciate their differences. Some writers suggest they might even "celebrate" the tension the irreconcilable differences hold. Prejudices are not viewed negatively, then; instead, they are incorporated into the model of common understanding.

An example may clarify this concept. One couple told their child that an architect named Bruce was going to visit them during the evening. A short time later, the child asked her father, "When is Punky coming?" Her father thought for a moment and then realized the child had creatively replaced "Bruce" with "Punky", probably because of the popularity of the "Punky Brewster (Bruce-ter)" television character in the child's life. His response was similarly creative: "Punky will be here in about 15 minutes, but you can call him 'Bruce.' " The father and the child now knew the man as "Punky Bruce," but agreed on calling him "Bruce."

John Stewart presents a table which summarizes interpretive listening and it is reprinted here with his permission.[14]

Table 4.1 Interpretive Listening

Focus	on mine and the other's verbal and nonverbal communicative action
Goals	a. to be present to the other and aware of the other's presence to me b. to affirm and use my prejudices as I co-produce with the other meanings that we share.
Mode of play:	
Action	engage in the to-and-fro do not expect closure or finality; stay open move in many directions at once
Outcome	fusion of horizons understanding—viewed as a tensional event; two persons subjectively build an understanding between themselves.

From Stewart, John, "Interpretive Listening: An Alternative to Empathy," *Communication Education,* 32, pp. 379–391. © 1983 Speech Communication Association, Annandale, VA. Reprinted by permission.

When we understand that effective listening is interpretive, we allow ourselves the opportunity to share meaning with another person. We do not perceive the world in exactly the same way other people do and we can never view their world in a manner that is identical to their experience with the world. Although we cannot have their experience, we can, through our interactions, share a newly created, joint experience.

Interpretive listening places both communicators in a similar position. Neither is superior or inferior to the other. One person does not patronize the other by talking "down to" him or her. Similarly, neither must struggle to "keep up" with the other individual's message.

When we listen interpretively, we do not feel the same emotions the other person is expressing. What we do communicate is an awareness, appreciation, and acceptance of their emotions. Interpretive listening requires sensitivity to others and an ability to demonstrate this sensitivity. When we are successful, we communicate to others we are one with them.

When we fail to interpretively listen to others, we are unable to understand them. In a very real sense, we are hurting ourselves. To the extent we cannot interpretively listen, we restrict ourselves to our personal experiences and feelings. Interpretive listening places us on true joint ventures with others with whom we communicate.

Interpretive listening is not an easy task. Frequently we need to demonstrate our interpretive skills when it is difficult to do so. When we disagree with others, we are called upon to come to a higher level of agreement or understanding. Our tendency in such situations is to spend a great deal of time and energy defending our own position and finding fault with other's point of view. We feel a compulsion to prove we are correct and others are wrong. And, yet, interpretive listening allows us to view both ourselves and others as correct. Interpretive listening is satisfying and enriching to both parties in an interpersonal relationship.

Interference with Our Ability to Listen

Studies cited earlier show we do not listen well. Understanding another by listening requires we hear both verbal and nonverbal messages; we understand the content, the intent, and the accompanying emotions; and we communicate our understanding. A number of difficulties and breakdowns in communication can occur on the way. Let us consider some of the factors that may interfere with our ability to listen.

The Message and the Occasion

A number of distractions occur both in the message itself and in the situation in which it is received—factual distractions, semantic distractions, mental distractions, and physical distractions.

Factual distractions occur because we tend to listen for facts instead of ideas. Perhaps our educational institutions encourage this tendency. Instead of looking at the whole, we focus on the parts. We can lose the main idea or the purpose behind a message if we jump from fact to fact instead of attempting to weave the facts together

Listeners are sometimes distracted and therefore cannot listen to the speaker's message.

into a total pattern. For example, a friend might relate an experience from her past in which she felt devastated by circumstances beyond her control. Friends may tell us stories about their childhood—stories of fear, frustration, or anger. We listen to the facts—she comes from a small town, he had a pet hamster—and we do not grasp the emotions.

Semantic distractions are similar to factual distractions in that they are also caused by elements of the message. Semantic distractions occur when someone uses a word or phrase differently or uses a word or phrase to which we react emotionally. Emotional reactions to words often occur when people are classified in a denigrating way—"girl" for a woman over twenty-one, "Polacks" for Polish people, "Jew" for anyone who tends to be thrifty. We examine the confusion words can cause in more detail in chapter 6.

Mental distractions occur when we engage in excessive intrapersonal communication (communicating with ourselves) when we are talking with others. The mental side trips, daydreams, counterarguments, and recollections that we engage in when someone is talking to us distract us from receiving the other person's message. These side trips can be suggested by something the other person says or by our own preoccupation. Mental distractions may occur because of the great difference between the speed at which we hear and the speed at which we speak. Most Americans talk at a rate of about 125 words per minute, but we are able to receive about 800 words per minute. This discrepancy allows us great freedom to consider other matters more important to us. A student can easily plan dinner while listening to a psychology lecture. Someone else can review the exciting events of the previous evening while listening to the news. We can decide whether to accept an invitation while listening to a friend's account of an argument with another friend.

Physical distractions include all the stimuli in the environment that might interfere with our focusing on the other person and his or her message. We can be distracted by sound—a buzzing neon light, loud music, or the speaker's lisp; by visual stimuli—a poster of a nude on the wall, bright sunlight, or the speaker's beauty; or by any other stimuli—an unusual odor, an uncomfortable article of clothing, or an unpleasant aftertaste in our mouth.

Ourselves

Other factors that interfere with our ability to listen are related to ourselves. Self-focus, defensiveness, experiential superiority, and egocentrism all interfere with our ability to understand another.

Self-focus, or a preoccupation with thoughts about ourselves, hampers listening and empathy. As we suggested in the exercise entitled "Who's Right?", we need to develop positive feelings about ourselves and about other people. Self-focus suggests we have developed regard for ourselves but we have failed to develop the same feeling toward others. In the conversation that follows, Tom is unable to empathize with Karen because he allows his personal concerns to dominate his thinking and his communication.

Karen has just received word that her grandmother has died. Tom is the counselor at the company where she works. Karen is extremely upset and goes to Tom because she needs to talk to someone. She has talked with him only casually in the past, but she feels he will understand because he is a trained counselor.

Karen:	Tom, do you have a minute?
Tom:	Sure, Karen, come on in.
Karen:	I wanted to talk to someone for a little while.
Tom:	Fine. What would you like to talk about?
Karen:	Well, I just got a phone call from home saying that my grandmother died, and I guess I just needed someone to talk to.
Tom:	Yeah, I know how you feel. I had a grandmother who died about eight years ago. She was the neatest lady I have ever known. Why, when I was a kid she used to bake cookies for me every Saturday. We used to go to the park on weekends for picnics. She sure was fun to be with.
Karen:	I'm sure you had a good time, but I sort of wanted to talk about my grandmother.
Tom:	Oh, sure. Well, what was she like?
Karen:	Well, she was a good lady, but . . .
Tom:	Yeah, I guess all grandmothers are pretty good.
Karen:	I guess so, but . . .
Tom:	You know, it's been a long time since I thought about my grandmother. I'm really glad you came in today.

Karen:	Yes, well, I guess my break is about over so I'd better get back to work.
Tom:	Okay. It's been nice talking to you. Stop by anytime.
Karen:	Sure.

A number of factors may account for a person's focus on himself or herself, rather than on the other person. **Defensiveness**, which was mentioned as an outcome of negative feedback, is a common reason. People who feel they must defend their position usually feel threatened. They feel that, in general, people are attacking them and their ideas, and they develop the habit of defending themselves. Sometimes, people who are championing a specific cause—such as the Ku Klux Klan, the National Rifle Association, the American Communist Party, or draft registration resisters—develop this attitude. They stand ready to respond to the least provocation, and they tend to find fault with other people.

In the interview that follows from the organizational setting, the supervisor demonstrates a defensive attitude and is consequently unable to listen to the employee. The supervisor is the director of operations in a social service agency. She has arranged this appraisal interview with the employee because she is evaluating his performance as a community organizer.

Supervisor:	As you know, after sixty days, we evaluate each new employee. That's why I've asked you to come here today. Here is the evaluation form I have filled out. Please read it.
Employee:	*(after reading)* I don't understand why you have marked me so low in dependability.
Supervisor:	Because you always ask so many questions whenever I tell you to do something.
Employee:	But the reason I ask questions is that I don't understand exactly what you want me to do. If I didn't ask the questions, I wouldn't be able to perform the task because your instructions usually are not clear to me.
Supervisor:	I marked you low in that area because you require so much supervision.
Employee:	It's not supervision I need, it's clear instructions, and I don't feel it's fair for you to mark me low in this area when I am not.
Supervisor:	It doesn't really matter what you think because I'm doing the evaluation.
Employee:	Don't I have anything to say about it?
Supervisor:	No. Now that you've read it, will you please sign here?
Employee:	Definitely not. I feel that it is unfair and inaccurate.
Supervisor:	Then check the box that indicates that you are not in agreement with the evaluation. All your signature means is that you have read it, not that you agree with it.
Employee:	This is the most ridiculous evaluation I have ever had in my entire life.
Supervisor:	That's unimportant at this point. If you don't have anything else to say, that will be all.

The defensive verbal behavior by the supervisor clearly interfered with her ability to listen to her employee. Defensiveness usually interferes with our ability to listen.

Another reason for self-focus is known as **experiential superiority.** People who have lived through a variety of experiences sometimes express this attitude toward people who have had less experience. Professors often cannot listen or empathize with a student who is explaining why an assignment was not completed on time; they assume the student is offering an excuse they have heard before. Parents sometimes fail to listen to their children's problems or to empathize with them; they feel, from their own experience with a similar problem, they can just give a pat answer.

Why do people engage in experiential superiority? We considered the role of past experiences in perception in chapter 2. Our past experiences lead us to expectations of the future. Thus, we sometimes fail to listen to others because we believe we can predict their messages.

A variation of experiential superiority occurs in long-term relationships, when people have a good deal of experience in the relationship and feel they can predict the other person's statements. Husbands may respond with an occasional "uh-huh" over the newspaper at breakfast; wives may repeat, "Sure, honey," while daydreaming about other matters. The characters in the "Hägar" cartoon typify people who no longer listen to each other—probably as a result of a long relationship.

Another reason people focus on themselves is simple egocentrism. **Egocentrism,** which is almost synonymous with self-focus, is the tendency to view yourself as the center of any exchange or activity. An egocentric person is overly concerned with self and pays little attention to others. This person appears to be constantly asking, "How do I look? How do I sound?" instead of responding to how the other person looks or sounds.

One place you can observe egocentric people is at a party. Egocentric people usually make a number of attention-getting moves that place them at the center of the stage. They may arrive late, talk loudly, dress flamboyantly, and stand in the center of the room to make others focus on them. They also move from person to person or group to group, but they do not give their full attention to the people with whom they are talking. They look around the room, glancing from one person to another. Rarely do they focus on anyone for more than a moment, and even then they do not concentrate on the other person's message.

Our Perception of the Other Person

Other factors that interfere with our ability to listen involve our perception of the other person and preconceived attitudes—such as status or stereotypes.

If we believe other people have **status,** we accept what they say easily, rather than listening carefully and critically. We usually do not listen carefully or critically when the speaker is an M.D., a Supreme Court justice, or a visiting expert. If we think other people have low status, we often do not listen to their statements at all, nor do we retain their messages. Seniors seldom listen to sophomores about study habits, and attractive people rarely take advice from people they consider unattractive. We dismiss statements made by people of lesser status. Thus, we tend not to listen carefully to persons whom we perceive to have either a higher or lower status than ourselves.

Our **stereotypes** also affect our ability to listen. Each of us place people into groups we respect and groups we do not respect. When people are within our respected groups, we tend to believe what they say. When they belong to a group for whom we have little regard, we tend to reject their messages. If we respect Volvo owners, joggers, or people who watch "The Cosby Show," we are more apt to listen to a person who falls into one of these groups than we are if a person owns a different automobile, does not exercise, or views different kinds of television programs.

Status and stereotypes affect our ability to listen. To demonstrate this for yourself, ask two people for a summary of a presidential address or of a statement made by a labor leader, a member of Congress, or the governor. If you ask two people who have different perceptions of the status of the speaker and different stereotypes of the groups to which the speaker belongs, you will probably end up with two entirely different versions of the same address or statement.

Improving Our Ability to Listen

Just as we can identify factors that interfere with our ability to listen, so can we identify ways of improving our listening ability. Let us reconsider the three sets of factors that interfere with our listening—the message and the occasion, ourselves, and our perception of the other person—and suggest methods of overcoming each.

As we mentioned earlier, a number of distractions occur both in the message and in the situation in which it is received. These distractions are factual, semantic, mental, and physical.

We can remove factual distractions by *focusing on the main ideas* the other person is presenting, remembering we can ask later for facts and details. It is far less offensive to another person to be asked for particular numbers, specific locations, or how to spell a particular name than it is to be asked, "What in the world are you talking about?"

Semantic distractions can be minimized if we keep in mind *words are arbitrary symbols*. They have no inherent or natural meaning shared by everyone. If another person uses a word that confuses us, the appropriate response is to ask the meaning of the word or to ask how she or he is using the word. If we cannot overcome our emotional reaction to a specific word, it is essential we explain the word's negative connotations for us to the person using it.

Instead of allowing mental side trips to distract us from another person's message, we should use the time to *identify the other person's central idea and to determine how the information fits into our own conceptual framework*. We can determine if the other person's ideas contradict or support what we already believe to be true. We can try to integrate the new information into the organized set of beliefs that is our own knowledge. By refusing to consider unrelated matters, our listening and our understanding can be greatly increased.

Physical distractions, like noise, bright lights, unusual odors, or provocative surroundings, can usually be handled easily. In most cases, a simple *move to another room or another location* solves the problem. If we cannot move, we may have to increase our concentration on the message and/or decrease our focus on the distraction.

In the previous section, we examined the distractions that result from ourselves and interfere with our ability to listen—self-focus, defensiveness, experiential superiority, and egocentrism. The habit of focusing on ourselves, rather than on the other person, is difficult to break. Nonetheless, we need to alter this behavior if we hope to listen to someone else, and, in turn, to understand that person.

Focusing on the meaning and experiences we share is helpful if we find that we usually react defensively to other people's messages. Other people may be attacking one of our pet beliefs or attitudes, but they may also be defending it from another perspective. Regardless of their point of view on the single issue, we usually can find a number of points of agreement. Maximizing our shared attitudes, values, and beliefs and minimizing our differences results in improved listening and better communication. In addition, if we do not react defensively to other people's disagreements with us, we may find ourselves being persuasive and encouraging them to agree with us.

Checklist for Effective Listening

To determine how effectively you listen to others, complete the following exercise after you have engaged in a conversation with another person:

_____ 1. Did you focus on the main ideas the other person was presenting, rather than on specific facts and details?

_____ 2. Did you avoid being distracted by an unusual word, by a word that offended you, or by a word used in an unusual manner?

_____ 3. Did you focus on the intent, as well as the content, of the other person's message?

_____ 4. Did you engage in the conversation in a place that was free of physical distractions, or did you move to such a place if your original setting was distracting?

_____ 5. Did you focus on the meaning and experiences that you shared with the other person, rather than on the meaning and experiences that are different?

_____ 6. Did you give the other person a full hearing, rather than exhibiting impatience with him or her?

_____ 7. Did you concentrate on the other person, rather than on yourself?

_____ 8. Did you suspend judgment until the other individual was finished speaking, rather than jumping to premature conclusions?

_____ 9. Did you focus on the other person as a valuable source of ideas and information, rather than categorizing and dismissing him or her?

If experiential superiority is the problem that interferes with your listening and empathizing, _give the other person a full hearing._ Impatience with a person who has no experience with a particular problem, and the poor listening that accompanies this attitude can result in a communication breakdown. Listening to this person will result in improved communication. You may even learn something new.

People who are continually concerned with their self-image and how that image is perceived by others have difficulty listening. Egocentrism is an ingrained attitude that is extremely difficult to change. Perhaps the best thing an egocentric person can do is to _attempt to concentrate on the other person._ There are appealing advantages to concentrating on the other person if you are egocentric. Concentrating on the other person when he or she is speaking will probably cause them to focus on you when you are speaking. Even more important, you will "come across" better if the other person perceives you to be a good and empathic listener. No amount of makeup, clothing, or other adornments will make you as attractive to others as the ability to listen.

To overcome problems related to our perceptions of other people, we need to *learn how to suspend judgment*. Rather than assuming other people's messages are acceptable or unacceptable without listening to them, we need to wait until we have heard them out. We can make grave errors by assuming that people who belong to a particular group are like all of the other members of that group. Bernard Gunther said, "Take a chance on getting slapped, you might get kissed!"

We can also overcome our perception problems of other people if we *focus on the other people as sources of feelings and thoughts, ideas, and information*. When we categorize other people, we can easily dismiss them. When we view them respectfully as valuable human resources, we find that our listening and our empathizing improve.

Behaviors Associated with Effective Listening

Along with the general guidelines for improving our ability to listen, there are specific verbal and nonverbal behaviors associated with effective listening. You may want to consider your own listening behavior to determine which of these behaviors you regularly demonstrate and which of these skills you may want to add to your repertoire.

Provide clear verbal responses. Do not provide ambiguous, complex, or overly simple verbal responses. Providing cliché responses like, "That's the way it goes," "I guess that's the way the cookie crumbles," and "You only get out of it what you put into it," add little clarity. Be as specific and detailed as you can in the verbal feedback you offer.

Employ descriptive statements. Evaluation leads to defensiveness. Descriptive feedback leads to a supportive communication climate. Descriptive comments add clarity and can suggest areas of disagreement without offending or insulting the other person. For example, the statement, "I understand your position, but I can also understand those who have the opposing view," does not threaten the other person.

Provide reflective statements. To provide a check on the accuracy of your understanding, you might try using reflective statements. Reflective statements are comments that "mirror" or "reflect" back to a speaker what the speaker has stated. You can simply restate what the other person has said, or you can put comments into your own words. In either case, reflective statements provide an opportunity for checking what the other person has stated or what the other person meant.

Demonstrate bodily responsiveness. A lack of movement suggests lethargy or a lack of interest; bodily movement and gestures suggest concern and interest. Alter your facial expression or the placement of your legs, arms, and head in appropriate response to the other person's message. Use touch to show your concern or your affection for the other person.

Establish eye contact. Direct eye contact allows you to observe the other person more carefully. We discuss the importance of nonverbal communication more fully in chapter 5. When you establish eye contact with the other person, you are able to receive the fullness of the other person's message—the nonverbal as well as the verbal elements. In addition, eye contact suggests you are focusing on the other person, rather than being distracted by other sights in the room.

Summary

In this chapter, we considered the importance of understanding other people when we communicate with them. We can increase our understanding of other people by improving our ability to listen. Listening is the process of receiving and interpreting aural stimuli.

Effective listening is active and interpretive. Active listening is involved listening with a purpose. Interpretive listening has understanding as its goal.

A number of factors interfere with our ability to listen and to empathize. These factors fall into three categories—those related to the message and the occasion, such as factual, semantic, mental, and physical distractions; those related to ourselves, including self-focus, defensiveness, experiential superiority, and egocentrism; and those related to the other person, such as status and stereotypes.

We can overcome these obstacles, however, and improve our ability to listen to others by: focusing on the main ideas; keeping in mind that words are arbitrary symbols; identifying the other person's central idea and determining how the information fits into our personal conceptual framework; moving when physical distractions interfere; focusing on the meaning and experiences that are shared; giving the other person a full hearing; concentrating on the other person; suspending judgment; and focusing on the other person as a source of feelings, thoughts, ideas, and information.

Five behaviors associated with effective listening are: providing clear verbal responses; employing descriptive statements; providing reflective statements; demonstrating bodily responsiveness; and establishing eye contact. Understanding another person is a difficult but worthwhile goal for each of us.

chapter 5

Nonverbal Codes: Sharing with Others

A smile is the shortest distance between two people.

> *Victor Borge*

You cannot shake hands with a clenched fist.

> *Indira Gandhi*

When one is pretending the entire body revolts.

> *Anais Nin*

Objectives

1. Identify the factors that make it difficult to interpret nonverbal behavior accurately.
2. Draw some conclusions about people that usually can be based on people's body orientation and position or their facial expression.
3. Discuss your own use of personal space, and explain why it differs when you are with a close friend or a stranger, at home or at a party.
4. Identify the factors that influence the meaning and use of touch.
5. Define six types of paralinguistics that can affect the meaning of a message.
6. Discuss your own use of objects in communication and the meaning you think the objects convey.
7. List some guidelines that can help you to interpret nonverbal behavior more accurately.

Key Terms

nonverbal codes	vocal cues
kinesics	pitch
proxemics	rate
territoriality	inflection
personal space	volume
intimate distance	quality
personal distance	enunciation
social distance	paralanguage
public distance	objectics
tactile	artifacts
communication	

In the past three chapters we have considered the process of understanding. In chapter 2, we considered perception, the process of understanding our world; in chapter 3, we considered self-awareness and self-concept, the process of understanding ourselves; and in chapter 4, we considered listening, the process of understanding others. In this chapter and in chapter 6, we shift our attention to sharing messages with others. One way we share messages with other people is through the nonverbal codes we use. As you shall determine in this chapter, communication often occurs without words.

Communication experts agree nonverbal communication is essential to understanding and sharing meaning.[1] *How* we say something is as important as *what* we say. Furthermore, the nonverbal aspects of our messages tend to add depth or additional meaning to the verbal aspects of our messages.

Problems in the Interpretation of Nonverbal Cues

Nonverbal communication provides the basis for much of the misunderstanding that occurs in communication. We have difficulty interpreting nonverbal cues for at least two reasons: we use the same cue to communicate a variety of different meanings, and we use a variety of cues to communicate the same meaning.

One Cue Communicates a Variety of Different Meanings

Examples of situations in which one cue communicates a variety of different meanings will clarify this problem. Raising your right hand may mean you are taking an oath, you are demonstrating for a cause, you are indicating to an instructor you would like to answer a question, a physician is examining your right side, or you want a taxi to stop for you. We may stand close to someone because of a feeling of affection, because the room is crowded, or because we have difficulty hearing. We may speak softly because we were taught it was the "correct" way for us to speak, because we are suffering from a sore throat, or because we are sharing a secret. We may wear blue jeans because they are an acceptable mode of dress, because they symbolize our rebellion against higher-priced clothing, or because they are the only clean clothes we have that day.

A Variety of Cues Communicate the Same Meaning

An example of a variety of nonverbal cues communicating the same meaning would be the many nonverbal ways adults have to express love or affection. We may choose to sit or stand more closely to someone we love. We might speak more softly, use a different vocal intonation, or alter how quickly we speak when we communicate with someone for whom we have affection. Also, we often dress differently if we are going to be in the company of a person we love.

The "Peanuts" cartoon shows an inappropriate way of communicating meaning. Yet, those of us who are parents or who have younger siblings are familiar with the tendency of young children to express affection or attraction through physical aggression. As children grow, they begin to experiment with more appropriate nonverbal indications of affection.

Definition and Identification of Nonverbal Codes

Nonverbal codes were defined in chapter 1 as codes of communication that consist of symbols that are not words. Bodily movements and facial expression, use of space, touching, tone of voice, and clothing and artifacts are all nonverbal codes. Let us consider these systematic arrangements of symbols that have been given arbitrary meaning and that are used in communication.

Bodily Movement and Facial Expression

Kinesics is the study of people's bodily movements and includes the study of posture, gestures, and facial expression. We communicate many of our feelings or emotions in these nonverbal ways. Ekman and Friesen determined our faces give others information about *how* we feel and our bodies suggest the *intensity* of the particular emotion.[2]

Nonverbal Codes: Sharing with Others   79

Best-selling self-help books have familiarized the general public with the importance of bodily movement in communication. Unfortunately, they have also left the impression that bodily movement is relatively easy to understand. Sitting in one way or another, substituting a new kind of posture for a more familiar one, and experimenting with novel bodily moves does not provide anyone with quick and easy solutions to personal or job-related difficulties. Understanding human movement is complicated. The meaning of a person's movement may be due to characteristics of that person, characteristics of the observer, characteristics of the environment, or a combination of these factors.

To make an accurate assessment of the meaning of another person's movements, we need consider the person's particular characteristics and circumstances. He may be grimacing because he has just left the dentist. Her quick pace may be due to lateness, rather than habit. He may regularly smile because of his optimistic disposition, while she may sit and stand close to others because she is warm and nurturing. We need to consider the physical, psychological, and emotional characteristics of the person being observed.

Our own particular characteristics must also be considered when we are observing another person. When we interpret another person's movements as unfriendly, we need to examine our own expectations. Are we expecting that person to be unfriendly and thus selectively perceiving what we want to perceive? If someone appears nervous to us, is it because we are feeling tension and projecting our feelings onto someone else? Our own attitudes, values, and beliefs, coupled with our current needs and goals, must be taken into account when we assign meaning to another person's movements.

Finally, we need to consider the particular characteristics of the environment. A person standing with crossed arms may feel cold. Someone who is moving around slowly might be sensitive to another person's headache and might be trying to avoid making noise. A clerk who is darting in and out of the storeroom may be waiting on customers who are hard to please. Environmental factors must be considered when we try to understand bodily movement.

Mehrabian found he could draw some general conclusions about a person's body position and orientation during communication by considering three variables: liking, power or status, and vitality or responsiveness.[3] If we keep in mind the particular characteristics of the person we are observing, our own particular characteristics, and the particular aspects of the environment, we can use Mehrabian's findings to help us interpret the movements of other people.

Mehrabian found liking was often expressed by leaning forward, a direct body orientation, greater closeness, increased touching, a relaxed posture, open arms and body, positive facial expression, and more eye contact. Consider your own body orientation and movement when you are with persons you like. You tend to sit closer to them, lean toward them, touch them more, relax physically, smile at them more, and look at them more. When you are with persons you do not know or do not like, you tend to sit farther away from them, you seldom touch them, you are physically tense or at least not relaxed, you smile less, and you establish only minimal eye contact.

Mehrabian found power, or status, was communicated by expansive gestures, relaxed posture, and less eye contact. When you consider persons in authority whom you know, you probably can recall their large gestures, the relaxed posture of their body, and their tendency to look at you less often. Supervisors, teachers, employers, and parents exhibit such behavior.

Mehrabian also found responsiveness or involvement with other people is shown by movement toward other people, spontaneous gestures, a shifting of posture and position, and facial expressiveness. Consider those persons whom you believe are highly responsive. They move a great deal, they are spontaneous in their gestures and movements, and their faces are very expressive.

Ekman and Friesen have presented a classification schema useful in understanding different types of bodily movements.[4] They base their categories of nonverbal movement on the functions, origins, and meaning of the behavior. Their five categories of nonverbal movement include emblems, illustrators, affect displays, regulators, and adaptors.

Emblems, according to Ekman and Friesen, are those nonverbal behaviors that directly suggest specific words or phrases. Emblems generally *substitute* for words, rather than accompany them. Among the most common emblems are the thumb and first finger held together to suggest "okay," the thumb in the air to identify a hitchhiker, and a beckoning first finger asking another person to "come here." Emblems, like the verbal language we use, are specific to individual cultures. In our culture, we ask someone to come toward us by beckoning with our finger; in another culture, the same gesture may be viewed as an insult.

Why do people rely on emblems when they could use words? Sometimes, you may wish to communicate something without interrupting another speaker or without being disrespectful. For instance, if someone asks you a question but does not allow you time to verbally answer, you can shake your head affirmatively or give them "thumbs up." Sometimes, you may use emblems because efficient communication is required. If you're working in heavy industry, you may only have time to signal to another person that he should pull a load, move a truck, or lift a rig. Finally, you may find emblems useful when someone may be able to see you but not hear you. Hitchhikers on the side of the road would have little success if they were required to discuss their need for a ride with passersby.

Ekman and Friesen define *illustrators* as those nonverbal behaviors that accompany and reinforce verbal messages. When you nod your head at the same time you are saying "yes"; when you point up, down, or in the direction that you are stating; and when you draw a picture in the air at the same time you are describing the shape of an object, you are using an illustrator. We might note that the same gesture that functions as an illustrator when it accompanies verbal language functions as an emblem when it replaces a verbal message. Illustrators have more universality from one culture to another than do emblems.

People who wish to add emphasis to their messages use illustrators. Similarly, persons who are concerned that the other person may not understand them use illustrators to validate their message. Effective communicators know the more channels they can use to express a message, the greater their chances for sharing meaning with another person and for gaining a common understanding.

Affect displays, according to Ekman and Friesen, are movements of the face and body that hold emotional meaning. The anger, the happiness, the surprise, or the love we show through the movements of our eyes, mouth, and other facial muscles are included in this category. Similarly, we use affect displays when we bang our fist on the table to show anger or when we jump up and down as an expression of joy or excitement. These displays may be conscious or unconscious. Just as illustrators tend to reinforce and clarify messages, affect displays similarly add another avenue for expression. Affect displays are more frequently associated with women than men; that is, women are more likely to show their feelings and emotions through nonverbal displays than are men.[5]

Ekman and Friesen define *regulators* as those nonverbal behaviors that monitor or control the communication of another individual. For example, the head nods, eye contact, blinking, smiling, looking away, and various sounds that we make while another person is speaking are regulators. We signal others to tell us more, to stop talking, to give us additional details, to give fewer specific incidents, or to continue talking in the same way. Among those nonverbal behaviors that discourage another from talking are neutral or negative facial expressions, physical movement away from the speaker, glances away from the speaker, and nonresponse to the speaker's message. Those nonverbal behaviors that encourage another to talk are positive facial expressions, smiles, physical movement or a physical lean toward the speaker, and changes or alterations in facial expression. For example, high school and college teachers generally know when to conclude their lectures even before a bell rings or before they examine their watches because of regulators students employ. Students generally begin to gather their books and put away their things shortly before the period is over.

Persons who use regulators to a great extent tend to be the "architects" of conversations. They are the people who introduce new topics, determine when a topic will not be discussed, encourage and discourage the participation of others in the conversation, and generally manage the interaction. People with a great deal of power or status are more likely to use regulators than are those with limited power and status.

Adaptors are the final category of nonverbal behaviors that were determined by Ekman and Friesen. Adaptors include movements we may fully perform in private, but only partially perform in public. For example, you may scratch an area of your body extensively when you are alone, but only rub the area lightly when you are in public. You may thoroughly massage a foot that has "gone to sleep" when in private, but only make a gesture toward doing so when with others. Adaptors serve a useful purpose, but are generally considered inappropriate in a public setting.

Adaptors are almost habitual behaviors we use to help make ourselves feel more comfortable in communication interactions. You may not be very conscious of your own adaptors. Some people are surprised to learn they regularly twist a ring or a lock of their hair; they stroke their chin or other area of the face; they pull a charm or other piece of jewelry back and forth; they play with cigarettes, cigars, or matches; or they chew on a toothpick or their fingernails.

Bodily movements and facial expression are important to the public speaker, just as they are important to the interpersonal communicator. As evidence, consider the finding that audiences who can view the speaker's visible behavior understand more of the speech than audiences who cannot see the speaker.[6] Gestures and facial expression should appear to be natural when you deliver a speech. You may find if you are sincerely concerned about the topic of a speech, you will gesture in a way that appears natural. In addition, you can practice delivering public speeches in front of friends, classmates, or even a mirror to determine if your gestures add to an understanding of your message.

Space

Edward T. Hall, an anthropologist, introduced the concept of **proxemics**, the human use of space, in 1966 in his book *The Hidden Dimension.* Robert Sommer analyzed the topic further in 1969 in *Personal Space: The Behavioral Basis of Design.* These researchers and others have demonstrated the role space plays in human communication.

Two concepts considered essential to the study of the use of space are territoriality and personal space. **Territoriality** is our need to establish and maintain certain spaces of our own. Territoriality has been studied more in animals than in humans, but it is recognized as a human need. People stake out their territory in various ways. Students leave coats or books on a library table while they search the stacks. Faculty members arrange their offices so their own chairs are identifiable. We all use fences, "no trespassing" signs, wedding rings, and other symbols that indicate our territory. We can purchase bumper stickers that read, "If you can read this, you're too close"; hotels and motels provide us with "Do not disturb" signs; and airlines offer us cards that state, "Sorry, this seat is occupied." Territoriality refers to territory that is generally immovable and typically separate from a person.

On the other hand, **personal space** is the area surrounding a person that moves with the person. Personal space is the amount of physical distance you maintain between yourself and other people. We seldom think about personal space until someone invades it, but such an invasion may create stress or evoke defensive behavior.

Edward T. Hall was the first to define four distances people regularly use. His categories have been useful in understanding the communicative behavior that might occur when two communicators are a particular distance from each other. Beginning with the closest contact and the least personal space and moving to the greatest distance, Hall's four categories are: intimate distance, personal distance, social distance, and public distance.[7]

Hall defines **intimate distance** as that distance which extends from touch to approximately eighteen inches. Intimate distance usually is used with people who are emotionally close to us. Frequently, this distance is used in private, rather than in public, situations. Intimate distance was the focus of Carole King in "Feeling Sad Tonight," when she sang, "There is a space between us which we cross to touch each other softly and so make up for our loss."[8] You may use intimate distance when you are showing affection to another person, when you are offering comfort to someone who has suffered a loss, or when you are protecting a person from real or imagined danger. In circumstances in which intimate distance seems inappropriate—on a crowded bus or elevator, walking on a narrow path, encountering others on a busy sidewalk—you may feel discomfort. In circumstances in which intimate distance is appropriate, you probably respond very positively to the other person. In general, we tend to stand and sit close to people for whom we feel interpersonal attraction.[9]

Personal distance, which, according to Hall, ranges from about eighteen inches to four feet, is used in a variety of different encounters. When people stand together at a range of about eighteen inches, they are probably signaling something more than a conversation is occurring. At four feet, conversations are the most likely interpersonal exchange to occur. This range of space allows intimate and nonintimate interpersonal exchanges. Crowded cocktail parties, informal social exchanges, and bars frequently encourage people to stand or sit at the minimum amount of space included in this distance. Such spacing encourages more intimate conversation than probably would occur if more space was available.

Hall defines **social distance** as extending from four to approximately twelve feet. Social distance is generally used by people conducting business. The closer social distances are commonly used in informal business settings—the boss speaking to an employee, a salesperson helping a customer, or a secretary addressing co-workers. The greater social distances are used in more formal and less personal situations. For example, we may use seven to twelve feet to separate ourselves from a college president, a potential employer, or other people with equally high status.

According to Hall, **public distance,** which exceeds twelve feet, is used primarily in public speaking situations. Your instructors probably stand twelve or more feet away from most of the class members. Ministers, lawyers, and public speakers usually use public distance when they address audiences. When others choose this distance to communicate, you can safely assume they are more interested in giving a speech than they are in having a conversation with you.

What implications can we draw about the four categories of space? We have already suggested they differ in privacy or intimacy as we move from closer and more personal distances to farther or more public distances. Should we assume that everyone with whom we communicate at eighteen inches to four feet simply wants a conversation and nothing more? Should we assume people who tend to sit or stand very close desire an intimate relationship? Such implications are not so easily drawn. Many variables affect the meaningfulness of the distance communicators use.

Personal space varies from person to person and from situation to situation. Among the variables that determine personal space are: (1) the characteristics of the individuals communicating, (2) the relationship between the individuals, (3) the physical setting, and (4) the cultural background of the individuals.

Two relevant characteristics of individuals are their size and sex. People who are larger require a greater amount of personal space, and people who are smaller—including children—require a smaller amount of space.[10] Women, for example, show the least discomfort when the space around them is small and tend to interact at closer

Conversational Space

Visualize your living room at home. Are the chairs and couches arranged to encourage or discourage conversations? How many conversational groupings are encouraged by the arrangement of the furniture? Do tables, lamps, and other objects interfere with conversations? How closely are chairs placed to each other? Does the lighting in the room, the colors of the walls, or the textures of the fabrics on the upholstered furniture add to, or detract from, the possibility people will enjoy conversations in the room?

Contrast your living room with a lounge in the student center on your campus. What similarities and differences exist? What general conclusions can you draw about the two rooms for communicative purposes?

range.[11] Women and children may be allowed less space and may therefore come to expect it. On the other hand, both women and children may desire more relational closeness than do men. Cause-effect relationships between size and use of space are difficult to prove, but do provide interesting avenues of speculation.

The relationship between the individuals who are interacting is also important in evaluating people's use of space. Generally, we stand closer to friends and farther away from enemies.[12] We also stand away from strangers, authority figures, people of higher status, physically handicapped people, and individuals from different racial groups. Several generalizations can be made here. We tend to use less space with people whom we perceive to be similar to us. If we stand close to other people, we tend to perceive them as friends, of equal status, and/or as generally more similar to us than different. In addition, we tend to use less space when we have little to fear. For instance, standing away from an enemy, someone who could do us physical or psychological harm, may be for self-protection. None of us consciously puts himself or herself in danger. Thus, people who stand close to us are communicating a sense of similarity and trust.

The physical setting also can alter our personal space. People tend to stand closer together in large rooms and farther apart in small rooms.[13] In addition, physical obstacles and furniture arrangements can affect personal space.

The cultural background of the people communicating also must be considered in the evaluation of personal space. Edward T. Hall was among the first to recognize the importance of cultural background when, in 1963, he was training American service personnel for service overseas. Hall wrote:

> Americans overseas were confronted with a variety of difficulties because of cultural differences in the handling of space. People stood "too close" during conversations, and when the Americans backed away to a comfortable conversational distance, this was taken to mean that Americans were cold, aloof, withdrawn, and disinterested in the people of the country. USA housewives muttered about "waste-space" in houses in the Middle East. In England, Americans who were used to neighborliness were hurt when they discovered that their neighbors were no more accessible or friendly than other people, and in Latin America, exsuburbanites, accustomed to unfenced yards, found that the high walls there made them feel "shut out." Even in Germany, where so many of my countrymen felt at home, radically different patterns in the use of space led to unexpected tensions.[14]

Cultural background can result in great differences in the human use of space and the interpretation, by others, of that use of space. As our world continues to shrink, more of us than ever will be working in multinational corporations, regularly traveling to different countries, and interacting with people from a variety of backgrounds. Sensitivity to space differences in different cultures and quick and appropriate responses to those variations may become imperative to survival.

Touching

Tactile communication is the use of touch in communication. Touch may be viewed as the most extreme form of invasion of personal space. Nonetheless, touch is essential to our growth and development. An insufficient amount of touching can result in health disorders such as allergies and eczema, speech problems, problems with symbolic recognition, and even death.[15] Researchers have found untouched babies and small children grow increasingly ill and even die. Schutz observes,

> The unconscious parental feelings communicated through touch or lack of touch can lead to feelings of confusion and conflict in a child. Sometimes a "modern" parent will say all the right things but not want to touch his child very much. The child's confusion comes from the inconsistency of levels: if they really approve of me so much like they say they do, why won't they touch me?[16]

Touch is one of the most powerful ways we have of communicating with others. The pleasure touch causes originates in infancy. For most people, touching is positive and enjoyable. The interpretation of the meaning of a particular touch depends, of course, on the type of touch, where a person is touched, and the cultural background of the people involved. Still, in most cultures, touch is associated with positive attitudes, and lack of touch is associated with negative attitudes. Touch is one of the clearest indications we like and accept others and they like and accept us.

Touch varies on the basis of one's culture. In general, North Americans are less touch-oriented than are persons in other cultures. Jourard determined the rates of touch per hour among adults. In a coffee shop setting, adults in San Juan, Puerto Rico, touched 180 times per hour while those in Paris, France, touched about 110 times per hour, followed by those in Gainesville, Florida, who touched about two times per hour, and those in London, England, who touched only once per hour.[17] A later study demonstrated North Americans are more frequent touchers than are the Japanese.[18]

Touch varies on the basis of subculture, too. Men and women, for example, do not touch each other to the same degree, nor are men and women touched to the same extent. Women value touching more than do men,[19] and most studies indicate females are touched by others more than males are from about the age of six months. Mothers tend to touch their female children more than their male children.[20] When college students reported the extent to which they were touched and the areas of their body that were touched, female students reported they were touched more and also more areas of their body were accessible to others.[21] In a final study, which investigated touching among fathers, mothers, daughters, and sons, it was found fathers and sons touched each other less than any other combination.[22]

Touch is essential to our growth and
development in communication.

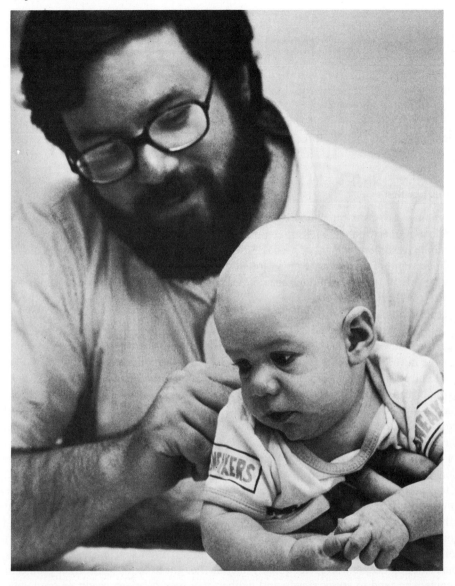

Men touch others more than women touch others. Gender differences in touch may
be based on the difference in sexual aggressiveness on the part of men in our culture.
Men generally have initiated and demonstrated sexual interest; therefore, they have
tended to touch others more. Henley has suggested the greater touching exhibited by
men may be an indication of power and dominance.[23] She explains touch is not a reciprocal act; that is, men have access to women's bodies but women do not have the

same access to men's bodies. Touching, according to Henley, may be a method of exerting status or power over another person since it represents an invasion of personal space.

Henley's interpretation of the differences in touching behavior by men and women may be more clear if we consider the differences in touching exhibited by subordinates and superordinates. The boss can put his hand on the secretary's shoulder, the teacher can pat the student's arm, and the doctor can touch the patient almost anywhere. Conversely, the secretary cannot put an arm around the boss, the student cannot hold the teacher's hand, and the patient is seldom allowed anything but a handshake with a physician. Persons with higher status are allowed the opportunity to touch others, and the opportunity is not reciprocal. Touch may be a sign of liking, it may suggest power or status differences, or it may be job related.

Vocal Cues

In chapter 1, we distinguished between nonverbal and nonoral communication. Nonoral communication includes all communication that is *not* oral. For example, written communication, sign language, and the use of touch are nonoral. While nonverbal codes include some of the nonoral or nonvocal codes, they also include pitch, duration of sound, rate of speech, and nonwords such as *eh* and *ah*. Nonverbal codes are all codes that do not consist of words. When we consider **vocal cues,** we include all of the oral aspects of sound except the words themselves.

We can categorize vocal cues into (1) **pitch**—the highness or lowness of a voice; (2) **rate**—how rapidly or slowly a person speaks; (3) **inflection**—the change or lack of change in the pitch of a person's voice; (4) **volume**—the loudness or softness of a person's voice; (5) **quality**—the pleasant or unpleasant characteristics of a person's voice, including nasality, raspiness, and whininess; and (6) **enunciation**—a person's pronunciation and articulation. In addition, vocal cues include specific sounds, such as *uh-huh, ah,* and *mmh,* as well as silences. All of these elements comprise **paralanguage,** the vocal or physical aspects of delivery that accompany the language used.

Vocal cues frequently convey a speaker's personal attributes and provide information about the speaker's current emotional state. Among the personal attributes are often communicated are the speaker's age, height, overall appearance, body type, status, and credibility (which is discussed further in chapter 13).[24] For example, we associate a high-pitched voice with someone who is female rather than male, someone who is younger rather than older, and someone who is smaller rather than larger. We visualize someone who uses a loud voice as being taller rather than shorter, and larger rather than smaller. People who speak quickly may be thought to be nervous rather than calm. People who tend to speak slowly and deliberately may be given credit as high-status individuals or people who have high credibility.

A number of studies have related various emotions to specific vocal cues. Joy and hate appear to be the most accurately communicated emotions, while shame and love are the least accurately communicated.[25] Joy and hate appear to be conveyed by fewer vocal cues, which makes their interpretation less difficult than the complex sets of vocal cues that identify emotions like shame and love. "Active" feelings like joy and hate are associated with a loud voice, a high pitch, a blaring timbre, and a rapid rate. Conversely, our "passive" feelings, which include affection and sadness, are communicated with a soft voice, a low pitch, a resonant timbre, and a relatively slow rate.[26]

Personality characteristics, too, have been related to vocal cues. Dominance, social adjustment, and sociability have been clearly correlated with specific vocal cues.[27] While the personality characteristics attributed to individuals displaying particular vocal cues have not been shown to accurately portray the person, as determined by standardized personality tests, our impressions affect our interactions. In other words, while we may perceive loud-voiced, high-pitched, fast-speaking individuals to be dominant, they might not be measured as dominant by a personality inventory. Nonetheless, in our interactions with such people, we may become increasingly submissive because of our perception that they are dominant. In addition, these people may begin to become more dominant as they are treated as though they have this personality characteristic.

Sex differences are also related to vocal cues. Women tend to speak in higher-pitched voices than do men. Men generally speak with greater intensity than women. Also, men and women demonstrate different intonational patterns. For instance, women tend to state even declarative sentences with an upward inflection to suggest a question rather than a declaration.[28]

Vocal cues can help a public speaker to establish credibility with an audience and can clarify his or her message. Pitch and inflection can be used to make the speech sound aesthetically pleasing, to accomplish subtle changes in meaning, and to tell an audience whether you are asking a question or making a statement, being sincere or sarcastic, being doubtful or assertive. A rapid speaking rate may indicate you are confident about speaking in public or you are nervously attempting to conclude your speech. Variations in volume can be used for emphasis or to create suspense. Enunciation is especially important in public speaking because of the increased size of the audience and the fewer opportunities for direct feedback. Pauses can be used in the public speech for dramatic effect and to arouse audience interest. Vocalized pauses—the *ahs, uh-huhs, ums,* etc.—are not desirable in public speaking and may distract the audience. Far better than vocalized pauses is silence. One observer noted, "Sometimes silence is best. Words are curious things, at best approximations. And every human being is a separate language. . . . [sometimes] silence is best."[29]

Clothing and Other Artifacts

Objectics, or *object language,* refers to our display of material things and includes clothing and other artifacts. **Artifacts** are ornaments or adornments and include jewelry, hairstyles, cosmetics, automobiles, smoking paraphernalia, umbrellas, expensive pens, briefcases, glasses, and even the choice of fillings in our teeth! Our clothing and other adornments communicate our age, gender, status, role, socioeconomic class, group memberships, personality, and our relation to the opposite sex. Dresses are seldom worn by men, low-cut gowns are not the choice of shy women, bright colors are avoided by reticent people, and the most recent Paris fashion is seldom seen in the small towns of

The importance of clothing and other artifacts play an important role in nonverbal communication.

mid-America. These cues also indicate the time in history, the time of day, and the climate. Clothing and artifacts provide physical and psychological protection and are used for sexual attraction and to indicate self-concept. Our clothing and artifacts serve to clarify for each of us the sort of person we believe we are.[30] They permit us personal expression,[31] and they satisfy our need for creative self-expression.[32] An interest in clothing predicts a high level of self-actualization.[33]

Many studies have established relationships between an individual's clothing and artifacts and his or her characteristics. In an early study, the personality traits of conformity, sociability, and nonintellectualism were positively correlated with *decoration* in dress; self-control and extroversion were positively correlated with *comfort;* compliance, stereotypic thinking, social conscientiousness, and insecurity were positively correlated with *interest;* social conformity, restraint, and submissiveness were correlated positively with *conformity* in manner of dress; and, finally, responsibility, alertness, efficiency, and precision were correlated with *economy* in dress.[34] A more recent study confirms these results; conforming to current styles is correlated with an individual's desire to be accepted and liked.[35] In addition, individuals feel that clothing is important in forming first impressions.[36]

Perhaps of more importance are the studies that consider the relationship between clothing and an observer's perception of that person. In an early study, clothing was shown to affect others' impressions of status and personality traits.[37] We also seem to base our acceptance of people on their clothing and artifacts. Women who were asked to describe the most popular women they knew used clothing as the most important characteristic.[38] Finally, brightly colored clothing is associated with sophistication, immorality, and physical attractiveness.[39]

Clothes Communicate!

Our clothing communicates who we are, what we value, how we see ourselves, and a number of other messages. Consider the clothing and jewelry you wear and what it might communicate about you. Keep a record for three or four days of all of the clothing, jewelry, and other adornments you wear. Record changes in clothing within the day. After you have compiled this record, suggest why you made these choices and what these particular clothes might communicate to others. Finally, ask two friends or acquaintances what your clothing communicates to them. Consider the similarities or differences in the perception you have of your clothing and the perceptions your friends or acquaintances have.

The importance of clothing and other artifacts on our perception of others cannot be overrated. A few years ago, the students in a male instructor's class told him clothing was a form of communication only among older people—like himself. They argued that young people made no judgments about other people's clothing and seldom even noticed other people's clothes. The instructor's arguments to the contrary fell on deaf ears. The next semester, while again lecturing on object language, the instructor told his new students about that previous discussion—but while he talked, he slipped off his jeans and sweater to reveal a t-shirt and running shorts. At the end of the hour, he gave a quiz on the material covered during the period. Not surprisingly, the students successfully answered the items on the material covered before he disrobed but did a poor job with the questions on material he covered afterward. These students agreed— they were distracted by his unusual and provocative attire and had difficulty concentrating on the lecture. The importance of clothing as a means of nonverbal communication, to young as well as older people, was established, at least in that second class.

Solutions to Problems of Interpretation of Nonverbal Codes

The difficulty of interpreting nonverbal codes appears insurmountable. The interpretation problems are serious, but they can be minimized if we use three sets of information: (1) we need to be sensitive to all of the variables in the communication situation; (2) we must attend to all of the verbal and nonverbal codes; and (3) we need to use descriptive feedback to clarify unclear codes.

Considering All of the Variables in the Communication Situation

Other people's nonverbal communication is only a small part of a communication situation. We must also consider other aspects of these other people—their ability to use words, their intentions, their immediate and past history, and so forth. We also need to consider ourselves and how our presence might affect the behavior of others. The relationship between ourselves and others is also important to take into account. Finally, we should consider the context and the reason for the conversation.

Considering All Available Verbal and Nonverbal Codes

Rather than focusing on another person's clothing or a specific facial expression, we should consider other nonverbal codes as well. We should not forget to listen to the verbal message. If we find contradictions between the verbal and nonverbal messages, we should recall the person's past communication behavior. When contradictions in verbal and nonverbal codes occurred in the past, what was the intended message? Is it likely that this is the intended message now?

Using Descriptive Feedback

Descriptive feedback, which we discussed in chapter 4, is one of the most accurate ways of solving the difficulty of interpreting nonverbal codes. By simply describing to the other person the conflict we find or suggesting the meaning we understand, we can clarify the communication. The other person can suggest reasons for the inconsistencies or supply the intended meaning. We can continue to request clarification until we understand and share the same message.

Descriptive feedback is a difficult skill to master. It requires attention to *describing,* not prescribing or evaluating, what has occurred. Suppose you are talking to a classmate about studying together for an upcoming exam. The classmate replies, "Sure, that would be fine." However, you notice he or she looks away, uses a neutral facial expression, and has no enthusiasm in his or her voice. If you wished to clarify your understanding of his or her response, you might descriptively state, "I am not sure if you wish to study together or not. You said it would be fine, but you did not look at me when you answered, you used a monotonous voice, and you did not display your agreement by showing positive facial expression." Descriptive feedback does not mean you are allowed to infer meaning that is captured from the nonverbal codes: "You say you would be willing to study together, but it's pretty clear you don't want to." Nor does it mean that you are allowed to evaluate the other person: "Why don't you ever say what you mean?" While descriptive feedback is difficult to master, it is well worth the effort! And, as we shall determine, descriptive feedback is important in solving verbal misunderstandings, too.

Summary

In this chapter, we considered the role of nonverbal codes in communication. We have difficulty in interpreting nonverbal codes because we use the same code to communicate a variety of different meanings and because we use a variety of codes to communicate the same meaning.

Nonverbal codes are all codes that consist of symbols that are not words. Bodily movements and facial expression, personal space, sounds other than words, and clothing and artifacts are nonverbal codes. Kinesics is the study of people's bodily movements, including posture, gestures, and facial expression. Five categories of bodily movements are emblems, illustrators, affect displays, regulators, and adaptors. Proxemics is the human use of space. Territoriality—our need to establish and maintain certain spaces of our own—and personal space—the amount of physical distance we maintain between ourselves and other people—are important concepts of proxemics. Tactile communication is the use of touch in communication and is essential to our growth and development. Vocal cues are all of the oral aspects of sound except the words themselves and include pitch, rate, inflection, volume, quality, enunciation, specific sounds, such as *huh, ah,* and *mmh,* and silences. Objectics, or object language, is our display of material things, including hairstyles, clothing, jewelry, and cosmetics. Our object language communicates our age, gender, status, role, socioeconomic class, group memberships, personality, and our relation to the opposite sex.

We can solve some of the communication difficulties in interpreting nonverbal codes if we consider all of the variables in the particular communication situation, if we consider all of the available verbal and nonverbal codes, and if we use descriptive feedback to minimize misunderstandings.

chapter 6

Verbal Codes: Sharing with Others

*C*alvin Coolidge don't say much—but
when he does—he don't say much.

Will Rogers

*I*f you don't say anything, you won't be
called on to repeat it.

Calvin Coolidge

*T*o say nothing, especially when speaking,
is half the art of diplomacy.

Will and Ariel Durant

Objectives

1. Discuss the relationship among words, codes, encoding, and decoding.
2. Explain the personal nature of language.
3. Give examples of how our verbal symbol system (English) gives us a different perception of reality than other verbal symbol systems (for example, French, Hopi, Russian, Eskimo).
4. Explain how words can be an obstacle to communication.
5. Discuss three ways in which we can improve our verbal skills.
6. Differentiate between paraphrasing the content and paraphrasing the intent of a message.
7. Discuss the relationship between the use of unconventional language and the skills of descriptiveness and concreteness.

Key Terms

code	euphemisms
encode	slang
decode	jargon
words	regionalisms
verbal	street language
symbol	Sapir-Whorf
semantics	hypothesis
general semantics	operational
syntactics	definitions
personal language	descriptiveness
subculture	inferences
denotative	implications
meaning	paraphrasing
connotative	concreteness
meaning	dating
colloquialisms	indexing
clichés	

The preceding three comments introduce this chapter on language. Words (verbal symbols) and sets of words (verbal codes) are basic to communication. However, misconceptions about the meanings of words may cause them to serve as barriers, rather than as bridges, to communication.

In this chapter, we explore the use of words in communication by discussing what verbal codes are, how verbal codes interfere with communication, and how we can prevent verbal codes from interfering with our understanding of ourselves and others and with our ability to share ourselves with others. We also examine how the verbal language that we choose provides others with information about how we conceive of ourselves, others, and the relationships between ourselves and others.

Verbal Codes: Sets of Words

Verbal codes consist of sets of words. In chapter 1, a **code** was defined as a systematic arrangement or comprehensive collection of symbols, letters, or words that have been given arbitrary meaning and are used for communication. When we use verbal codes to communicate, we **encode** (as senders), or put our feeling or thought into a verbal code, and we **decode** (as receivers), or assign meaning to the verbal codes we receive.

Words as Verbal Symbols

We define **words** as verbal symbols. **Verbal** refers to anything associated with or pertaining to words. A **symbol** is something that stands for or represents something else, either by association or convention.

A word is a symbol in the same sense a wedding ring is a symbol for marriage, and a flag is a symbol for a particular country. Words symbolize events, people, and ideas by agreement among the people who use them and through conventional use. They do not necessarily resemble the thing they represent; they are arbitrary representations of the thing they represent. Statements like, "The word is not the thing," and "Words don't mean, people do," allude to this arbitrary nature of words.

Some examples may clarify the symbolic nature of words. Suppose you were thirsty and asked a friend for a drink. How would you feel if your friend returned with the word *drink* written on a piece of paper? Suppose a friend said she loved you, but treated you disrespectfully or ignored you? Or, suppose your boss said he had good news and you were going to get a raise. On payday, you might be very disappointed to find your regular check and a sheet of paper with the word *raise* written on it in the pay envelope. In each of these cases, the other person was behaving as though "the word was the thing." However, words are not the same as the things they represent; they only serve as symbols for them.

An entire science has been devoted to the examination of the relationship between words and meaning. **Semantics** is the study or science of meaning in language forms. Semanticists study the ways in which individuals use language to respond to certain meaningful notions. They are especially interested in how relationships between words and meaning change over time.

Someone in semantics, for example, might be interested in how the words that refer to women and men have changed in the past twenty years. For instance, twenty years ago, adult females were usually referred to as "girls" or "ladies"; they were almost never discussed as "women." Today, it is more common for adult females to be called "women." To give another example, thirty years ago, invitations asked people to join others in a "gay event." Today, such an invitation would have an altogether different and specific meaning.

Alfred Korzybski originated the field of **general semantics.** General semanticists emphasize improving human behavior through a more critical use of words and symbols. Although this theoretical perspective is but one approach to language, we subscribe to its goals and guidelines in this text. While other approaches stress the power of natural and/or metaphoric language, general semantics recommends we use words and language in a more precise manner. Later in this chapter, we consider indexing and dating, which are two devices suggested by general semanticists for clarifying meaning among people. In general, people who endorse the principles of general semantics recommend we replace abstract, overly general terms with words that are more concrete and specific.

How does the symbolic nature of language operate? We name or label things in our environment by observing them, by identifying certain characteristics or qualities about them, and then by classifying them into one group or another. For example, if you are shopping for furniture and you spot, in the corner of a furniture store, a rolltop desk to which you want to draw your companion's attention, you would probably say, "Look at that desk over there," and gesture toward it. You named it *desk* after observing it and determining it had the essential characteristics you associate with desks.

Language provides an important function in this regard. It allows us to order all of the stimuli that bombard us into meaningful groups or classes. If we did not have the word *desk,* for example, you might have to say to your friend, "Look at that wooden object that has four legs, six drawers, a tabletop surface on which to write, about twenty or thirty small pigeonholes in which to file papers and other materials, and that is about five feet wide, four feet high, and two feet deep."

When we classify objects, persons, or situations, we are stating, in effect, they have characteristics similar to other members of a particular group. We determine the rolltop desk has sufficient essential characteristics to call it *desk* instead of *chest,* or *buffet,* or *table.* In doing so, we neglect the differences between the object—the rolltop desk, in this instance—and other members of the class, other desks. By naming the piece of furniture *desk,* we fail to take into account the pigeonholes, the size, and other unusual features.

Classifications are neither right nor wrong. Instead, the classifications we make reveal to others the criteria we are using in naming the person, object, or situation. All of us have had the experience of trying to point out a particular person to others and of having them fail to locate the person we are describing. A conversation, as you are waiting for class to begin, might go something like this:

"Look at that woman!"　　　　　　　　　　　　"No, the short woman over on the right."

"Do you mean the blonde?"　　　　　　　　　　"Do you mean the one with the blue eyes?"

"No, she has brown eyes."

"Is it the one in the red T-shirt?"

"It looks like orange to me."

"Is she heavy?

"I wouldn't call her heavy at all. . . ."

"Now she's moving to the front of the room."

"Why didn't you say it was the instructor?"

"I guess I never thought about it."

Both of the communicators used a variety of classes into which to place the person they were discussing—gender, hair color, eye color, weight, clothing, position in the room, and, finally, occupation. This example is a particular favorite because it illustrates a phenomenon that has been experienced a number of times. Students—regardless of their age or gender—tend to classify instructors as instructors, rather than by gender, attractiveness, or other physical features.

Words Organized into Larger Units

We usually do not use individual words to express our thoughts. Instead, we use groups of words. We might choose to express ourselves through phrases, sentences, or longer units of related words. **Syntactics** is the study of how we put words together to form phrases and sentences.

Languages are made up of words and the organization among those words, and languages have rules for organizing thoughts into meaningful units. Although we may not consciously consider all of these rules when we speak to others, we generally notice when someone breaks such a rule. An individual from Germany may be accustomed to speaking in the form, "Did you the memo bring?" but such a pattern would be noticed and labeled incorrect in English.

You can probably think of countless examples of different ways to organize the same words that result in different meanings. For instance, the sentence, "You will go to the store later," consists of the same words as, "Will you go to the store later?" but the meaning is quite different because of the ordering of the words. "Sam loves Sally" is not the same as "Sally loves Sam." The garbled, "Most university students desire commitment, have a few to fail, and to completing their college education," probably would not be construed as, "Most university students have a commitment to completing their college education, and few desire to fail."

Language Is Personal

To support the argument, there are more than three billion different languages in the world is easy. Each of us talks, listens, and thinks in a unique language (and sometimes we have several) that contains slight variations of agreed-upon meanings and that may change each minute.

Language usage is personal and is learned over time. You already know that, if you had grown up in Poland, rather than the United States, your language usage would be quite different. But have you ever stopped to recognize how other factors affect your language usage? Our **personal language** is shaped by our culture, country, neighborhood, job, personality, attitudes, values, moods, gender, experiences, and age.

Figure 6.1
How would you describe this picture?

An experiment illustrates the differences in our personal language usage. The photograph in figure 6.1 was shown to three people—a sophomore enrolled in a speech communication course, a Ph.D. in speech communication, and a veterinarian. Each person was asked to define or describe the picture. Their descriptions follow:

> It is a deerlike animal with a white belly and horns. The ears appear relatively large, and the rump is higher than the shoulders.
>
> *Student*
>
> A four-legged mammal of indeterminate size with hooves, variegated horns, large ears, elongated neck, and a two-toned torso. The rear legs are larger than the front legs, as if the animal were designed for running. Its relatively large eyes are on the sides of the animal's face, so it is probably among the grazing, hunted animals, rather than the carnivorous hunters.
>
> *Speech communication professor*
>
> *Gazella dorcas.*
>
> *Veterinarian*

The student used relatively simple and straightforward language, the professor used a larger vocabulary and (perhaps because of her academic training or interest) a greater number of words, and the veterinarian used the fewest, but most precise and technical words. If you had only been given the three descriptions of figure 6.1 and been told the three individuals involved in this experiment were a student, a speech communication professor, and a veterinarian, you probably would have been able to match the correct description with the correct individual. All of us draw conclusions about others on the basis of the language that others use.

The personal nature of language may be a means of coming closer to others and to ourselves. The uniqueness of each individual's language provides valuable information in our attempts to achieve some common form with all involved. Nonetheless, the personal nature of language also provides some difficulties in our communication with others. As we have already observed, each of us has a unique language shaped by a variety of factors. The possibility that even a few people will share most of these characteristics at the same time in the same way is really quite remote. The personal nature of language, then, obstructs, as well as enhances, communication.

Let us examine the influence of cultures, subcultures, the individual, and the situation and context on personal language usage and some of the misunderstandings that can occur when people do not recognize the influence of such variables.

Cultural Influence on Language Usage

Language usage varies among different cultures for the obvious reason that different cultures have different languages. A family we know spent a summer in Europe several years ago. As they traveled from country to country—sometimes crossing two or three borders in a single day—the wife noticed a striking similarity in the behavior of the Europeans they met. Although her husband is fluent in a number of European languages, the children and she are not. After successfully communicating with the husband, the European would turn to the wife and attempt to make small talk or social conversation. She would shrug her shoulders to indicate she did not understand. The European would repeat the remark, but a bit more loudly. She would again try to say she could not understand the language. The other person would stand closer to her, use more gestures, and repeat the message very loudly. Generally, the husband intervened at this point and explained she really did not understand the language. This happened everywhere the family went. People in the Netherlands, France, Germany, Spain, Italy, and other countries all shared the assumption that speaking more loudly and more enthusiastically would result in understanding.

This European experience is similar to experiences all of us have had in this country. People often assume their words have an inherent, intrinsic meaning that is universally understood. Unfortunately, they do not.

Subcultural Influence on Language Usage

Differences in language seem obvious when we consider different cultures. The examples, however, are more subtle *within* a culture. A variety of **subcultures,** or cultural subgroups differentiated by status, age, ethnic background, religion, or other factors, exists within each culture, and each uses unique words and provides distinctive meaning for some words. Consider language differences in our own country between poor and wealthy people, older and younger people, black and white Americans, and women and men. Too often, we assume, if we just talk louder, people from other subcultures will understand us, but *bad* means bad, unless it means "very good," regardless of how loudly we talk.

People in subcultures rely on differences in language for two purposes. First, they often need a specialized language in which to conduct their business. For instance, women have traditionally been able to identify such colors as *puce, aquamarine, lavender,* and *persimmon* because they have been involved in occupations or have fulfilled jobs that require sensitivity to color. Also, women, rather than men, have usually decorated the home and chosen clothing for the family. As men have become increasingly involved with professions or positions that require color knowledge, however, they have become increasingly aware of colors and have developed a larger vocabulary of color names.

Cultural subgroups establish specialized
language among themselves to establish a
subculture identity.

A second reason for establishing a specialized language among subculture members
is to establish a subcultural identity. On a number of occasions, the black community
has provided interesting terms and unique jargon that have been subsumed in the larger
culture. The statement made earlier that *bad* means bad unless it means "very good"
is a good example. In the early 1970s, a young Minnesotan who was about six months
pregnant began teaching in an integrated high school in Columbus, Georgia. After she
had been teaching in the school for about a month, one of the black males in the senior
class told her that he and his buddies thought that she was "bad." He explained, "Mama,
we think you are *so* bad—especially for a white chick." The woman was not sure if
"mama" referred to her pregnant condition or what would occur now that a consensus
of students had decided she was "bad." Needless to say, the young man was attempting
to compliment her on her ability to communicate with the students.

The word *bad* is no longer used in all black communities. When people from other
subcultures began using the term *bad,* some blacks dropped the term. The same phenomenon occurs in other subcultures. For instance, the first time you heard one of your
parents use the jargon of your subculture— *cool, rad, wick, boss, jerk,* or *choice*—
you probably vowed never to use the word again. When other subcultures begin to use
the specialized language of one group, the word no longer serves the purpose of distinguishing the subculture from others, and members of the subculture drop the word.

Individuals' Influence on Language Usage

We can demonstrate again that words do not have inherent meaning by considering the differences in personal language usage among individuals within the same subculture. If, for example, you find yourself in conflict with the idea that *lady* is a sexist term, you are demonstrating a difference among individuals within a subculture. You might find yourself arguing, "But I am a woman, and I don't feel that way," or "I consider myself a feminist, and I don't think that," or "I'm proud to be known as a lady." All of these statements point up the different meanings a word can have and the idea that words vary in meaning from person to person.

A distinction is frequently made between the denotative and connotative meanings of words. **Denotative meaning** refers to an agreed-upon meaning or a dictionary meaning for a term. **Connotative meaning** refers to an individualized or personalized meaning that may be emotionally laden. Denotative meanings are understood and shared by a large number of people. They are meanings people have come to hold because of a common social experience with a word. For example, the word *chair* is generally understood similarly by others through their essentially common experience with the objects we call *chairs*. Connotative meanings are limited to a single person or to a very small number of people. They are meanings others have come to hold because of a personal or individual experience with a word. For example, the word *love* holds vastly different meanings for people because of their unique experiences with the concept.

In general, people feel they use words as though they are using the denotative, or the "real", meaning. On the contrary, although the dictionary contains a number of accepted (denotative) meanings for words, we always use them connotatively, based on our understanding of and experience with them. Even when we are using a dictionary definition of a word, we must keep in mind two principles: (1) a word's meaning is constantly undergoing change, and the meaning printed in an old dictionary may not represent the current usage; and (2) the connotative meaning of the word, which may well be the meaning that another person intended, is not in the dictionary.

Unfortunately, we do not usually recognize the limited value of "dictionary definitions." People frequently will rely on historical, denotative definitions to defend sexism, racism, or other prejudices. For instance, a great deal of research has demonstrated that the use of man-linked words (postman, chairman, fireman) communicates that men *exclusively* are the referent and that "no women need apply." Pleas that "man" means all people, regardless of gender, are largely unheard. Dictionaries, at best, offer an historical account of meaning among powerful subcultures.

In chapter 1, we considered the notion that communication is a *process,* that it is dynamic and always changing. One of the most obvious examples of the dynamic nature of communication lies in each individual's verbal usage. Terms become outdated, new words or *neologisms* come into usage, and specialized language is coined. The study of language provides an interesting and informative history of our culture and identifies those phenomena we once felt were important, unique, or revered. Language does not stay the same from one year to the next; it is alive and filled with change.

PEANUTS

© 1976 United Feature Syndicate, Inc.

The Influence of the Situation and Setting on Language Usage

Not only do the meanings of words vary in different cultures and subcultures and among different individuals, they also vary with the same person, depending upon the situation and the setting. We can see how this happens by looking at the number of denotative meanings for a word provided in a dictionary. For example, the *Oxford English Dictionary* provides us with twenty-one separate definitions and many more subtypes for the word *close;* the word *clear* has twenty-seven definitions and many subtypes; the word *head* has sixty-six definitions with two to four subtypes of each definition; and the word *come* has sixty-nine definitions, but nearly two hundred definitions when all the subdefinitions are counted.

We gain a clue about the particular denotative meaning a person has in mind for a particular word from the setting in which the word is used. For example, if someone asked us for bread, we would probably hand them something to eat if we were sitting at the dinner table, but a small amount of cash if we were standing in the parking lot.

An additional problem with spoken English (not as great in written English) is the number of words that sound the same but have different spellings and/or meanings. The "Peanuts" cartoon calls to mind *tail* and *tale*. Unless we are sensitive to the setting and the situation, we can easily receive the unintended definition.

Words as an Obstacle to Communication

In this section, we consider how language can actually be a major obstacle to communication. We will see that people sometimes use language in unconventional ways or to distort or alter meaning.

Unconventional Language Usage

People sometimes use language in highly unusual ways, and clear communication is almost impossible when individuals do not follow language conventions. For example, people sometimes break the semantic and syntactical rules that others agree upon, and sometimes they replace cultural language rules with those from a particular subculture. At other times, more personal decisions operate in the choice of words and the structuring of them. For instance, we use language in an unconventional way when we make errors in grammar, word choice, or the structure of our sentences; or when we use colloquialisms, clichés, euphemisms, slang, jargon, regionalisms, or street language.

Some errors in language usage have become fairly commonplace; nonetheless, they still cause confusion. For instance, if someone states, "Look—a black dog walking on both sides of the street!" what does she mean? She might mean that there is one black dog who is alternately walking on one side of the street and then on the other, or she might mean that there are two dogs, each walking on a different side of the street. The statement would have been clear if she had said, "Look, there is a black dog on each side of the street!"

Similarly, incorrect syntax creates problems. If someone told you, "I like to write on my book," you might not be sure if he liked to write and scribble on the cover of his book or if he liked writing and was authoring a book. The statement he made suggests the former conclusion. If he had been trying to express the latter, he should have said, "I like writing my book."

Colloquialisms include words and phrases that are used informally, but not formally. Sometimes, colloquial words and phrases are ambiguous, unclear, or out-of-date. Some typical examples of colloquialisms are, "Have a happy day," "Good to see you," "Take care now," "How you doin'?" and "See you." The excessive use of colloquialisms may confuse others.

Clichés are words or phrases that have lost their effectiveness because of overuse. Examples include, "Don't lose any sleep over it," "I could put him on my dresser and look at him all night," "As good as gold," "Give them an inch and they'll take a mile," "Watch him like a hawk," "You can't take it with you," and "Skeleton in the closet." In addition to being overused, clichés may be unclear to individuals who are unfamiliar with the underlying ideas of a particular cliché.

Euphemisms are inoffensive words substituted for words considered offensive. These, too, confuse others. For instance, we may ask for the "ladies' room," the "powder room," the "lounge," or the "little girls' room." Or, we may talk about another person "going to the final reward," "passing away," or simply "passing." Euphemisms are frequently substituted for short, abrupt words, the names of physical functions, or the terms for some unpleasant social situation. Although euphemisms are frequently considered more polite than the words for which they are substituted, they also distort reality. For example, we find it easier to discuss "substandard living" than the horrors of starvation, and we can soften the reality of child and spouse abuse by calling it "intrafamily conflict." Communication based on delusion allows us to ignore real human problems and to avoid unpleasant situations.

Slang refers to a specialized language of a group of people who share a common interest or belong to a similar subculture. While slang is understood by many people, it is generally not used in formal oral or written communication. Slang is often associated with teenagers, blacks, and women. It is temporary in nature. In the 1950s, the terms used by young women and men were "scuzz" and "zilch." In the 1960s, young people said "pig," "groovy," and "uptight." In the 1970s, young people used the terms "turkey," "gross," and "queer." In the 1980s, they have used "really," "I mean," "rad," and "wick." By the time this text is published, even these terms will be out-of-date.

Unconventional Language

Each of us uses a variety of unconventional language forms. Try to list at least two clichés, two euphemisms, two slang expressions, and two examples of jargon you use. If you have difficulty identifying such forms in your own language, use someone else's expressions. It is sometimes easier to identify unconventional language in other people's communication.

Clichés   1. _____

                 2. _____

Euphemisms   1. _____

                 2. _____

Slang   1. _____

                 2. _____

Jargon   1. _____

                 2. _____

Jargon is the technical language developed by a professional group, such as physicians, educators, electricians, economists, and computer operators. Some examples of jargon include "angina," "duodenal," "dyadic interaction," "bytes," and "CPU." Jargon can be an efficient and effective aid in communicating with those who share an understanding of the terms. However, like slang, it can lead to confusion when individuals who understand such terms attempt communication with others who do not.

Regionalisms are words or phrases specific to a particular region or part of the country. The word *coke* in Texas has the same meaning as the word *soda* in New York and the word *pop* in Indiana. When people from different parts of the country try to talk with each other, clarity may break down.

Street language consists of words or phrases specific to one section of one city. To clarify their unity as a group, individuals of a particular ethnic background may create language that is unique to them. For instance, one group of people used the phrase "over the hill" to refer to going across the railroad tracks that served as a boundary between the wealthier and poorer sections of one city. In another city, an avenue served as the area in which teenagers tended to "hang out." When the adolescents were going to that particular avenue, they would tell their friends they were going to "the stroll." Individuals from different cities or from different sections of the same city may have different meanings for such words or phrases.

Distorted Language or Language That Alters Meaning

All of us confuse ourselves and others with language. For example, a friend asks, "How do I look?" and we respond with a compliment rather than with an honest response. People sometimes press us to state a point of view before we have had time to think it through. If pressed too hard, we may make a vague response to gain more time to

Metaphoric Language

As you have seen in this chapter, language is fluid and continually changing. In this exercise, you will have an opportunity to rely upon this notion. Metaphors are figures of speech in which a word is transferred from the object it ordinarily represents to an object that it designates only by implicit comparison. For example, we may talk about the "autumn of one's years," the fog which comes in on "tiny cat feet," or "the song of the sea." Metaphors are generally fresh and lively comparisons; they are not to be confused with cliches which are overworked or overused terms. For each of the concepts listed below, try to determine one to three metaphors. Compare your phrases or words with those of your classmates.

1. Springtime _____

_____

2. Love _____

_____

3. Friendship _____

_____

4. Twilight _____

_____

5. Anger _____

_____

6. Success _____

_____

7. Human babies _____

_____

8. Surprise _____

_____

9. Old age _____

_____

10. Death _____

_____

consider the issue. We also sometimes hedge when someone asks for information we do not have. Through ambiguity, we attempt to convey the idea that we really know more than we do.

Politicians provide abundant examples of language intentionally used to obstruct communication. People running for political office often use abstract terms and vague phrases to say nothing or everything. They recognize specific and concrete terms will offend one group or another, so they seek the safety of empty and meaningless language.

Advertisers, too, often intentionally use language to confuse the consumer. Words like "better," "improved," and "new," and phrases like "revolutionary change," "a taste worth smoking," "a real taste," "real satisfaction," "more than just low tar, this is ultra-low tar," and "We're Number One" are typical. Such words and phrases, like the sign in "The Wizard of Id" cartoon (page 107) that advertises a "100-foot pool," do not convey a clear message.

Improving Verbal Skills

We have observed words are symbolic and highly personal. In addition, we have noted that sometimes we use language in unconventional ways and we intentionally attempt to confuse others with our language. Words need not be obstacles to communication, however. We can make specific changes in our verbal usage that will help us to become more effective communicators. But before we discuss those specific changes, we should observe two warnings.

First, we are limited in our language changes by factors we do not always understand and we do not always control. Before you read this chapter, you may have been unaware of all of the different influences—such as your culture, subculture, religion, gender, and neighborhood—on your language. Even now, you may be influenced by factors we have not fully discussed or of which you are unaware.

For example, the intimate relationship between language and perception creates difficulties for us in changing our language and, simultaneously, in changing our perceptions. Edward Sapir, a linguist, and Benjamin Lee Whorf, a fire-insurance expert, first discussed the relationship between language and perception. The **Sapir-Whorf hypothesis,** as it has become known, states our perception of reality is determined by our thought processes and our thought processes are limited by our language; therefore, our perception of reality is dependent upon our language.[1] To understand how the Sapir-Whorf hypothesis works, we can consider the difference in perception and language when an optometrist examines our eyes and when we look at our own eyes in the mirror. Whereas we may see our eyes only as "nice" or as "bloodshot," the optometrist might note the dilation of the pupil, the lack of perceptual acuity, the apparent distortion of the eyeball, and the accuracy of depth perception. Why does the optometrist see so much more? According to the Sapir-Whorf hypothesis, it is because the optometrist has been given training that includes the language for such phenomena.

Another example may help to clarify the Sapir-Whorf hypothesis. In your lifetime, you have engaged in countless conversations. However, before you read the material on nonverbal communication in chapter 5, you may not have "seen" those interactions in the same way. Now you may notice the bodily movement of others, their use of space, the amount of touching in which they engage, their paralanguage, and the influence of their clothing on the many "messages" they provide. Your familiarity with the language of nonverbal communication may create greater sensitivity in your perception of interactions.

THE WIZARD OF ID by permission of Johnny Hart and Field Enterprises, Inc.

The second warning we must consider when experimenting with new language behavior concerns the purpose of the former behavior and the purpose of the new verbal patterns. Sometimes, ambiguous, colloquial, or distorted language serves an important purpose for an individual. We may use such practices to protect ourselves—to establish a healthy self-concept or to maintain a distorted self-concept, to deny self-awareness or to gain time to develop self-awareness. We also use such forms to protect others— to help them maintain a selective view of reality, to help them distort their world, or to help them acknowledge successes or deny difficulties. A *late bloomer* does not have to admit being a decade or two older than the other students. An *underachiever* can't really expect high grades. The existence of a *word processing center* allows us to alter our perception of jobs in a typing pool. A discussion of *low-rent housing* denies the real situation in the inner-city slums. Similarly, clichés like "Fat people are always so jolly," and "Anything worth doing is worth doing right," may allow us to justify excessive weight or to be overly methodical in whatever we attempt.

Our choice of language provides information to others about how we see ourselves, how we see others, and what relationships we believe are established between ourselves and others. You may relax around friends and use language deemed "inappropriate" by your parents or co-workers. If you are being interviewed for a job, you may use language that is particular to your profession and be careful to use correct grammar. You may use words with special meaning with an intimate or lover.

Changes in your verbal behavior must occur within the context of the situation in which you find yourself. You must consider what you wish to share with others through your language and how clearly you wish to be known. Your prior relationships with others and your current goals in the interactions are important considerations. Understanding and sharing are the ultimate benefits of verbal clarity; you must decide the extent to which such goals are possible and important. With these considerations in mind, let us consider how we can improve our verbal skills.

Avoid Intentional Confusion

Some of the verbal patterns we fall into have become so habitual we no longer feel we are intentionally confusing; rather, we believe "everyone" speaks the way we do. We take comfort in our clichés. Edwin Newman, television news personality, talks about his own use of clichés in his books *Strictly Speaking* and *A Civil Tongue:*

> One thing that happened to me, as a reporter on the air, was that I realized I was pushing along ideas that had no substance. I was taking phrases and using them as if they had substance, and they didn't.[2]

We should strive to become increasingly sensitive to our own use of empty language, ambiguities, clichés, and euphemisms. It is often helpful to have someone else monitor our statements and point out the problem areas. After someone else has sensitized us to our confusing phraseology, we can "take the reins in our own hands." (Er, that is, do the job ourselves!) Our goal, at all times, is to keep it simple.

Confusion can also arise when we use unusual terms or if we use a word in a special way. If we suspect someone might not understand the terminology we are using, it is essential to define the term. We need to be careful not to offend the other person, on the one hand, and to offer a definition that is clearer than the term itself, on the other. Similarly, we need to ask others for definitions when they use words in unusual or new ways.

Operational definitions, or definitions that point to the behavior, action, or properties a word signifies, are sometimes very useful. When Alice asked the Dodo, in *Alice's Adventures in Wonderland,* what he meant by a Caucus-race, he wisely replied, "Why, the best way to explain it is to do it."[3] We use operational definitions when we explain, "For me, a good day is any day I don't have to go to classes or go to work," or when we explain outlining to a friend by stating the basic steps that are involved. Operational definitions are one form of descriptiveness.

Use Descriptiveness

Descriptiveness is the practice of describing observable behavior or phenomena instead of offering personal reactions or judgments. This skill was discussed in chapter 4 in the section on feedback and the section on behaviors associated with effective listening.

We can be descriptive in different ways. One of the most important ways involves making simple checks on our perception. To communicate effectively with another person, it is important to have a common understanding of an event that has occurred or of the definition of a particular phenomenon. We can check with other persons to determine if their perceptions are the same as our own. We ask another person, "Do you feel a draft?" or "Don't you get tired, studying and working at a full-time job?" Many disagreements occur because people do not stop to make these simple checks on their perception.

For example, each of us confuses **inferences**—the drawing of a conclusion from or about things we have observed—with observations. One of the most obvious examples of this occurs when we walk through a dark room at night. We cannot see the furniture or other obstacles, but we conclude they are still where they were, and we walk around them without turning on the light. We have no problem with this kind of simple exchange of an inference for an observation—unless someone has moved the furniture or placed a new object in the room, or unless our memory is not accurate. Even simple inferences can be wrong. Many shins have been bruised because someone relied on inference rather than observation.

Problems in communication occur when people draw different inferences from similar observations. Researchers have been known to perform the same experiment and conclude entirely different things. Lawyers have lost cases in the courtroom because none of the witnesses could agree upon critical details. Spouses face marital discord when they reach different inferences from the same observations.

In the following conversation between a young married couple, the difficulty they are experiencing arises from different inferences from the same observation:

Jane: (noticing that John has not eaten very much of his dinner) Don't you like this new recipe for chow mein?

John: No, it's fine.

Jane: Well, I get bored with the same things over and over.

John: Me, too.

Jane: It's really hard to plan meals when food costs so much.

John: I'm sure it is.

Jane: You never want to experiment. All you want is steak or pork chops every night.

John: No, I like casseroles and most of the things you make.

Jane: Maybe you should make dinner instead of breakfast. You know, the breakfasts that you make are so easy that anyone could make them. I can put cold cereal on the table, too! Dinner is the tough meal!

John: I would be happy to make dinner, but there's nothing wrong with your cooking.

Jane: Then why aren't you eating your chow mein?

John: (sheepishly) Well, it was one guy's birthday at work, and I ate two big pieces of chocolate cake at about four o'clock. You know how I love chocolate.

Jane: Why didn't you say so—I thought you didn't like your meal.

Difficulties in communication can also ensue when persons fail to separate their inferences from their observations. Obviously, we have to make some assumptions when we make statements about observable data. If we walk into a classroom and observe a person who appears to be about twenty-five years old, male, and Caucasian, standing at the front of the room behind a lectern, we draw a number of conclusions. Most of us assume that the person is human, male, of an approximate age, and of a particular race. Some of us might also conclude he is the instructor. A few people might decide he is a graduate assistant, a boring lecturer, too formal, poor, unaware of current clothing styles, or a host of other characteristics. All of these conclusions are inferences, but they are not all verifiable by observation to the same degree. All of the conclusions rely on assumptions. We assume a person with relatively short hair in a three-piece suit is a man. We assume persons who are blond and blue-eyed are Caucasian. We assume a certain stance, a certain body position, and a lack of wrinkles indicate a certain age. These assumptions are generally shared, and we usually agree persons who display these characteristics are of a specific sex and race and in a specific age bracket.

As the number of assumptions we make increases, the likelihood we are accurate decreases. In addition, as we move from generally agreed-upon assumptions to more questionable ones, we move from the area of observation to the area of inference. Sometimes, we fail to recognize we are drawing inferences based on many questionable assumptions and believe we are simply stating observations shared by others. If you observed the person described in the previous paragraph and concluded he dressed in an outdated style, you might feel uncomfortable when the student sitting next to you told you how good you would look if you bought a similar suit. Agreement between you and the other student might not be possible until you both recognized your statements reflected individual inferences based upon your separate perceptions, attitudes, values, and beliefs.

In the same way we draw inferences that go beyond what we see, we also draw inferences from the words others offer. For instance, suppose you were sharing your opinion on the outcome of elections for a state representative in your district. The person to whom you were speaking responded with such phrases as, "Yes," "Right," and "I know." What would you conclude? You would probably infer his or her opinion on the elections was the same as your own. In reality, however, this person may hold a different opinion but simply have been affirming your right to hold your opinion. Observe how two different inferences might be drawn from the following conversation:

Paula: I'm really surprised the incumbent was defeated in the race for representative.
Peter: I am, too.
Paula: I worked to unseat him.
Peter: Yes, you did.
Paula: Just think—the incumbent was in office for twelve years, and he was replaced by someone who was far less experienced.
Peter: That's right.
Paula: I feel like celebrating—how about if I buy you a drink?
Peter: I'd like a drink.

The listener in a conversation draws inferences based on the speaker's verbal and nonverbal cues. In this case, Paula may have assumed that Peter agreed with her because he was generally positive and did not offer contrary evidence.

The speaker can do a great deal to eliminate or encourage erroneous inferences. In the same way the listener draws conclusions from the evidence with which he or she is presented, the speaker provides **implications.** When we imply something, we do not directly express it. Instead, an implication consists of information is inherent or suggested. In the preceding dialogue, we might conclude Peter was implying he felt the same way as Paula because he did not disagree and because he agreed to have a drink with her. Peter may have eliminated this inference by stating, "I would like to have a drink with you, but for me it's not a celebration. I supported the other candidate."

The implications offered by the speaker and the inferences drawn by the listener relate to perception. Suppose you are a fun-loving person who frequently uses sarcasm as humor. If you kiddingly tell one of your instructors you would like to present a speech that is longer than the assignment, you might perceive your statement as an obvious joke. The instructor who does not understand your statement as banter may consider the request seriously. Your differences in perception affect the implications and inferences.

In addition to making simple checks on our perception, a second way we can be descriptive is to utilize descriptive feedback, which was introduced in chapter 4. *Descriptive feedback* consists of nonevaluative, nonthreatening statements about our observations of other people and their communication with us. These comments should be free of evaluation and judgment. Examples of descriptive feedback include statements like, "You appear to be preoccupied and unable to concentrate on what I'm discussing with you," "I perceive an edginess in your voice," and "You seem enthusiastic when you talk about him." Statements like, "You're a real slob," "I don't like the way you talk to me," and "You sure could improve your relationship with your boyfriend if you wanted to," are not appropriate descriptive feedback because of their evaluative, threatening, judgmental nature.

Descriptive feedback provides a method of indicating to other people what we do and do not understand from their messages. It allows the other people the opportunity to validate accurate perceptions and to correct misunderstandings.

Paraphrasing—one form of descriptive feedback—allows increased understanding between two people. Simply stated, **paraphrasing** is the restatement of the other person's message. It is not merely repetition, however, since repetition only shows you have received the words, not that you have really understood the message.

Suppose a student says, "I don't understand descriptiveness." The teacher can respond by repeating, "I heard you say you don't understand descriptiveness," or "Do you mean my explanation of that skill wasn't clear?" or "Do you mean you would like me to explain the skill further to you?" In the first case, the teacher is merely repeating the message and has only shown the words were heard. The second reply shows the content of the student's message has been understood. The third reply shows the intent of the message has been understood. The first response is mere repetition; the second and third are two levels of paraphrasing.

Be Concrete

Earlier in this chapter, we observed the general semanticists recommend individuals improve their verbal behavior by using words more critically. Concreteness is one of their specific recommendations. **Concreteness** is specificity of expression. A person whose language is concrete uses statements that are specific, rather than abstract or vague. "You have interrupted me three times when I have begun to talk—I feel as though you do not consider my point of view as important as yours," is specific; "You should consider my viewpoint, too," is not.

In the following conversation, notice that the student becomes increasingly concrete as she describes her reactions to a textbook:

Student: I don't like the book.
Instructor: What book is that?
Student: The book for this class.

Instructor:	We have three required books—to which book are you referring?
Student:	The big one.
Instructor:	Do you mean *Professional Speaking?*
Student:	Yeah, that's the one.
Instructor:	Why don't you like it?
Student:	Well, it doesn't say anything to me.
Instructor:	Do you mean it's not relevant to your needs?
Student:	Yeah, I guess so, but it's more than that.
Instructor:	Could you explain why you don't like it?
Student:	Well, the chapters are so long and boring.
Instructor:	Do you find the examples helpful?
Student:	No.
Instructor:	Are there specific chapters that you find to be too long?
Student:	I've only started to read the first one, but it's pretty long.
Instructor:	Why do you find it boring?
Student:	There aren't any cartoons, pictures, or anything but words!
Instructor:	In other words, you find chapter 1 of *Professional Speaking* to be long and boring because it has so few or no illustrations?
Student:	Right. I don't like the book because the first chapter is over forty pages long and has only one diagram, which is of a model of communication that doesn't make any sense to me. I like books that have short chapters and lots of illustrations that I can understand.

Concreteness is any form of more specific expression. Two of the more interesting subtypes of concreteness are dating and indexing. **Dating** is a skill based on the idea that everything is subject to change. Often, we view things as remaining the same. We form a judgment or point of view about a person, an idea, or a phenomenon, and we maintain that view, even though the person, idea, or phenomenon has changed. Dating is a method of avoiding this kind of frozen judgment. Instead of saying something is always or universally a certain way, we state *when* we made our judgment and state our perception was based on that experience.

For example, if you had a course with a particular instructor four or five years ago, it is essential your judgment about the course and instructor be qualified as to time. You may tell someone, "English 100 with Professor Jones is a snap course," but it may no longer be true. Or, suppose you went out with a man two years ago, and now your best friend is looking forward to her first evening with him. You might say he is quiet and withdrawn, but it may no longer be accurate: the time that has passed, the person he is with, and the situation have all changed. Statements like, "English 100 with Professor Jones was a snap course for me in 1986," and "Joe seemed quiet and withdrawn when I dated him two or three years ago," will create fewer communication problems.

Indexing is a skill based on the idea that all members of a subset do not share all of the characteristics of the other members of that subset. Stereotyping—making conventional, oversimplified generalizations about a group, event, or issue—is the opposite of indexing. Earlier in the chapter, we discussed the importance of being able to generalize and classify. Nonetheless, problems can arise when we generalize and classify.

Paraphrasing

For each of the following dialogues, identify the response as repetition, paraphrasing of content, or paraphrasing of intent. Place an "R" in the blank if the dialogue is a repetition, a "C" if it paraphrases content, and an "I" if it paraphrases intent.

1. *Question or statement:*   If you had to do it over again, would you do the same thing?

   Response: _____ Do you mean, would I state my disagreement to my employer?

2. *Question or statement:*   Will your wife move to the new location with you if you secure this promotion?

   Response: _____ Are you asking if my wife will move with me to the new location if I get the job?

3. *Question or statement:*   I'm always afraid I'm going to make a mistake!

   Response: _____ What do you mean, you feel like you're going to make a mistake?

4. *Question or statement:*   I've lived here for three months, but I still don't know my way around the city.

   Response: _____ Would you like me to show you some of the principal landmarks and the main streets?

5. *Question or statement:*   I really appreciate the time you have spent talking to me.

   Response: _____ I would like to encourage you to come in and see me whenever you have a problem—I understand how important it is to be able to talk to your supervisor.

We sometimes have a tendency to assume the characteristics of one member of a class apply to all of the members of the class. For example, you may incorrectly generalize that since your Hyundai uses very little gas, all Hyundais use little gas. Or you may incorrectly believe that, since your older brother is more responsible than you, all firstborn children are more responsible than their younger siblings.

A second problem occurs when we assume a characteristic of one member of a group is true of another member of the same group. If you delegated the characteristics of your Hyundai to your friend's Hyundai, or if you assumed somebody else's older brother was responsible because your older brother is, you would be making this error.

Indexing assists us in avoiding these pitfalls. Indexing is simply recognizing differences among the various members of a group. Instead of grouping all automobiles together and assuming a characteristic one car has is shared by all of the others, we recognize that the car we own could be unique. Instead of assuming all firstborn children are alike, we exhibit openness and an inquiring attitude about firstborn children, other than the ones we know.

We are indexing when we make statements like, "I have a Hyundai that uses very little gas. How does your Hyundai do on gas mileage?" or "My older brother is far more responsible than I. Is the same true of your older brother?" We lack an ability to index when we state, "Hyundais get good gas mileage—I know, I own one," or "Firstborn children are more responsible than their younger brothers and sisters."

Practicing Concreteness

To gain some practice in being concrete, rewrite each of the following statements to make the statement more specific, to date the statement, or to index the statement. For instance, if you were given the statement, "I don't like algebra," you would date it by stating, "I don't like the algebra course I have this quarter." If you were asked to index the statement, you might write, "I don't like the algebra course taught by Professor Smith." If you were asked to make the statement more specific, you might write either of the previous alternatives, or you might write something similar to, "I don't like the algebra course required at this university."

1. "I love 'The Cosby Show.' "

Dated alteration: _____

2. "My mom is my friend."

Indexed alteration: _____

3. "My roommate never listens to me."

More specific alteration: _____

4. "My boyfriend is hard to get along with."

Dated alteration: _____

5. "Tom is really jumpy."

Indexed alteration: _____

6. "Sue never dates any good-looking guys."

Dated alteration: _____

7. "I have a woman professor for statistics—women instructors are always so hard!"

Indexed alteration: _____

8. "Did you meet the good-looking guy in chemistry class? He's from the northern part of the state—people from there are always so stuck-up!"

Indexed alteration: _____

_____

9. "Who's the redhead?"

More specific alteration: _____

10. "Where's my book?"

More specific alteration: _____

Summary

In this chapter, we have explored the use of words in communication. Words are symbolic; that is, they stand for something else. Verbal codes consist of sets of words. Semantics is the study or science of meaning in language forms. General semanticists emphasize improving human behavior through more critical, concrete use of words and symbols. Words are organized into larger units known as languages. Syntactics is the study of how we put words together to form phrases and sentences.

Language is personal. Each of us possesses a unique language, although we share some meanings with others. Denotative meaning refers to an agreed-upon meaning or a dictionary meaning, while connotative meaning refers to an individualized or personalized meaning for a term. The culture, the subculture, the individual, the situation and setting all influence our language usage.

Words can be an obstacle to communication because we sometimes use language in an unconventional way, such as when we make structural and grammatical errors, or when we use colloquialisms, clichés, euphemisms, slang, jargon, regionalisms, or street language. Words can also be an obstacle to communication when we use language to distort or alter meaning.

We sometimes have limited success in improving our verbal skills because we are unaware of the factors that affect our language or we cannot control those factors. In addition, we sometimes purposely distort what we state to protect ourselves or to protect others. Nonetheless, we can change and improve our use of language.

We can use language to communicate more effectively by first defining the terminology we use and by avoiding unconventional usage. Second, we can check our perception of something by becoming increasingly descriptive. We need to recognize others may draw inferences about what we are stating and we provide implications in the messages we share with them. Practicing descriptive feedback (providing nonevaluative, nonthreatening statements about our observations of the other person and his or her communication with us) is an effective way to increase our descriptive ability. Paraphrasing the intent and content of others' messages—one form of descriptive feedback—can be highly useful in our attempts at verbal clarity. Third, we can improve our verbal skills by making an effort to be more concrete; that is, we should try to use statements that are specific, rather than abstract or vague. Both dating and indexing are useful methods of being increasingly concrete.

part 2

Interpersonal Communication

Interpersonal communication is the process of understanding and sharing between at least two persons. This type of communication situation is highlighted in this section of the text. The roles of self and other in communication are explored.

Our examination of interpersonal communication begins with chapter 7, "Interpersonal Relationships," which focuses on the nature of interpersonal relationships, self-disclosure, conflict, and improving communication in interpersonal relationships. Chapter 8 considers communication with friends and family, which are of increasing concern to people in our culture. Chapter 9 examines the nature of interviewing, questions and questioning, answers and answering, organizing the interview, and purposes of interviews. In chapter 10, "Small Group Communication," we discuss the importance, the nature, and the process of small group discussion. Chapter 11, "Leadership in the Small Group," examines a variety of approaches to leadership. This chapter also provides information about how to participate in leadership in the discussion group.

Interpersonal Relationships

L *ife is truly a boomerang. What you give,*
you get.

Dale Carnegie

S *eeing ourselves as others see us would*
probably confirm our worst suspicions
about them.

Franklin P. Jones

C *onsidering how dangerous everything is*
nothing is really very frightening.

Gertrude Stein

Objectives

1. Define interpersonal relationships and explain their importance.
2. Identify Knapp's ten relational stages and describe each.
3. Define self-disclosure and explain its importance.
4. Explain how conflict can be used constructively in an interpersonal relationship, and identify some of the positive outcomes of conflict.
5. Discuss the role of behavioral flexibility in effective interpersonal relationships.

Key Terms

interpersonal relationships	differentiation
uncertainty principle	circumscribing
	stagnating
inclusion	avoiding
affection	terminating
control	relational development
complementary relationships	relational maintenance
symmetrical relationships	relational deterioration
cost-benefit theory	self-disclosure
bargaining	defensiveness
social penetration theory	assertiveness
initiating	interpersonal conflict
experimenting	behavioral flexibility
intensifying	androgynous
integrating	
bonding	

In this chapter we will consider the importance of communication in interpersonal relationships. The skills and concepts discussed thus far in this text are particularly relevant to successful interpersonal communication. For example, how we see ourselves is largely dependent upon the relationships we have with others, and the interpersonal relationships we have with others help us to define who we are. Also, perceptual differences are often apparent as we engage in interpersonal relationships and may lead to the deterioration of a relationship. Our ability to listen is another skill critical to the development of an interpersonal relationship. Finally, we rely upon verbal and nonverbal codes to express our understanding of others and to share ourselves with others.

The Nature of Interpersonal Relationships

Definition of Interpersonal Relationships

On the simplest level, relationships are associations or connections. Interpersonal relationships, however, are far more complex. **Interpersonal relationships** may be defined as associations between two or more people who are interdependent, who use some consistent patterns of interaction, and who have interacted for some period of time. Let us consider the different elements of this definition in more detail.

First, interpersonal relationships include two or more people. One person does not comprise a relationship. Often, interpersonal relationships consist of just two people—a dating couple, a single parent and a child, a married couple, two close friends, or two co-workers. But interpersonal relationships can also involve more than two people—a family unit, a group of friends, or a social group.

Second, interpersonal relationships involve people who are interdependent. Interdependence refers to people being mutually dependent upon each other, having an impact upon each other. In a married couple, for instance, the husband might be dependent upon his wife for her concern and empathy. The wife might be dependent upon her husband for acceptance and trust. When individuals are independent of each other, or when dependence only occurs in one direction, the resulting association is not defined as an interpersonal relationship.

Third, individuals in interpersonal relationships use some consistent patterns of interaction. These patterns may include behaviors generally understood across a variety of situations and also behaviors unique to the particular relationship. For example, a husband may always greet his wife with a kiss. This kiss is generally understood as a sign of warmth and affection. On the other hand, the husband may have unique nicknames for his wife not understood beyond the confines of the relationship.

Fourth, individuals in interpersonal relationships generally have interacted for some time. When you greet someone on the street with, "Hello! Great day, isn't it?" when you discuss with a salesperson a purchase you wish to make, or when you meet a friend's parents, you do not have an interpersonal relationship. Although participants use interpersonal communication to accomplish these events, onetime interactions do not constitute interpersonal relationships. We should note, however, interpersonal relationships may last for varying lengths of time—some are relatively short, and others extend for a lifetime.

Communication is central to the
development of interpersonal relationships.

Importance of Interpersonal Relationships

Interpersonal relationships are essential for all of us. Five reasons we engage in interpersonal relationships are: (1) to understand ourselves, (2) to understand others, (3) to understand our world, (4) to fulfill our needs, and (5) to increase and enrich positive experiences.

To Understand Ourselves

We learn about ourselves through our interpersonal relationships. Sometimes, we find our perceptions of ourselves are not the same as are others' perceptions. At other times, our self-concepts are strengthened by the confirmation we receive from others' reactions. We do not share the same perspective as others, and we learn more about ourselves as we listen to the alternative perceptions others hold of us.

The Johari Window, examined in chapter 3, is useful in illustrating how we come to understand ourselves better through interpersonal relationships. To review, the *open self* consists of information about yourself known to you and known to other people; the *blind self* consists of information about yourself known to others but not known to you; the *hidden self* includes information you are aware of about yourself but you have not shared with others; and the *unknown self* includes information about yourself unknown both to you and to others.

Through our interpersonal relationships, we can increase the size of the open self and decrease the size of the other three quadrants. For example, in talking about a

We develop interpersonal relationships in
order to understand other people.

number of happy experiences you have had, you may suddenly realize why they were
all happy. This learning more about yourself decreases the unknown self and increases
the open self. In discussing clothes with a friend, you may discover that others view
you as a style-setter. Since your friends, and perhaps others, hold this perception of
you, and you were unaware of it, you reduce the blind self on the Johari Window and
increase the open self.

We should observe the "self" is different in each relationship in which we are involved. We share more of ourselves with some people than we do with others. Consequently, the open self is different in size for each relationship. A different Johari Window
would be necessary to depict each of our relationships. Nonetheless, the Johari Window
illustrates our interpersonal relationships result in greater understanding of ourselves.

To Understand Others

Similarly, interpersonal relationships assist us in learning about others. Many times,
we may feel we "know" someone before we have a relationship with them. We make
judgments, draw inferences, and reach conclusions about others without really knowing
very much about them. Berger and Calabrese label this phenomenon the **uncertainty
principle.**[1] This principle simply suggests when we initially meet others, we know little
about them, and we rid ourselves of this uncertainty by drawing inferences from the
physical data with which we are presented. This tendency is similar to the process of
closure discussed in chapter 2. Additionally, the urge to lessen uncertainty motivates
additional interpersonal communication.

When we actually involve ourselves in a relationship with another person, however, we may find our initial reactions were inaccurate. For instance, the beautiful woman who appeared to be arrogant might actually be shy. The small, thin man may actually be a marathon runner and a strong athlete. The elderly person who appears angry may actually care a great deal for others but be suffering from physical pain.

People can be quickly stereotyped, categorized, and forgotten; however, we cannot learn about others through snap judgments and initial interactions. Interpersonal relationships allow us to continue to grow in our knowledge of other persons. In the same way others help us to increase our open self in the Johari Window, we can, through our interpersonal relationships, expand the open self of others.

To Understand Our World

In addition to learning more about ourselves and about others through interpersonal relationships, we also learn more about our world—our environment. Our environment is made up of other people, physical objects, events, and circumstances. Our knowledge of the environment comes largely through the interactions we have in our relationships. For instance, how did you get to know your best friend? How did you come to hold your attitudes about sexuality? Who influenced your feelings about higher education? Why do you hold certain beliefs about how a husband and wife should interact? Your responses to these questions probably indicate you learned about these people, ideas, and issues through your interpersonal relationships with acquaintances, friends, and family.

In addition to developing interpersonal relationships to learn more about our environment, we often develop interpersonal relationships to *cope* with our environment. For example, a far greater number of people today than ever before are single parents. Single parenthood is difficult for a variety of reasons. Single parents complain of the role shifting they must perform as they serve as both mother and father. They discuss the difficulties of living without other adults and having no one with whom to share their problems. It is not surprising single parents often express interest in remarrying or establishing other interpersonal relationships to gain some assistance in coping with their worlds.

As another example, consider another family type that is on the rise—the dual-career couple with children. Dual-career couples consist of individuals who must manage traditional household and child-raising duties as well as perform adequately in two separate occupations. The stress for dual-career couples is obvious. Individuals may find they have little time for themselves, each other, and for recreational activities. Dual-career couples may find establishing relationships with others—their parents who can assist with child care, friends who can share their anxieties about their busy lives, and co-workers who are sympathetic to the pushes and pulls of an overloaded life—may help them to cope with their environment.

To Fulfill Our Needs

Individuals have many needs. In chapter 3, we discussed Maslow's hierarchy of needs, which included physical, safety and security, social, esteem, and self-actualization needs. According to William Schutz, we also have three basic interpersonal needs that are satisfied through interaction with others. These are: (1) the need for **inclusion,** or becoming involved with others; (2) the need for **affection,** or being cared for by others; and (3) the need for **control,** or the ability to influence others, our environment, and ourselves.[2] Although we may be able to fulfill some of our physical and safety and security needs through interactions with relative strangers, we can only fulfill the other needs through our interpersonal relationships.

The interdependent nature of interpersonal relationships suggests people mutually satisfy their needs in this type of association. Interdependence suggests one person is dependent upon another person or persons to have some need fulfilled and the other person or persons are dependent upon the first to have the same or other needs fulfilled. For instance, if you are dating someone who comes from a large family and she and her family make you feel involved with them, your need for inclusion may be fulfilled. At the same time, you may be fulfilling your girlfriend's need for affection in the manner in which you show her you care.

Complementary relationships—those in which each person supplies something the other person or persons lack—provide good examples of the manner in which we have our needs fulfilled in interpersonal relationships. The popular male involved with the intelligent female is an example of a complementary relationship, since the woman may find herself involved in the social events she desires, and the man may find himself increasingly successful in his classes. The person providing assistance on a project to a well-known celebrity in exchange for being viewed as that celebrity's friend is another example of a complementary relationship.

Our needs also may be fulfilled in **symmetrical relationships**—those in which the participants mirror each other or are highly similar. Two attractive individuals may pair up because they both value physical beauty. A research scientist may marry an individual with a similar background so they can conduct research together.

Whether the other person or persons are similar to us or highly discrepant, our needs are generally fulfilled through the relationships we have with others.

To Increase and Enrich Positive Experiences

We also enter into interpersonal relationships to increase and enrich positive experiences and/or to decrease negative experiences. One theory, the **cost-benefit theory,** suggests individuals will only maintain relationships as long as the benefits of the relationship outweigh the costs.[3] Some of the benefits of a relationship include personal growth, improved feelings about self, increased self-knowledge, assistance with particular tasks, greater resources, and an improved capacity for coping. The costs include the amount of time spent on the relationship, the amount of energy that goes into the relationship, psychological stress created by the relationship, perhaps physiological stress, and social limitations. According to the cost-benefit theory, if the costs begin to outweigh the benefits, we may decide to terminate the relationship. If the benefits appear to outweigh the costs, we may escalate relationship development.

Interpersonal relationships are not so simply translated into a cost-benefit model, however. More often, we engage in *bargaining* in our interpersonal relationships. **Bargaining** occurs when two or more parties attempt to reach an agreement as to what

Interpersonal communication involves
bargaining with the other person.

each should give and receive in a transaction between them. Bargains may be explicit and formal, such as the kinds of agreements we reach with others to share tasks, to attend a particular event, or to behave in a specified way. Bargains may also be implicit and informal. For instance, you may agree not to use profane language around your parents in exchange for their respect and positive regard for you. You may not even be aware of some of the implicit, tacit agreements you have with others with whom you communicate.

In a study on interpersonal bargaining, three essential features of a bargaining situation were identified:

1. All parties perceive the possibility of reaching an agreement in which each party would be better off, or no worse off, than if no agreement is reached.
2. All parties perceive more than one such agreement that could be reached.
3. All parties perceive the other or others to have conflicting preferences or opposed interests with regard to the different agreements that might be reached.[4]

What are some examples of bargaining situations? Perhaps the person you are dating suggests you go to a ball game on a night when you want to go to a party. Or, your spouse may want to go to bed early, and you may prefer to stay up late. Suppose one of your friends uses the word *several* to mean "two or three," while you reserve the word *several* to refer to "six or more" items, thereby precipitating regular arguments about what time you were to meet or how many items you were to bring. In each of these instances, the disagreement can be resolved through bargaining.

Bargaining may be obvious to you in those communication situations in which people are arguing over a particular phenomenon, behavior, or person. However, bargaining also occurs, to some extent, in nearly every interaction and may be almost invisible.

For example, in the following conversation, the two individuals have a different conception of the word *hard,* but they never appear to disagree:

"How was the physics exam?"
"Hard—really hard."
"Do you think you failed it?"
"Oh no."
"Well, do you think you got a *D*?"
"I don't think I did that poorly."
"What grade do you think you will get?"
"Maybe only a *B*."

The first person in this interaction perceives the word *hard* to mean the second individual received a *D* or *F* on the exam. The second person has the idea that a *B* grade results when one takes a difficult exam. While the two bargain in this conversation, no harsh words are exchanged, and neither becomes angry.

Two researchers underlined the importance of bargaining in interpersonal communication:

> The point should be made . . . that whatever the gratifications achieved in dyads, however lofty or fine the motives satisfied may be, the relationship may be viewed as a trading or bargaining one. The basic assumption running throughout our analysis is that every individual voluntarily enters and stays in any relationship only as long as it is adequately satisfactory in terms of rewards and costs.[5]

This statement emphasizes the central role of bargaining in interpersonal relationships, and it also underlines the notion of cost-benefit analysis.

Stages in Interpersonal Relationships

Communication and relationship development are symbiotic; that is, communication affects relational development and relational development affects communicative behavior.[6] The association between communication and relational development have encouraged communication researchers to study **relational development, relational maintenance,** and **relational deterioration.**

Current theories rest on the original work of Altman and Taylor. These authors developed the **social penetration theory,** which explains the development and deterioration of interpersonal relationships. In essence, the theory states interpersonal exchanges move from superficial, nonintimate information transfers to exchanging more intimate information through the process of revealing personal information. The amount of interaction increases as the relationship develops. Further, cost-reward considerations determine how quickly or slowly relationships develop. Finally, dissolution or depenetration is the reverse process of development or penetration.[7]

For their part, Altman and Taylor identified four stages of relationship development, including orientation, exploratory affective exchange, affective exchange, and stable exchange. Each stage is distinguished on the basis of eight characteristics: (1) richness or breadth of interaction; (2) uniqueness of interaction; (3) efficiency of exchange; (4) substitutability and equivalency; (5) synchronization and pacing; (6) permeability and openness; (7) voluntariness and spontaneity; and (8) evaluation.

These eight qualities need further clarification. *Breadth* means more topics are covered and they are covered in more ways. *Uniqueness* means individuals interact with intimates as particular people and they use idiosyncratic ways of communicating with them. *Efficiency of exchange* is contrasted with the difficulty of exchange that occurs in early conversations with others. *Substitutability* refers to the variety of ways a person develops of communicating the same message to the other person. The individuals rely more frequently on alternative nonverbal and verbal cues to provide the same meaning. *Synchronization* means the partners better coordinate their ideas, and *permeability* suggests they become more physically and emotionally accessible to each other. *Spontaneity* means partners become more informal and comfortable with each other. Finally, *evaluation* refers to the idea the partners become increasingly evaluative of each other.

Knapp expanded upon Altman and Taylor's levels of relationship development by identifying ten interaction stages of interpersonal relationships. These stages are depicted in Table 7.1. Baxter and others have experimentally attempted to validate these

Table 7.1 An Overview of Interaction Stages

Process	Stage	Representative Dialogue
	Initiating	"Hi, how ya doin'?" "Fine. You?"
	Experimenting	"Oh, so you like to ski . . . so do I." "You do?! Great. Where do you go?"
Coming Together	Intensifying	"I . . . I think I love you." "I love you too."
	Integrating	"I feel so much a part of you." "Yeah, we are like one person. What happens to you happens to me."
	Bonding	"I want to be with you always." "Let's get married."
	Differentiating	"I just don't like big social gatherings." "Sometimes I don't understand you. This is one area where I'm certainly not like you at all."
	Circumscribing	"Did you have a good time on your trip?" "What time will dinner be ready?"
Coming Apart	Stagnating	"What's there to talk about?" "Right. I know what you're going to say and you know what I'm going to say."
	Avoiding	"I'm so busy, I just don't know when I'll be able to see you." "If I'm not around when you try, you'll understand."
	Terminating	"I'm leaving you . . . and don't bother trying to contact me." "Don't worry."

From Knapp, Mark L., *Social Intercourse: From Greeting to Goodbye.* © 1978 Allyn & Bacon, Inc., Newton, MA. All Rights Reserved.

stages. While they have found the termination stages are not reverse images of the developmental stages, the model that Knapp presents generally appears valid.[8] Furthermore, this developmental model helps to organize and explain relational changes.

The first five stages are developmental. **Initiating** is stage one, and involves the short beginning period of an interaction, which includes such matters as first impressions, assessment of the other person, and attempts to begin a conversation. In the cartoon, "Ziggy" illustrates the difficulty of initiating a relationship. **Experimenting** occurs next as partners attempt to discover unknown information. They may exchange demographic information or small talk. **Intensifying** involves more active participation and greater awareness of the process of relational development. The two partners exchange more personal information, they address each other less formally, they begin to develop private symbols, and they use more direct expressions of commitment. **Integrating** occurs when the two begin to mirror each other's behavior, manner, dress, and/or verbal codes. The partners may merge their social circles, designate common property, or state shared interests or values. **Bonding** is the final stage and generally suggests some kind of public ritual, which announces their commitment to outsiders. The couple may marry, cohabit, or sign a legal agreement.

The second five stages occur as the relationship moves toward termination. **Differentiation** occurs when the partners emphasize their individual differences rather than their similarities. **Circumscribing** is evidenced by decreased interaction in terms of duration and depth. **Stagnating** suggests a lack of activity. Generally the partners engage in minimal interaction and the interaction in which they do engage is difficult, awkward, and hesitant. **Avoiding** includes antagonistic or unfriendly messages and a general reluctance to interact. Finally, **terminating** occurs when the couple demonstrates both distance and disassociation. Psychological and physical barriers may be erected. Concern for each person's interests rather than concern for the pairing is apparent.[9]

Knapp acknowledged individuals do not move in a linear way through these escalating or de-escalating stages. He suggests people might move within stages in order to maintain their equilibrium or stability. In other words, people might behave in a way that is more characteristic of one stage even though they are generally maintaining the interaction patterns of another stage.

Although Altman and Taylor as well as Knapp briefly consider relational maintenance, neither cover it in very much detail. Wilmot felt Knapp's notion of movement within relationship stages were "minor adjustments" and that features characteristic of stable relationships need to be identified. He suggests relationships stabilize when the partners reach at least some level of agreement about what they want from the relationship. In addition, he states relationships can stabilize at any level of intimacy. Finally, he observes even "stabilized" relationships may have internal movement.[10]

Other writers have criticized those theorists who have equated relational development with the communication of personal information. Parks, for instance, believes such an ideology devalues less intimate, but more prevalent relationships.[11] Similarly, others have suggested the view of relationship development should be refocused.[12] Nonetheless, relationship development, maintenance, and deterioration have guided a great deal of contemporary theorizing. Furthermore, they are a useful way to demonstrate the relevance of communication to relationship development.

Self-Disclosure

Definition of Self-Disclosure

The relationship development stages change as the revealing of personal information changes. The term **self-disclosure** broadly includes any statement a person makes about himself or herself. A few researchers have narrowed this definition to include only statements that are intentional, conscious, or voluntary. Other writers have suggested the term *self-disclosure* should be reserved for statements about ourselves another person would be unlikely to know or discover. Because we are more interested in intentional communication, rather than in random and unplanned statements, and because we are more interested in those revelations about ourselves others are unlikely to discover through observation, we will focus on the most limited definition of self-disclosure. For our purposes, self-disclosure consists of those verbal and nonverbal statements about ourselves that are intentional and that the other person or persons are unlikely to know. Self-disclosure can be as unthreatening as saying how you feel about a particular movie or how much studying you have been doing, or it can be as difficult as telling someone her use of obscenity makes you feel uncomfortable or that you have allowed your baby to be adopted.

Self-disclosure can be analyzed on the basis of a number of dimensions. Two important dimensions are valence (positive or negative information) and amount. Although we cannot supply prescriptive answers to the desirable amount of self-disclosure, self-disclosure should be reciprocal. In other words, you should use the other person's disclosure as a guide to the amount of information you should disclose. We usually provide positive information to others about ourselves before we provide negative information. An extremely high level of negative information can create problems in developing relationships.

Importance of Self-Disclosure

Self-disclosure is important for two reasons. First, it allows us to establish more meaningful relationships with others. And, second, self-disclosure allows us to establish more positive attitudes toward ourselves and others. Let us examine these two reasons for self-disclosure in more detail.

To Establish More Meaningful Relationships

Consider your communication with the person to whom you feel closest. Have you engaged in a great deal of self-disclosure? Now consider what you say or write to someone with whom you have only an acquaintanceship. How does your self-disclosure differ? Self-disclosure is offered most frequently and regularly to close friends. Self-disclosure allows relationships to grow in depth and meaning. If we use self-disclosure appropriately, our relationships move from being fairly superficial to being deeper and more meaningful. We find when we self-disclose more to others, they, reciprocally, disclose more to us.

An inability to self-disclose, on the other hand, can result in the death of a relationship. One of the common explanations for divorce given by women is their need to self-disclose. Divorced women are increasingly identifying their own lack of opportunity to express who they are as the cause of the breakup of their marriages. Without opportunities for self-disclosure, relationships appear to be doomed to shallowness, superficiality, or death.

To Establish More Positive Attitudes toward Ourselves and Others

In an article entitled "Shy Murderers," Lee, Zimbardo, and Bertholf discuss people who are overcontrolled and shy, and who, because of their frustration, attack others. They suggest these people need to learn how to express feelings directly to others. They continue:

> The social skills we've outlined should be learned by every child as a normal part of socialization. Children should be encouraged to express their feelings and to like themselves. They should come to see other people as sources of positive regard and interest, not as critical, negative evaluators who might reject them. They, and we, must be seen *and* heard.[13]

Both positive and negative self-disclosure can result in more positive attitudes about ourselves and others. If we disclose positive information about ourselves, we share the joy we feel about ourselves. When we tell others about our hopes and dreams, when we share happy moments, and when we recall exciting experiences, we feel encouraged. Others reinforce our feelings by offering their support, enthusiasm, and encouragement.

Although it may seem paradoxical, negative self-disclosure can also result in more positive attitudes about ourselves and others. When we are able to expose our negative qualities, our mistakes, our failings, and our shortcomings to others, and when others are able to do the same with us, we recognize we are all fallible, no one is perfect. We become more understanding and forgiving, and we develop more positive attitudes about all humankind.

Interference with Self-Disclosure

If self-disclosure is an aspect of interpersonal communication important to the way we view ourselves and others, we should consider why we are often unwilling to self-disclose to others. In general, we can say people are reluctant to self-disclose because of their negative feelings about themselves or their negative feelings about others. In other words, they do not respect themselves, they do not trust others, or both.

Many contemporary writers have discussed the risk involved in self-disclosure. For example, in *The Shoes of the Fisherman,* Morris L. West wrote:

> It costs so much to be a full human being that there are very few who have the enlightenment or the courage to pay the price. . . . One has to abandon altogether the search for security and reach out to the risk of living with both arms. One has to embrace the world like a lover. One has to accept pain as a condition of existence. One has to court doubt and darkness as the cost of knowing. One needs a will stubborn in conflict, but apt always to total acceptance of every consequence of living and dying.[14]

In *Why Am I Afraid to Tell You Who I Am?* John Powell writes he asked a number of people the question, "Why are you afraid to tell me who you are?" The response of one of his friends was to the point. He answered, "Because if I tell you who I am, you may not like who I am, and that's all that I have."[15] In essence, his friend was stating he did not respect himself enough to trust others with the information. Frequently, our lack of positive feelings about ourselves or about others contributes to our inability to self-disclose.

We are probably taught very early in our lives to avoid self-disclosure. The same kinds of responses that interfere with our self-awareness (see chapter 3) contribute also to our difficulty in self-disclosing. Our parents taught us positive self-disclosure was bragging. Significant others responded negatively when we made negative self-disclosures. The message we seemed to hear was self-disclosures should be avoided.

Men and women might avoid disclosure for different reasons. One study suggested men avoid self-disclosure in order to maintain control over their relationships, while women avoid self-disclosure in order to avoid personal hurt.[16] Another investigation showed men were shown to disclose more to strangers and casual acquaintances while women were more willing to disclose to intimates. The authors state stereotypically successful men are expected to compete and win, and competitiveness is not conducive to intimacy. They conclude one form of winning is exploiting another person's weakness, so men may cut themselves off from others in order not to expose their vulnerability.[17]

Self-disclosure may be avoided because of people's negative feelings about themselves or about others.

Two communication behaviors are related to our unwillingness to self-disclose. If we feel insecure about ourselves, we may be overly defensive. If we are unsure of our own responses and believe others are superior to us, we may be nonassertive.

Defensiveness, the tendency to protect oneself against danger or injury, was mentioned in connection with feedback and listening in chapter 4. We observed in chapter 4 that defensiveness may occur when individuals receive negative feedback and they may not listen effectively to others because of their defensive posture. Defensiveness is also relevant to self-disclosure. Defensiveness may occur because we believe the kind of person we are is not consistent with the kind of person we are supposed to be. In other words, our "real" self is discrepant from our "idealized" self. The difference between these two selves causes us to feel uneasy because we are concerned we will show others our "real" self and be discounted.

Six behaviors have been identified as contributing to defensiveness in individuals. These behaviors and their counterparts, which lead to a supportive communication climate, are listed in table 7.4. Let us consider each of these categories in more depth.

Evaluation refers to comments or statements that tend to be judgmental in tone. For instance, "I wouldn't wear my hair like that!" and "I never wait until the last minute to study for an exam like you do," are examples of evaluative statements. Another example of evaluation is your instructors' feedback about your work. You may receive a letter grade or comments that suggest you did "good" or "poor" work. *Descriptive* statements, on the other hand, are not evaluative, but merely reflect the

Table 7.4 Defensive Versus Supportive Communication Behaviors.

Defensive Behaviors	Supportive Behaviors
1. Evaluation	1. Description
2. Control	2. Problem orientation
3. Strategy	3. Spontaneity
4. Neutrality	4. Empathy
5. Superiority	5. Equality
6. Certainty	6. Provisionalism

speaker's perceptions. "That hairstyle is attractive on you, but I couldn't wear it because my face is so long and narrow," and "Some people seem to study better under pressure; I find I do my best work when I am done far in advance," replace the previous evaluative statements. Similarly, you may find you feel far less defensive when instructors provide you with descriptive comments about their reactions to your work than when they offer evaluative responses.

Control refers to statements aimed at commanding behavior. For instance, statements like, "If you would get up a half hour earlier, you would be better able to start the day with breakfast," and "Don't you think you would be a lot happier if you became a speech major like I am?" tend to be controlling statements. At the other end of the continuum is *problem orientation,* which suggests the speaker does not have the one best solution in mind when he or she speaks. Instead, the speaker suggests the two communicators attempt to find a solution together. Examples of problem-oriented statements are, "How do you think you should start the day?" and "What major do you think would make you happy?"

Strategy refers to statements that attempt to manipulate the other person into behaving in certain ways. If you tell some friends you will go shopping with them, but then ask them to make three or four stops on the way so you can take care of some business or academic matters, they may feel you have manipulated them into driving you around the city. *Spontaneity* refers to honest expression of your current feelings. Spontaneity is not preplanned or considered in terms of its potential effect. When you are spontaneous, you allow yourself to be influenced by the interaction. In other words, you are open to the communication process. Spontaneous expression leads to supportiveness, while strategic expression leads to defensive communication.

Neutrality is contrasted with *empathy*. Neutrality refers to a lack of interest or a lack of concern for another person and is exemplified in such statements as, "I don't care what you do," "I'm not interested in what happened to you," and "Your problems are none of my concern." Empathy, is trying to understand a situation from the other person's perspective and is demonstrated in such statements as, "I understand how you feel," "You know I am interested in you" and "Your problems are important to me, too."

Superiority refers to those comments that suggest one person is of higher status than the second and that he or she wants to relate in a superior-subordinate relationship. Comments like, "Well, it's about time you realized how our company works," "I guess you're finally growing up," and "Perhaps when you have had more experience, you will begin to understand," suggest superiority from the speaker. Conversely, comments like, "I don't always understand how this company works either," "We all have more to learn," and "No matter how much experience we have, we can be surprised with the way that things turn out," suggest *equality* between the communicators. Underlying the notion of equality is the idea that, although we are not all of equal status, expertise, or experience, we are all equally valuable human beings and thus have equal value as communicators.

Certainty is reflected in statements that suggest the speaker has all of the answers; *provisionalism* suggests the speaker may not know all of the answers. An example of certainty is the assertion that others are failures at communicating with you, they will never improve, and future interactions are out of the question. On the other hand, an example of provisionalism is suggesting you and another person appear to be having communication problems and you would like to investigate some means of resolving them.[18] Key terms that reflect provisionalism include *perhaps, maybe, might, try, could do,* and so on.

Defensiveness may be a regular response pattern resulting from strong negative feelings about self, or it may be a function of current statements from others. Occasionally feeling defensive as a result of people making evaluative, controlling, strategic, neutral, superior, or certainty statements is a natural response. However, recognizing you respond defensively may assist you in altering your behavior in these occasional circumstances.

We may dismiss occasional defensiveness on the basis it occurs on rare occasions, it occurs in response to another person's comments, or it is not overly destructive to effective communication. Regular defensiveness, however, can be a problem. Never being open and honest in communication can lead to shallow interpersonal relationships and a distrust of others. Further, regular defensiveness can lead to a communication climate in which people learn to expect such behaviors as evaluation, control, strategy, neutrality, superiority, and certainty.

If you feel you use defensiveness as a regular response to others, you may want to consider ways to overcome your negative feelings about yourself to be free of the potential negative effects of defensiveness in your communication behavior.

Assertiveness, the ability to communicate feelings, attitudes, and beliefs honestly and directly, is a communication skill associated with a positive self-concept. Nonassertiveness, conversely, is associated with a negative self-concept and indicates an inability to stand up for one's own rights, or, to stand up for oneself in a dysfunctional way. Nonassertive people do not acknowledge self. They do not accept the notion of personal rights and are inhibited in their expression of feelings, attitudes, and beliefs. Nonassertive people rarely achieve their goals and may often be hurt by other people. Perhaps nonassertive people feel their goal in life is to appease others or to serve others.

While they may gain some satisfaction out of caring for another person, their joy is short-lived if they do not enjoy a reciprocal relationship in which their own needs are met.

Assertiveness is different from aggressiveness. Aggressiveness involves standing up for one's rights at the expense of others. Aggressive people care little about anyone's needs, other than their own. They strive to win, regardless of the cost to others. People who interact with aggressive persons often feel a great deal of frustration. As a consequence, the "victories" of aggressive people may be only temporary because they lose their friends and do not develop meaningful relationships with others. Aggressive people, like nonassertive people, probably suffer from a negative self-concept. They may feel insecure or unworthy of acceptance and believe they must compete to be accepted by others. Unfortunately, their intense competitiveness often denies them the acceptance they seek.

Assertiveness falls between aggressiveness and nonassertiveness. Assertiveness, as we pointed out earlier, is associated with a positive self-concept. People who are assertive are concerned with their own needs and rights, as well as the needs and rights of others. Assertive individuals trust themselves and their responses. They are able to create a supportive communication climate marked by openness and honesty. The acceptance of personal rights and the lack of inhibition surrounding self-expression on the part of the assertive communicator encourage effective communication.

As we have observed, both defensiveness and nonassertiveness are related to an unwillingness to self-disclose. Fear of situations not under our control, and our lack of trust of other people can result in our refusal to share ourselves with others. In time, this fear and lack of trust become permanent, and our refusal to self-disclose becomes habitual.

Interpersonal Conflict

The Nature of Interpersonal Conflict

Conflict may occur in relationships because of differences in individuals' abilities to self-disclose or for other reasons. Conflict is inevitable in relationships and may be constructive as well as destructive. Conflict may have the same sort of driving force as do hunger, thirst, pain, and other physically based phenomena. Physical arousal may occur, which produces more efficient learning, a sharpening of faculties, and a motivation to act. In this section, we consider the role of conflict and conflict resolution in interpersonal relationships.

Definition of Interpersonal Conflict

According to Hocker and Wilmot, **interpersonal conflict** is "an expressed struggle between at least two interdependent parties who perceive incompatible goals, scarce rewards, and interference from the other parties in achieving their goals."[19] By "an expressed struggle," the authors suggest both (or all) communicators understand a conflict is present. If one individual feels a problem exists but the other or others are

Interpersonal conflict is inevitable in relationships and may be destructive or constructive.

unaware of it, no interpersonal conflict is present. For example, suppose you feel a great deal of anger toward others with whom you carpool because they are never on time. You spend a great deal of time waiting, but the other carpoolers continue to be oblivious to the time. Can we define this as a situation of interpersonal conflict? No, this is not interpersonal conflict unless you communicate your feelings to the others, and they understand the situation.

"Perceived incompatible goals" suggests the parties believe they cannot achieve their goals without causing the other persons to lose. For instance, if you and a date want to go to different movies on the same evening, you might perceive the situation as one that includes incompatible goals. The situation need not be truly incompatible for people to perceive it that way. For instance, you might be able to go to two movies in one evening. However, if the parties involved believe the goals are incompatible, then interpersonal conflict is present.

"Perceived scarce rewards" suggests people perceive an insufficient amount of a certain resource to satisfy everyone. For example, family members may perceive conflict when they observe the small amount of ice cream available for all of them to share. The amount of ice cream may seem to be sufficient to another family, but the group involved may not view it as sufficient, and, thus, we can define the situation as one involving interpersonal conflict.

"Interference from other parties in achieving their goals" suggests one person in a relationship will not allow the other person or persons to achieve their goals. The wife who perceives her husband as trying to sabotage her diet by bringing home candy and other fattening treats perceives interference from him in achieving her goals. Similarly, the little brother who changes the television channel each time his siblings are quietly sitting before the set provides interference.

Outgrowths of Interpersonal Conflict

At the beginning of this section, we suggested conflict may be constructive as well as destructive. Conflict is destructive when individuals do not understand the value of conflict, when it is perceived as a win/lose game in which only one person is the winner and one person is the loser. Similarly, if people act aggressively, if they withdraw from each other, if they repress their feelings, or if they project blame on others, conflict can be destructive.

Conflict is constructive when individuals feel some commitment to each other. If two people care more about their relationship than about day-to-day disagreements, they will probably be able to use conflict constructively in their relationship. Conflict is used constructively when the individuals involved confine their disagreements to the issues, rather than bringing up old issues or unresolved matters from other disagreements.

What positive outcomes result when conflict is used constructively? First, the people involved may find they have reached a better understanding of the nature and implications of the problem they face. Before the interaction, the individuals involved may have had different ideas about the cause of the other person or persons' angry, hurt, or taciturn behavior. After the interaction, they might clearly understand both the cause and the implications of the problem.

Second, the individuals may actually increase the alternatives from which they can select a solution. Before the conflict, the individuals involved might have had limited ideas about how to solve their problem. They may see the situation as involving one extreme solution or another and not be able to perceive a variety of compromises between the extremes. For example, one member of a couple may want to go on vacation to some-place warm to enjoy the sunshine and the beach. The other member may want to go somewhere close to home and fish. The two may feel their goals are mutually incompatible—they cannot go far away to a warm climate and at the same time stay relatively close to home and fish. After the conflict, they may realize they might go somewhere warm that offers deep-sea fishing. Or the two might go on separate vacations, with each person enjoying what he or she desires. They may decide to do what one person desires this year and what the other person wishes the next year. Or they may choose an entirely different vacation spot that offers totally different opportunities they both enjoy.

Finally, the individuals involved in constructive conflict may find interaction and involvement have been stimulated. Perhaps one or more of the individuals involved felt very apprehensive about the particular issue and was reluctant to talk to the other individual or individuals. This withdrawal may have led to both or all of the individuals in the relationship being quiet. The raising of the issue encourages an end to the silence and more communication among the individuals. A decrease in interaction and a lower level of involvement frequently result in individuals having unspoken disagreements.

Resolution of Interpersonal Conflict

How do people resolve interpersonal conflict? The methods of conflict resolution can be categorized in a variety of ways. In this text, however, we suggest five common conflict resolution patterns individuals use: denial, suppression, power, compromise, and collaboration.

Denial

Individuals who use denial generally withdraw from conflict and do not acknowledge a problem exists. Even though denied, however, the problem does not go away. The cause of the conflict remains, and individuals feel increasingly uncomfortable. Sometimes when denial is used, the problem becomes unmanageable. For instance, suppose a husband dominates conversations with his wife. He interrupts, he cuts off her sentences, and he generally talks louder and faster. If the wife refuses to acknowledge a problem exists and she withdraws, does the situation improve? Probably not. The husband may continue to dominate until the behavior is brought to his attention.

Suppression

When people suppress conflict, they try to smooth over the problem and minimize their differences. In denial, they do not acknowledge a problem exists. In suppression, they are aware of a problem, but they choose to minimize its importance. Individuals who generally rely on suppression may feel effective communicators simply do not resort to conflict. They may also fail to recognize the positive aspects of handling conflict in an open manner. Suppression may be employed when it is more important to preserve the relationship than it is to deal with a seemingly insignificant issue. People who suppress conflict, however, should consider whether suppression is a general response to conflict, rather than a response based on a highly important relationship and an unimportant issue. An example of suppression would be the situation in a family when only one person generally takes out the garbage. Perhaps a number of people are strong enough and capable of removing the garbage, but the job seems to fall regularly to one member of the family. This person may resent always having to perform this task but decide his or her relationships with other family members are more important than arguing about who should do the job.

Power

Power is used in conflict resolution in a variety of ways. First, people may use the power vested in their authority or position. For instance, a mother might argue she is the "head" of the household and thus gets to make final decisions on matters. Second, people may use power in the form of a majority. Children may gang up on an unsuspecting parent by determining how the parent should spend some unexpected money and claim "majority rules." Third, power may take the form of a persuasive minority. A family, returning from a long vacation, may begin to discuss where the family should have dinner on its first night back in town. The person who does the cooking in the family may want to go out to eat, while the others are too tired to think about dressing appropriately and making the necessary moves. The cook may persuasively argue his or her position, even though he or she is the only one who is initially in favor of going out to eat.

The problem with conflict resolution based on power is that, too often, power plays result in winners and losers. When a father has the final say on every matter, when the children in a family determine how some extra money is spent, or when the cook always determines what is eaten and where it is eaten, they all win. At the same time, the other members in the relationships all lose. The losers may begin to resent the person or people wielding power, they may not support the final decision, and they may actually interfere with the decision.

Compromise

When individuals use compromise to resolve a conflict, they each state their position, and then some middle ground is determined. Compromise is highly effective in some situations and the last resort in other situations. Compromise is not without problems, however. First, when people know they are going to resolve their conflict through compromise, they may begin with inflated positions. Suppose a couple is discussing going out for dinner and the woman wishes to go to a more elegant restaurant than the man. She may suggest a five-star restaurant, and he may suggest a fast-food restaurant, rather than their actual choices. Second, compromise may be weakened to a point it is not effective. Remember the couple who had different vacation plans? Suppose the woman's idea was to go to the Caribbean on a cruise and the man's idea was to rent a canoe on the local river. How satisfied would either be if they floated down the Mississippi on a steamboat? Finally, there is often little real commitment by any of the parties to a compromise. Perhaps a couple decides to go to the vacation spot of one person one year and to the other person's choice the next year. Freezing in Colorado may be highly dissatisfying to the one the first year, and baking in Jamaica may be equally displeasing to the other the second year. Neither may be very committed to either trip.

Collaboration

The essential characteristic of collaboration is communication. When individuals collaborate to resolve a conflict, they talk with each other and attempt to negotiate a situation satisfactory to all. When collaboration is used, all of the individuals involved recognize the abilities and expertise of the others. In this situation, the emphasis is on the problem, rather than on defending one's position. The assumption is the group or dyad's decision is superior to that of any one individual. The problem orientation leads to a supportive communication climate, rather than a defensive communication climate, which is caused by controlling behavior.

Collaboration can break down when conflict is offered as an "either-or" statement or if the conflict is resolved due to a lack of resources. For instance, if the members in a relationship do not have sufficient time, money, or understanding, a dissatisfying decision is often reached.

Collaboration can be used to resolve interpersonal conflict among family members.

How does collaboration operate? Suppose you are the mother of two sons. One of your sons wants to spend the afternoon at the local swimming pool, and the other wants to go to a nearby wooded park and hike in the woods. What do you do? The ideal situation, in this case, might be to have the two boys and yourself discuss the situation, with each boy carefully explaining his choice and the rationale for it. As the two listen to the advantages of each plan and as you add clarification and suggestions, a decision may be arrived at that is mutually satisfying.

To illustrate all five conflict resolution patterns, suppose you find evidence one of your older children is taking illegal drugs. The child is in high school, and you have noticed a drop in academic grades, sharp mood swings, and an unhealthy appearance in recent weeks. What do you do? If you denied the situation, you might not acknowledge the problem—even to yourself. If you suppressed it, you might keep an eye on the child but say nothing. If you used power, you might tell your child as long as he or she was living in your house, no drugs would be permitted, and if the child wished to continue to use drugs, his or her only option would be to move out. If you used compromise, you might suggest the child use some drugs, but not others, or that the child use drugs at home, but not in public places. To use collaboration to resolve the conflict, you might interact with the child directly, tell him or her what you suspect and why, ask for an explanation, and assure the child you will help in any way that is desired.

Improving Communication in Interpersonal Relationships

We all want to have successful interpersonal relationships. We want to be able to trust others and to self-disclose to them. We want to be able to handle conflict and to use conflict resolution techniques that are mutually satisfying. Nonetheless, countless people find themselves in dissatisfying and unhappy relationships.

The Possibilities for Improvement

Can we improve our communication in interpersonal relationships? Until relatively recently, many people felt we could not learn to relate more effectively to others. Today, most individuals feel such a possibility does exist. Are such changes easy? Generally, they are not. We should not expect to take an introductory course in communication and solve all of our relational problems. Self-help books that promise instant success will probably result only in permanent disillusionment. Courses on assertiveness training, relaxation techniques, and marital satisfaction provide only part of the answer.

If we wish to improve our communication within our interpersonal relationships, we must have a commitment to learning a variety of communication skills. We must understand the importance of perceptual differences among people, the role of self-concept in communication, the nature of verbal language, and the role of nonverbal communication. We must be willing to share ourselves with others as we self-disclose, and we must be willing to attempt to understand another person through our careful and conscientious listening. In addition, we must recognize that, even when we thoroughly understand these concepts and are able to implement them in our behavior, our interactions with others may not be successful. Communication is dependent upon the interaction between two communicators, and one person cannot guarantee its success. Others may have conflicting goals, different perspectives, or less ability to communicate effectively.

Learning individual communication concepts and specific communication skills is essential to effective interaction. But we also need to understand the impact of setting upon these skills. For example, we know we do not communicate at home the way we do in the classroom. Self-disclosure, which is especially appropriate and important within the family context, may be out of place in the classroom. Preparation and planning are important in an interview, as we will observe in the next chapter, but they may be seen as manipulative in a conversation between a husband and wife.

Behavioral Flexibility

In addition to communication concepts, skills, and settings, our interactions may be greatly enhanced by an underlying approach to communication behavior called behavioral flexibility. **Behavioral flexibility** is defined as "the ability to alter behavior in order to adapt to new situations and to relate in new ways when necessary."[20] This global concept may be central to increased success and decreased failures in relationships.

Flexibility is important in a variety of fields. For example, biologists and botanists have demonstrated extinction of certain living things often occurs because of an organism's inability to adapt to changes in the environment. Psychologists have suggested women and men who are **androgynous**—who hold both male and female traits—are more successful in their interactions than are people who are unyieldingly masculine or absolutely feminine. Flexibility in our psychological sex roles is more useful than a static notion of what it means to be a man or a woman in our culture. For instance, if you are a single parent, you may be called upon to behave in a loving and nurturing way to your child, regardless of your biological sex. If your goal is to be a successful manager in a large corporation, you may have to exhibit competitiveness, assertiveness, and a task orientation, regardless of your biological sex. As you move from interactions with co-workers to interactions with your family and friends, you may need to change from traditionally "masculine" behaviors to those which have been considered to be "feminine."

Behavioral flexibility is especially important in interpersonal communication today because relationships between people are in constant flux. For example, as we shall discuss in the next chapter, the family structure has gone through sharp changes in recent years. In addition, the United States today has a growing older population. Also, changes in the labor force require new skills and different ways to interact with others. Too, people travel more often and move more frequently. As a result of these types of changes, people may interact differently today than in the past.

What kinds of changes might you expect in your own life that will effect your relationships with others? You may change your job ten or more different times. You may move your place of residence even more frequently. You probably will be married at least once, and possibly two or three times. You probably will have one child or more. You will probably experience loss of family members through death and dissolution of relationships. You may have a spouse whose needs conflict with your needs. Other family members may view the world differently than you and challenge your perceptions. When your life appears to be most stable and calm, unexpected changes will occur.

How could behavioral flexibility assist you through these changes? A flexible person has a large repertoire or set of behaviors from which to draw. This individual is confident about sharing messages with others and about understanding the messages that others provide. The flexible person is able to self-disclose when appropriate but does not use this ability in inappropriate contexts. The flexible person can demonstrate listening skills but is not always the one who is listening. The flexible person can show concern for a child who needs assistance, can be assertive on the job, can be yielding when another person needs to exercise control, and can be independent when called upon to stand alone. The flexible person does not predetermine one set of communication behaviors he or she will always enact. The flexible person is not dogmatic or narrow-minded in interactions with others.

It is also important to remember that changes are not always negative. In fact, a great deal of change is positive. For instance, when we graduate from college, the changes that occur are generally perceived as positive. When we enter into new relationships, we generally encounter positive change.

Behavioral Flexibility

For each of the three situations given, suggest how a behaviorally flexible person and a person who is not behaviorally flexible might respond.

1. You are a man who believes women and men are different and men should be the final arbiter of decisions. Your wife believes the two of you should reach decisions together by talking about the situation until a solution is determined. How might you respond to your wife if you were behaviorally flexible? If you were behaviorally inflexible?

2. You are a woman who cares a great deal about children. As a consequence, you take a job in a day-care center. You find you form many attachments to the children who come each day and you suffer a certain amount of anguish and sadness each time one of the children is moved to a different school. You try to resolve the problem by becoming even closer to the new children who enroll. However, you know this is no solution since these children too will at some time leave the day-care center. What would you do if you were behaviorally flexible? If you were behaviorally inflexible?

3. You are a person who likes to date only one other individual at a time. You have had several fairly long-term relationships, but each relationship has ended with the other person gradually fading out of the picture. You do not know why others leave you, but you feel a certain amount of distress that you cannot maintain a relationship. What would you do if you were behaviorally flexible? If you were behaviorally inflexible?

Change is stressful, however, even when it is positive. Nonetheless, we cannot remain the same; we must change. As Gail Sheehy, author of *Passages: Predictable Crises of Adult Life,* writes:

> We must be willing to change chairs if we want to grow. There is no permanent compatibility between a chair and a person. And there is no one right chair. What is right at one stage may be restricting at another or too soft.[21]

Summary

In this chapter, we examined interpersonal relationships, one context in which people communicate with each other. Interpersonal relationships are associations between two or more people who are interdependent, who use some consistent patterns of interaction, and who have interacted for some period of time. We establish interpersonal relationships for a variety of reasons, including to understand more about ourselves, to understand more about others, to understand our world, to fulfill our needs, and to increase and enrich our positive experiences. Relationships go through definable stages in development, maintenance, and deterioration, which affect self-disclosure.

Self-disclosure consists of verbal and nonverbal intentional statements about ourselves that the other person is unlikely to know. Self-disclosure is important in interpersonal relationships because when we tell others about ourselves, we become closer to them and are able to establish more meaningful relationships. Self-disclosure also allows us to establish more positive attitudes about ourselves and about others. Women and men exhibit different self-disclosure patterns. Some people choose not to self-disclose because they have negative feelings about themselves, do not trust others, or both. Two communication behaviors related to an unwillingness to self-disclose are defensiveness and nonassertiveness.

Conflict appears to be inevitable in interpersonal relationships. Interpersonal conflict is an expressed struggle between at least two interdependent parties who perceive incompatible goals, scarce rewards, and interference from the other parties in achieving their goals. Conflict can be constructive or destructive, depending upon how the communicators view it. Constructive conflict may allow the interactants to reach a better understanding of their disagreements, may increase the number of alternatives individuals have from which to select a solution, and may result in increased interaction and involvement. Interpersonal conflict is resolved in a number of ways, including denial, suppression, power, compromise, and collaboration. In many circumstances, collaboration appears to be the superior method of resolution.

Communication can be improved in interpersonal relationships but it is not a simple matter. In addition to understanding communication concepts, skills, and settings, we need to develop behavioral flexibility. Behavioral flexibility refers to our ability to alter our behavior in order to adapt to new situations and to relate in new ways when necessary. Interpersonal relationships are constantly changing, and individuals who wish to be successful in them must demonstrate flexibility.

Communication with Friends and Family

T he only way to have a friend is to be one.

Ralph Waldo Emerson

W e fall in love with a personality, but we must live with a character.

Peter DeVries

A ll happy families resemble one another; every unhappy family is unhappy in its own way.

Tolstoy, Anna Karenina

Objectives

1. Define and identify the characteristics of friendship.
2. Explain how we can improve our communication with friends.
3. Define and explain the definition of a family.
4. Identify and explain some types of contemporary American families.
5. List communication behaviors that are related to family satisfaction.

Key Terms

friendship
availability
shared activities
caring
honesty
confidentiality
loyalty
understanding
empathy
family
couples with no
  children

single-parent
  families
cohabitating
  couples
blended families
dual-worker
  families
nuclear families
extended families
family satisfaction

In the last chapter we considered the nature and importance of interpersonal relationships. In this chapter we focus on two particular kinds of interpersonal relationships, those that occur among friends and those that occur among family members. These settings of interpersonal communication are familiar to each of us, but we will separately consider how people communicate in each setting.

Friends

Definition of Friendship

The relationship that exists between friends has been examined poetically and scientifically. We might distinguish between friendships and acquaintanceships on the basis of *choice* and of *positive regard.* We choose our friends; we do not accidentally have friendships. You might strike up a conversation with a stranger in a public place; you may have an acquaintance because you are enrolled in the same class or work at the same place. Your friends are persons you have singled out for a relationship. Similarly, you generally show positive regard for your friends. You may talk to a stranger for whom you have little positive or negative feeling, and you may have mixed feelings about some of your acquaintances, but your friends generally receive your positive regard. A recent definition of friendship seems particularly appropriate. **Friendship** is "an interpersonal relationship between two persons that is mutually productive, established and maintained through perceived mutual free choice, and characterized by mutual positive regard."[1]

Characteristics of Friendships

On what basis do we choose our friends? You may have a variety of very distinctive people whom you consider as your friends. You may be able to account for your choice in selecting a person as a friend, or you may be less certain about why your relationship with that person is so positive. In *The Heart of Friendship,* Muriel James and Louis Savary suggest eight descriptors that identify a friendship.[2] Considering these eight characteristics will help us understand why we enter into friendships with others.

One characteristic of friendships is **availability.** We expect friends to be available to us, or we expect to have access to them. If we call friends when we are in trouble, we expect them to respond. Carole King probably popularized this concept best in her song, "You've Got a Friend":

When you're down and troubled
And you need some loving care,
And nothing, nothing is going right
Close your eyes and think of me
And soon I will be there
To brighten up, even your darkest night
You just call out my name
And you know wherever I am
I'll come running, to see you again.

Friendships are developed through communication.

Winter, Spring, Summer, or Fall,
All you have to do is call
And I'll be there—You've got a friend.[3]

Similarly, the often-quoted sentiment, "You can't *make* friends, you have to be a friend and then others will make *you* a friend," suggests that our availability and access to others is why they may perceive us as a friend.

A second characteristic of friendships is **shared activities.** We expect to engage in common activities with our friends. A recent study provided some interesting results in this regard. The study examined whether friends and strangers could be distinguished from each other on the basis of shared activities or on the basis of shared attitudes. Perhaps surprisingly, the study demonstrated friends can be identified by their shared or common activities, not by their shared or common attitudes. For instance, a friendship may develop between two people who enjoy jogging together, even though one is a staunch Republican and the other is an avowed Democrat. Or, a good friendship may include a person who was opposed to the national Equal Rights Amendment and a person who worked diligently in favor of it because they both are writers and enjoy co-authoring books and articles. Friends are more similar in their activities than in their attitudes and more accurate in estimating activity preferences of their friends than they are in identifying attitudes of their friends. For example, friends would be able to accurately predict the leisure activities, but would be unable to predict the religious values, of their own friends. In this study, attitudes tended to be as dissimilar among friends as among strangers.[4] Friends could belong to different churches, different political parties, and support entirely different causes, just as strangers might be expected to do.

A third quality associated with friendships is **caring.** We expect our friends to sincerely care about us. Caring involves such behaviors as attentiveness, interest, forethought, and watchfulness. We expect verbal and nonverbal sensitivity from our friends. We assume they will observe the manner in which we behave and respond to our behavior. When persons neglect us, disregard our feelings, show indifference or inattention, we assume they do not care about us and are not among the group of people we would identify as our friends.

A fourth quality of friendship is **honesty.** We expect our friends to be honest and open in their communication with us. If you make a serious error in judgment, if you drink too much alcohol, or if you have a smudge on your face, you would expect a friend to redirect, guide, or tell you. This does not mean being someone's friend allows you the privilege of disregarding that person's feelings and beginning statements with, "I know this might hurt you, but . . ." "I'm telling you this for your own good . . ." and "You might be angry now, but some day you'll thank me for what I am about to tell you." We need to be cognizant of the other person's feelings and not take license to be brutally or hurtfully forthright. As we explained in chapters 4 and 6, we use the technique of descriptive, not evaluative, feedback. Using descriptive methods, we can grant honest feedback. As a friend, we grant honest feedback and sincere responses that may result in improvement for the other person, but we do not show unnecessary cruelty nor do we impose our values on our friends.

We generally expect **confidentiality** from our friends. We self-disclose more to our friends than to acquaintances. One recent study examined the patterns of self-disclosure that existed between pairs of college roommates and college hallmates (nonroommates on the same floor) in first-year dormitories. The study determined friendship was related to intimate self-disclosure and proximity, or physical closeness, was related to superficial self-disclosure.[5] In other words, we self-disclose more personal information—how we feel about our body, our religious values, and our sexual behavior—to persons we consider friends while we self-disclose superficial information—our major, when we hope to graduate from college, and the places we have lived—to persons who are in our physical proximity. One of the reasons we are able to make intimate and negative self-disclosures to our friends is we expect them to consider the information confidential. We trust our friends not to disclose our idiosyncrasies and embarrassing moments to others. Jane Howard, in *Families,* recounts a meeting with one of her close girlhood friends:

> "Do you still hold your wet head out the window of a cold winter's night so you'll catch cold and sound sexy like Tallulah Bankhead?"
> "I only did that once, when I was fifteen. Do *you* still hide your dirty dishes in the oven? Or was it the bathtub?" Our friendship is a cobweb of such frail legends.[6]

Howard's reunion with her friend is filled with stories and experiences the two have shared with each other, but before the publication of Howard's book, probably few other people knew of such stories. The proverb, "It is better to have friends learn of your faults than your enemies," alludes to the confidential nature of friendship that does not extend into the relationship between enemies.

A sixth quality associated with friendship is **loyalty.** We expect our friends to be loyal; we do not expect them to betray us or to show disloyalty, even under difficult circumstances. Perhaps we define those persons who stay with us "through thick and thin" as our friends while we define people who are only interested in us when we are successful as acquaintances. Friends remain loyal to us regardless of our circumstances.

We expect some level of **understanding** in our friendships. This understanding may be in the form of a friend recognizing why we respond in an unusual way to another person as a result of some past experience. Or, a friend may show his understanding of us by withholding negative judgments about idiosyncratic behavior on our part. Nonverbally, a friend may communicate understanding by a nod, a wink, or a smile others do not notice or do not acknowledge.

Finally, we desire **empathy** from our friends. We want our friends to view the world as though they were seeing it from our perspective. We are very disturbed when we make a comment about an event, an idea, or another person and a friend appears unwilling or unable to perceive the phenomonen from the perspective we offer. For instance, if you comment, "I think my physics professor is unable to teach in an interesting and effective manner," and your friend responds she believes you don't understand physics, the particular professor is the best in the college, or you don't know how to discriminate between an effective and an ineffective instructor, you would be surprised, and perhaps, upset. We expect our friends to attempt to see the world through our eyes, from our perspective.

We choose our friends and we have positive regard for them. Among the characteristics of friendship are availability, shared activities, caring, honesty, confidentiality, loyalty, understanding, and empathy. How do you communicate your friendship to others? Nonverbally, you can demonstrate your feelings of friendship proxemically, by sitting and standing close to the other person. You may reach out and physically touch your friend. You may use increased facial expression and gestures to demonstrate your feelings. You may develop specialized gestures that have meaning for the two of you, but for no one else. You may look at your friend more than you look at a stranger or acquaintance. You may even share each other's clothing, jewelry, and other belongings.

How is friendship transmitted verbally? You may develop special verbal codes with which to communicate. Words may be used in unique, but mutually understood ways, between friends. You may self-disclose more intimate information to a friend than to a stranger. You may discuss negative as well as positive aspects of your self-concept. You will want to behave assertively as you express yourself honestly and completely without imposing your views on your friend. You will demonstrate your understanding and empathy by those verbal skills discussed in Chapter 6. Topics of conversations with friends will include those shared activities or common perspectives that originally contributed to your friendship.

When we do not communicate our friendship to those persons whom we classify as friends, what occurs? The relationship may deteriorate as was discussed in Chapter 7, or one person may continue to maintain the relationship. Friendships cannot last in one-sided situations, however, and they frequently deteriorate if one person refuses to communicate her commitment to the relationship. Friendships may deteriorate to become acquaintanceships, or they may change and become intimate or even family relationships which we will discuss later in this chapter.

Improving Communication with Our Friends

We communicate with our friends every day. Our proficiency with conversational skills can affect the relationships we develop or fail to develop, the tasks we are able to accomplish or fail to accomplish, and the way other people view or fail to view us. In this section we will offer some suggestions on how to improve in this communication setting. You have already read about some of the specific nonverbal and verbal skills you should develop.

Before beginning this discussion, we should dispel the myth about conversational ability that people are "naturally" good or poor conversationalists. The person who always has a ready illustration or an apt anecdote may be a popular guest at cocktail and dinner parties, while the person who "doesn't know what to say" or is reticent may find she receives few invitations. Are good conversationalists born and not made? No research has demonstrated inherited traits rather than learned skills contribute to an individual's ability to interact with friends. People can improve their informal interactions with others.

The nature of communication with friends may cause us to believe we cannot improve in this skill area. We may agree public speaking skills, radio and television broadcasting, and even interviewing techniques can be learned but may seriously question whether we can become better conversationalists. Some of the other communication skills appear to be more formal, that is, they are more ceremonial, more methodical, and more precise. Conversations, on the other hand, are more informal or common, ordinary, and conventional. The formality or informality of an activity should not be the determinant of whether improvement is possible, however. Consider other informal activities in which you engage. For example, a number of books have suggested we can become better gardeners, better carpenters, and better "fix-it-up" people. We learn how to raise our house plants, how to purchase and return items more successfully, and even how to improve our eating habits. Similarly, we can learn how to improve our ability to hold conversations with persons we consider to be friends.

We may find we are better able to communicate with others if we adopt three perspectives. First, we need to understand the differences among our relationships and adjust our behavior and speech accordingly, and operationalize differences in relationships. We cannot treat everyone the same way in our communicative behavior. We must be clear about the mutually understood nature of the relationship. Do you perceive a person as a friend while he views you merely as a business acquaintance? Can you self-disclose intimacies to your roommate?

We communicate differently with people depending on the relationship we have with them.

An important feature of relational definition lies in the mutually accepted definition of the relationship. In other words, one person cannot impose the definition of the relationship on both people. We cannot, independently, determine the nature of the relationship. As a consequence, we cannot introspectively determine what the relationship shall be and then impose that view on another. Clarification of a relationship often requires sharing your feelings with your partner, particularly when you feel the other person is a friend. You may consider discussing the quality, depth, or focus of your relationship with the other person who is involved if disagreement about the definition of the relationship seems to exist. Are you using verbal and nonverbal messages that are mutually understood? Do you demonstrate assertiveness skills and an ability to self-disclose appropriately? Do you practice active listening? Reviewing the material in chapters 2 through 7 may be useful in improving your ablty to communicate in this setting.

Third, we must accept change and adapt our behavior appropriately. You will recall the discussion of behavioral flexibility in Chapter 7. It is important to understand relationships *do* change. We do not remain friends with everyone for our entire lives. Both acquaintances and lovers can become friends while friends may become strangers. Our relationships with others need not be bound by age, sex, or other subcultural differences. You may find a relationship with someone much older than yourself is very rewarding or that men and women can be "just friends." You may develop a more personal relationship with a colleague or classmate. You may find that a friend with whom you ride to school every day has become a stranger when she moves to a different city. You may feel exhilarated when a stranger becomes a close friend. The point is that relationships do change as they meet the expectations or fail to meet the expectations of the participants, as the partners grow at similar or different rates, as needs are satisfied or fail to be satisfied, and as pleasure is increased and pain is decreased or as pleasure is decreased and pain is increased. Our task is to be sensitive and responsive to those changes. To the extent we are able to be creative in our definitions of relationships, caring in our interactions with others, and courageous in taking the first step, we will develop satisfying interpersonal relationships with our friends.

Families

Jane Howard, author of the best-seller, *Families,* underlined the importance of the family when she wrote:

> Call it a clan, call it a network, call it a tribe, call it a family. Whatever you call it, whoever you are, you need one. You need one because you are human. You didn't come from nowhere. Before you, around you, and presumably after you, too, there are others. Some of these others must matter. They must matter a lot to you and if you are very lucky, to one another. Their welfare must be nearly as important to you as your own. Even if you live alone, even if your solitude is elected and ebullient, you still cannot do without a clan or tribe.[7]

None of us can do without a family. Unlike our friendships, we do not always choose the relationships that constitute our family. Family relationships may vary from other interpersonal relationships in their relative lack of fluidity and their lack of freedom of choice.

Families may provide extreme joy or sorrow. Sven Wahlroos writes "the deepest satisfaction" may come from "being a member of a loving family."[8] On the other hand, Jules Henry, author of *Pathways to Madness,* paints a bleak picture of family life. He discusses the way children are shielded from the truth, the lack of tenderness among family members, the lack of availability of parents to children, and our lack of understanding or comprehending messages of love.[9] Clearly, there is great variance in the potentialities of family life.

Family communication is important because of the omnipresence of the family unit and because it may provide the difference between the family which affords "deep satisfaction" to its members and the family which disintegrates through mental or physical illness, separation, or other causes. These two characteristics—family communication being everywhere and so varied—may explain why individuals have not devoted very much attention to the topic.

Family communication is a relatively new area of inquiry. Both researchers and practitioners have demonstrated concern for the dysfunctional family—the family which has sought counseling or professional assistance—for some time. However, the functioning family has been shown little interest until recently. The first text which considered the functioning family was *Family Worlds: A Psychological Approach to*

Family Life which was published in 1959.[10] Subsequent to *Family Worlds,* a number of other books have been published which consider the communication that occurs in "normal" families. As you might expect, a great deal of disagreement still occurs about what constitutes a "normal" family. Authors variously define the term to refer to "non-dysfunctional," "functioning," "stable," and "homeostatic" families. Let us begin our consideration of the family as an interpersonal communication setting by defining the term "family."

Definition of a Family

Families have changed dramatically in the last two decades. Jane Howard adds,

> They're saying that families are dying, and soon. They're saying it loud, but we'll see that they're wrong. Families aren't dying. The trouble we take to arrange ourselves in some semblance or other of families is one of the most imperishable habits of the human race. What families are doing, in flamboyant and dumbfounding ways, is changing their size and their shape and their purpose.[11]

Howard suggests families vary in definition, and our past conceptions of families, still depicted to a great extent in the media, are outdated.

The differing configurations of families require us to adopt a broad definition that will include all of the variety of families in which we will find ourselves during our life times. Bochner offers the beginning points of such a definition. He writes a **family** is "an organized, naturally occurring relational interaction system, usually occupying a common living space over an extended time period, and possessing a confluence of interpersonal images which evolve through the exchange of messages over time."[12] We will delete the words "naturally occurring," replace the word "interaction" with "transactional," replace the word "system" with "group," and replace the word "messages" with "meaning" to define the family as "an organized, relational transactional group, usually occupying a common living space over an extended time period, and possessing a confluence of interpersonal images which evolve through the exchange of meaning over time." Let us examine each of the components of this definition.

Families are organized. Individual family members play particular roles within the unit. You may play the role of mother, sister, daughter, aunt, grandmother, or father, brother, son, uncle, or grandfather. Families are also organized as the behavior among individuals does not occur in a random or unpredictable fashion. We generally can predict, within a range of possibilities, how family members will act and react to each other. For example, when the six-year old son and the twelve-year old daughter are watching television together, we can predict they will get into a disagreement about which show to view. Similarly, the behavior of other family members can be predicted within a range of possibilities.

Bochner suggests the family "naturally occurs", which suggests it is not an artificially created group. We do not choose our parents and we do not choose our family of origin; however we generally do choose at least one member or more of our current families. For instance, if you are married, you probably chose your own spouse. If you have adopted children, you chose them. If you have dissolved a previous marriage, you

Family members play specific roles within
the family unit.

may have made choices about who would be in your current family, too. We agree with Bochner, we do not choose everyone in our families; however, some choice is possible and inevitable. Consequently, we delete the definitional phrase a family "naturally occurs" from our definition. Nonetheless, we observe the limited choice about who is defined as a member of our family affects our interactions with them.

The family is a "relational transactional system." Relationships may be defined simply as associations or connections. However, relationships are far more complex than such a definition suggests. Silverman and Silverman explain,

> Consider for a moment a passenger ship in New York harbor, whose destination is Southampton. It is a "ship," of course, because we choose to call it "a ship," and an entity because we define it as one. It is also, among other things, engines, cabins, decks, and dinner-gongs—these are some of its parts or components. If we were to rearrange the components, or lay them out side by side, the entity would no longer be a ship, but perhaps look more like a junk-yard. The "parts," then, may be said to "make up" the whole, but the whole is defined by these parts in a particular relationship, each one not only to those attached to it, but also to the whole itself.[13]

Similarly, families are relationships that include the individual members, their associations with each other, and their connection with the whole unit.

Families are transactional. This notion suggests members share with each other; all participants are actively engaged in the communicative process. When we view communication as transactional, it is viewed as a dynamic process that varies as a result

Communication in Your Family

Every family has different rules or norms governing their communication patterns. Complete the following exercise in order to determine the patterns in your family.

1. What communication topics *can* be discussed? _____

   _____

   _____

2. What topics *cannot* be discussed (for instance, sex, money problems, religious convictions, drug use)? _____

   _____

   _____

3. *When* can you communicate with others? _____

   _____

   _____

4. When can you *not* communicate with family members? _____

   _____

   _____

5. What emotions are you allowed to communicate (anger, hostility, sadness, hurt, joy, sorrow, fatigue, enthusiasm)? _____

   _____

   _____

6. What emotions are you *not* allowed to communicate? _____

   _____

   _____

of context and situation. For example, the same people would behave differently if they were placed in another family. Similarly, the same family behaves differently when they are in different places or when they are facing a traumatic experience rather than normal day-to-day events.

Families usually occupy a common living space over an extended time period. Whether the dwelling is a flat, a tenement, a large old farm house, a contemporary suburban home, an eight-bedroom "mansion" complete with swimming pool and tennis courts, university married student housing, a furnished apartment, an attic in someone else's home, or a cabin, families generally share a common living space. However, the newly emerging dual career couple is frequently seeking other living arrangements. Although families generally share a common living space, they do not always do so. Many individuals in the dual career marriage have adopted the commuter marriage, which includes two separate living quarters.

7. In what verbal and nonverbal behaviors do you participate in your family that you rarely, or never, participate in outside of your family unit? _____

_____

_____

8. Do you have family "secrets" you are not allowed to discuss with others? _____

_____

_____

9. List some specific words you cannot use in your family (jargon, clichés, profanity, nicknames).

_____

_____

10. List some specific nonverbal behaviors you cannot use in your family (nonverbal behaviors that have a specific meaning in one of your membership groups, nonverbal behaviors that have a profane meaning within your family, etc). _____

_____

After you have completed this inventory, compare your list with a person whom you trust. Do you see similarities? Explain why your family unit has different communication patterns than does another family unit. To what extent do nationality, region of the country, and other subcultural differences affect your family communication? Consider *who* the primary "rule maker" is in your family. Does this affect the communication patterns? What conclusions can you draw from this exercise?

Families possess a confluence of interpersonal images which evolve through the exchange of meaning over time. Each of us gains an understanding of the world by interacting with others. In other words, we learn to stereotype others because people we trust or respect stereotype them. We learn to be open and to share our feelings with others because our family members behave in such a manner. We view such matters as appropriate levels of intimacy, the amount of ambition to demonstrate, desirable earnings, and kinds of futures to expect based largely on our interactions with our family members. Just as George Herbert Mead observed one cannot separate the person from his or her society,[14] we observe we cannot separate the individual from family.

Types of Families

John Naisbitt, author of *Megatrends,* offers an optimistic prediction about the family. He views changes in family life to be consistent with his "megatrend" of movement from the either/or choice to multiple options. He writes,

> Personal choices for Americans remained rather narrow and limited from the postwar period through much of the 1960s. Many of us lived the simple lives portrayed in such television series as "Leave It to Beaver" and "Father Knows Best": Father went to work, mother kept house and raised 2.4 children. There were few decisions to make; it was an either/or world:
> Either we got married or we did not (and of course, we almost always did).
> Either we worked nine to five (or other regular full-time hours) or we didn't work, period.
> Ford or Chevy.
> Chocolate or vanilla.[15]

He goes on to note the time of few decisions has been replaced with an age of diversity: "The social upheavals of the late 1960s and the quieter changes of the 1970s, which spread 1960s values throughout much of traditional society, paved the way for the 1980s—a decade of unprecedented diversity."[16] In this section we will define the most common types of families that exist in contemporary America, and we will consider some of the unique communication problems and patterns that exist in these family forms.

Couples with No Children

Couples with no children are included within our definition of a family. Families have fewer children today than they have in the past. Beginning families in the early 1980s are expected to average 2 children.[17] In addition, couples are waiting longer to have children. Finally, some couples choose voluntary childlessness.

Single-Parent Families

A **single-parent** family has one adult and may include adopted, natural, step-, or foster children. The single-parent family typically occurs when one parent dies or leaves the family unit; however, an increasing number of individuals choose to parent by themselves from the start. This includes women in their thirties or forties who have careers, but do not wish to pass up parenting, as well as teenagers who may "overestimate the benefits of child-bearing."[18]

Cohabitating Couples

When two unrelated adults share living quarters, with or without children, the family unit is defined as a **cohabitating-couple household.** Nonmarital cohabitation is not a new phenomenon, but it has become more prevalent and more openly practiced by Americans in recent times. The research on unmarried-couple households has been largely limited to college students; however, cohabitation is not limited to those in college.

Family satisfaction is related to our ability
to communicate with family members.

Cohabitors may not really be experiencing a "trial" marriage as many suggest. The cultural demands and the role expectations placed on married couples may far outweigh the relational rules the cohabiting couple has established. Although a couple may feel they are creating lifetime relational patterns during cohabitation, they may find these patterns are dramatically altered when they become husband and wife. Cohabitation appears to have its own unique set of characteristics and the communication patterns that occur between and among cohabitors are not generalizable to all family types.

Blended Families

The **blended family,** reconstituted family, stepfamily, or remarried family consists of two adults and step-, adoptive, or foster children. This family type is also numerically increasing in our culture. One of the difficulties of the blended family is that it is fairly new so we have neither the terminology to discuss it nor the research which explains the complex nature of this family unit.

Communication is very difficult in the blended family. In the nuclear family, communication patterns are established with the family members, beginning with the marital couple and including children as they are born or adopted. In the blended family, communciation patterns have already been established among a group of people, or among groups of people (the previous nuclear, single-parent, or blended families). Past family histories from the previous relationships are brought forward, and these must be revised as the blended family establishes its new identity.

Dual-Worker Families

The **dual-worker family,** which includes two working adults, has also increased in size in our recent history. Norms concerning the appropriateness of wives working out of the home were reversed with a single generation.[19] The dual-worker couple is a marital arrangement which may be based on economics, egalitarianism, and technology, among other factors. This new family form calls into question basic assumptions concerning one's sex role and one's function within the family unit.

Nuclear Families

Nuclear families are conventionally "nuclear," with breadwinning fathers, home-making mothers, and resident children. In 1976 fewer than 7 percent of all husband-wife families were traditionally nuclear. Current figures would probably demonstrate this figure has dropped even further. Nonetheless, some families remain nuclear. Pressures on individuals in this familial arrangement may include their minority status as a family type.

Extended Families

Extended families include families in which not only parents and children are part of the family unit but in which grandparents, aunts, uncles, cousins, and others are included. Extended families, like nuclear families, no longer occur with the frequency they once did in our history. Increased mobility encourages second and third generations to live in separate homes, even in separate states.

Family Satisfaction

At the beginning of this chapter we observed Tolstoy wrote, "All happy families are alike; every unhappy family is unhappy in its own way." We did not note Nabokov responded, "All happy families are more or less dissimilar; all unhappy ones are more or less alike." As you have been reading this chapter, you may have wondered if any families are alike. In this section we will try to untangle the contradictory and complex nature of interaction in the family to try to offer some suggestions on how individuals can improve their marital and family life. This section will consider **family satisfaction**—one's positive or negative assessment of the marriage or family.

Communication is related to family satisfaction. Research in this area allows six general conclusions: 1) Family satisfaction is related to the family members' ability to favorably perceive the communication behavior of the other family members; 2) Family satisfaction is related to the family members' ability to provide both verbal and non-verbal messages to each other; 3) Family satisfaction is related to the family members' ability to understand the messages sent by other family members; 4) Family satisfaction is related to the family's ability to provide supportive, understanding, and positive comments to each other; 5) Family satisfaction is related to the family's ability to reach consensus and agreement, to resolve differences, and to avoid or minimize conflict; and 6) Family satisfaction is related to the family members' flexibility. Let us consider each of these generalizations briefly.

Family satisfaction is related to the family members' ability to favorably perceive the communicative behavior of the other family members. Both the family's perceptions of their interactions and their interactive behavior contribute to our understanding of family satisfaction. Families who positively distort other members' communicative behavior are generally more satisfied about their families than are families who do not distort other members' behavior.[20] In other words, to the extent families perceive their members' behavior more favorably, they also are more favorably disposed to rating their family satisfaction.

The conclusions of this study suggest people who view events more favorably consistently view both their family members' communicative behavior and their family satisfaction more favorably. Such a result may seem somewhat trivial; positive people are positively disposed across a variety of measures. However, it may also suggest if we are concerned with increasing family members' self reports of their family satisfaction, one tack may be to increase an individual's overall positive outlook. If therapists and practitioners can improve people's perceptions of various aspects of their family members' behavior, they may find an added benefit is more positive scores on family satisfaction measures. The study suggests people who intervene in distressed marriages not only may need to work on behavioral change, but, perhaps more importantly, also need to work on changing the perceptions of that behavior.

The notion that happy families tend to positively distort the communicative behavior of their family members is also related to another finding we will discuss later in this section. We will find family satisfaction is related to our ability to send positive and supportive messages to each other. Family members who perceive other members as being more effective communicators may be more likely to send more positive messages in return. An individual who positively distorts his or her family's messages may reciprocate with equally positive interactions. Thus the positive distortion may serve as a cue to escalate effective and positive interactions.

Family satisfaction is related to the family members' ability to provide both verbal and nonverbal messages to each other. In other words, communication, in and of itself, is related to family success. Families who talk to each other tend to be more satisfied than do families who do not talk to each other. Open and interactive communication affects the quality of the family relationship.[21] Overall family satisfaction is highly related to the family members' ability to discuss problems effectively and to share their feelings.[22] Wives who rate high on communication competence similarly state they have high levels of family satisfaction.[23]

Family satisfaction is related to the family members' abilities to send messages which indicate understanding and to their actual understanding of the messages sent by their family member. Understanding and demonstrating understanding are both related to family satisfaction. Through identification and empathy the family members come to define themselves as a unit.[24] Building such a relationship is not possible without understanding. We cannot identify with a person nor show him or her empathy unless we first understand that person.

Families mature as members become increasingly sensitive to each other's views and to their own views of other families.[25] Maturing families continue to integrate and reintegrate each individual's view into a common set of understandings and conceptions. Less healthy, adaptive, or satisfied families fail to reconcile the varying perceptions and conceptions of their members. Sensitivity to the often differing needs and views of family members and an ability to integrate them into a new structure may be essential for satisfaction among family members.

Family satisfaction is related to the family members' ability to provide supportive and positive comments to each other. In general, satisfied families provide more positive, supportive, and agreement statements. This behavior extends to the nonverbal arena as well and is even more apparent in the family members' nonverbal cues. Nondistressed families provide fewer negative comments than do distressed famlies.[26] Satisfied families are more likely to positively reinforce each other.[27] Nondistressed families also enjoy more humor and laughter.[28] In a review of literature on agreement and disagreement, Riskin and Faunce prescribed that families should have more agreements than disagreements if they wish to be fully functioning.[29] The communication behavior of dissatisfied families is characterized by such behaviors as defensiveness,[30] quarreling, nagging, arguing,[31] aversive control and coercion,[32] expressions of hostility,[33] and attempts to humiliate and threaten.[34]

Families that include a delinquent child use less positive and more negative interactions than do families that do not include a delinquent child.[35] Families with delinquent children include three times as many negative statements than do families without such children. Furthermore, the positive or negative nature of the comments appears to affect delinquency as delinquent behavior decreased when the balance of positive and negative occurred, but it increased when more negative statements were offered.[36]

Family satisfaction is related to the family's ability to reach consensus and agreement, to resolve differences, and to avoid or minimize conflict. Agreement is a hallmark of satisfied families and a key to successful marriages. One area in which agreement may be essential is the family's agreement about their relationship, itself. Two researchers demonstrated that couples who share a similar definition of their relationship are likely to agree on more relational issues and to be more cohesive than are couples who do not share relational definitions.[37] Another researcher suggests marital satisfaction may be more highly related to the couple's ability to resolve their differences or to achieve consensus than any other communicative behavior. He writes,

> . . . of all the relationship variables that could be selected for understanding marital satisfaction, the couple's ability to arrive at consensus in resolving differences may be of central importance. There are two ways in which a couple could arrive at consensus. One possibility is that they share normative conflict resolution rules transmitted culturally or from parental models. The other possibility is that they are able to construct their own decision rules.[38]

Family satisfaction is related to the family members' flexibility. Throughout this text we have considered the importance of flexibility and adaptability. Concepts such as flexibility and trust are salient in conflict resolution and in family satisfaction. Scanzoni and Polonko hypothesize a relationship between trust, risk-taking ability, fairness, and flexibility. They state when one family member trusts the other, the other member is more likely to increase their trust of the first family member, which will lead to mutual flexibility. Similarly, if one family member is fair to the second, the second is likely to be more flexible and thus be viewed to be fair by the first.[39]

Summary

This chapter considered interpersonal communication with family and friends. You may not have recognized we can improve our communication skills with persons whom we consider to be friends or family. If you are typical, you probably have experienced some difficulties in the conversations you have had in these settings.

We defined friendship as "an interpersonal relationship between two persons that is mutually productive, established and maintained through perceived mutual free choice, and characterized by mutual positive regard." Friendship is characterized by availablility, shared activities, caring, honesty, confidentiality, loyalty, understanding, and empathy.

We can improve our conversations with friends by understanding the specific verbal and noverbal cues appropriate for each of the different relationships in which we engage. In addition, we will experience vast improvement if we (1) understand and operationalize differences in relationships, (2) are aware of and practice the communication skills discussed in this text, and (3) accept change and adapt our behavior.

Families are defined in this text as "organized, relational transactional groups, usually occupying a common living space over an extended time period, and possessing a confluence of interpersonal images which evolve through the exchange of meaning over time." The contemporary American family is not of one type. Among current family types are the couple with no children, single-parent families, cohabitating couples, blended families, dual-worker families, nuclear families, and extended families.

Satisfaction within the family unit has been studied by researchers. Six communicative behaviors are related to satisfaction. First, satisfaction is related to the ability to perceive the communicative behavior of other family members favorably. Second, satisfaction is related to the ability to provide both verbal and nonverbal messages to each other. Third, satisfaction is related to the ability to send messages which indicate understanding. Fourth, satisfaction is related to the ability to provide supportive and positive comments to each other. Fifth, satisfaction is related to the ability to reach consensus, to agree, to resolve differences, and to avoid or minimize conflict. Sixth, satisfaction is related to the flexibility.

Each of us can improve communication with others in our families by practicing the communicative behaviors outlined in this text and in other well researched material on interpersonal relationships. Changing our behavior is usually risky, but the rewards are well worth the effort.

chapter 9

The Interview

*I*t is better to know some of the questions than all of the answers.

James Thurber

*F*acts do not cease to exist because they are ignored.

Aldous Huxley

*T*he closest to perfection a person ever comes is when he fills out a job application form.

Stanley J. Randall

Objectives

1. Distinguish interviewing from other forms of communication.
2. Define and give examples of open and closed, primary and secondary, and neutral and leading questions.
3. Identify five guidelines for effective answers in the interview setting.
4. Explain the three major divisions of the interview, and distinguish among organizational patterns for the body of the interview.
5. Prepare and conduct an informational interview, an employment interview, and a performance appraisal interview.

Key Terms

interview
open questions
closed questions
primary questions
secondary
  questions
neutral questions
leading questions
opening of the
  interview
body of the
  interview
closing of the
  interview

funnel approach
pyramid approach
tube approach
hourglass
  approach
diamond approach
informational
  interview
employment
  interview
performance
  appraisal
  interview

In the last chapter we considered our informal communication with friends and family. In this chapter we shift our attention to a relatively more formal setting of interpersonal communication, the interview. Each of us participates in interviews from time to time. We are interviewed by employers, doctors, instructors, friends, counselors, parents, and people taking surveys. We interview our peers, our customers, and our neighbors. We participate in the interview to understand another person. Through the process of questions and answers, we gain insight into another's world.

In this chapter, we consider the interview as one type of interpersonal communication. The same principles of effective interpersonal communication we have identified in previous chapters are essential to our success in the interview. For example, the relationship between listening and successful interviewing is particularly important. The effective interviewer is the individual who is able to understand not only the content, but also the intent, of the interviewee's responses. In fact, one technique for improving listening is the interview, with its careful use of questions. Differences in perception also are relevant to interviews since we observe those differences in unusual or unexpected answers to questions. Verbal communication is very important in interviewing because we must carefully write and plan both questions and answers. Nonverbal communication is important, too, and we must consider "accidental" nonverbal messages as well as purposive nonverbal behavior. Finally, the way in which we see ourselves can affect the interaction during an interview. We need to be sensitively attuned to ourselves in order to focus on, and understand, another person.

In addition to understanding the communication concepts presented earlier, we, as competent interviewers or interviewees, must understand the specific features and nature of this form of interpersonal communication. How do we define interviewing? What kinds of questions can be included in an interview? What kinds of answers are most effective? How are interviews organized? What are the unique features of the informational and employment interviews? We attempt to answer all of these questions in this chapter. One author observed,

> Interviewing is very much like piano playing—a fair degree of skill can be acquired
> without the necessity of formal instruction. But there is a world of difference in the
> craft, in the technique, and in the finesse between the amateur who plays "by ear" and
> the accomplished concert pianist.[1]

Although you may feel you already know the keyboard, you should be more successful when you complete this material.

Interviewing is planned communication between two parties which has a predetermined purpose and involves the asking and answering of questions arranged in some order. Interviewing is more formal than the conversations in which we engage but less formal than other types of communication, such as public speaking. Interviews are generally planned; they are not spontaneous occurrences as are many of our conversations with others. Interviews occur between two parties, often between two people. One party serves as the interviewer, and the other serves as the interviewee. Some interviews include more than one person as the interviewer (a presidential press conference, celebrity interviews, oral graduate student exams), and some interviews include more than one person as the interviewee (television talk shows, interrogations, screening employment interviews). Generally, however, one person serves as the interviewer, and one person serves as the interviewee. Interviews usually have a specific purpose—to gain information, to provide information, to persuade another person, to get a job, to make a judgment about the work of another person, or to provide counseling. Interviews, like public speeches, usually are organized into the opening or introduction, the body, and the closing or conclusion. Almost all interviews involve the asking and answering of questions. Indeed, questions generally form the basis of the interview.

Questions and Questioning

In planning an interview, the interviewer must determine the most appropriate kinds of questions for the purpose. Questions fall roughly into three categories—open or closed, primary or secondary, and neutral or leading; that is, every question is either open or closed, primary or secondary, *and* neutral or leading.

Open or Closed Questions

Open questions are broad and generally unstructured. They often simply suggest the topic under discussion. The respondent, or interviewee, is offered a great deal of freedom in answering. Examples of open questions are, "How do you feel about our president?" "What is Chicago really like?" "What are your feelings on reverse discrimination?" and "What is your problem?"

Open questions do not allow for a yes-or-no answer. They allow other people to see we are interested in them. They generally create a supportive communication climate and allow the interviewer to establish good rapport with the interviewee.

Closed questions are restrictive. They offer a narrow range of answers; often, all of the possible answers are included in the question. Sometimes, the possible answers are limited to *yes* and *no*. Examples of closed questions include, "Do you attend the university at this time?" "Do you plan to drop out of school if you get this job?" "What is more important to a social worker—the ability to relate to people or the administrative experience that allows the handling of a large number of cases?" and "Have you the time to do the work necessary to complete this class?"

Closed questions are useful if we want a specific response. If the closed question is threatening, the interviewee may become defensive; if it is without threat, a short answer is easy to give. Closed questions are appropriate when the interviewer has sufficient information about the respondent and the respondent's point of view; when the question contains or permits an appropriate response; and when the respondent has information, an opinion, or a point of view about the matter under discussion.

Primary or Secondary Questions

Primary questions introduce a topic or a new area within a topic under discussion. Examples of primary questions include, "Shall we turn to the topic of summer employment?" "Could we begin the interview by discussing your experience in welding?" and "Let's go back to your grades for a minute—how's your algebra?"

Secondary questions are used to follow up primary questions. When an interviewee does not answer fully or completely, the interviewer asks another question to secure the desired information. Secondary questions are often short: "Shall we go on?" "Can you tell me more?" "How did you feel then?" and "Is there anything you would care to add?"

Neutral or Leading Questions

Neutral questions do not contain any correct or preferred answer. They do not suggest any particular response or direction. They are usually open. Examples of neutral questions are, "What did you do last summer?" "How did you like your last job?" "What kind of music do you listen to?" and "How do you spend your weekends?"

Leading questions suggest a preferred answer—they ease the way for one answer and make any other answer difficult. Examples of leading questions created from the previous neutral questions are, "I suppose you worked last summer. What at?" "Even if you liked your last job, there's no harm trying to better yourself, is there?" and "I guess you play a lot of ball on weekends, like most young people. What is your game?"

Leading questions are very useful in persuasive interviews, as when you are attempting to convince people they want an additional insurance policy, they want to enroll in a particular course, or they are prepared to accept your religious beliefs. But leading questions can create a defensive climate when the interviewer is not attempting to persuade the interviewee and assumes an inaccurate response. For example, you and your spouse may expect to go bowling, but you meet a friend who says, "You and your spouse would like to go to the symphony tonight with me and my spouse, wouldn't you?" Or you go to your professor's office to drop the class, but before you can ask, you hear, "You really do enjoy my class, don't you?" Both the friend and the professor make you defensive by asking a leading question instead of a neutral question.

Answers and Answering

Typically, we focus on the questions asked in the interview, rather than on the answers given. This is no different than our focusing on what is *said* in a conversation, rather than what is *heard*. Nonetheless, the skill of answering questions is as important as the skill of asking questions. For some situations—the employment interview, for example—you may be more interested in learning how to answer questions than in learning how to ask them. The role of the interviewee in the employment interview is considered in more detail later in this chapter, but some general answering guidelines are important at this point.

Five guidelines are useful in considering effective answers in the interview setting. First, interviewees are advised to always *answer the questions* that are asked of them. Communication theorists point out that people, even when they do not say anything, are communicating some messages. For example, they may be suggesting they are bored, disinterested in the other person, or confused through their kinesics or proxemics. Similarly, in the interview, interviewees who do not answer a question suggest they are embarrassed, do not know the answer to the question, are confused by the terminology, are fearful of communicating, have something to hide, are dishonest, or

Answering and asking questions is an
important communication skill.

are attempting to fabricate an elaborate answer. None of these impressions is desirable
for interviewees. If you are confused by the language the interviewer uses, do not understand the importance or relevance of the question, or believe the question is not
within the legal guidelines recommended by the Equal Employment Opportunity
Commission, which we will discuss later in this chapter, you should explain your reluctance to answer or ask for further clarification. An open, straightforward response
is viewed more positively than hesitation, a reluctance to answer, or complete silence.

Second, interviewees should *not provide inaccurate or distorted answers*. Stating
you have completed your college education when you are really in the last term, explaining you already own a set of encyclopedias to a salesperson when you do not, or
pretending to understand all of the ramifications of a recent constitutional amendment
only lead to trouble. If you do not know what a term or concept means, ask for an
explanation. If you know a job description included specific qualifications you do not
have, be straightforward in stating those qualifications you do not have. If you do not
want to make a purchase or to be persuaded by a persuasive interviewer, state directly
and honestly why you do not want his or her product or service. Honesty is an ethical
consideration and one that will make you a more effective interviewee.

Third, interviewees should *provide complete answers*. This guideline is often related
to the honesty and accuracy of your response. Do not provide half of the picture so the
interviewer obtains a distorted view of your reality. Explain your position, your background, or your experience fully and completely. Occasionally, a factor you may feel
is less important will be perceived as highly important to the interviewer. This guideline
does not mean you should tell an interviewer every detail about yourself. You can also
err by saying too much. But be aware of the tendency to say far too little or to provide
incomplete answers.

Fourth, interviewees should *offer specific, concrete responses*. Speaking in plati-
tudes or using a large number of clichés or euphemisms only distorts your messages.
You may want to review chapter 6 to determine how to avoid ambiguity and how to
be increasingly concrete and descriptive in your responses. Ambiguous language is confusing and may suggest you are attempting to be dishonest.

Types of Questions in a Health Clinic Interview

To determine whether you understand the three categories of questions, complete the exercise that follows. Mark each question in this interview *O* or *C* for open or closed, *P* or *S* for primary or secondary, and *N* or *L* for neutral or leading.

		Open/ Closed	*Primary/ Secondary*	*Neutral/ Leading*
Client:	I came in because I can't sleep and I was wondering if you would give me something for it.			
Nurse:	Why do you think you are having trouble sleeping?	_____	_____	_____
Client:	I don't know.			
Nurse:	Have you had any problems at school or at home that might be affecting your sleep?	_____	_____	_____
Client:	Well, not really.			
Nurse:	What might account for your sleeplessness?	_____	_____	_____
Client:	Well, my mom and dad have been fighting a lot.			
Nurse:	Does that worry you?	_____	_____	_____
Client:	Sometimes I hear them when I go to bed— their bedroom is right next to mine.			
Nurse:	Do they argue at night when you're trying to sleep?	_____	_____	_____
Client:	Well, yes, but they're not real loud.			
Nurse:	Are you concerned that their marriage may be in trouble?	_____	_____	_____
Client:	I guess so.			
Nurse:	Do you think it would help if your family talked to one of the case workers in this county or to a family counselor?	_____	_____	_____
Client:	I don't know if my mom and dad would do it.			
Nurse:	How about if I call them and offer to make a referral?	_____	_____	_____
Client:	What about the sleeping pills?			
Nurse:	Let's see if we can solve your problem without medication. I will call your parents and then you come back and see me next week.			
Client:	I guess that will be OK.			

Fifth, *relevant answers* are important. If you are asked about purchasing a new cologne, you should not respond with a comment about foreign automobiles. If you are asked about your background in accounting, you should not detail all of the courses in speech communication you have taken. If you are asked about your feelings on the mandatory helmet laws for motorcycle drivers, you should not talk about the rights of the unborn child. Offering a *non sequitur* may suggest you are confused, you have difficulty concentrating, or you are unwilling to answer the question asked. If you are unwilling or unable to answer a question, you should explain your reluctance or your position rather than surreptitiously attempting to avoid the question.

Organizing the Interview

Interviews have a predetermined purpose and are preplanned. They are not sponta-neous interactions like many of our conversations. Interviews, like other preplanned communication, are organized. As we mentioned earlier, the interview, like the public speech, is organized into the opening or introduction, the body, and the closing or con-clusion. We examine these three major divisions first, and then we consider the variety of organizational patterns possible within the body of the interview.

Major Divisions: Opening, Body, Closing

The **opening** or introduction of the interview sets the tone for the rest of the interview. It is generally quite short and may consist of only one or two questions and answers, although in a long interview, the opening may extend for several minutes.

One purpose of the opening is to introduce the two parties. For instance, the inter-viewer might say, "Hi, I'm Dave Bennett. Are you Jo Edwards?" or "Are you Ellen Bonaguro?" or "Linda Davis, I'm happy we've finally met!" Another purpose of the opening is to establish a cordial and warm atmosphere. The interviewer might say, "I understand you're from Minnesota," "I heard you had some stormy weather on your flight this morning," or "I know you've been interviewed about this topic several times before."

The questions or comments in the opening should be easy to answer or to respond to and should put both parties at ease. The interviewer should consider ways of estab-lishing rapport with the interviewee and should try to identify comments or questions that will motivate the interviewee to willingly participate in the interview.

The **body** usually consumes about two-thirds of the interview. During the body, the purpose of the interview is either achieved or not achieved. The body may be organized in a variety of different ways, and we discuss some of these methods in the next section.

The **closing** or conclusion of the interview usually is parallel to the opening in both length and purpose. The closing may range from one or two comments in the short interview to several questions and sentences in the longer interview. The purpose of the closing, like the purpose of the opening, is to create goodwill and to establish a positive atmosphere, but also to clarify for the interviewee what will occur next. For example, the interviewer in an informative interview may wish to remind the interviewee how

Figure 9.1

Organizing the body of the interview.

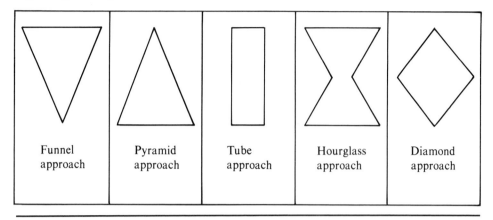

| Funnel approach | Pyramid approach | Tube approach | Hourglass approach | Diamond approach |

the interview information will be used and that a copy of the report will be available to the interviewee. A reporter may wish to tell the interviewee when and where the story will appear. Some typical comments from the interviewer include, "Thanks for helping me today," "I appreciate the time you spent talking with me," "When I finish my paper, I will send you a copy," "I will let you know within two weeks if you are a finalist for our position," and "My story should appear in Friday's edition of the paper. I will call you with my copy tomorrow night to make sure I have not misquoted you."

Organizational Patterns for the Body of the Interview

We observed earlier the body of the interview can be organized in a number of different ways. Some of the more common ways to organize this part of the interview are the funnel approach, the pyramid approach, the tube approach, the hourglass approach, and the diamond approach (see figure 9.1). As we shall determine, the openness or closedness of the questions accounts for the open or closed spaces in the diagrams in figure 9.1.

The **funnel approach** begins with broad, open questions, becomes restrictive as more closed questions are asked, and finally concludes with very closed questions. This approach is useful when the interviewer has done little preparation, does not fully understand the topic, or knows relatively little about the interviewee. An interviewer who is facing a hostile or defensive interviewee might consider this approach since the openness of the first questions can reduce the anxiety or defensiveness of the interviewee. Sometimes, employment interviewers use the funnel approach when they are interviewing applicants who are unknown to them or who appear especially nervous.

The **pyramid approach** is organized in the opposite way from the funnel approach. It begins with tightly closed questions, gradually becomes more open, and concludes with broad, open questions. This approach is useful when the interviewee is nervous, embarrassed, or finds the topic distasteful. The short one- or two-word answers required by the closed questions sometimes encourage the interviewee to respond more fully as the interview progresses. The interviewee may feel the topic is less distasteful or she or he can overcome nervousness or embarrassment once the interview is underway.

The **tube approach** involves questions generally either all closed or all open. The relative similarity in the openness or closedness of the questions gives the diagram of this approach its uniform structure (see figure 9.1). The tube approach is generally used in interviews being conducted as part of a survey or a study. Individuals using this approach frequently analyze their information in a statistical or systematic manner. The tube approach has the advantage of being virtually the same from beginning to end, thereby allowing systematic analysis.

The **hourglass approach** and the **diamond approach** are variations on the funnel and pyramid approaches. The hourglass approach begins with open questions that become increasingly restrictive and then become increasingly open. The diamond approach begins with closed questions that become increasingly open and then become restrictive again.

The hourglass and diamond approaches are more complex than the other three approaches already discussed and are sometimes used in persuasive interviews. For example, the hourglass approach may be appropriate if a salesperson is uncertain if the other person is truly interested in the product or uncertain about which of several products the interviewee may show interest. The salesperson may begin with open questions to determine which product to attempt to sell or if a sale should be attempted at all. After the salesperson has gained information from some open questions, he or she may ask closed questions to make the sale. Then, the salesperson may conclude with open questions to establish a positive rapport or to gain information useful in making future sales. The diamond approach also is sometimes useful for a salesperson or someone conducting a persuasive interview. For example, the salesperson can begin with closed questions, use some open questions to get information, and then restrict the questions to make the sale.

The information we have just presented on questions and questioning, answers and answering, and organizing the interview may seem a little abstract. As you read the next section on the purposes of interviews, with special emphasis on the informational interview, the employment interview, and the performance appraisal interview you should be able to directly apply this information.

Purposes of Interviews

People engage in interviews for a variety of purposes—to provide information, to gain information, to persuade, to counsel, to receive advice, to offer an assessment, to receive an evaluation, to gain employment, and to identify an appropriate candidate for a job or another kind of position. Our foci in this section are on the informational interview, the employment interview, and the performance appraisal interview, since these three types of interviews are particularly relevant for most college students. The informational interview occurs frequently in the journalism and health fields. The employment interview and the performance appraisal interview occur most often in the organizational communication setting.

Informational Interviews

We enter into **informational interviews** when we are collecting information, opinions, or data about a specific topic. You have probably already participated in this kind of interview in completing an assignment for a class. You may have interviewed someone who is knowledgeable about a particular topic or well-known in a specific field. Two examples of informational interviews follow.

The first interview was conducted to gain initial knowledge about a small, local business. The interviewer wanted to know how the business was started, to learn about the personnel, and to gain some preliminary accounting information as the basis for an in-depth study later. The interview was moderately scheduled. Each question is categorized as open or closed, primary or secondary, and neutral or leading. Notice the interview included many closed questions. Earlier, the interviewee told the interviewer he had very little time to discuss his business with her, so she attempted to adapt her interview to the limited time.

Opening   Good afternoon, Mr. Williams. My name is Kris Cook. I spoke with you a few days ago about doing an accounting systems analysis of your business. I will need to work with your accounting personnel, but I need about fifteen minutes of your time to find out some preliminary information.

Body
Objective: To find out the history of the business

	Type of Question		
1. How was the racquet club started?	Open	Primary	Neutral
2. When was it opened?	Closed	Secondary	Neutral
3. It has been a fairly successful business venture, hasn't it?	Closed	Primary	Leading
4. How is it owned—sole proprietorship, partnership, or corporation?	Closed	Primary	Neutral
5. Does a partnership or corporation own the club?	Open	Secondary	Neutral

Objective: To find out about the staff

6. What is the makeup of the staff and their responsibilities?	Open	Primary	Neutral
7. What is the makeup of the staff during odd hours, after 5:00 P.M., and on weekends?	Open	Secondary	Neutral

8. What portion of these employees are full-time, and what portion are part-time?	Closed	Secondary	Neutral
9. Are employees screened and trained for positions?	Closed	Secondary	Neutral
10. Are the employees who do accounting work bonded?	Closed	Secondary	Neutral
11. Are employees required to take vacations or to rotate jobs?	Closed	Secondary	Neutral
12. How often are appraisal interviews held to evaluate employee progress and to resolve any problems?	Closed	Secondary	Neutral
13. Do you have an organizational chart?	Closed	Primary	Neutral
14. If not, could you describe the organizational structure?	Open	Secondary	Neutral

Objective: To find out about the basic accounting structure

15. Describe the main sources of receipts.	Open	Primary	Neutral
16. How do these rank in terms of income generated?	Open	Secondary	Neutral
17. Are the records for the pro shop kept separate from the other records?	Closed	Primary	Neutral
18. Do you use an accrual or a cash accounting system?	Closed	Primary	Neutral
19. Explain the budget system.	Open	Primary	Neutral
20. How often are audits done?	Open	Primary	Neutral

Closing Thank you, Mr. Williams. I will be in touch with your bookkeeper next week to complete my field study.

In the second informational interview, which follows, the interviewer was seeking information about job satisfaction at a particular company. The interview began with an open question, switched to a series of closed questions, and concluded with the same open question with which it began.

		Type of Question		
Interviewer:	We are conducting a study of job satisfaction at this company. We are particularly interested in why people came to work here originally, and why they stay for such a long time. How long have you been with us?	Closed	Primary	Neutral

Interviewee:	About four years, I guess.			
Interviewer:	Why did you choose this company?	Open	Primary	Neutral
Interviewee:	Gosh, that was quite a while ago. Let me think.			
Interviewer:	Yes, it was some time ago. Who were you working for before you joined us?	Closed	Primary	Neutral
Interviewee:	Midwest Machines.			
Interviewer:	Why did you leave that company? Were you dissatisfied?	Open Closed	Primary Secondary	Neutral Leading
Interviewee:	It really wasn't a very pleasant place to work.			
Interviewer:	Did they offer a pension plan, a job rotation plan, training for automation, a family health plan, or any other special benefits?	Closed	Primary	Neutral
Interviewee:	No, they didn't have any of those things.			
Interviewer:	Did your wife think that you should continue to work for Midwest Machines?	Closed	Primary	Neutral
Interviewee:	No, she was the one who suggested I try to get another job.			
Interviewer:	Did you hear about our plant through the paper or from someone you knew?	Closed	Primary	Neutral
Interviewee:	I spent a lot of time looking at the ads in the paper.			
Interviewer:	Why did you finally choose us?	Open	Primary	Neutral
Interviewee:	This is a progressive company. It has a lot of personnel policies that I like. My wife is satisfied that it's the best job for me.			

In the preceding interview, the importance of asking effective questions is apparent in the lines spoken by the interviewer. Because the interviewer's intention was to find out whether the employee was satisfied with the company, the questions focused specifically on why the employee was or was not satisfied. The employee's answers were nearly all declarative, but in an informational interview, the interviewer has to be careful not to invite the desired answers. In this interview, for instance, the interviewer may have been perceived by the interviewee as part of the company's management. The interviewee may have known at the outset that employees were being questioned about their job satisfaction, or he might have gotten the drift of the interview by listening carefully to the questions. Reporters, government employees, survey takers, and others who interview other people regularly should realize many interviewees simply tell them what they think they want to hear. Is there any way that we could determine, for instance, that the employee being interviewed was worried about his job and was simply giving the interviewer the answers he thought were the "right" ones? In other words, is it possible that the interviewee interpreted as leading questions some that were coded as neutral?

Employment Interviews

The purpose of **employment interviews** is to select people for employment and to place them in certain positions or jobs. In the past, employers may have selected people because of their personality characteristics, their style, or their sex. Today, guidelines from the federal and state levels and recommendations from experts in the area of employment interviewing suggest such criteria are illegal or irrelevant.[2] The Equal Employment Opportunity Commission (EEOC) has developed strict guidelines for interviewing and testing applicants. The five major provisions in the EEOC guidelines are: (1) discrimination on the basis of race, sex, or ethnic group cannot occur, (2) no one part of the interview may affect the evaluation of the whole, (3) validation of decisions must be demonstrated, (4) documentation must be provided, and (5) affirmative action should be taken to enact the guidelines. Both employers and employees should be familiar with these federal guidelines, as well as state laws govern hiring and firing.[3]

The Role of the Interviewer

Planning is essential for a successful employment interview. Coffina has proposed two distinct models of the employment interview: the ideal and the dysfunctional.[4] The ideal model assumes the employment interviewer is prepared for the interview, conducts the interview in an unhurried and uninterrupted manner, and devotes his or her full attention to the employment candidate. The dysfunctional model assumes the employment interviewer has not read the candidate's resumé before the interview, allows interruptions, glances at his or her watch and other distractions, and generally makes the candidate uncomfortable.

Thorough planning by the employment interviewer can ensure a legal, effective interview. One method of planning includes the creation of an *employment interview guide*. This guide can be used in the actual interview, although the interviewer might want to deviate from it slightly, depending upon the answers of the interviewee. The employment interview guide should consist of a general purpose, an opening or introduction, a schedule or list of questions (body), and a closing or conclusion.

The general purpose identifies the objective of the interview, such as finding a manager for a local fast-food restaurant. The opening or introduction should be brief but should introduce the employment interviewer, develop a congenial atmosphere, and provide an orientation for the interview. The early questions in the opening should be relatively easy to answer and should serve to put the interviewee at ease. An example of an opening follows:

Interviewer: Good afternoon. You're John Anderson, right?

Interviewee: Yes, I am.

Interviewer: May I call you John?

Interviewee: Sure.

Interviewer: As you know, I'm Betty Wright, the owner of Hamburger Haven. Feel free to call me Betty, if you wish.

Interviewee: I'm happy to know you, Betty.

Interviewer: Please sit down. I appreciate your being free at this time to talk with us about the possibility of managing our local store. I'd like to begin the interview by talking to you about your interests and background. Then we will proceed to what managing our store has to offer, and finally, I will answer any questions you may have. Please feel free to ask any questions about the position.

Interviewee: That sounds reasonable.

Interviewer: John, I see that you were a fry cook and a cashier for two other similar restaurants. I am not sure how they operate. Please tell me about the general operation at each of the two restaurants. What were your specific responsibilities at each?

The body of the employment interview should include questions designed to measure the individual's qualifications for the position. The employment interviewer should examine the responsibilities the person will have and then determine the qualifications necessary for the job. Responsibilities for the management position at Hamburger Haven, for example, probably would include hiring counter personnel, ensuring a particular level of quality in service and food, and suggesting promotional campaigns. Qualifications probably would include being responsible, organized, creative, and relating well with people.

After determining general qualifications, the employment interviewer should determine more precisely what he or she needs by concretely and specifically describing the qualifications. For instance, being creative could be defined as "someone who can use language in a thought-provoking way for advertisements and promotional slogans." The description of this definition would be, "Knows how to write jingles, rhymes, or alliterated phrases," or "Knows currently used jargon that could be incorporated into a successful slogan."

Next, the employment interviewer creates sets of questions to help obtain information to determine if the potential employee can meet the needs of the firm. In the Hamburger Haven example, questions might include, "Have you ever written advertisements, slogans, or other promotional materials?" "What kinds of words do you associate with a *good* hamburger?" or "Can you think of some ways in which Hamburger Haven could be marketed more successfully?"

During the interview, the objectives should always be clearly stated, specifically defined and concretely described, relevant to the job, and ordered in importance. The

An employment interview invites good
communication skills.

questions should be within the EEOC guidelines, should be designed to seek information specified in the objectives, should use information already available on the resumé or application form, and should be sufficient in number to accurately assess applicant qualifications.

The employment interviewer should also inform the applicant about the company. Before doing so, however, it is wise to ask the applicant if he or she has any information already. A direct question, "What do you know about Hamburger Haven?" is usually most successful in determining the applicant's level of knowledge.

Finally, the employment interviewer should allow the applicant the opportunity to ask questions about the position. Again, a simple request, such as, "What questions do you have?" or "Do you have questions about this position that have not been answered?" is sufficient.

The closing of the interview should maintain a positive climate and provide the employment interviewee with information about what will occur next. An example of a closing follows:

Interviewer: Thank you for having interviewed with me. The information that I obtained will be very useful in making a decision. We have two more applicants to interview, and we will be finished with the interviewing process at the end of this week. I will call you on Monday of next week to let you know our decision. If you have any questions, don't hesitate to call. Also, if you have another offer or a change in your plans, please let us know. Thanks again for coming in to interview today.

In addition to preparing an employment interview guide, the employment interviewer should demonstrate *good communication skills* during the interview. He or she should listen carefully and maintain eye contact, should word comments and questions in a careful manner, and should encourage the interviewee to answer freely.

The Role of the Interviewee

The employment interview can be viewed from the perspective of the employment interviewer, as we just did, or from the perspective of the employment interviewee, or applicant. Applicants can do a great deal to make the employment interview a positive experience. Galassi and Galassi suggest the interview preparation process can be divided into four phases.[5] First, interviewees should develop realistic expectations about the particular job. Second, they should develop interviewing skills. Third, they should be able to demonstrate their skills and to assess how they meet the needs of the job. And fourth, interviewees should be prepared for rejection. Most interviews do not conclude with the applicant being hired.

Employment Interviewers' Criticisms of Interviewees

Employment interviewers frequently complain interviewees demonstrate poor communication skills, appear ill-prepared for the interview, express only vague interest, lack motivation, and hold unrealistic expectations.

Poor communication skills include long, rambling responses, lack of description, nervousness, and talking too much or talking too little. A recent study demonstrated poor communication skills could be perceived as dishonesty. Interviewees who used short answers with long intervals between answers, vagueness, constant smiling, postural shifting, and grooming behavior were perceived as lying.[6]

Interviewees are perceived to be ill-prepared for the interview when they have no information about the company with which they are interviewing and when they have no questions to ask the interviewer during the interview. Lack of concern or lack of commitment are suggested by the interviewee who has not done the necessary homework before the interview.

Interviewees demonstrate vague interest when they are not clear about their lifetime goals or when they cannot specify their career goals. Applicants who offer vague or ambiguous responses to questions about where they see themselves in ten years or how they expect their career to progress are viewed as holding unclear interests.

Lack of motivation also is sometimes perceived in job applicants. In one interview, a woman who was graduating from college was asked why she enjoyed her previous part-time employment. She responded, "Because that job was close to home, and it started late in the day. It was easy to get to and didn't interrupt my sleep." The woman did not get the job because, "She didn't seem to have any motivation—she seemed to want something that was easy and that would meet her own particular schedule." Lack of motivation can also be shown by lack of enthusiasm, lack of interest, and apathy. In addition, the applicant who is *too* agreeable may also be perceived as lacking motivation. For instance, if you are willing to take low pay, poor working hours, bad working conditions, and no security, an employer might wonder about your ambition.

Finally, some employment interviewers have criticized interviewees for holding unrealistic expectations. The beginning college professor who expects a private secretary, the new clerk-typist who expects a private office, and the young physician who refuses to work at night or on weekends all serve as examples. Interviewees who are overly concerned with salaries or expect luxurious offices may be rejected because they lack realistic expectations.

Overcoming the Criticisms of Employment Interviewees

The average person spends about two thousand hours each year at work. In forty years, the average length of time most people work, the average person will have spent over eighty thousand hours at his or her chosen profession. Our time commitment to our employment warrants adequate preparation for the employment interview. Four essential steps in preparation include (1) knowing yourself; (2) knowing about employment opportunities in general, and especially at the specific company with which you are interviewing; (3) knowing the steps involved in getting a job with a particular company; and (4) developing successful communication skills.

Knowing yourself is the first step to success in the employment interview. It is important to assess your skills, knowledge, and experience. It is sometimes helpful to list these assets and to rank them in terms of importance and enjoyment to you. You might want to consider your *wants*—those things you would like to be able to obtain in a position—and your *musts*—those things imperative before you accept an offer. A review of chapter 3 on understanding yourself may be useful.

Second, you should *know about employment opportunities* in general and especially at the specific company with which you are interviewing. Many people consider only a relatively small number of occupations. A thorough search of potential positions might surprise you. Over twenty thousand jobs are currently available in the United States. A visit to your local placement office or library may provide you with useful information about the many careers open to you. Other opportunities available on many campuses, such as internships, externships, cooperative positions, and summer work, may also be beneficial.

You will impress an employment interviewer if you do a little homework before the interview. You can learn about the particular company with which you are interviewing from a variety of sources, including placement offices, the Better Business Bureau, the Chamber of Commerce, and Dunn & Bradstreet, or you can write to the Security Exchange Commission for an annual corporate report or a 10-K, which outlines the financial situation of corporations. A little knowledge about the company to which you are applying will demonstrate your interest and commitment.

The third step in preparing for an employment interview is *knowing the steps involved in getting a job* with a particular company. Are you required to send a resumé, send a letter of application, complete an application form, have references, send letters before the interview, take a screening or aptitude standardized test, participate in role-playing situations, complete personality inventories, participate in screening and selection interviews, or provide a copy of your portfolio? The steps involved and the order of these steps vary from company to company. You should know the basic steps of the company to which you are applying and learn about unusual procedures.

Finally, you should develop good communication skills useful to you in the interviewing situation. Providing unambiguous nonverbal cues, self-disclosing appropriately, demonstrating empathy and active listening, and being descriptive and clear in your verbal comments are all important. In addition, you should rehearse your answers to some possible questions to be thoroughly prepared. The twelve questions asked most frequently by employers are:

1. What brings you to this agency?
2. What sort of job are you looking for?
3. What other efforts have you made to find a job?
4. Why do you want to leave your present job?
5. What percentage of college expenses did you earn yourself?
6. What do you think of your present job?
7. What makes you think you would be good at the new job?
8. This question is unspoken. The interviewer simply falls silent, a device to test the applicant. Some applicants feel that they must keep the ball rolling.
9. What sort of money are you looking for?
10. What do your parents do?
11. What are your best qualities?
12. Since no one is perfect, what are your worst qualities?[7]

Local placement offices in your community or college may be able to provide other typical sample questions that employers will ask, such as:

What are your future vocational plans?

Why do you think you would like to work for our company?

What jobs have you held?

Why did you leave your previous jobs?

What courses did you like best in college (or in high school)?

Why did you choose your particular area of work?

What do you already know about this company?

What kind of salary do you expect?

What kind of person do you like to work for?

Do you like to travel?

Would you be willing to work overtime?

What special skills do you possess?

Were you involved in extracurricular activities in college?

Why did you go to college?

Do you like routine work?

Which cities in which to work seem particularly attractive to you?

Do you have an analytical mind?

Do you plan on doing any graduate work?

Do you prefer to work with others or alone?

Are you interested in research?

What kind of writing ability do you possess?

Do you believe your oral communication skills are above average?

Providing complete answers to these two sets of questions would thoroughly prepare an applicant for the interview situation.

As an interviewee in the employment setting, you should effectively present your qualifications. This includes taking the initiative to present your major personal characteristics that meet the job qualifications; providing specific details about your background and qualifications; stressing skillfully, but honestly, your favorable characteristics; and treating questionable or weak factors in a tactful, positive, and candid way. Good communication skills will be displayed in comments that are well organized, appropriately worded, and smoothly presented with confidence and enthusiasm. You should listen carefully, maintain good eye contact, and generally present an effective style. Your physical and mental image should include a neat, clean, conservative appearance; and you should demonstrate a thorough knowledge of yourself, including career objectives and personal goals, and a good knowledge of the potential employer and the position available.

In the employment interview that follows, emphasis was on the background, experience, training, and other interests the applicant had. In this situation, an application for the position had been previously submitted. (Each question is categorized in parentheses as open *(O)* or closed *(C)*, primary *(P)* or secondary *(S)*, and neutral *(N)* or leading *(L)*.)

Interviewer: Good morning, Bob. Bob Johnson, is that correct? *(C/P/L)*

Interviewee: Yes, that's correct.

Interviewer: I'm Dave Selking, employment interviewer here at the company. Come over here and have a seat. Do you smoke, Bob? *(C/P/N)*

Interviewee: No, thank you. I've never had the urge to start.

Interviewer: Well, I think you used good judgment in regard to your health and well-being, according to all recent medical reports. I see by your application you have some college training. Are you currently enrolled? *(C/P/N)*

Interviewee: Yes, but only part-time now.

Interviewer: What are you studying? *(C/S/N)*

Interviewee: Industrial management. I have twenty-one hours in the program.

Interviewer: Do you enjoy this field enough to continue and complete the program? *(C/S/N)*

Interviewee: I've enjoyed the studies so far, but I have met some students who are enrolled in a supervision program. I'm going into that some more because I think I would do well working with people. I'm more at ease with the human, rather than the technical, side of industry. And my credits would count toward a supervision degree.

Interviewer: Have you had any experience either in technical work or in a supervisory position? *(C/P/N)*

Interviewee: Not really; I haven't been out of high school that long. However, I led a Boy Scout troop for five years and really enjoyed working with people. After becoming aware of the supervision courses, I feel that would suit me better.

Interviewer:	Have you had any other leadership positions? *(C/S/N)*
Interviewee:	Not really in *leading* people, but I coach Wildcat baseball teams every year and help to schedule the year's games.
Interviewer:	Do you enjoy working in community affairs? *(C/P/N)*
Interviewee:	Yes, but I need a job, and that doesn't help me in getting one.
Interviewer:	It doesn't hurt your situation any, let me assure you! Our organization, like every other industrial plant, exists in a community. We encourage our employees to participate and to show an interest in community projects.
Interviewee:	In that case, I would like to point out I helped form and organize the Decatur Youth Center and helped secure the use of the old county building for our activities. We canvassed for funds and assistance in remodeling the interior to meet our needs. Oh, yes, I also helped organize girls' softball three years ago. We had four teams then, and last summer we had sixteen full teams in the league with full sponsors. That took a lot of work, but it was rewarding. That's about all I've helped to start.
Interviewer:	This has been a highly informative interview. We are not hiring at present, but when we do, I assure you that you'll be given every consideration. Thank you for your time, Bob. I appreciate your promptness in coming in when we called you.

The interviewer in the previous employment interview tried to draw out as much information as possible from the applicant. Notice how the interviewer reinforced the applicant every time the applicant disclosed additional information about his activities. The result was the applicant felt good about telling the interviewer even more about his experience. In general, the applicant should try to anticipate the interviewer's questions. In this interview, the interviewer had to work to get the applicant to supply relevant leadership experience. Perhaps the interviewee was interpreting neutral questions as leading questions and was reluctant to disclose information that might hurt his opportunity for future employment with the company. It is essential to answer questions as openly and fully as possible in the employment interview situation. It is especially important to point out any employment and any social, community, or campus activities that have taught you how to organize time and people, to manage resources, to accept and execute responsibility, and to build communication skills.

Performance Appraisal Interviews

Performance appraisal interviews occur whenever one person evaluates the work of another person. In general, these interviews occur between an evaluating superior and an evaluated subordinate, but sometimes subordinates evaluate their superiors, as well. A number of purposes are achieved in the performance appraisal interview. Some of these include:

1. To build a better relationship between the interviewer and the interviewee.
2. To determine the interviewee's perspective on how well he or she is performing.
3. To give the interviewee another perspective on how well he or she is performing.

4. To recognize interviewee accomplishments.
5. To discover the interviewee's aspirations.
6. To clarify interviewer expectations.
7. To develop some plan for improvement.
8. To set objectives for future performance.[8]

The evaluative nature of the performance appraisal interview suggests a potentially emotional situation. For instance, if one of your professors announced oral evaluations of your classroom work in her office, rather than providing written feedback, you might have an emotional response to the situation. The performance appraisal interview can have disastrous results if a defensive communication climate occurs. In order to avoid such a calamity, the interviewer should be aware of supportive communicative behaviors. You will recall we contrasted behaviors that lead to defensiveness and supportiveness in chapter 7. Interviewees are well advised to use description, problem orientation, spontaneity, empathy, equality, and provisionalism rather than evaulation, control, strategy, neutrality, superiority, or certainty. You may wish to review the information in chapter 7.

Norman R. F. Maier outlined three general approaches to the appraisal interview distinguished on the basis of the defensiveness they are likely to engender. Maier's approaches are provided in his well-known book, *The Appraisal Interview,* which is recommended for the student who wishes to gain a more detailed understanding of this type of interview.[9] The three approaches—Tell and Sell, Tell and Listen, and Problem Solving—are provided in Table 9.1.

The Tell and Sell approach occurs when the appraiser provides an evaluation to the appraised and then attempts to convince the appraised of that evaluation. Of the three approaches, it is the most likely to make the appraised feel defensive, and he or she has no opportunity to rid himself or herself of these feelings. The Tell and Sell approach assumes the appraiser knows best and must simply convince the appraised of his or her evaluation.

The Tell and Listen approach occurs when the appraiser provides an evaluation to the appraised and then encourages the appraised to release any defensive feelings he or she may have. The Tell and Listen approach assumes the appraiser knows best, but recognizes the appraised may feel defensive and must vent emotions. While the appraised is not an initiator in the evaluation process, he is allowed an opportunity to respond. Defensiveness may occur when this approach is used, but an opportunity is provided for it to be dissipated before the interview is completed.

The Problem Solving approach is distinctive, as the appraiser must listen to the appraised and reflect her feelings and ideas. The appraiser asks questions and summarizes rather than offering an own evaluation. Together the appraiser and the appraised attempt to come to some solution for problems perceived by either party. The Problem Solving approach assumes both the appraiser and the appraised have valuable perspectives and may each contribute to an improved performance on the part of the appraised. This approach leads to the least amount of defensiveness of the three approaches.

Table 9.1 Maier's Three Types of Appraisal Interviewing

Approach	Tell and Sell	Tell and Listen	Problem-Solving
Goal	To communicate evaluation.	To communicate evaluation.	To stimulate growth and development.
Assumptions	Appraised can choose to improve; a superior is qualified to judge a subordinate.	Appraised will change if he/she does not feel defensive.	Change occurs without alienating appraised.
Reactions	Defensive behavior is suppressed; attempts to avoid hostility.	Defensive behavior is expressed; person feels acceptance.	Problem solving behavior.
Gain	Success is likely when appraised respects appraiser.	Favorable attitude toward appraiser develops which increases likelihood of success.	Some improvement is almost inevitable.
Risk	Loss of loyalty; independent judgment inhibited; face-saving problems are created.	Need for change may not be developed.	May lack ideas; change may be different from appraiser's idea.

Kindall and Gatza have suggested a five-step process may eliminate the defensiveness and negative feelings that sometimes accompany the performance appraisal interview. The process is based on open communication between the individual being appraised and his or her appraiser throughout a performance period. This process eliminates surprises and also allows both the appraiser and the appraised to be part of the appraisal process. Although it may be used with any of the approaches outlined by Maier, it may work best with the third approach which attempts to minimize defensiveness. They suggest:

1. The appraised and the appraiser discuss the job description and the two agree on the nature of the job and the relative importance of appraised's major duties.
2. The appraised establishes performance targets for each responsibility.
3. The appraised and the appraiser meet to discuss the target program.
4. Checkpoints and other ways of measuring progress are selected.
5. The appraiser and the appraised meet at the end of the period to discuss the results of the appraised's efforts to meet his or her previously established goals.[10]

You may have already been involved in a performance appraisal interview; if not, you are likely to be involved in such an interview in the future. In any case, it is an important interview within the organizational setting, and your understanding of the process is likely to help you to succeed in the workplace. In addition, it is also possible to use the principles of performance appraisal in the family setting, especially between parents and children. In cases of behavior problems or recurring arguments over such as household chores, parents have successfully used the Problem Solving performance appraisal method. Problems that could not be solved by the Tell and Listen approach or the Tell and Sell method, which parents usually use, have been eliminated.

Summary

In this chapter, we explored one form of interpersonal communication, the interview. An interview is planned communication between two parties which has a predetermined purpose and involves the asking and answering of questions that are arranged in some order. Interviews are more formal than conversations and less formal than most small group discussions and public speeches.

The interviewer must determine the most appropriate kinds of questions for the interview. Open questions are broad and generally unstructured, while closed questions are restrictive and offer a narrow range of answers. Primary questions introduce a topic under discussion, while secondary questions are used to follow up primary questions. Neutral questions do not contain any correct or preferred answer, while leading questions suggest a preferred answer.

The interviewee needs to comprehend five guidelines for providing appropriate and effective answers: (1) answer the questions asked; (2) do not give inaccurate or distorted answers; (3) provide complete answers; (4) offer specific and concrete responses; and (5) respond with relevant answers.

Interviews generally are organized into three major divisions: the opening or introduction, the body, and the closing or conclusion. The body of the interview can be organized using the funnel approach, the pyramid approach, the tube approach, the hourglass approach, or the diamond approach. Successful interviewers are aware of the characteristics of each of these organizational approaches and select the approach best suited to the outcome desired.

Interviews occur for a variety of purposes, but our foci in this text are on the informational interview, the employment interview, and the performance appraisal interview. People engaging in informational interviews collect information, opinions, or data about a specific topic. The purpose of employment interviews is to select people for employment and to place them in certain positions or jobs. Employment interviewers should be aware of all federal and state guidelines for interviewing and testing applicants and also should thoroughly plan the interview. Interviewees should prepare themselves for an employment interview by: (1) knowing themselves; (2) knowing about employment opportunities in general, and especially at the specific company with which they are interviewing; (3) knowing the steps involved in getting a job with a particular company; and (4) developing successful communication skills. The purpose of the performance appraisal interview is to make a judgment of an individual's performance and to assist that person in improving performance. The evaluative nature of the appraisal interview encourages defensiveness on the part of the appraised, but a number of techniques and processes exist that can reduce defensiveness.

Small Group Communication

The world must be made safe for democracy.

Woodrow Wilson

Talented administrators know that they do not know all there is to know.

Unknown

The average executive spends about 60 percent of his [her] time in meetings and conferences. This recent survey finding points up the fact that ability to work in and through small groups is one of the most useful skills a manager can have.[1]

Louis Cassels

Objectives

1. Define small group communication.
2. Define and explain the relevance of the terms *norms, roles, productivity, cohesiveness, commitment, consensus, member satisfaction,* and *communication networks.*
3. Identify how women and men may behave differently in a small group.
4. List the steps necessary in the preparation for, and presentation of, a problem-solving group discussion.
5. Suggest some important qualities for effectiveness as a participant in a small group discussion.

Key Terms

small group
  communication
norms
roles
productivity
cohesiveness
commitment
consensus
member
  satisfaction
communication
  networks
psychological
  gender
panel

symposium
forum
brainstorming
questions of fact
questions of value
questions of policy
primary research
secondary
  research
consensual
  validation
Dewey's method
  of reflective
  thinking

These three quotations serve as a good introduction to small group communication. The Woodrow Wilson quotation reminds us decisions are often made by groups, rather than by individuals. The second quotation emphasizes one of the reasons why small group communication is important—none of us knows everything, and we all should rely on others for additional information. Groups often make better decisions than individuals because more information is available. The final quotation suggests the importance of small group discussion skills for individuals entering businesses and organizations. As we shall see, individuals in many occupations rely upon small group communication.

We all participate in small groups on a regular basis. Some of these interactions focus on problems we share with others, and some are for sharing information with other people. Sometimes, we communicate in small groups as a sociable way to spend time.

In this chapter, we consider the small group context of interpersonal communication. The small group is interpersonal communication because individuals have an equal opportunity to serve as receivers or listeners and as sources or speakers. The same principles of effective interpersonal communication identified in previous chapters, such as listening and self-disclosure, are essential to success in the small group discussion. In addition, we must understand the specific features of this form of interpersonal communication if we want to be competent in small group interactions.

The Importance of Small Group Communication

The significance of small group communication is probably apparent to most college students. Students are frequently assigned to small groups to solve problems or to work on projects in a variety of classes. Students regularly serve on academic and social committees. Interaction in the classroom often occurs within small groups. You may participate in small group interaction with roommates, other students, instructors, and possible employers. Communicating in small groups is a common, everyday occurrence for most of us. An ability to communicate well in the small group—to have fruitful discussions, to solve problems efficiently and easily, to have interesting and relaxing conversations—is important to each of us.

While you may understand the importance of small group communication for students, you may question how important this form of communication will be after you graduate. Small group communication may be the most important form of interpersonal communication used by college graduates.[2] After you graduate, you will be involved in small group communication when you participate in social groups, civic committees, local government, and problem-solving groups. Open discussion is essential in a free, democratic society. The complexity of our culture requires that, to cope, each of us must spend a great deal of time in small groups. Group discussion allows us to retain our humanity in a time marked by major social changes and a media-constructed reality.

Organizational Groups

If you are interested in the relevance of small group communication to your future career or occupation, you may be interested to know small group communication is of increasing importance in the structures of many business and government organizations. The most common kinds of small groups in the workplace include conferences, committee meetings, quality circles, information-sharing meetings, decision-making meetings, and problem-solving meetings.

Committee meetings may become more familiar to you than you wish in your current or future occupation. Many business people report they are involved in too many meetings and the meetings require more time than they deem necessary. Research shows formal committees exist in 94 percent of those organizations who have more than ten thousand employees. Executives routinely spend about ten hours each week involved in meetings. Goldhaber reported most faculty members spend an average of eleven hours per week in university, college, and departmental committees. One of the faculty members he interviewed stated he "barely had time left to prepare for his classes."[3] The information in this chapter may lead you to become a more productive group member in your current or future occupation.

Health Care Groups

Small groups have been shown to be increasingly important in the health care setting. Among these are self-help groups, such as Weight Watchers and Alcoholics Anonymous, and rehabilitation groups that include health providers. An engaging report of such a health care team is provided in a popular new text on health communication. The account is reprinted here with permission.

Dr. G. S. Edwards is a well-known oncologist who is determined to make the detection and treatment of cancer bearable and even humane. She has developed an effective team approach, utilizing the particular skills of a receptionist with counseling training and three nurses trained in oncological nursing. This approach is designed to do much more than treat the purely physiological aspects of the tumor and to include the patient and his or her family's well-being.

The doctor's office serves as the hub of a wheel. The receptionist and chemotherapy room are within steps and Dr. Edwards is almost instantly available for consultation if necessary. The nurses and the receptionist-counselor are trained by the doctor in communication, cancer, and chemotherapy. These members of the team often answer initial client questions or serve as intermediaries if the doctor is out of the office. Clients calling the office are always able to talk to a member of the oncology team. Quite often, Dr. Edwards will interrupt whatever she is doing to take these phone calls. At least a majority of the same staff sees the client on each visit.

The examining room is in the doctor's cheerful office and family members stay in the room with a curtain separating them from the doctor and the client during the examination unless the client directs otherwise. Notetaking is common. Family members are encouraged to accompany the client. Often, hours are spent educating the family regarding the various treatment alternatives. The theory utilized is that well-educated clients and family members can be capable participants in the decision-making and treatment phases. Families are taught to become active in the treatment process. If shots are required, for example, they learn to give these shots in Dr. Edwards' arm, which psychologically removes much of the threat of this procedure. During the twenty-four hours after the first treatment, the doctor often makes a house call to check on both client and family. Later, during treatment, the receptionist-counselor might also visit the client in home or hospital settings.

The members of the oncology team are chosen carefully. The receptionist-counselor has conducted support groups and worked in other health care settings. The nurses were carefully picked for their concern about clients, their relaxed manner, and their ability to communicate. The team members report that they like each other and feel trust in their professional relationships. Meetings are held on a daily basis and the doctor listens carefully as well as participates. She is quite aware that the client provides different kinds of information to each team member and it is during the meetings that all the information is integrated and put to use for the client's benefit.

Family members also report feeling part of the extended family effort. They credit the initial time spent educating them regarding the illness as reassuring during the whole treatment. Additionally, being involved gives them something to do at a time when most of them are feeling useless and frustrated. They also note that neither they nor the client have to call the doctor often during the treatment process because of the adequate preparation (even though the doctor has provided them with her home telephone number).

The report of the client and the family, however, is most important. Dr. Edwards' clients do not follow the usual national pattern where large numbers drop out of chemotherapy during the treatments. Rarely do her clients refuse to complete the treatments. In addition, they report reduced side effects. The clients credit open communication and the team process with giving them needed support and more bearable treatments.

Dr. Edwards is candid about the advantage of the team system. Time spent initially with the client and the family prevents excessive phone calls to the physician, and having a fully functioning team shares pressure, and allows her to supervise and be more aware of the overall client regime and profile. It also frees her to keep up to date professionally and to work with her colleagues. She particularly stresses that the time taken with clients by team members induces client cooperation during the treatment regime, which in turn reduces morbidity and raises the response rate to the treatment because of better patient toleration. Clearly, this physician's office operates as an effective health-related small group.[4]

Kreps and Thornton report this health care team is located in Santa Barbara, California, at the Santa Barbara Clinic and they have used actual names. Now that we have explored the importance of small group communication, let us consider a definition of small group communication and the basic components of the small group.

The Nature of Small Group Communication

Definition of Small Group Communication

Many definitions of small group communication have been proposed. Brilhart combined elements from various definitions to present five minimal characteristics all small group communication must meet. He asserted small group communication involves:

1. A sufficiently small number of people (from two to rarely more than twenty) so that each group member is aware of and has some reaction to each other group member.
2. A mutually interdependent purpose, and the success of each person is contingent upon the success of the small group in achieving this goal.
3. For each person, a sense of belonging or membership.
4. Oral interaction (not all of the interaction is oral, but a significant characteristic of a discussion group is reciprocal influence exercised by talking).
5. Behavior based on norms, values, and procedures accepted by all members.[5]

To summarize, **small group communication** consists of a relatively small number of persons who have a mutually interdependent purpose and a sense of belonging, demonstrate behavior based on norms and values, use procedures accepted by the group, and interact orally. We discount small numbers of people who do not have shared interests, do not communicate regularly with each other, and do not all contribute to the functioning of the group.

All small groups have two primary concerns: (1) accomplishing the task and (2) maintaining healthy relationships among the group members. Groups have distinctive tasks they accomplish: to solve a problem, to share information, to determine a policy, to clarify values, or to introduce social opportunities. Regardless of the task, all groups also have a relational function as they attempt to encourage individuals to establish and maintain positive associations with the others in the group.

Appropriate Use of Small Group Communication

Although small group communication is an essential part of our lives, we need to observe it is most appropriate under certain conditions. Among these conditions are:

1. *When a variety of different ideas is preferable over a smaller number of less diverse ideas.* Individuals working together in a group setting are likely to encourage each other to come up with a larger number of different ideas than will individuals attempting to generate ideas by themselves.
2. *When differing amounts and levels of information, expertise, or experience are necessary to solve the problem.* The group setting is ideal for combining people with different information, ideas, and backgrounds.
3. *When time constraints are not present.* Groups often take longer than individuals to reach a decision.
4. *When individuals desire an opportunity to be involved in the information sharing or decision making.* If people wish to be part of the decision-making process or the information-sharing opportunity, it is wise to include, rather than exclude, them from the possibility.

5. *When members' commitments are needed to implement decisions.* If decisions cannot be put into place unless most group members agree and feel some sense of commitment, a group rather than one individual or a small sub-group should be used. If a manager determines a new production schedule without consulting his or her subordinates, he or she may be surprised by the resistance that is present.

6. *When a group decision is a requirement.* If a group—rather than an individual—decision must be made, the group setting is a superior place in which to have that decision made. Asking individuals privately about their opinions will result in a different and less useful outcome than will occur if the entire group is allowed to interact. Examples of required group decisions include a jury selecting a "foreman," an ongoing group selecting a chairperson, or an intact group determining how it shall be governed.

A group is more than the sum of its members, just as a whole is more than the sum of its parts. Groups consist of people who individually have energy, information, abilities, and ideas. When these people are placed together in a group, the psychological combination leads to a level of productivity the members could not achieve if they were working alone. Small groups are useful and important. Let us consider a definition and the basic components of the small group discussion.

Concepts Important in Small Group Communication

Although the small group discussion shares characteristics with other forms of interpersonal communication, it also has some unique features. The terms *norms, roles, productivity, cohesiveness, commitment, consensus, member satisfaction,* and *communication networks* are applied in a special way to the small group setting. Let us consider each of these concepts as it relates to the small group.

Norms

All small groups establish norms. **Norms** refer to how members "ought" to behave. They include those behaviors, attitudes, and values identified as acceptable. Norms may be stated openly, or they may only be implied by patterns of behavior in the small group process. Norms actually help orient people to each other. They provide the guidelines for how interpersonal issues are to be managed by group members. Norms provide a basis for predicting the behavior of others in the group context and can also help unify the small group.

A typical nonverbal norm is mode of dress. You may dress differently for class than you do when you are going to spend an evening with a group of your friends at a local bar. You may dress differently when you are with your parents at home than you do when you attend church with them. A verbal norm is style of language. You may use more colloquial language when you are with your friends than when you answer a question in class. You may speak more ambiguously to your parents about how you spent the past school term than to a group of same-sex friends. The group determines norms and may enforce them with negative responses if a member does not conform to these standards.

Roles

Similarly, persons are placed in particular roles in the small group context. A **role** is a pattern of behavior perceived, expected, or enacted by a member of a small group. This pattern of behavior comes to be expected by other group members and may be the only pattern of behavior permitted. For instance, if you add humor at a time when the group appears to be particularly tense, you may be viewed within the group as a "tension-reliever" or as a "clown." If other members interpret your behavior as useful in the group, they will look to you to relieve the situation whenever the discussion appears to be particularly heavy and in need of "lightening up." On the other hand, if they view your behavior as disruptive, they may ignore your comments or show no respect for your contributions to the group. In either case, you are cast in a role associated with a specific pattern of behavior.

Earlier, we observed groups have two primary concerns—that of accomplishing the task and that of maintaining relationships among the group members. Some roles are particularly good for accomplishing the task, and some roles are especially helpful in maintaining the relationships. Individuals play maintenance-functional roles when they raise other people's status, offer help to others, and reward others' behaviors; when they provide tension releases, such as jokes, laughter, or satisfaction; and when they agree or show understanding, compliance, or concurrence. Individuals play task-functional roles when they offer suggestions, opinions, orientation or information, repetition, clarification, or confirmation; or when they ask for suggestions, opinions, or orientation.

Most of us play one role very well, regardless of the group. For instance, we may always be a task leader who attempts to move the group forward by providing transitions, asking the group to move to another point, and seeking closure on the discussion. Or, we may be a person who provides information throughout the discussion. On the other hand, we may be a person who creates conflict in the small group by being highly evaluative and using an attacking tone of voice. Any of these roles may be useful under certain circumstances. Similarly, any of them may be destructive to the productivity or cohesiveness of the group under other circumstances. Each of us needs to sensitively assess the role the group needs us to play. We also should try to establish a wide repertoire of roles so we can alter our patterns of behavior.

Productivity

Productivity refers to the relative success the group has in completing a specific task. A group of faculty members that meets for an entire academic year to determine which courses should be included in a particular curriculum and concludes the year with the report "more study is needed" was not very productive. Conversely, if the same group of faculty members meets for an entire year to determine how the university is going to alter all of its courses from a quarter system to a semester system and does not conclude its work within an academic year, we might not be as harsh in our assessment. Productivity is a measure of the dimension of the task. We can determine a group has productivity that ranges from low to high; we cannot properly conclude a group has no productivity at all.

Our interactions in a group establish our role.

Cohesiveness

Cohesiveness refers to the "stick-to-itiveness" of the small group. Small group members must feel a sense of belonging. This sense of unity with the group depends on the individual member's attraction to the group. Small groups sometimes are very cohesive because group members feel they have a great deal in common with the other members. They perceive their needs and interests as matching the needs and interests of the others. The group also may reinforce individuals for belonging to the group, which increases a feeling of cohesiveness.

Commitment

Commitment is closely related to cohesiveness. Group members feel commitment to a group when the group is cohesive. Commitment to a group may arise because of interpersonal attraction among group members; because of commonality in beliefs, attitudes, and values; because of fulfillment of needs; or because of the reinforcement the group offers. Groups that meet to solve a problem or to share information should also feel a commitment to their task. A lack of commitment to an assigned task can be very disruptive to the functioning of a small group.

Consensus

Consensus refers to agreement among members, due to active participation in the process, to implement and support group decisions. Consensus is more than no one objecting to a particular decision. Occasionally, a group will make a decision that appears to be unanimous because no one voices a dissenting opinion. Later, members resign from the group or show their disapproval by not assisting the group in carrying out the decision that was made. They may privately report they felt obligated to "go along" with the decision because of the vociferous arguments made by the proponents or that they felt unable to articulate their own position. Such decisions cannot be considered to be achieved by consensus. Consensus requires genuine agreement and commitment by group members. Groups high in cohesiveness, commitment, and productivity often achieve consensus; similarly, when groups are able to reach decisions by consensus, they typically find increases in cohesiveness, commitment, and productivity.

Member Satisfaction

Member satisfaction refers to the positive or negative evaluation of the group by the members. For example, members of a local chapter of the National Organization for Women may feel their chapter has an obligation to contribute time and money toward eradicating or decreasing wife and child abuse. If the group provides primarily social functions, member satisfaction will be low; if the group is highly productive when it comes to the wife and child abuse issue, member satisfaction will probably be quite high. Member satisfaction is dependent upon the extent to which a group fulfills the expectations of its members. Member satisfaction can result in increased cohesiveness, and cohesiveness may be a contributing factor to member satisfaction. Similarly, member satisfaction may be positively related to productivity in the group as both a cause and an effect.

Communication Networks

Communication in the small group is complicated by the number of individuals involved. In the dyad, the two people can only interact with each other; in the small group, interaction is possible in a variety of combinations. The phrase **communication networks** is used to refer to the patterns of communication possible among group members. Five different possibilities have been identified, including the chain, the Y, the wheel, the circle, and the all-channel network. These five possibilities are depicted in figure 10.1.

The chain communication network allows each member to communicate with one or two other members, but not with everyone in the group. The chain is often present in business organizations in which the president speaks only to the vice-president, who, in turn, speaks only to senior managers, who pass information on to subordinates. The Y communication network similarly allows communication only among two or three members.

The wheel communication network often occurs when one person serves as the leader and is very dominant in his or her interactions with others. This person communicates with everyone else, but the others in the group have the privilege of speaking only to him or her. The dominant person is depicted by the middle position in the wheel. Group discussions, which can be depicted as wheels, are often characterized by satisfaction being demonstrated by one person (the dominant center) and dissatisfaction shown by the others. The wheel is generally faster in information flow than the other networks, but the decreased member satisfaction often outweighs this consideration.

Leaderless discussions are depicted in the circle and the all-channel communication networks. The circle is similar to the chain in that each person can only speak with two others rather than with the entire group. The all-channel network may be the slowest interaction system of the five shown here, but it generally results in the highest member

Figure 10.1

Communication networks.

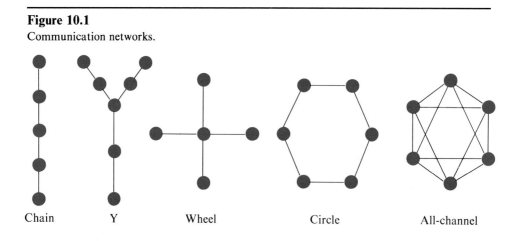

Chain   Y   Wheel   Circle   All-channel

satisfaction. In the all-channel network, each person is allowed the opportunity of speaking with all others.

Research on these five communication networks has resulted in some interesting conclusions. Centralized networks, which are exemplified by the chain and the wheel, appear to be superior in simple problem solving, but decentralized networks, such as the circle and the all-channel network, are clearly superior if the problem is complex. In general, the decentralized circle and the decentralized all-channel network allow faster and more accurate solutions and greater member satisfaction.[6] Examine the communication patterns of the groups in which you are involved to determine the typical interaction patterns that occur. As you will determine in the next section, a small group's gender composition may be one reason for differing communication patterns.

Gender Differences in Small Group Communication

Just as no two people are completely alike, no two small groups are identical. Small groups vary as a function of the size and purpose of the group, and characteristics of its members. One of the most interesting findings in the past few years concern gender differences in the small group. We will briefly review some of the conclusions researchers have offered.[7] You should keep in mind these are general differences, and all men and all women do not behave in these ways. In addition, you should know we are not recommending persons behave in such gender differentiated ways.

Some research has shown men talk more in the small group setting than do women, and they demonstrate more task-related behavior than do women. Women offer more positive responses than do men and they are also more opinionated than men. Men, on the other hand, are more informative, objective, and goal-oriented.[8] If the interaction is not pleasant, women are more likely to withdraw while men are inclined to talk even more.[9]

A common task of the small group is to solve problems. Some early research suggested women were superior at tasks which were personally interesting, but men were superior at abstract multiple-choice problems.[10] Although men may be superior to women in solving problems, this difference is reduced when mixed-sex groups are examined, and when women are highly motivated to solve problems.[11] Motivated women may be just as effective at problem-solving as motivated men. Further, mixed-sex groups may produce superior outcomes to all-male or all-female groups.

Nonetheless, women are sometimes perceived to be less competent than men in problem solving or decision making in the small group.[12] What can women do when they are placed in such situations? Bradley suggested women can overcome negative perceptions by increasing their demonstrated competence. She showed women who demonstrated high task-related competence were treated with friendliness, reason, and relatively few displays of dominance from their male counterparts. However, she also found these women held low interpersonal attraction for the men in the group.[13] The competent woman is perceived as effective as a small group member, but she is not seen as an attractive social partner.

Risk taking occurs with more frequency in the small group than it occurs in individual behavior. Studies on individual risk taking by women and men suggest men take more risks than women when they are behaving individually.[14] Mixed-sexed groups are most likely to take risks, followed by all-male groups, then all-female groups.[15] Consistent with individual behavior, women tend to take fewer risks in a small group. The higher incidence of risk taking in the mixed-sex groups allows for interesting speculation, however.

Cooperation and competition are important in the small group setting. Most studies suggest women tend to be more cooperative than men, and they are more willing to share their resources with their opponents than are men.[16] Women appear to be more interested in fair outcomes than in winning.[17] Some writers have suggested men play to win while women play to avoid losing. Why do men and women behave differently in this area? Females may have a greater "fear of success," a higher need for acceptance and affiliation, or less need for dominance and achievement.

Men and women engage in and resolve conflict differently, as well. Men are more likely to engage in aggression than are women.[18] They are also more likely to gain their own way through deception and deceit than are women.[19] Men are more likely to use antisocial modes of behavior, including revenge, verbal aggression, and physical violence.[20] Women, on the other hand, are more likely to engage in socially acceptable behavior, including reasoning and understanding, to resolve conflict than are men.[21]

Coalitions, or subgroups, sometimes form in the small group. Both women and men tend to join the majority coalition, but they do so in different situations. Women are more likely to do so when they are weak, while men are more likely to do so when they are strong.[22] When three men are placed together in a group, the men tend to engage in a dominance struggle in which the two strongest males tend to form a coalition and the weakest male is excluded.[23] When three person groups include two men and a woman, the men compete for the woman's attention.[24] When women are in the majority, they tend to include any person who may be left out, regardless of his or her biological sex.[25]

Do men and women prefer to work in same-sex or mixed-sex groups? Women prefer to work with all women if the group is small; they prefer the inclusion of men only when the group is large. Men, conversely, prefer to have women present regardless of the size of the group. In addition, cohesiveness within a small all-male group takes a longer time to materialize than in mixed-sex or all-female groups.[26]

As our culture changes, women and men may behave differently in the small group than they have in the past. Some recent studies suggest such changes are already occurring.[27] One's **psychological gender**—an individual's internalization of characteristics associated with men or women in a particular culture—may be more relevant to understanding gender in the small group than one's biological sex. Masculine individuals compete for control in predictable patterns of relational interaction while feminine individuals use equality and submissiveness in unpredictable patterns, and androgynous individuals—persons who are both masculine and feminine—are more moderate and use patterns of idea initiation.[28]

The Process of Small Group Discussion

A variety of types of public presentation formats are possible for the small group discussion. Among the primary formats are the panel, the symposium, and the forum. The **panel** is the most familiar type of public discussion. It involves a discussion among people who attempt to solve a problem or to make a policy decision. A panel generally includes one person whose job is to moderate the discussion by asking questions, encouraging everyone to participate, and keeping the discussion orderly.

The **symposium** is more formal than the panel and is closer to being public communication than it is to being interpersonal communication. The symposium is actually not a discussion if we define a discussion to be an opportunity for equal give-and-take among members. The symposium generally includes a number of speeches oriented around a topic. Each symposium speaker typically addresses one part of the topic.

The **forum** occurs when audience members participate in a public discussion. A forum may follow a speech, a symposium, or a panel discussion. A forum may also occur without a prior discussion. For instance, town meetings, in which a moderator simply calls on anyone who wishes to speak, would qualify as a forum, even though no prior small group discussion occurred.

In your class, you may be asked to participate in a panel discussion, a symposium, a panel-forum (a discussion followed by questions and answers from the audience), or a symposium-forum (a symposium followed by participation from the audience). Within these presentation formats, you may be involved in either information sharing or problem solving. Since the problem-solving discussion is more complex than the information-sharing discussion, and since the preparation for, and presentation of, a problem-solving discussion requires more steps than that of an information-sharing discussion, we discuss the problem-solving discussion here in detail. If you are able to understand and carry out the suggestions for the problem-solving discussion, you should have no difficulty adapting the suggestions to an information-sharing discussion.

Preparation for the Discussion

The steps involved in preparing for the problem-solving discussion include: (1) selecting a topic, (2) wording the question to be discussed, (3) researching the topic, (4) evaluating the research, and (5) organizing the discussion. Let us discuss each of these steps in detail.

Selecting a Topic

The first step in preparing for a group discussion is to select a topic. The method most often recommended is brainstorming. **Brainstorming** is a technique in which you list or name as many ideas as you can within a stated period of time. Alex Osborn, who introduced the technique nearly a quarter of a century ago, listed four rules governing brainstorming: (1) don't criticize any ideas, (2) no idea is too wild, (3) quantity is important, and (4) seize opportunities to improve on, or add to, ideas suggested by others.[29]

Wording the Question to Be Discussed

After you have selected a topic, the next task is to word the question to be discussed. The wording of the question is very important—it can lead to a fruitful or a wasted group discussion. The question clarifies the purpose of the discussion, suggests the avenues of research, and largely determines the agenda.

Categories of Discussion Questions

In general, questions to be discussed can be placed into one of three categories. **Questions of fact** deal with truth and falsity. They are concerned with the occurrence, the existence, or the particular properties of something. Examples of questions of fact include: "How much water does the United States require to meet normal needs?" "How much marijuana is harmful to the human body?" "How do women's opportunities for employment differ from men's in the United States?" and "What measures need to be taken by large electric companies to forestall additional blackouts in the future?"

Questions of value require judgments of good and bad. Such questions are grounded in the participant's motives, beliefs, and cultural standards. Desirability and satisfaction are often central to questions of value. Examples of questions in this category are: "To what extent is a college education desirable for everyone?" "To what extent are older Americans discriminated against?" "What is the desirability of beauty contests?" "What are the pros and cons of open visitation hours in the dormitories?" and "To what extent do we need to reform tax laws in the United States?"

Questions of policy concern future action. The purpose of a policy question is to determine a course of action to be taken or supported in a specific situation. The word *should* often appears in a question of policy. Examples of questions of policy include: "What rules should exist concerning nepotism?" "To what extent should seniority systems be eliminated?" "Which specific courses should students be required to take?" and "How should cocaine users be penalized?"

Identifying Categories of Discussion Questions

Place the following questions into one of the three categories of discussion questions. Mark each question *F* for fact, *V* for value, or *P* for policy.

1. How much oil does the United States need to import? _____
2. To what extent has the United States become the graduate school of the world? _____
3. To what extent should pornography be prohibited? _____
4. To what extent is a person's social standing related to his or her wealth? _____
5. How much money should the United States spend on defense? _____
6. To what extent should employees determine their own work schedules? _____
7. To what extent should the rights of gay individuals be protected? _____
8. How does regular exercise affect the length of your life? _____
9. To what extent should artificial sweeteners be banned? _____
10. Should small amounts of marijuana possession be legalized? _____
11. To what extent should the federal government regulate the use of energy? _____
12. How liberal should abortion laws be? _____
13. To what extent does unemployment fall disproportionately on the young? _____
14. To what extent should computer training be included in the primary and secondary school curriculum? _____
15. To what extent are day-care centers adequate to meet the developmental needs of small children? _____

Characteristics of Good Discussion Questions

All discussion questions should meet a minimum set of standards. Characteristics of good discussion questions—whether they are questions of fact, value, or policy—are that they should be simple, neutral, open, and controversial. By *simple,* we mean the question should be written with the fewest number of words possible and should be easily understood by all who read or hear it. In addition, the question should be appropriate for the time available, the research available, and the individuals who will be discussants. A discussion question such as, "How do most people anticipate the advent of androgyny vis-à-vis the economic structure?" does not meet the criterion of simplicity. This question is lengthy, difficult, and complex.

A discussion question should be written *neutrally.* It should not imply "correct" answers. Persons reading the question should be able to suggest alternative answers. The question, "Should the U.S. economic structure, which favors the rich and discriminates against the poor, be changed?" does not meet the criterion of neutrality. The wording of this leading question suggests that "yes" is the only appropriate answer.

A discussion question should be *open* rather than closed. In chapter 9, we discussed the distinction between open and closed questions. Open questions allow a number of alternative answers. Closed questions allow only a "yes" or "no" response. Discussion questions should be able to be answered in a variety of different ways, more than simply "yes" or "no."

Finally, the discussion question should be controversial. It should not be a question with a predetermined answer. Nor should it concern a matter that has an already agreed-upon solution. The question should be timely—of current international, national, or local concern; interesting to the group members; and worthwhile to those involved. The following questions are not suitable: the question, "Should the E.R.A. be passed?" is out-of-date for many Americans; the question, "Should homosexuals be allowed to marry?" may be irrelevant to the members of a particular discussion group; and the question, "Should students be given more course selection in their higher education?" would probably receive a unanimous "yes" from a group of college students.

Researching the Topic

After selecting a topic and wording the question, you must research the topic. You must *discover the information,* and then you must *evaluate it.* Among the sources you should consider for securing information are interviews with people close to the problem, surveys of the people involved, and secondary sources available in the library. Interviewing was discussed in chapter 9. Surveys and library research are discussed in chapter 14; you may want to read ahead to familiarize yourself with them. You may choose one or more avenues of research. The nature of your question will dictate the kind of research necessary.

It is equally important, in research, to evaluate the information you find. Too often, we assume simply collecting information concludes the research task. An abundance of unevaluated information may be worthless.

Evaluating Primary Research

We evaluate **primary research**—interviews, surveys, and personal experience—differently from **secondary research**—information we find in books, magazines, and similar sources. Three questions should be asked about primary research:

1. *Are eyewitness accounts confirmed?* In chapter 2, we discussed the role of perception in communication. We stated people can observe the same phenomena but have greatly divergent perceptions and draw entirely different conclusions. **Consensual validation**—checking our observations with others—is a remedy for such differences. When we engage in primary research, we should validate the perceptions of one person with the perceptions of others.

2. *Is the authority competent?* In other words, is our source a recognized expert? Do others agree he or she is knowledgeable and experienced about the question under consideration? People can be experts in one area but may know little about other areas. The football player who testifies to the quality of women's clothing, for example, may be out of his league.

3. *Is the source unbiased?* Sometimes, people have a vested interest in a particular point of view. They may realize some real or intangible gain if others can be convinced to see things in a certain way. For instance, a speech teacher would very likely believe speech should be a required course for all students. Alumni or experts in college administration would be better sources on this issue because they are less likely to be biased.

Finding information and evaluating it are
important in researching a topic.

Evaluating Secondary Research

A different set of questions should be asked if we are evaluating secondary research:

1. *Is the information consistent?* Two types of consistency are important in evaluating
   secondary research. Is the information internally consistent? Does the author suggest two
   or more conflicting conclusions? Do the conclusions follow logically from the material
   reviewed? Second, is the information externally consistent? That is, is the information
   consistent with other sources? Does it agree with other findings? Are there startling
   conclusions that violate previously known facts? Differences between one author's point
   of view and another's do not render the information inaccurate or the conclusion false,
   but you must consider why the disagreement exists.

2. *Is the information current?* The publication date of a source may be either unimportant
   or crucial. In some cases, the date can resolve conflicts of evidence.

3. *Is the information complete?* The reference should be complete in two senses. The source
   should not take information from other sources out of context or report someone else's
   work only partially in order to make a point. The reference work should be an
   examination of the entire problem or area under consideration, rather than a tangential
   view. In other words, the secondary source should include the comprehensive statement
   or conclusion offered by another and should cover all of the ground promised.

One more point is important with regard to secondary research: you should keep a
written copy of the information. You should record the author's name, the name of the
article and magazine or the name of the book, when and where it was published, and
other important bibliographic information. A sample style of recording this information is provided in chapter 14. When, during the discussion, you present the information you have collected via secondary research, remember to provide an oral footnote.
An oral footnote is simply your oral acknowledgment of where the information came
from.

Organizing the Discussion

Each category of discussion questions requires a different kind of discussion organization. A question of fact requires you (1) define key terms in the question, (2) gather relevant information, and (3) compare your information to the terms and classifications you have made. A question of value requires you (1) define key terms in the question, (2) establish criteria of "goodness" or value for the question, (3) gather relevant information, and (4) compare your information to the criteria you have established.

For many years, it was believed a discussion involving a question of policy could only be organized according to **Dewey's method of reflective thinking,** which required discussants to:

1. *Recognize the problem.* The group must acknowledge a problem exists and group members are concerned about that specific problem.

2. *Define the problem.* The group must identify the nature of the problem and define the critical terms.

3. *Analyze the problem.* The group must suggest the cause of the problem, the extensiveness of the problem, the limits of the problem, the implications or effects of the problem, and who the problem affects.

4. *Establish criteria for evaluating solutions.* The group must decide by which criteria a solution will be evaluated and whether the solution must solve the problem entirely or if a partial solution will be acceptable. The group decides whether the efficiency of the solution is an important criterion and makes other similar decisions. In addition, the group ranks criteria in some hierarchical order to determine which criteria are mandatory and which are not. Examples of criteria include amount of concern and limitations of money and time.

5. *Suggest solutions to the problem.* By brainstorming or other techniques, the group lists possible solutions to the problem.

6. *Select the best solution.* After many solutions have been offered, group members subject the solutions to the previously established criteria (step 4). They select those solutions that best fit the criteria. They consider combining two or more possible solutions. Finally, they identify the best solution.

7. *Test the solution.* The final step in the Dewey method of reflective thinking is testing the solution, which is often done by trying out the solution in practice. Decisions can then be made about the effectiveness of the solution.

More recently, authors have suggested a strict adherence to this organizational pattern results in planned performances rather than decision-making processes. These authors have demonstrated that many questions are not susceptible to solution by Dewey's method of reflective thinking, and a number of alternative organizational patterns have been created for the use of small groups. But, basically, all problem-solving discussions must include two questions: (1) What is the nature of the problem? and (2) How can we solve it? Subsidiary questions can be added to this most simple organizational pattern to meet the group's needs.

For example, a group may find the problem it is considering requires a very loosely structured pattern. Or group members may find they require a very prescriptive pattern of organization. The appropriate organizational pattern will depend on the nature and composition of the group as well as on the nature of the problem. Regardless of what specific organizational pattern seems appropriate, it is essential the discussion be organized.

Participation in the Discussion

You can interact more effectively in the small group if you consider your role as a participant and if you are sensitive to the interaction patterns that occur in the group. Participants, like leaders of small groups, have responsibilities in the small group context. In general, you should review the earlier chapters on self-awareness, self-disclosure, and listening. A positive self-concept, an ability to share your feelings and experiences, and critical, active, and empathic listening are all important to the effective small group participant.

In addition to these general skills, you may wish to consider five other specific abilities that contribute to the success of the small group. First, you should try to develop a sense of cohesiveness or "groupness" with the group. Each group member should feel as though he or she is part of the group and identifies with the group's goals and needs. We have all observed athletes who demonstrate a great deal of individual talent but who are unable to play as a "team" member. The basketball player who dribbles, passes, and shoots well but refuses to hand off the ball so a team member can make a basket; and the tennis player who plays singles well but tries to cover the entire court when playing doubles and consequently loses the game are examples. Similarly, an effective communicator who cannot cooperate with the group and who views small group communication as an individual competitive event negatively affects the entire group. An individual who helps to develop cohesiveness and commitment within the group may exert a strong positive effect.

Another skill that contributes to the success of the small group is an openness to others and to new ideas. You need to be willing to hear other people, just as you expect them to hear you out. You may need to develop patience in dealing with specific individuals in the small group and in dealing with the sometimes seeming slowness of the small group process. You should listen carefully and thoughtfully to ideas that may seem, at first, to hold little merit. Sometimes, the most successful ideas are created by combining two or more unworkable ones. Try to avoid premature dismissal of ideas or of individuals in the small group.

If you and the other discussants listen openly to each other, you should be able to reach a solution acceptable to all of you. Earlier in this chapter, we noted consensus is related to cohesiveness and commitment. Consensus is also far more likely in a group in which people listen to each other. As you open yourself to other people and to other ideas, you may find better solutions to problems and better relationships among the group members.

A third skill that contributes to the success of the small group is a willingness to communicate appropriately. You should not monopolize the small group. Small group communication should allow for *equal* opportunity for the communication of all members. However, you should also avoid becoming the "silent member" or the person who regularly responds, "I don't care." Neutrality can result in defensiveness. It is important that you do care and that you are willing to state your views and to support them. Be willing to share your ideas and to make appropriate contributions, and encourage others to similarly participate.

Appropriate communication is related to the concept of roles. Each of us has developed both useful and useless communication skills. For instance, you may have learned how to paraphrase the ideas of others carefully and to self-disclose appropriately, but you might also tend to interrupt others and to dominate conversations. In a small group setting, you may be perceived as a person who moves the group on to the solution of the problem quickly. However, imagine the group is made up of three other individuals who have similar communication behaviors. Each of you tries to get the floor, interrupts others when they talk, spends some time paraphrasing, and even more time elaborating on your point of view. How effective would the interaction be? Or, suppose your group consisted of four people who were all shy, good listeners, and supportive. The discussion might involve your statements and the others' quiet assent. Would that discussion be evaluated as highly successful?

Effective communication in the small group does not mean you should simply "be yourself," even if you have developed some important skills. It also does not mean all communication skills are equally important. Sometimes, you may be called upon to be a good listener and a supportive communicator, and at other times, you may be called upon to be talkative and assertive.

Effective communication in the small group means you should sensitively determine the skills that are important given the nature of the group and the topic under consideration. Just as you should shift the role you play to meet the needs of the group, you should reconsider the communication skills paramount in a particular group. One role or one set of skills, just like one pair of shoes, is not always right for the occasion.

The fourth ability you should attempt to cultivate for effective small group communication is sensitivity to the other group members. Listen carefully to the feelings being expressed as well as to the ideas. Become a sensitive observer of nonverbal communication. Do others look bored, tired, angry, confused, or frustrated? What are some of the possible causes for their reactions? How can you alter or alleviate a negative situation? How can you sustain or encourage a positive situation? Be observant of verbal and nonverbal messages, and try to determine how you can react. Member satisfaction is likely to increase when individuals in the group feel they are being heard and their point of view is important.

Fifth, and finally, you should be sensitive to the context of small group communication. Can you alter some of the patterns of communication, the roles that members are playing, the agreements that are being reached, or the rules that govern communication in your small group? Do physical features, such as the size of the room, the arrangement of tables and chairs, and so on, affect the interaction in the group? What other factors unique to the small group setting should be considered and possibly altered? Can you initiate some of these changes?

Summary

Small group communication is a form of interpersonal communication familiar to each of us. In this chapter, small group communication is defined as communication among a relatively small number of persons who have a mutually interdependent purpose and a sense of belonging, demonstrate behavior based on norms and values, use procedures accepted by the group, and interact orally. All small groups have two primary concerns: (1) accomplishing the task and (2) maintaining healthy relationships among the group members.

A number of concepts are important in understanding small group communication. Norms refer to how members "ought" to behave. Roles are patterns of behavior demonstrated by individuals in the small group setting. Productivity refers to the relative success the group has in completing a task. Cohesiveness refers to the sense of belonging individuals feel toward the small group. Commitment is the level of attraction the group holds for an individual. Consensus is the complete agreement among members and their support of group decisions. Member satisfaction refers to the positive or negative evaluation of the group by the members. Finally, communication networks refer to the five possible patterns of communication among group members: the chain, the Y, the wheel, the circle, and the all-channel network.

Essential steps in the preparation for, and presentation of, the problem-solving small group discussion include selecting a topic, wording the question to be discussed, researching the topic, evaluating primary and secondary research, and organizing the discussion.

Leadership in the Small Group

*Without leadership, there is no focus
about which a number of individuals
may cluster to form a group.*[1]

Cecil Gibb

*The successful organization has one major
attribute that sets it apart from
unsuccessful organizations: dynamic and
effective leadership.*[2]

*Paul Hersey and
Kenneth Blanchard*

Power is the great aphrodisiac.

Henry Kissinger

Objectives

1. Define and explain nine approaches to leadership.
2. Differentiate between laissez-faire, democratic, and autocratic styles of leadership.
3. Name some functions of leadership.
4. Distinguish between the power approach to leadership and the organizational approach to leadership.
5. Explain how the visionary approach to leadership and the ethical approach to leadership are similar.
6. Suggest some leadership behaviors that are important to leadership in the discussion group.

Key Terms

leadership
trait approach
styles of
 leadership
 approach
laissez-faire
 leadership
autocratic
 leadership
democratic
 leadership

situational
 approach
functional
 approach
power approach
organizational
 approach
visionary approach
ethical approach
eclectic approach

These three quotations introduce us to the topic of this chapter—leadership. The first quotation states leadership serves as a necessary prerequisite for a group to form. In other words, without leadership, small group communication may be meaningless. The second quotation underlines the importance of leadership in businesses and organizations. The third quotation reminds us of the importance of power, or leadership, from a contemporary American politician.

We all participate in leadership. Sometimes, we share leadership functions with others, and sometimes, we serve as appointed leaders for groups and organizations to which we belong. We may choose to be a leader, or others may choose us. In this chapter, we consider leadership in general terms, and we will apply the concept specifically to the small group context.

Leadership may be defined generally as influence. Whenever an individual influences another person, he or she is exhibiting leadership behavior. Leadership in the small group is defined as verbal and nonverbal communication behavior that influences the group to move in the direction of its goal or goals. The leader helps the group to clarify and attain its goals. Leadership is often shared by the members of a group. An ideal situation may be one in which a number of people share leadership functions.

Groups may function with one or more emergent leaders, or they may have an appointed leader. An emergent leader is an individual who is not selected to be the leader by others, but who emerges as the group continues to meet and work. The emergent leader may be a person who talks a great deal, who is highly responsive to the ideas of others, who initiates many new ideas, or who summarizes carefully and correctly. The appointed leader, on the other hand, is a person who is formally selected to lead.

People are selected to be leaders for a variety of reasons. An individual may be an appointed leader because of personal prestige, resources, or other factors. The appointed leader may or may not have effective small group communication skills. The emergent leader, by definition, is effective in the small group setting. Group members respond differently to emergent and appointed leaders. In general, group members agree more with statements made by appointed leaders than by emergent leaders.[3]

Approaches to Leadership

With which of the following statements would you agree?

(a) Leaders are born.
(b) Leaders exhibit a particular style.
(c) Leaders are made.
(d) Leaders are powerful.
(e) Leaders are organized.
(f) Leaders are visionary.
(g) Leaders are ethical.
(h) Leaders creatively combine all of the above and more.[4]

Leadership is increasingly important in our contemporary society.

Leadership Characteristics

What characteristics or traits do you believe leaders should possess? Check eight to ten of the following characteristics you feel best describe an effective leader.

_____ 1. Aggressive	_____ 11. Self-confident
_____ 2. Passive	_____ 12. Subjective
_____ 3. Tactful	_____ 13. Independent
_____ 4. Talkative	_____ 14. Emotional
_____ 5. Gentle	_____ 15. Objective
_____ 6. Dominant	_____ 16. Supportive
_____ 7. Religious	_____ 17. Active
_____ 8. Logical	_____ 18. Submissive
_____ 9. Competitive	_____ 19. Worldly
_____ 10. Insecure	_____ 20. Ambitious

What traits do you associate with leadership? Do you observe a pattern to the characteristics that you checked? Do you see leaders as being generally aggressive, talkative, and dominant, or do you see leaders as being tactful, gentle, and supportive? Do effective leaders combine these somewhat contradictory sets of behaviors? How many of the characteristics that you checked are associated with stereotypical male behavior? How many are associated with stereotypical female behavior? What implications can you draw? Which of the characteristics do you believe that you possess? To what extent do those characteristics that you possess lead you to believe that they are ideal characteristics for leaders? In other words, if you are tactful, gentle, and supportive, do you have an inclination to view these characteristics as the ideal?

Leadership is a topic which has fascinated people for centuries. As we will determine in this section of the chapter, a variety of approaches have emerged. We may study leadership using (1) the trait approach, (2) the styles of leadership approach, (3) the situational approach, (4) the functional approach, (5) the power approach, (6) the organizational approach, (7) the visionary approach, (8) the ethical approach, or (9) the eclectic approach. Let us consider each of these in more detail.

Trait Approach

The **trait approach** to leadership in the small group is perhaps the oldest perspective. This approach suggests leaders have certain personality traits or characteristics that allow them positions of leadership. For example, according to this approach, persons who are strong, resourceful, forthright, and aggressive might be viewed as successful leaders, while persons who are quiet, shy, weak, and unimaginative might be viewed as poor leaders. Physical attributes, too, may contribute to an individual's leadership ability, according to the trait approach. For instance, it seems tall people and men are placed in positions of leadership more often than are shorter people and women.

Within the past three decades, an interest in gender differences in leadership has emerged. Although we cannot go into all of the findings, we will summarize a few of the conclusions offered by researchers. First of all, men emerge as leaders in small groups more often just as they emerge as leaders in other spheres of life. In addition, men are ranked higher than women as group leaders in a variety of different tasks.[4] Men may emerge as leaders because they tend to initiate more verbal acts, make more suggestions, defend their ideas more strongly, yield less readily to interruptions, and, in general, dominate in the group setting.[5]

However, simple dominance does not predict leadership. Dominant women and men and submissive women and men were placed in small groups. The following results occurred: 1) dominant males and females emerged as leaders over their same-sexed submissive partners; 2) in mixed-sex groups, dominant males emerged over submissive females; 3) in mixed-sex groups, submissive males emerged over dominant females.[6] In general, females yield to males regardless of whether they are dominant or not.

Women are as capable of serving in leadership roles as are men. For instance, no gender differences emerge in high task clarity conditions.[7] Although traditional sex stereotyping is pervasive, the idea that women are inferior leaders does not appear to be true in actual behavioral situations.[8] Nonetheless, one study demonstrated even though men and women perform equally well as leaders, group members still perceive men to be more successful than women in leadership roles.[9] In sum, while women can be effective leaders, they are often perceived as though they cannot.

The traits identified most frequently for the leader in small group communication include:

1. An ability to communicate clearly and effectively
2. An ability to listen for the content and the intent of the other group members' comments
3. An ability to think quickly—to follow closely what is being said and to think ahead of the group
4. Knowledge about the topic under discussion
5. Knowledge of group process

Figure 11.1
Styles of leadership.

| Laissez-faire | Democratic | Autocratic |

The trait approach to leadership suggests leaders are "born, not made." This approach has been rejected for many reasons. First, relationships between specific traits and leadership ability have not been demonstrated. For instance, the relationship between creativity and effective leadership is largely insignificant.[10] While some traits are positively related to leadership ability in some cases, they are negatively related to effective leadership in others. Second, the measurement of personality traits is difficult. Persons who score high on one quality or trait may score low on the same quality on a different measure or at a different time. Finally, most studies that have dealt with the relationship between specific traits and leadership have not distinguished between effective and ineffective leadership. Traits associated with leadership do not necessarily identify the successful leader.

Styles of Leadership Approach

The **styles of leadership approach** suggests if we examine an individual's influential communication, patterns of behavior emerge that typify a particular leadership style. Styles of leadership have been placed on a continuum from *laissez-faire* to autocratic (figure 11.1). Halfway between these extremes is democratic leadership. Since these three positions exist on a continuum, many other leadership styles fall between them, but we only deal with these three basic styles.

In general, the *laissez-faire,* democratic, and autocratic leadership styles are defined in terms of the amount of control exercised by the leader. **Laissez-faire leadership** is the most permissive, and group members are offered almost no direction. **Autocratic leadership** contrasts sharply with *laissez-faire* leadership in that the leader has complete control and group members have very little freedom. **Democratic leadership** allows the leader some control, but group members also have some freedom.

Style of leadership may be a function of many variables. The personality of the leader may affect style of leadership. For example, firstborn children are more likely to develop task-oriented, directive leadership styles, while later-born children are more interpersonal, relationship-oriented leaders.[11] In other words, firstborn children are more likely to fall on the end of the continuum between democratic and autocratic leadership, while later-born children are more likely to fall on the end of the continuum between *laissez-faire* and democratic leadership.

What style of leadership is superior? *Laissez-faire* leadership results in the least amount of work and the poorest quality of work. Autocratic leadership generally produces more work than does *laissez-faire* leadership, but member satisfaction is diminished since hostility and aggression often result. In many situations, democratic leadership seems to be the most successful because work motivation is higher, more originality in ideas is demonstrated, and group members indicate a preference for this kind of leadership.

Past research suggested democratic leadership frequently promoted more friendliness, permissiveness, and member satisfaction than did other styles of leadership, even though it took longer.[12] However, a number of limitations of these studies should be noted. First, our cultural bias in favor of democratic leadership may skew the results of the older research. Particularly in the 1940s and 1950s, people may not have wanted to believe ruling in an autocratic manner was preferable to the democratic style. Second, the democratic leader has been defined in terms of culturally preferred characteristics. Third, the democratic leader has been positioned halfway between the two extreme positions. This style of leadership may merely represent a "happy medium" between two extremes. Fourth, the ambiguity of leadership styles that fall between the democratic style and the extreme ends of the continuum calls into question the meaningfulness of the research findings. Finally, it appears intuitively incorrect that one style of leadership would always be superior in all situations and with all people, and current research supports this. For instance, a small group that must act quickly and has a highly informed person as a leader might find the autocratic style of leadership is more effective. The democratic style of leadership is no longer seen as superior for all situations.

More recent evidence suggests the preferred style of leadership is dependent upon the type of task, the context of the small group, and the individuals involved.[13] For example, effective leadership styles vary for women and men. A directive, autocratic leadership style has been rated even more unfavorably when displayed by a female than a male, and male workers have stated a woman who employs such a style would be less effective. The rated effectiveness of a leader and the satisfaction of subordinates may decrease to the extent the leader adopts a style inconsistent with the expected stereotype.[14] Women who are directive and men who are *laissez-faire* may find others rate them as ineffective.

Because of these kinds of problems, the styles of leadership approach no longer enjoys a central role in our understanding of leadership that it once did.

Situational Approach

A few years ago, at a large midwestern university, the chair of a respected department passed away. The department was small in total number of faculty but was considered to be one of the finest in the country. All nine members of the department held Ph.D. degrees from prestigious universities, all were well published, and all were experienced teachers with national reputations. In addition, all were male and over fifty years of age. The chair who passed away was similarly well published, well-known, male, and sixty-four years of age.

When the position of chair was announced, many people across the country applied for the job. Among the candidates were people who were similar to the past chair and to the current faculty. Nonetheless, the faculty chose a young woman who had just

received her Ph.D. and had few publications. The woman was not automatically given tenure when she arrived at the university, but she soon received it because of her excellent work. Less than thirty years of age, with little experience, and no job security, this woman provided the *laissez-faire* leadership the department sought.

This example illustrates the **situational approach** to leadership, which suggests the interrelationship of the demands of the situation allow or disallow people success in leadership. Characteristics of one situation may call for entirely different leadership skills, traits, or styles than another situation. Among the more important situational factors are the personalities of the group members. Among the less important situational factors are the physical setting, the nature of the task, and the size of the group. The "Peanuts" cartoon illustrates the situational approach.

The situational approach to leadership received some support in the popular book by Kenneth Blanchard, Patricia Zigarmi, and Drea Zigarmi, *The One Minute Manager*. This book states a leader knows when to behave in different ways. He or she knows if coaching, supporting, directing, or delegating is appropriate. The authors suggest leaders must serve the people they supervise by doing for the followers what they cannot do for themselves in a given situation. Situational leaders thus need instruction in diagnosing situations and knowing how to apply particular skills to specific situations. The importance of audience analysis, discussed later in this book, is clear.

Group Leadership Functions Scale

What functions do you serve in the small group? This exercise allows you to determine the functions you are most likely to serve. *Instructions:* Respond to each of the items below with respect to your general and actual interpersonal behavior effectiveness. Consider the entire 1 to 7 scale for each item.

As a member of a small group I . . .

	very low		moderate			very high	
1. reveal my feelings to others	1	2	3	4	5	6	7
2. show understanding of others	1	2	3	4	5	6	7
3. clarify others' feelings	1	2	3	4	5	6	7
4. suggest or set limits	1	2	3	4	5	6	7
5. offer my friendship to others	1	2	3	4	5	6	7
6. challenge others' behavior	1	2	3	4	5	6	7
7. conceptualize ideas	1	2	3	4	5	6	7
8. elicit others' reactions	1	2	3	4	5	6	7
9. manage my time and that of others	1	2	3	4	5	6	7
10. confront others	1	2	3	4	5	6	7
11. interpret others' statements	1	2	3	4	5	6	7
12. praise others	1	2	3	4	5	6	7

The situational approach to leadership is attractive, but it is not without problems. First, few generalizations can be offered to a potential leader about how he or she should lead particular groups of persons. Second, the great number of situational variables and the relative importance of these variables disallow easy rule making about the situational perspective. The contribution of the situational approach is it reminds potential leaders they must adapt to the situation, rather than identifying and following specific adaptive behaviors.

13. accept others	1	2	3	4	5	6	7
14. exhort others	1	2	3	4	5	6	7
15. manage activities involving others	1	2	3	4	5	6	7
16. explain situations involving others	1	2	3	4	5	6	7
17. participate actively with others	1	2	3	4	5	6	7
18. question others	1	2	3	4	5	6	7
19. give emotionally to others	1	2	3	4	5	6	7
20. summarize others' statements	1	2	3	4	5	6	7
21. suggest procedures	1	2	3	4	5	6	7
22. am genuine with others	1	2	3	4	5	6	7
23. take risks with others	1	2	3	4	5	6	7
24. translate behavior to ideas	1	2	3	4	5	6	7
25. develop close relationships with others	1	2	3	4	5	6	7
26. deal with decision-making	1	2	3	4	5	6	7
27. help others understand their experience	1	2	3	4	5	6	7
28. inspire others	1	2	3	4	5	6	7

Functional Approach

The **functional approach** to leadership suggests leaders are made, rather than born, and views leadership as a composite of certain behaviors groups need to achieve their goals. While the other approaches to leadership focus on the *person,* the functional approach focuses on the *behaviors* of the person or persons. The functional approach suggests individuals can improve their leadership abilities and a number of people can contribute to leadership in a single group.

Specific leadership functions have been identified by authors who take a functional approach to leadership. Hersey and Blanchard suggested leadership includes both a task function and a socio-emotional function. Task leaders insure the job is completed, and socio-emotional leaders insure the group members are satisfied with the group process and the group outcome.[15] Homans, similarly, has suggested two functions identify leadership: (1) attaining the purposes of the group and (2) maintaining a balance of incentives, both reward and punishment, sufficient to induce the group members to obey the leader.[16]

Early studies suggested men were more likely to satisfy the task function while women were more likely to serve the socio-emotional function.[17] Contradictory results in more recent times have encouraged researchers to rethink this fairly simplistic conclusion. Current research suggests femininity predicts socio-emotional leadership and masculinity predicts task leadership.[18] In other words, the functions an individual plays is not based on biological sex, but on an internalization of specific personality characteristics.

Other researchers have offered longer lists of functions leaders must serve in the small group setting. Hemphill has stated leaders have five functions: (1) to advance the group's purposes, (2) to administer, (3) to inspire activity or to set the pace, (4) to make members feel secure within the group, and (5) to act without regard to their own self-interest.[19] Stogdill has identified six functions of a leader: (1) to define objectives and maintain goal directions, (2) to provide means for goal attainment, (3) to provide and maintain group structure, (4) to facilitate group action and interaction, (5) to maintain group cohesiveness and member satisfaction, and (6) to facilitate group task performance.[20]

Power Approach

Individuals who encourage us to consider the **power approach** to leadership state the essence of leadership is power. In other words, one's position is not as important as is his or her ability to make something happen. The definition of leadership provided at the beginning of this chapter is consistent with this notion. In the small group setting, the person who is appointed the leader may or may not have actual power; instead, another person may serve as an "emergent leader." Emergent leaders are not assigned the role, instead they exhibit leadership.

Using this approach, leadership is defined as "making a difference." The skills of the leader would include "persuasion, conflict analysis, resolution, strategizing, organizing, manipulation, assessment of [the] opponents' vested interests, and the development of winning strategies."[21] Communication skills are basic to leadership as power.

A second school of power theory suggests the empowerment of followers is more important than the leaders' power. To the extent leaders can offer their followers a sense of power, they are more likely to be viewed as leaders. This second view suggests community organizing and coalition building may be more important than persuading, resolving conflicts, manipulating, and formulating strategy. The work to be accomplished is completed by empowered followers rather than by the leader.

Jacobson published a text in which he outlined the principles of leadership from the perspective that leadership is equivalent to power. Although we cannot outline all of

Communication skills are basic to leadership.

the principles here, the following list provides a representative sampling. The reader is encouraged to refer to the original book, *Power and Interpersonal Relations,* which is cited in the footnotes for the complete set of axioms.

1. The power recipient is the crucial part of any power attempt, because power resides implicitly in his or her dependency.

2. The amount of dependency of the power recipient on the power agent is directly proportional to the power recipient's motivation to accomplish the power agent's goals.

3. The amount of the power recipient's dependence on the power agent is directly proportional to the goal availability outside of the relationship.

4. The power recipient will conform to a power attempt if it is consistent with his or her own beliefs and values.

5. The power recipient will conform to a power attempt if he or she admires the agent exerting power, or if he or she wishes to be like him or her.

6. Power is a property of the social relationship rather than an attribute of a person.

7. The group's power over its members is increased if the members perceive common outcomes for each of them.

8. The group's power over its members has special significance because there is a tendency for group products to be superior to individual efforts.

9. There must be a time lag between one person's attempt to exert power and the other person's response.

10. Members who are less accepted and who rate others highly will conform to power attempts, while the highest and the lowest power members will be the most resistant to power attempts.[22]

Organizational Approach

The **organizational approach** suggests leadership is a function of one's role or position in a particular organization, thus the leader in a small group is the person who is designated as a leader while the leader in a corporation is the person who is designated as the corporate executive officer.

Warren Bennis and Burt Nanus recently published a popular book entitled *Leaders: The Strategies for Taking Charge.* These authors do not state they subscribe to the organizational approach to leadership, but their research on leaders was conducted on sixty chief executive officers, over half of whom were from the *Fortune* 500 list. Their definition of "leader" thus suggests one who is designated as a group's "boss" or "chief".

Probably the group that subscribes most strongly to the notion that leadership is an assigned role rather than an emergent role is the military. All branches of the military rely upon a strict allegiance to the concept that the "officer in charge" is the leader. U.S. Army lieutenants are expected to respond to the requests of captains who pay attention to majors who listen to lieutant colonels, and so on.

Visionary Approach

Although proponents of the **visionary approach** recognize power is related to leadership, they hold the crucial factor in the definition of leadership is vision. As one author notes, "Leadership articulates directions for human action. Leadership scans current trends and points people toward a meaningful future."[23] A variety of groups across the country hold that vision is the key to leadership, and they are working on programs that will actually teach people specific visionary skills such as holistic, as opposed to atomistic, thinking; future imaging, or envisioning events that may occur; and intuition. You might note such skills are related to left-brain hemispheric activity which is more often well developed in women.

Bennis and Nanus advocate vision as a key to leadership. One of their four strategies to leadership is "attention through vision." They begin their explanation of this strategy with a poem from T. E. Lawrence:

> All men dream; but not equally.
> Those who dream by night in the dusty
> recesses of their minds.
> Awake to find that it was vanity;
> But the dreamers of day are dangerous men,
> That they may act their dreams with open
> eyes to make it possible.[24]

These researchers found leaders were able to "create focus." They were highly result-oriented, and they knew results would gain attention from others. Bennis and Nanus noted,

Leadership points people toward a
meaningful future.

Their visions or intentions are compelling and pull people toward them. Intensity
coupled with commitment is magnetic. And these intense personalities do not have to
coerce people to pay attention; they are so intent on what they are doing that, like a
child completely absorbed with creating a sand castle in a sandbox, they draw others
in.[25]

Vision, suggest people within this perspective, is the key, if not identical, to leadership.

Ethical Approach

The **ethical approach** to leadership builds upon the theory that vision is essential. The
ethical approach suggests leadership is not only visionary, but it also must involve some
ethical assessment, reflection, and action. In other words, the leader must be an ethical
person. He or she should behave in accordance with the acceptable principles of right
and wrong. Individuals who subscribe to this approach view ethics as the center of
human action. Bennis and Nanus appear to subscribe at least partly to the ethical
approach as their book jacket proclaims, "Managers do things right. Leaders do the
right thing."

We may agree that leadership is tied up with ethical judgments, but we may strongly
disagree about which decision is the ethical or unethical one. Political leaders, for instance, often claim, and believe, that their position is the "ethical one" even when their

opponents make the same value claims for the opposite position. Politics, like other aspects of our lives, contains a gray area that makes the "ethical choice" difficult to discern. Contemporary leadership must fit a complex, morally ambiguous world. Contemporary leaders must consider both the ideal and the real in their judgments.

Eclectic Approach

The final approach to leadership is one which embodies all of the other approaches. The **eclectic approach** chooses the best from the other approaches. This approach suggests leadership is based on traits, styles, situations, functions, power, organizations, vision, and ethical assessment. Leadership, as you have probably determined, is a complex activity and cannot be easily categorized as theorists and researchers have sometimes attempted to do.

Robert Terry, director of the Hubert H. Humphrey Institute of Public Affairs Education for Reflective Leadership Program, at the University of Minnesota, has best articulated this point of view. He observes each view of leadership is "partially true when tied to one feature of action, but each view alone distorts a total picture."[26] He explains the eclectic view,

> It is grounded in traits, yet the required skills are not exhausted by traits. It is sensitive to shifting situations, yet it recognizes complexities beyond situation theory's reach. It is shaped by roles and position, yet is greater than any organization hierarchy. It is activated by power, yet challenges the primacy of power. It is driven by vision, yet is not satisfied with just any direction. It is ethical, yet tempered by an awareness of existence, ambiguities, and unforeseen consequences. . . . Leadership empowers human beings to claim ultimate fulfillment.[27]

Terry's perspective is very compelling as it synthesizes the diverse approaches that have been taken in our understanding of leadership. Although you may find the next section of the chapter to be less profound, the information should be useful to you as you specifically prepare to serve as a leader in the small group setting.

Participation in Leadership in the Discussion Group

You may be asked to share leadership functions in a small group discussion or to exhibit your leadership abilities in a problem-solving or information-sharing group discussion in your speech communication class. Your role in the group discussion may be as an appointed leader or as someone who shares leadership functions with others.

What leadership functions are important in the group discussion? Brilhart suggests the functions of leaders can be categorized into "initiating, organizing, spreading participation, stimulating both creative and critical thinking, facilitating understanding, promoting cooperative interpersonal relationships, and developing the group members.[28] While this list may sound overwhelming, these classes of behaviors are comprehensive and may be shared among members.

Identifying Different Approaches to Leadership

Do you understand the different approaches to leadership that have been discussed? To test your understanding, complete the following exercise. Next to each statement write T if it exemplifies the trait approach, ST for styles approach, S for the situational approach, F for the functional approach, P for the power approach, O for the organizational approach, V for the visionary approach, Et for the ethical approach, and E for the eclectic approach.

_____ 1. Sue can envision the future.

_____ 2. Tom always does the right thing.

_____ 3. "You'll do it because I'm the boss!"

_____ 4. Hal has the skills to be in charge, he always does the right thing, and he was elected as Director.

_____ 5. Somehow Julie always gets her way.

_____ 6. Leaders are born, not made.

_____ 7. Successful leaders are those who are sensitive to the needs of the group and the context and respond accordingly.

_____ 8. The autocratic leader gets the job done!

_____ 9. Mary's not the boss, but she's the one who gets things done.

_____ 10. The President is the Commander of the Army

_____ 11. Pope John Paul II is truly a pious leader.

_____ 12. Harry S Truman was in the right place at the right time.

_____ 13. The successful leader considers the personalities of the group members as she or he determines the most appropriate way to lead.

_____ 14. Everyone likes the *laissez-faire* leader.

_____ 15. Women can never be as effective in leadership as can men.

_____ 16. The effective leader is someone who is outgoing and talkative.

_____ 17. The democratic leader generally has more positive outcomes than do the autocratic or *laissez-faire* leaders.

_____ 18. We should not look for a *person* to lead us, but we should examine the *behaviors* of the person.

Initiating may include icebreaking activities or other action by which the members of the group learn the names of the other members and are introduced to each other. During this stage, procedures, purposes, and other plans should be outlined. Opening remarks may be made, and necessary arrangements, such as securing and running a tape recorder, appointing a secretary, or arranging the room, should be handled. The group members should be made to feel comfortable during this initial phase.

Organizing refers to orderliness. The group leader should help to keep the group moving toward its goal by summarizing, making transitions, and bringing the group to a conclusion. When the group digresses from the topic, the leader should direct the group back to the topic. When the group repeats itself, the leader should be sensitive to the need to move on. When the group spends a great deal of time on one aspect of

ANIMAL CRACKERS

Reprinted by permission: Tribune Media Services, Inc.

the problem, the leader should remind the group of time constraints and help the group to budget its time appropriately.

Spreading participation means the group leader should help to equalize or divide participation among group members. Individuals in the group should not feel obliged or forced to speak if they have nothing to contribute, but talkative members should not be allowed to prevent the contributions of other members. The leader should carefully observe members to determine if they wish to speak and should listen actively to determine what points need extension or clarification. The leader should ask questions to encourage participation and should use follow-up questions or probes to gain additional information. Acceptance should be shown toward the contributions of all group members—no matter how trivial the remark. Highly evaluative verbal or nonverbal responses may serve to discourage individuals from future participation.

Stimulating both creative and critical thinking refers to simultaneously encouraging novel and unique ideas and also careful analysis of ideas. While it is difficult to encourage both at once, both kinds of thinking are essential to the successful small group discussion. Criteria by which solutions or answers will be measured should be uniformly understood; ideas should not be dismissed until they have been carefully and thoughtfully measured against existing criteria; and new approaches should be encouraged.

Facilitating understanding means the leader models active and empathic listening and he or she encourages others to engage in this kind of listening as well. Pointing out areas of agreement, stressing commonalities, suggesting visualizations, and offering analogies all contribute to understanding among members.

Promoting cooperative interpersonal relationships is another function of the leader. Tension within the group should be reduced so group members can work together effectively. Disallowing conflict over personalities or personal issues is useful. The leader can encourage humor as a tension-reliever in groups that are particularly serious or have an especially difficult task. When conflict does arise, using conflict-reduction methods, such as compromise, negotiation, consensus, or arbitration, may be helpful.

Developing the group and its members suggest the leader helps the group and group members to grow and change. Sometimes, these goals are at cross-purposes, but, usually, helping individuals to develop their repertoire of roles within a group or to learn more about a certain topic also helps the group to develop and grow. Similarly, helping the group to develop by establishing consensus and member satisfaction frequently results in individual growth in the members. Growth of the group at the cost of the individuals has short-term benefits. Also, helping individuals to grow and develop without regard to the group's goal has limited benefit.

Effective leadership is essential to successful problem solving in the small group. As we stated earlier, the leadership of a small group discussion is generally shared, but the designated leader has the responsibility of ensuring that all of the leadership functions are performed. If you are selected as the leader of a small group or if you emerge as the leader, you will want to review the functions that must be provided by leadership and ensure that you or someone else is fulfilling them.

Summary

In general, leadership is defined as influence; in the small group, leadership is defined as verbal and nonverbal communication behavior that influences the group to move in the direction of its goal or goals. A group may have one or more emergent leaders, or it may have an appointed leader.

A number of approaches to leadership have been offered, including the trait approach, the styles of leadership approach, the situational approach, the functional approach, the power approach, the organizational approach, the visionary approach, the ethical approach, and the eclectic approach. The trait approach suggests leaders have certain personality traits or characteristics that allow them positions of leadership. The styles of leadership approach suggests, if we examine an individual's influential communication, patterns of behavior emerge that typify a particular leadership style. Leadership styles include *laissez-faire,* democratic, and autocratic. The situational approach suggests the interrelationship of the demands of the situation allow or disallow people success in leadership. The functional approach suggests leaders are made, rather than born, and views leadership as a composite of certain behaviors that groups need to achieve their goals. The power approach equates power with leadership and minimizes an individual's assigned or given role. The organizational approach takes just the opposite position and suggests one's role or position determines if he or she is a leader. The visionary approach suggests leaders must have vision while the ethical approach requires the leader to offer an ethical assessment. The eclectic approach combines all of these approaches and may currently be the most useful way to view leadership.

part 3

Public Communication

Public communication is the process of understanding and sharing that occurs in the speaker-to-audience situation. Public communication, like interpersonal communication, is a transaction in which people simultaneously give and receive meaning from each other.

Our exploration of public communication begins with chapter 12, "Topic Selection and Audience Analysis," which provides methods of discovering good speech topics and explains how to interpret information about the audience. Chapter 13, "Speaker Credibility," begins by discussing fear of public speaking and then examines the dimensions of credibility and means of improving credibility as a public speaker. In chapter 14, "Finding Information," we explain where to find information in written sources and from people. Ways to develop sentence and key-word outlines and a number of patterns of speech organization are presented in chapter 15, "Organizing Your Speech." Chapter 16, "Delivery and Visual Aids," discusses vocal and bodily aspects of public speaking—including voice, eye contact, gestures, and movement. This chapter also has an expanded section on why and how to use visual aids in your speech. In chapter 17, "The Informative Speech," we provide detailed directions on how to compose a speech whose primary purpose is to increase the audience's knowledge. Preparing a speech that is designed to change an audience or to invite the audience to action is the subject of chapter 18, "The Persuasive Speech."

chapter 12

Topic Selection and Audience Analysis

*T*here are no uninteresting things; there are only uninterested people.

G. K. Chesterton

*O*ne of the finest accomplishments is making a long story short.

Kin Hubbard

*N*one are so deaf as those who will not hear.

Matthew Henry

Objectives

1. Employ brainstorming techniques to generate a list of possible speech topics.
2. Use personal inventories to find subject areas for possible topics.
3. Limit your topic to fit the subject, the audience, and the time allowed.
4. Analyze your audience for demographics, interest, knowledge, attitudes, values, and beliefs.
5. Deliver a speech in which you exhibit audience sensitivity.

Key Terms

brainstorming
personal
  inventories
involvement
audience analysis
captive audience
heterogeneous
voluntary
  audience
homogeneous
demographic
  analysis

audience interest
audience
  knowledge
attitude
belief
value
observation
inference
questionnaire

The selection of a topic for a public speech may emerge from your own interests or experiences.

Choosing a topic for a speech can be a problem, unless you know what you are doing. You may have already discovered that, when you are assigned to write a paper or to deliver a speech, the beginning step of finding something to write or speak about is difficult. You may not be able to think of a topic as soon as you hear the assignment. Instead, you may find yourself mulling over the assignment for days, sharpening your pencil, drinking water or coffee as you think, and only selecting a topic after most of your time for completing the assignment has slipped away.

In this chapter, we illustrate two methods of selecting topics for speeches. We also examine how to link topic selection to audience analysis; that is, how to select topics with your particular audience in mind so the topic is appropriate for you, for your audience, and for the situation in which you are going to deliver the speech.

Selecting and Limiting the Topic

Let us begin by examining some methods of finding a topic. The two methods discussed here are individual brainstorming and conducting a personal inventory.

Individual Brainstorming

Group **brainstorming** is a useful technique for selecting a topic for group discussion. Individual brainstorming can be equally effective for finding a topic for your public speech.

What is "individual brainstorming," and how can you use it to help you find a topic? First, give yourself a very limited time, say five minutes. Without trying to think of fancy titles or even complete thoughts, write down as many topics as you can. When your time is up, you should have a rough list of the ideas or topics easiest to arouse in your mind. This step can be repeated if you want to have an even larger list from which to choose. The second step is to select three items from your list that have the most appeal as topics for you. Third, choose one of these three topics you feel would be appealing not only to you, but also to your audience.

This technique of individual brainstorming can generate many speech topics from which you can choose. Many students find this method more productive than trying to think of one topic for their speech.

Personal Inventories

Another way to find a topic for your speech is to conduct **personal inventories** of your reading and viewing habits. Choosing one topic from thousands of possible topics requires some self-analysis.

You make choices every time you read or watch something. You can discover your own interests by examining carefully what you choose to read or watch. What kind of books do you read? The person who reads science fiction exhibits quite a different interest than the person who reads biographies, autobiographies, or mysteries. Do you watch films? The person who watches international films is reflecting quite a different interest than the person who watches horror films, musicals, or X-rated movies.

Public speaking starts with the self, with what you know, have experienced, or are willing to learn. The two inventories that follow demonstrate how self-analysis can help you to assess those areas in which you are qualified to speak. You could do the same kind of inventory with music, books, films, plays, and art.

Your personal inventories of television and newspaper reading habits are just two rough indications of your own interests. Other inventories that you could conduct, besides those already mentioned, might include:

hobbies	jobs
leisure activities	elective courses
organizations	talents
magazines	academic major courses

Personal inventories should help you to identify your own interests and preferences—including some you may not have been fully aware you have. How the topic relates to self is an early step in topic selection; how the topic relates to the listeners comes later. Now, however, you are ready to assess your personal involvement in and knowledge of the topic.

Television Inventory

Note the items you watch often (+), sometimes (0), and rarely or never (−).

_____	Television news	_____	Game shows
_____	Sports news	_____	News channel
_____	Local news	_____	Entertainment/interview (for
_____	National news		example, "The Tonight Show")
_____	International news	_____	News/interview (for example,
_____	Weather		"Meet the Press")
_____	Movie channel	_____	Variety shows
_____	Music channel	_____	Soap operas
_____	Religion channel	_____	Drama shows
_____	Health channel	_____	Situation comedy shows

Newspaper Inventory

Take the local newspaper and note the sections you read often (+), sometimes (0), and rarely or never (−).

_____	Front-page news	_____	Birth and wedding announcements
_____	Comics	_____	Home and family
_____	Sports	_____	Art and music
_____	Editorial page	_____	Books
_____	Letters to the editor	_____	Travel
_____	Obituaries		

Involvement in the Topic

After you have selected a possible topic area, you should evaluate the topic to see if you have the appropriate involvement in and knowledge of the subject. **Involvement** is simply a measure of how much a topic means to you.

Your brainstorming and personal inventories might have shown that you have an interest in many items. However, you may not be involved in these items. For example, you could be interested in sports because they allow you a kind of escape from everyday concerns, but you might not be highly involved in sports. How can you tell the difference between mere interest and involvement? And what difference does it make whether a speaker is involved in a topic?

One measure of involvement is how much time you put into a topic area. What if one of your interests you find through brainstorming and conducting personal inventories is computers? You could probably consider yourself involved in computers if you spend time around them, learn how they work, read books about them, and spend time around computer shops to see what new hardware and software is available. The amount of time you spend with your topic is, then, one measure of your involvement.

A second measure of involvement is how much effort you expend with a particular interest. The person who is really involved in politics is much more than a passive observer. He or she knows the candidates and politicians, works on campaigns, helps bring out the voters, reads about politics, talks with other interested persons and joins groups with a similar interest. Involvement, then, is measured by the time and effort committed to your subject.

To tell whether or not a speaker is involved in a speech topic is easy. An involved speaker speaks with more conviction, passion, and authority. The involved speaker gives many verbal and nonverbal indications that he or she cares about the topic. The person who is only trying to fulfill an assignment cannot convey the sense of involvement so important in public speaking. Usually, you will find the speaker who really cares about the topic being discussed is often successful at getting you involved in the topic as well.

Knowledge of the Topic

After you have selected a topic area and determined your own involvement in the subject, you need to assess your personal knowledge of the subject. What do you know about the subject that can and should be communicated to your audience? Your knowledge about the topic comes primarily from three sources: yourself, other people, and resources like books, films, magazines, and television.

First, determine what you know about your subject from *your own experience*. Do you have experience that has not been shared by many other people? Have you raised children, worked at interesting jobs, served in the armed forces, traveled to unusual places, or done things that few can claim?

The importance of speaking from personal experience was demonstrated at a large university where over seven hundred students were invited to select the best speeches made in their individual speech classes. The winners delivered their speeches in a runoff contest, and the three best speakers gave their speeches to everyone taking the course. Those three speakers, selected by their classmates, were two black males and a handicapped white female—but, of the seven hundred competitors, very few were black and even fewer were handicapped. All three spoke about topics in which they were highly involved and to which they were committed: the two black men spoke about being black students in a predominantly white university, and the woman told what it was like to be a student confined to a wheelchair. The black men told about being stared at in class, having classmates constantly asking them about being black, and being misunderstood. The handicapped woman told of having practically nobody speak to her no matter where she was, of people moving to the other side of the sidewalk when she approached, and of being considered an oddity. All three students had special knowledge of and experience with the topics on which they based their speeches.

After determining what you know about a topic from your personal experience, you should *turn to other people* who might know more about the topic than you do. You can make your speech stronger by talking to people in your community or in your college or university who are knowledgeable about your topic. A telephone call or personal interview can often provide you with some ideas and quotations for your speech that will show you cared enough about the subject to bring your audience current expert information. Chapters 9 and 14 give additional information about how to interview other people for information that you can use in your speech.

You can also bolster your knowledge of a topic by *turning to resources* like magazines, books, films, newspapers, or television. These resources can help you to fill in information about your topic that you do not already know, and they will increase your credibility as a speaker. Finding such information is discussed in more detail in chapter 14.

It is important to remember that, when you get information from another person or from some resource, you must credit that person or resource. In other words, you must tell your audience that you got the information from someplace other than your personal experience.

Narrowing the Topic

Brainstorming techniques and personal inventories can yield topic areas appropriate for you. However, these topics are probably too large or abstract for a brief speech. A personal inventory may show that a speech on the topic of welfare reform is a good one for you because you are involved in the topic, and you read and know about it. Unfortunately, a speech on welfare reform could take days or weeks to deliver because so much information is available on the subject. You might try *narrowing the topic* so much that, at first glance, it might appear you would never be able to find enough information on the topic. The advantage in starting with a very narrow topic is it renders much information on the subject irrelevant. Only a small amount of the available information will be related to your narrowed topic. Thus, your research on the topic will be highly focused, and you will not end up spending a lot of time to obtain information you cannot use.

The most common way to narrow a topic is to make it more specific and concrete. For example, the welfare reform topic can be narrowed geographically to welfare reform in the state of New Jersey, welfare reform in Polk County, or welfare reform in Rock City. Even then, the topic is broad so the category *welfare reform* might have to be reduced to a smaller, more manageable category, such as aid to dependent children, funds for widows and orphans, or support for the disabled. After carefully considering the audience's interests in the various geographies and in the various kinds of welfare reform, you might end up delivering a speech on problems with aid to dependent children in Polk County.

One method of narrowing a topic is suggested by the welfare reform example just described. An abstract category discovered through brainstorming or personal inventories can be narrowed by listing smaller categories directly related to that topic. The abstract topic *business,* for instance, might yield the following smaller categories directly related to it:

Securing a job in business
Securing a job in local businesses
Where to find jobs in local businesses

How to get job interviews with local businesses

How to get interviews for summer jobs with local businesses

A slightly different approach to narrowing a topic involves taking a broad category, like *sports,* and listing as many smaller topics as you can that are at least loosely related to that topic:

Special treatment of football recruits

Tutoring of athletes

Scholarships for athletes

Keeping score in wrestling

New opportunities for women in golf

Financing our athletic program

Is our proposed stadium worth the expense?

The track program for women

Injury: The unpublicized problem in college football

What happened to our basketball stars of the past?

The lists of more specific and concrete topics can be extended until you have a large number from which to choose.

How will you know if your topic is narrow enough? There is no easy answer. Several things to consider are: (1) how much information is available on the narrowed topic, (2) how much information can be conveyed within the time limits for the speech, and (3) can the narrowed topic be discussed with enough depth to keep the audience interested and to increase their knowledge?

The advice in this section on how to find and narrow a topic should help you to choose a topic for your speech. If all of these suggestions fail, then you may have to examine the lists of topics that appear in chapters 17 and 18 on informative and persuasive speaking. These topics were taken from some excellent student speeches.

Now we turn from selecting a speech topic to adapting your topic to an audience.

Analyzing Your Audience

Why should you analyze your audience? Especially, why should you analyze your audience if it consists of your own classmates? Before we start talking about *how* to analyze an audience, we need to explain *why* we analyze an audience.

One professor who used this text commented he never used the chapter on audience analysis because his students spoke only to their own classmates and therefore did not need to analyze the audience. Naturally, the authors were startled because they assumed a public speaker always needs to know about an audience before knowing how to state a message. Would you give the same speech in the same way no matter who constituted the audience?

Let us say you are going to give an informative speech on interest rates. Would you give that speech in the same way to a beginning speech class that consisted mainly of business majors as you would if the class consisted mainly of arts and sciences majors? Or let us say you are going to give a persuasive speech on birth control. Would it matter

Classroom speakers generally face a captive audience.

to you that the audience consisted of many persons whose religious beliefs prohibited the use of birth control? In short, how would you know the majors, religious beliefs, and interests of your audience unless you analyzed the audience in some way?

Audience analysis can be as simple as "eyeballing" a group to estimate age, gender, and race, or it can be as complicated as polling people to discover their predispositions on your topic. The information that follows is designed to make you more insightful about how you approach an audience and to invite you to think carefully about the people to whom you speak so that you can be as effective as possible.

To begin, we survey four levels of **audience analysis.** The categories are called *levels* because the first is relatively easy and the last is the most difficult to understand and to use. In that sense, the levels are like grade levels in school; the ideas and concepts increase in difficulty. The four levels begin with the distinction between captive and voluntary audiences.

Level 1: Captive and Voluntary Audiences

A **captive audience,** as the name suggests, is an audience that did not choose to hear a particular speaker or speech. The teacher of a required class addresses a captive audience. A disc jockey who broadcasts commercial announcements between the songs you want to hear addresses a captive audience. Similarly, a student who addresses fellow students in a required speech class is addressing a captive audience.

Why should a public speaker distinguish a captive from a voluntary audience? One reason is a captive audience did not choose to hear from you or about your subject—you may have to motivate them to listen. Another is that captive audiences are **heterogeneous,** characterized by the wide variety of differences among the individuals. The speaker must adapt the topic and the content of the speech to a wider range of information and to more diverse attitudes toward the subject. One of the advantages of a captive audience is it gives the speaker an opportunity to present ideas to people who, under ordinary circumstances, might never have heard the information or the point of view embodied in the speech.

The **voluntary audience** chooses to hear the particular speaker or speech. The most important characteristic of the voluntary audience is the participants have some need or desire to hear the speech. The people who go to listen to a politician are usually sympathetic to the speaker's ideas. The students who stop to hear a traveling evangelist speak on the campus lawn are usually curious about, or perhaps even committed to, the speaker's religious beliefs. The advantage of a voluntary audience is the speaker addresses an audience that is more **homogeneous,** that is, audience members are more like one another. Addressing a captive audience is like attempting to attract new customers to a product; addressing a voluntary audience is like attempting to please customers who have purchased the product before. Both salesperson and speaker are helped by knowing whether the audience is voluntary or captive because the nature of the audience affects the topic, the rationale, the approach, and the goal.

The task of determining the character of an audience is far from simple. A specific example can demonstrate its complexity. At first, you might guess a congregation is a voluntary audience—people choose to attend a particular church to hear a particular minister. But what about the children in the congregation? Did they choose to hear the sermon, or did their parents make them go to church? What about some of the husbands and wives? How many people are there because their spouses wanted them to come along? To what extent did social pressures persuade some of these people to attend church? Did the audience members really know what the minister was going to say, or are they captives of the message that is being delivered? Even this first level of audience analysis is more challenging than it appears. The minister of a congregation addresses an audience that is in some ways voluntary and in some ways captive, and must adapt the message to those differences.

How can you, in your speech class, make the distinction between the voluntary and the captive audience? You may find your audience is more captive than voluntary—the members of the audience did not enroll in the class to hear you or your speech. On the other hand, they are there to learn how to give and to listen to speeches. You may have to adapt to your student audience by ensuring they know why *you* are speaking to *them* about *this* particular subject. You will actually find yourself more dependent than most speakers on the other kinds of audience analysis covered in this chapter. Most public speakers work with voluntary audiences. They know, from experience and investigation, what their audience wants to hear and what they can do. You will probably have to learn about your audience through the methods suggested in this chapter.

Level 2: Demographic Analysis

Demographics literally means "the characteristics of the people." **Demographic analysis** is based on the kind of characteristics you write on forms: name, age, sex, hometown, year in school, race, major subject, religion, and organizational affiliations. Such information can be important to public speakers because it can reveal the extent to which they will have to adapt themselves and their topics to that audience.

Occupation

Name

Race

Age

Sex

Religion

Major

Organizations

A closer look at one item might demonstrate the importance of demographic information about the audience. Let us see what the effect might be of your audience's majors. Suppose you plan to speak about the cost of littering in your state. Your audience consists of twenty-two students: seven have not chosen a major subject, three are mathematics majors, four are biology majors, six are majoring in business administration, and one is an English major. This information gives you no reason to assume that any of them knows much about littering, but you can assume from nine to thirteen audience members have a basic understanding of numbers. The six business majors may have a better understanding of costs than the others, and the students majoring in math and science may find the cost-benefit approach attractive as well.

If you add to that small bit of information more demographic information, then you can find even more to guide you. Does your college attract students who are likely to be concerned about the expense of littering? Is your audience likely to be knowledgeable about rural or urban littering? Do any students in your audience belong to organizations concerned about conservation? Whatever your topic, the demographic characteristics of your audience can imply the audience's receptiveness to your topic.

Public speakers usually rely heavily on demographic information. Politicians send personnel ahead to find out how many blue-collar workers, faithful party members, elderly people, union members, and hecklers they are likely to encounter. They consult opinion polls, population studies, and reliable persons in the area to discover the nature of a prospective audience. Conducting a demographic analysis of your class can serve a similar purpose—it will help you to design a speech is better adapted to your audience.

Level 3: Audience Interest in and Knowledge of the Topic

As you move up the levels of audience analysis, the information you are asked to discover becomes more difficult to find. On level 3, your task is to determine the degree of **audience interest** in your topic and **audience knowledge** of the topic. Another way to ask the same question about interest and knowledge is: How familiar is your audience with the topic? This question is important because if your audience is disinterested in, or unfamiliar with, your topic, you will have to generate that interest in your speech.

One means of finding an audience's interest in, and knowledge of, a topic is to consider the age of the topic. Age and familiarity are closely related because the longer a topic has been around, and the more recently it has gained importance, the more likely the audience is to know about it. Your classmates may know much about a topic that has been a burning issue in the student newspaper, but they may not know a great deal about nuclear fusion, power satellites, or the latest fashions. A topic that is old to a middle-aged person can be new to a nineteen-year-old student. If you were addressing classmates of mixed ages, you would have to adapt to those persons who are familiar with the topic and to those who are not. Fortunately, old topics have new variations. Topics, like people, live, change, and die—some have long and varied lives, while others pass quickly.

How can you gauge the audience's interest in, and knowledge of, your topic? One way to find out is to ask. You can ask demographic questions to help assess audience interest in your topic. The audience members' ages, majors, year in school, and organizational memberships can suggest their familiarity with, knowledge of, and interest in your topic. Ask your fellow students before and after classes, in the hallways and the cafeteria. Ask them in writing, through a questionnaire, if your instructor encourages that kind of analysis. You can even ask for some indication of interest during your speech, by asking your classmates to raise their hands in response to such questions as: How many of you watch television news? How many of you have been to Washington, D.C.? How many of you have read an unassigned book in the last three months?

Level 4: The Audience's Attitudes, Beliefs, and Values

An **attitude** is a tendency to respond favorably or unfavorably to some person, object, idea, or event. The attitudes of audience members can be assessed through questionnaires, by careful observation, or even by asking the right questions. If your audience comes from a place where many attitudes, beliefs, and values are shared, your audience analysis may be easy. A speech about birth control would be heard in some colleges with as much excitement as a speech on snails, but at other colleges, the same speech could be grounds for dismissal. Attitudes toward politics, sex, religion, war, and even work vary in different geographical areas and subgroups. Regardless of the purpose of

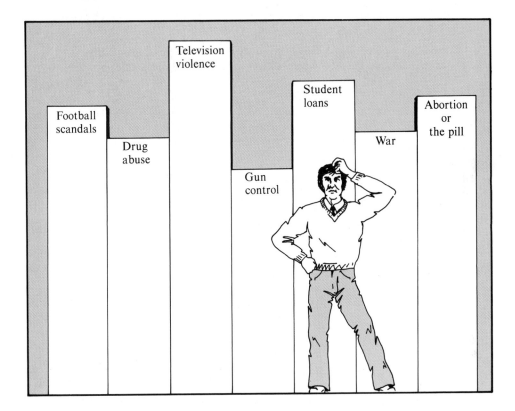

your speech, the attitudes of audience members will make a difference in the appropriateness of your topic. Examples of different attitudes are:

Pro-war   Anti-pollution
Anti-Communist   Anti-immigration
Pro-government   Pro-business
Anti-gun control   Anti-materialism
Pro-conformity

A **belief** is a conviction. Beliefs, or convictions, are usually considered more solid than attitudes, but our attitudes often spring from our beliefs. Your belief in good eating habits may lead to a negative attitude toward overeating and obesity and to a positive attitude toward balanced meals and nutrition. Your audience's beliefs make a difference in how they respond to your speech. They may believe in upward mobility through higher education, in higher pay through hard work, in the superiority of the family farm, in a lower tax base, or in social welfare. Or they may not believe in any of these ideas. Beliefs are like anchors to which our attitudes are attached. To discover

Consider the appropriateness of some of these subjects with your instructor and your classmates. The answers you receive will tell you a lot about your classmates' attitudes.

Gun control	Divorce
Birth control	Interest rates
Abortion	Swearwords
Weapons	AIDS
Secret societies	Gambling
Sexual mores	Equal pay
Value of a college education	Gay rights
Marriage	Drugs and alcohol

the beliefs of our audience, we need to ask questions and to observe carefully. Some examples of beliefs are:

Hard work pays off.	The Bible is God's word.
Minority persons cannot get a fair trial.	Democrats are spenders.
No one is concerned about crime victims.	Women are discriminated against.
Taxes are too high.	War is natural.
Anyone can get rich.	The world gets better and better.
There is an afterlife.	

Values are the deeply rooted beliefs that govern our attitudes. Both beliefs and attitudes can be traced to some value that we hold. (Relationships between attitudes, beliefs, and values are illustrated in figure 12.1.) Learned from childhood through the family, the church, the school, and many other sources, values are often so much a foundation for the rest of what we believe and know they are not questioned. Sometimes, we remain unaware of our primary values until they clash. For example, a person might have an unquestioned belief that every individual has the right to be and do whatever he or she wishes—a basic value in individuality and freedom—until it comes to homosexuality. Sexual identity as an aspect of individual freedom may clash with the person's value for individuality. Some examples of values are:

Marriage	Beauty	Salvation
Love	Self-expression	Pleasure
Friendship	Law and order	Equality
Courage	Sexual freedom	Wisdom
Freedom	Work	Happiness
Individual rights	Privacy	Freedom
Patriotism	Family	Excitement
Religion	Competition	Peace

Figure 12.1
Relationships between attitudes, beliefs,
and values.

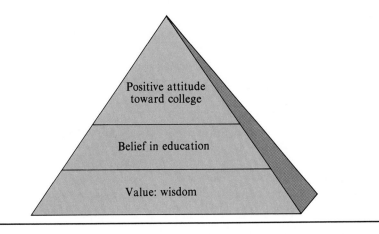

The public speaker must consider
differences in values among audience
members.

The values held by your audience and the order in which these values are ranked
can provide valuable clues about your audience's attitudes and beliefs. The speaker
who addresses an audience without knowing the values of audience members is taking
a risk that can be avoided by careful audience analysis.

Three Methods of Audience Analysis

Method 1: Observation

Effective public speakers must engage in active **observation** of the behavior and characteristics of their audience. An effective lawyer selects an audience by questioning prospective jurors. The lawyer asks questions designed to discover prejudice, negative and positive attitudes, beliefs, and values. Later, as the witnesses testify, the lawyer observes their verbal and nonverbal behavior and decides which arguments, evidence, and witnesses are influencing the jurors. Evangelists know, from their many sermons, which Bible verses, parables, and testimonials bring sinners to the altar. People who speak on behalf of business associations, unions, political parties, colleges, and the underprivileged have usually spent years watching others and learning which approaches, arguments, and evidence are most likely to be accepted by an audience.

You can learn to do the same thing in your speech class. For every speech you give, you might listen to twenty or twenty-five. You have a unique opportunity to discover your classmates' responses. Do they respond well to speakers who come on strong and authoritatively, or to speakers who talk to them like equals? Do they like speeches about work, leisure, getting ahead, or getting the most out of their education? Do they respond well to numbers and statistics, stories and examples, graphs and posters, or pictures and slides? As a listener in the classroom, you have a unique opportunity to observe your own and your classmates' responses to a variety of speakers.

You can also observe some demographic characteristics of your classmates: age, sex, race, and group affiliations (athletic jackets, fraternity pins). You can see how they respond to a speaker who keeps his or her eyes on the audience and how they respond to one who depends heavily on notes. You can observe whether you and the audience respond favorably when the speaker is deeply involved in the speech. Every speech you hear will, in some way, indicate the speaker's attitudes, beliefs, and values, and the response of the audience.

Even though your audience may be more captive than most, you have an advantage over most public speakers. How many public speakers have an opportunity to hear every one of their listeners give a speech? Instead of sitting back like a passive observer when you are a member of the audience, take advantage of the situation by listening actively, taking notes about the speaker's characteristics, and recording the audience's responses. You can analyze your audience continually during a round of speeches by careful observation.

Method 2: Inference

To draw an **inference** is to draw a tentative conclusion based on some evidence. We draw an inference when we see someone dressed in rags and tentatively conclude the person is poor. Our inferences are often accurate—we infer from his wedding band a man is married, from the children tugging at his sleeve he is a father, and from the woman holding his arm she is his wife. We are basing these inferences on thin data, but they are probably correct. Inferences may also be incorrect. The more evidence on which you base an inference, however, the more likely it is to be true.

You can base inferences on observed characteristics in your audience, on demographic information, and on questionnaires. You can also draw inferences either indirectly or directly. An indirect way to draw inferences is by observation. For instance, you might be in a school where male students do not hold hands with female students (an observation). You infer public displays of affection are discouraged by administrative edict, by custom, or by the students' own preference. You might also infer, from your limited information, that most of the students in this school have a negative attitude toward displays of affection, believe education comes before dating and courtship, believe a person should only marry once, and value families.

A more direct way to gather data on which to base inferences is to ask questions. You could, for example, ask either orally or in writing, to determine how many students in the class have part- or full-time jobs; how many are married, have families, have grown children; how many plan to become wealthy; whether they were raised in an urban or rural setting; and how many have strong religious ties. The answers to these questions would provide valuable information about your audience.

To illustrate how this method works, let us examine one question, one answer, and some inferences that could be drawn from the information. The question is: How many students in your speech class have full- or part-time jobs? The answer, perhaps, is two-thirds—thirteen out of twenty students—are employed. The inferences that can be drawn from this data include the facts the students are probably older than the usual eighteen- to twenty-one-year-olds who attend college, the students' or their parents' income is insufficient to allow them to attend school full-time, and the students are very ambitious or intelligent and can handle both jobs and classwork.

How can these inferences help you in preparing your speech? If the best-supported inference is that your classmates cannot afford to go to school full-time, then certain topics, lines of argument, examples, and approaches will be more attractive to them than others. Speeches on how to save money and how to manage time would probably be welcomed by this audience. On the other hand, speeches on yachting, owning your own racehorse, or taking a cruise might get you hooted out of the room.

Method 3: The Questionnaire

A more formal way to collect data on which you can base inferences is to ask your audience to fill out a **questionnaire** you or others have developed to determine demographic and attitudinal information. Demographic information can be easily gathered and summarized from questions similar to those that follow:

_____ 1. I am *(a)* a first-year student.
           (b) a sophomore.
           (c) a junior.
           (d) a senior.
_____ 2. I am *(a)* under 18.
           (b) 18–21 years old.
           (c) 21–27 years old.
           (d) over 27.
_____ 3. I am *(a)* single.
           (b) married.
           (c) divorced or separated.
           (d) widowed.
_____ 4. I have *(a)* no children.
           (b) one child.
           (c) two children.
           (d) more than two children.

The audience members do not have to identify themselves by name to provide this information. Keeping the questionnaires anonymous (no blank for the name) encourages honest answers and does not reduce the value of the information.

Attitudinal information can be collected in at least three ways. One way is to ask questions that place audience members in identifiable groups, as these questions do:

_____ 5. I *(a)* am active in campus organizations.
           (b) am not active in campus organizations.
_____ 6. I see myself as *(a)* conservative.
           (b) liberal.
           (c) independent.
_____ 7. I see myself as *(a)* strongly religious.
           (b) moderately religious.
           (c) unreligious.

A second method of gaining attitudinal information is to ask people to rank values such as hard work, higher education, high pay, and security. People's ranking of their values can suggest additional information about their attitudes and beliefs.

The third method of collecting data about people's attitudes involves listing word-concepts that reveal attitudes and then asking your respondents to assess their attitudes toward these specific issues. One way to do this involves using an attitudinal scale like the one in the activity above. The reactions to these and similar words or phrases can provide information that will help you to approach your audience successfully. For

Attitudinal Scale

Indicate, next to each word or phrase, your attitude toward it by writing in the appropriate number: (1) strongly favor, (2) mildly favor, (3) neutral, (4) mildly disfavor, or (5) strongly disfavor.

Compile data that indicate the attitudes within your class on one of these topics. What does this information tell you about how to approach your audience about this topic?

_____ a. Sexual freedom   _____ h. Alcohol consumption
_____ b. Born-again Christians   _____ i. Welfare
_____ c. Gun control   _____ j. Military
_____ d. Minority groups   _____ k. Recreational drugs
_____ e. Divorce   _____ l. Religion
_____ f. Government controls   _____ m. Individual rights
_____ g. Women's rights   _____ n. The U.S. President

example, if most persons in your audience are neutral to mildly favorable toward abortion, then your speech advocating abortion could be designed to raise their attitudes to mildly favorable to strongly favorable. If the responses are mixed, then you may have to work just to move your audience closer to a mildly disfavorable attitude or toward neutrality.

Adapting to the Audience

Analysis of an audience yields information about your listeners that enables you to adapt yourself and your verbal and nonverbal codes to that audience. A speech is not a message imposed on a collection of listeners; a speech is a compromise between a speaker and an audience designed to inform, entertain, inspire, teach, or persuade that audience. This compromise is based on your analysis of your audience.

An important question to consider in *adapting to an audience* is: How do I adapt to an audience without letting the audience dictate my position? The answer is you do not analyze the audience to discover your own position but to discover theirs—how much do they know about the topic? What approach is most likely to persuade persons with their attitudes, beliefs, and values? To find, for example, an audience is likely to be utterly opposed to your position is not an indication you should alter your position on the issue; instead, it is an indication that you may have to adopt a more gradual approach to changing them than you would have liked to use. Similarly, to discover the audience is even more ignorant of the topic than you thought only indicates you will have to provide more background or more elementary information than you had originally planned. In short, you have to adapt yourself, your verbal and nonverbal codes, your topic, your purpose, and your supporting materials to the particular group of people you will face in your speech.

The public speaker must adapt to the audience through both verbal and nonverbal codes.

Adapting Yourself

In previous chapters, you learned about self-concept and about how people in interpersonal contexts and small group settings adjust to each other. In public speaking, the speaker also has to adjust to information about the audience. Just as the senior who is preparing for a job interview adapts to the interviewer in dress, manner, and language, the public speaker prepares for an audience by adapting to its expectations. How you look, how you behave, and what you say should be carefully adjusted to an audience you have learned about through observation, experience, and analysis. As you will discover in chapter 13 on speaker credibility, there are ways in which you can help an audience to perceive you as a credible person.

Adapting Your Verbal and Nonverbal Codes

The language you employ in your speech, as well as your gestures, movements, and even facial expressions, should be adapted to your audience. Does your experience, observation, and analysis of the audience's attitudes indicate your language should be conversational, formal, cynical, or technical? Does your analysis indicate your listeners like numbers and statistics? Do your observations indicate you should pace the stage or stand still behind the lectern? Does your analysis indicate you should not use taboo words in your speech lest you alienate the group, or does the audience like a little lively language?

Adapting Your Topic

Public speakers should be permitted to speak about any topic that fits the assignment. In the classroom, at least, you should select a topic that relates to you. But, remember, you will be giving your speech to an audience of classmates. Therefore, the topic you select must be adapted to them. Audience analysis is a means of discovering the audience's position on the topic. From information based on observation, description, and inference, you have to decide how you are going to adapt your topic to this audience.

Audience analysis can tell you what challenges you face. If you want to speak in favor of nuclear energy and your audience analysis indicates the majority of your listeners are opposed to that position, you need not conclude the topic is inappropriate. But you may adapt to the members of your audience by starting with a position closer to theirs. Your initial step might be to make audience members feel less comfortable about their present position so they are prepared to hear your position.

Your analysis might indicate your audience already has considerable information about your topic. You then may have to adapt by locating information they do not have. For example, you may want to deliver an informative speech about the latest world crisis, but your analysis may indicate the audience is not only already interested but also it has sufficient information of the sort you planned to offer. You can adapt your topic by shifting to an area of the subject about which the audience is not so well informed: What is the background of the situation? What are the backgrounds of the personalities and the issues? What do the experts think will happen? What are the possible consequences?

Adapting Your Purpose

You should also adapt the purpose of your speech to your audience. Speech teachers often ask a student to state the purpose of a speech—what do you want your audience to know, to understand, or to do? It may help you to think of your speech as one part of a series of informative talks your audience will hear about your topic. They have probably heard something about the topic before and are likely to hear about the topic again. Your particular presentation is just one of the audience's exposures to the topic.

Still, your immediate purpose is linked to some larger goal. The goal is the end you have in mind. In the "Doonesbury" cartoon, Ms. Slade's immediate purpose is to announce her candidacy for the United States Congress; her larger goal is to be elected to office. Some examples of immediate purposes and long-range goals will illustrate the difference. In an informative speech, the immediate purposes and long-range goals might be:

Immediate Purpose	**Long-Range Goal**
To help the audience remember three reasons why we should adopt nuclear power plants as a source of energy	To increase the number of people who will read articles and books about nuclear power as an energy source
To teach the audience six expressions that are part of the street language used by urban blacks	To help the listeners understand and appreciate the language employed by some black students

DOONESBURY

Copyright, 1977, G. B. Trudeau/Distributed by Universal Press Syndicate

In a persuasive speech, the immediate purposes and the long-range goals might be:

Immediate Purpose

To have the audience remember three positive characteristics of the candidate for mayor

To reveal to the audience the nutritional value of two popular junk foods

Long-Range Goal

To have some of the audience members vote for the candidate at election time

To dissuade the listeners from eating junk food

The more specific your purpose, the better you will be able to determine whether you accomplished it. Also, you should employ audience analysis to help you discover whether your purpose is appropriate. Suppose half the people in your class are going into fields where knowledge of food and nutrition is important. They already know more than the average person about nutritional values. Consequently, it is probably not appropriate to deliver a speech about junk food. It may also not be wise to speak to a group of athletes about the importance of exercise. You should adapt your purpose to the audience by considering the level of their information, the novelty of the issue, and the other factors discussed in this chapter.

Adapting Your Supporting Materials

Your personal knowledge, your interviewing, and your library research should provide more material for your speech than you can use. Again, audience analysis helps you to select materials for this particular audience. Your analysis might reveal, for example, your classmates do not have much respect for authority figures. In that case, you might be wasting your time informing them of the surgeon general's opinion on smoking; your personal experience or the experience of some of your classmates might be more important to them than an expert's opinion. On the other hand, if your audience analysis reveals parents, teachers, pastors, and other authority figures are held in high regard, you may want to quote physicians, research scientists, counselors, and health-service personnel.

As a public speaker, you should always keep in mind the choices you make in selecting a topic, in choosing an immediate purpose, in determining a long-range goal, in organizing your speech, in selecting supporting materials, and even in creating visual aids are all *strategic choices*. All of these choices are made for the purpose of adapting the speaker and the subject to a particular audience. The larger your supply of supporting arguments, the better your chances of having effective arguments. The larger your supply of supporting materials, the better your chances of providing effective evidence, illustrations, and visual aids. Your choices are strategic in that they are purposeful. The purpose is to choose, from among the available alternatives, the ones that will best achieve your purpose with the particular audience.

Summary

This chapter has two purposes: to help you select a speech topic appropriate for you and for your audience and to help you analyze and adapt to your audience.

Brainstorming and personal inventories are two methods of topic selection. Involvement in, and knowledge of, a topic are two means of evaluating the topic's appropriateness for you. Once you have chosen a topic, it is important to narrow the topic to fit the subject, the audience, and the time allowed.

To discover if a topic is appropriate for your audience, you have to analyze your audience at four levels. Level 1 distinguishes between voluntary and captive audiences. Level 2 is demographic analysis, in which the characteristics of the audience members are evaluated. Level 3 analyzes the audience's interest in, and knowledge of, a topic. Level 4 determines the audience's attitudes, beliefs, and values.

Three methods of analyzing an audience are observation, inference, and the questionnaire. Observation involves actively watching your audience and learning from its behavior. Inference uses incomplete data to draw tentative conclusions about an audience, conclusions that may make the audience's response more predictable. The questionnaire can be used to garner demographic and attitudinal information about the audience.

Adapting to an audience after audience analysis requires you carefully adapt yourself, your verbal and nonverbal codes, your topic, your purpose, and your supporting materials to the particular group of people you will face in your speech.

Speaker Credibility

N *o one can make you feel inferior without your consent.*

Eleanor Roosevelt

Y *ou can't build a reputation on what you are going to do.*

Henry Ford

I *n the future everyone will be world-famous for 15 minutes.*

Andy Warhol

Objectives

1. Recognize the effects of fear on a speaker.
2. Understand how to reduce fear.
3. Describe the four dimensions of speaker credibility.
4. State some ways in which a speaker can influence his or her credibility.

Key Terms

communication
  apprehension
systematic
  desensitization
eye contact
vocalized pauses
credibility
competence
trustworthiness
dynamism
co-orientation
sleeper effect

In this chapter, we cover two areas of great concern to students of public speaking. The first area is fear. Many people are afraid of public speaking. In fact, at least one source reports it as the most common phobia in this country.[1] The person who does not feel some fear as a beginning public speaker is rare, so if you look forward to public speaking with some apprehension, you are normal. On the other hand, some students exhibit a more serious problem as they face the prospect of giving public speeches. Their problem is called speech or communication anxiety. This chapter explores the normal and more serious fears people have about public speaking and also looks at some of the ways of coping with this fear.

The second area of concern to students of public speaking is speaker credibility. Why will people listen to a particular speaker when he or she speaks? What do audiences perceive as the signs a speaker is believable? And can a speaker do anything to help an audience recognize he or she has earned the right to speak on a topic? These and other dimensions of credibility focus our attention on sharing ourselves with an audience.

Fear of Public Speaking

The fear of speaking in public goes by many different names. One of the early terms for this fear was "stage fright" because it was a fear most often seen in beginning actors or speakers who acted or delivered orations from the stage. Other names that have achieved popular usage over the years are "speech anxiety" and "**communication apprehension**." The latter term is, perhaps, the most useful of the current terms because it covers many kinds of communication fears in diverse situations: fear of talking on the telephone, fear of face-to-face conversations, fear of talking to authority figures or high-status individuals, fear of speaking to another individual, fear of speaking in a small group, and fear of speaking to an audience, whether small or large.

Why should you know about communication apprehension? Even the question is controversial. Some teachers of public speaking feel that talking about communication apprehension—even in a textbook—is questionable because students who read about the fear of public speaking may see themselves as more apprehensive than those who do not know about it. In earlier editions of this book, little was discussed about communication apprehension, and nothing was said about how it relates to public speaking. As more and more teachers find out about communication apprehension, however, more and more of them want the subject discussed in the text.

There are at least two reasons why you should know about communication apprehension. The first is you need to be able to see the difference between the normal fear most people experience before they give a speech and high communication apprehension, which is a more serious problem. The second reason is people who are highly apprehensive about communication should receive special treatment for their problem, lest they spend a lifetime handicapped in many ways by their fear.

Let us look first at the scope, the symptoms, and the effects of high communication apprehension. Then we examine some solutions or remedies to this malady.[2]

High Communication Apprehension

About one out of every five persons is communication apprehensive, that is, 20 percent of all college students. Fortunately, that statistic means that four out of every five students, or between 80 and 90 percent, are not apprehensive. Communication apprehensive people may not appear apprehensive unless they are engaging in a particular type of communication. High communication apprehension seems unrelated to anxiety and intelligence. They may show no overt signs of anxiety in activities like playing football, studying, eating, watching television, or walking to class. However, the high communication apprehensive (HCA) has such strong negative feelings about communicating with other people that he or she typically avoids communication or exhibits considerable fear when communicating. The scope of the communication apprehension problem may not appear large, but millions of people suffer from the fear of communicating.

One symptom of communication apprehension is the HCA tries to avoid communication situations. Pearson and Yoder conducted a study to find out what would happen if HCA students had a choice of an interpersonal communication course or a public speaking course. They found HCA students overwhelmingly chose the interpersonal communication course. The researchers suspected students perceived the public speaking course as much more threatening than the interpersonal communication course.[3] Similarly, in small group communication, HCA students tend to be nonparticipants in the class or to repeatedly register for, and drop, the class. HCA students try to avoid participating in the kind of communication that arouses their fears.

What are some other choices characteristic of HCA people? They will choose rooms away from other people at the ends of halls in dormitories or housing away from busy streets and playgrounds in a housing development. HCA people will sit away from others or in places in which leadership is not expected (along the side of the table, far from the end). When HCA persons do find themselves in a communication situation, they talk less, show less interest in the topic, take fewer risks, and say less about themselves than their classmates do. HCA people are difficult to get to know. Even when they do find themselves in a situation where communication is unavoidable, they discourage talk with disinterest and silence.

The effects of high communication apprehension can be serious. HCA persons are not perceived as leaders. They are seen as less extroverted, less sociable, and less competent than their peers. They are not perceived as desirable partners for courtship or marriage. They are viewed as less composed, less attractive socially, and less task-attractive. In some cases, they are even seen as less physically attractive. Because they do not communicate much and seem so uneasy when they do, HCA people are perceived negatively by others. They therefore tend to do poorly in interviews and tend not to get the same quality of jobs as nonapprehensive people do. The consequences of being a HCA seem serious enough to encourage us to look next at solutions.

One remedy for high communication apprehension is professional help. The negative feelings about communication in the HCA person have often been developing since childhood. They do not disappear easily. Many schools and colleges have psychologists and counselors who have had professional training in reducing students' fears about speaking in public. If you think you are among the small minority of people who have unusually high fear in a public speaking situation, then you may want to talk to your speech teacher about any services available to you.

Another remedy for fear of public speaking is called **systematic desensitization.** Systematic desensitization is the repeated exposure to small doses of whatever makes one apprehensive in a situation that is designed to reduce or eradicate that fear. A public speaking student might be asked over a number of weeks to think of what is frightening (for example, going to the front of the room to speak) and then to immediately follow the frightening thought with thoughts that please. This process repeated over time tends to diminish a person's anxiety about communicating. Some schools and colleges have taped messages using this method that a student can use alone. Other places have this method built into their basic speech communication course for any students with an unusually high fear of public speaking. Finally, some speech communication professors are trained in this technique, as are many persons in counseling.

So far, this section on fear of public speaking has concentrated on the individual with extreme fear. What about the vast majority of persons who have a normal fear of public speaking? What are the signs of normal fear, and what can you do about reducing this normal fear—or even getting it to work for you instead of against you?

Normal Communication Apprehension

Most human beings feel fear when they speak in public. New teachers march into their first classes armed with twelve hours worth of material—just to be sure they will have plenty to say in their one-hour class. Experienced speakers feel fear when they face audiences that are new to them. Nearly all of the students in a public speaking class feel the classic symptoms of fear when they think about giving their speeches and when they deliver them.

What are the classic symptoms of communication apprehension for the public speaker? One of the authors of this book has given hundreds of speeches but still cannot sleep well the night before an important speech—one sign of anxiety or fear. Another common symptom is worry: you can't seem to get the speech out of your mind, you keep thinking about what giving the speech is going to be like, and you keep feeling inadequate for the task. When you actually give the speech, the common symptoms of fear are shaking—usually the hands, knees, and voice; dryness of the mouth—often called cottonmouth; and wetness—usually on the palms of the hands. One wit noted public speakers suffer so often from dryness of the mouth and wetness of the palms that they should stick their hands in their mouth. But for the public speaker, fear is no laughing matter. Let us turn from what the normal speaker *feels* to how the normal speaker *behaves* when afraid.

The speaker who is afraid—even with normal fear—tends to avoid **eye contact,** speak softly, utter **vocalized pauses,** ("Well," "You know," "Mmmmm"), speak too slowly or too quickly, not know what to do with hands or feet, stand as far away from the audience as possible, and place as many obstacles as possible between the speaker and the audience (distance, lecterns, notes). The speaker who is overcoming fear looks at the audience; speaks so all can hear easily; avoids vocalized pauses; speaks at a normal rate; moves body, arms, and feet in ways that do not appear awkward; stands at the usual distance from the audience; and uses the lectern to hold notes instead of as a hiding place.

The research on audience responses to public speakers indicates the importance of overcoming fear of public speaking for improved effectiveness. For example, one study shows that speakers who look at their audience are judged as credible and are seen as more persuasive than those who do not.[4] Another study shows apprehensive speakers who employ more vocalized pauses or hesitations are less persuasive.[5] Finally, speakers who appear unusually slow or powerless are perceived as less knowledgeable about the topic and, therefore, as less credible.[6]

Now that you understand the fear of public speaking and the way a speaker acts when afraid, you need to focus on the more positive topic of what to do about reducing fear.

Reducing the Fear of Public Speaking

The first thing you need if you expect to overcome your fear of public speaking is a strong desire to overcome it. You need incentive, motivation, and determination. The Dale Carnegie organization has taught public speaking skills to millions of adults who did not believe in the merits of public speaking until they got out of school. An executive from the Dale Carnegie organization once admitted, before he took the Dale Carnegie course, he was so afraid of public speaking, and so outraged that his fear limited his life in so many ways, he decided to overcome his fear by sheer determination. Ironically, the man who was so afraid of public speaking ended up devoting his life to teaching others how to become effective public speakers.

Fortunately, there are some other things besides sheer determination you can do to help overcome normal fears of public speaking. You can:

1. *Know your topic.* Know more than most of your audience about the topic, find information and interview others about the topic, and organize your speech into the time allowed.
2. *Know your audience.* Know who the students are in your audience, what they are majoring in, how much education they have had, what they are interested in, and how they are likely to respond to your topic.
3. *Know yourself.* If you feel good about yourself—your intelligence, talents, and competence—then you will be more secure and less afraid.
4. *Know your speech.* Practice your speech so you know the ideas, the order in which they appear, and the main messages you want to communicate to the audience.
5. *Focus on communication, not yourself.* If you have selected a topic important to you and your audience and you see your purpose as successfully communicating that message to the audience, then you will not be thinking about your hands, your mouth, or your knees—and neither will your audience.
6. *Recognize your value and uniqueness.* You are the only one who can share what you have with audience members—they can not get it anywhere else.

Anxiety about public speaking can be reduced if you have a strong desire to overcome the fear.

Your instructor may be able to suggest some additional ideas for reducing your anxiety about public speaking, and you may be able to think of some ideas for reducing fear yourself. When some students in a beginning public speaking class were asked what they did to reduce their fears, they mentioned the following ideas:

1. Walk to the podium calmly and confidently because acting confident and poised can make you feel confident and poised.
2. Do not start talking until you feel comfortable up in front. Look at the people in your audience before you start talking to them, just as you would in a conversation.
3. Focus on the friendly faces in the audience—the people who nod affirmatively, smile, and look friendly and attentive—they will make you feel good about yourself and your speech.
4. Have your introduction, main points, and conclusion clear in your head and practiced. The examples and supporting materials come to mind easily when the important items are remembered.

Perhaps you will not find this information startling, but the best cure for normal fear of public speaking is exactly what you are doing: take a course in which you are invited to deliver a number of supervised public speeches to an audience that is sympathetic because audience members have to speak too. In other words, the speech classroom is a laboratory in which you can work systematically to reduce your fears. Your instructor's comments and those of your classmates can help you to discover your strengths and weaknesses. Repeated experiences in front of an audience tend to reduce fear and to permit the learning of communication skills that have application both inside and outside the classroom. In short, you are now in the process of reducing your normal fear of public speaking.

Fear of public speaking is a burden for the few who suffer from high communication apprehension. For most of us, however, the fear can be reduced to levels where it helps, rather than hinders. Ask anybody who has to deliver the same lecture three times a day. Often, the second lecture is the best because of the confidence borne of practice. The third lecture is usually the worst because there is so little fear left that delivering the lecture becomes a bit boring, even to the speaker.

You *can* learn to control and reduce your fear of public speaking. You can look your audience members in the eye, move and gesture with purpose, speak conversationally but with strength, and focus on the reason for your speech: to communicate your message to your audience.

Source Credibility

More than twenty-three hundred years ago, Aristotle noted a speaker's "character may almost be called the most effective means of persuasion he possesses."[7] Scholars have continued to study the importance of the source or speaker since that time because they correctly believed who says something determines who will listen.

In the public speaking classroom, you are the source of the message. You need to be concerned about how the audience will perceive you. You may feel you do not have the same credibility as a high public official, a great authority on some topic, or an expert in some narrow field. That may be so. However, you can still be a very credible source to your classmates, fellow workers, or friends. A line supervisor may be credible to those who work for her; a boss may be credible to his employees; and a physician may be credible to her patients. But the same line supervisor may not be credible in her church; the boss may not be credible at his country club; and the physician may find she cannot even get patients to quit smoking. So who is credible?

To understand the concept of source **credibility,** you must first recognize it is not something a speaker possesses, like a suit of clothes. Instead, the audience determines credibility; the audience sees a speaker as credible or not. "Credibility," like beauty, "is in the eye of the beholder."[8] A speaker's credibility depends in part on who the speaker is, in part on the subject being discussed, in part on the situation, and in part on the audience. You might be highly credible to an audience about your major, your adventures, or your hobbies, but you might be low in credibility when you speak on nuclear fission, water conservation, or economics. You might be more credible in some situations than in others—you might be highly credible as a student who can achieve high grades and very low in credibility as a person who can tell others how to repair a car. Similarly, you might be more credible to some audiences than you are to others— your classmates might find you credible and the local Teamsters Union might not. Some people are like Woodstock in the "Peanuts" cartoon; they think a certain characteristic will give them credibility. The concept of credibility is much more complex.

How do we gain credibility with an audience? The answer is public speakers *earn* the right to speak. They earn the right through their lives, their experiences, and their accomplishments. As one person observed, "Before you express yourself, you need a self worth expressing." You may have earned the right to speak on a number of subjects. Have you worked in a fast-food restaurant? You may have earned the right to comment on the quality of fast food and service. Have you raised children? You may have earned the right to speak on the problems and pleasures of family life. Have you gone without work for a period of time? You may have earned the right to give a firsthand account of what it is like to live without your usual income. Think about it. What have you experienced, learned, or lived through that has earned you the right to speak?

Four Aspects of Credibility

What do audience members perceive that gives them the idea a speaker is credible? If credibility is based on judgments by individuals in the audience, then what is the basis for those judgments? On what will your classmates be rating you when they judge your credibility? According to recent studies, four of the most important aspects of credibility are competence, trustworthiness, dynamism, and co-orientation.[9]

Competence

The first aspect of credibility is **competence.** A speaker who is perceived as competent is perceived as qualified, trained, experienced, authoritative, expert, reliable, informed, or knowledgeable. A speaker does not have to live up to all of these adjectives; any one, or a few, might make the speaker credible. The machinist who displays his metal-work in a speech about junk sculpture as art is as credible as the biblical scholar who is demonstrating her ability to interpret scripture. They have different bases for their competence, but both can demonstrate competence or expertise in their own areas of specialization.

Your own competence as a speaker is conveyed by your words, your visual aids, and your air of authority. What can you build into your speech that will help the audience to see and understand the basis for your air of authority? What experience have you had that is related to the subject? What special training or knowledge do you have? How can you suggest to your audience you have earned the right to speak about this subject? The most obvious way is to tell the audience the basis of your authority or expertise, but a creative speaker can think of dozens of ways to hint, and suggest, competence without being explicit, without seeming condescending, and without lying.

A speaker also signals competence by knowing the substance of the speech so well the speech is delivered without reading from notecards, without unplanned or vocalized pauses, and without mispronounced words. The speaker who knows the technical language in a specialized field and who can define the terms for the audience is signaling competence. The speaker who can translate complex ideas into language the audience can understand, who can find ways to illustrate ideas in ways the audience can comprehend, and who is familiar with people who know about the subject and with books and articles about the subject are all signaling competence to the audience.

Trustworthiness

The second aspect of credibility is **trustworthiness.** How honest, fair, sincere, friendly, honorable, and kind does the audience find the speaker? These descriptors are also earned. We judge a person's honesty both by past behavior and present estimates. Your classmates will judge your trustworthiness when you speak in front of them. How do you decide whether or not other speakers in your class are responsible, sincere, dependable, or just? What can you do to help your audience perceive you are trustworthy?

The speaker who uses facial expression, gestures, movements, and voice to make a point exhibits dynamism.

You may have to reveal to your audience why you are trustworthy. Have you held jobs that demanded honesty and responsibility? Have you been a cashier, a bank teller, or a supervisor? Have you given up anything to demonstrate you are sincere? The person who pays her own way through college ordinarily has to be very sincere about education and the person who chooses a lower-paying job because he feels a sense of public service is displaying sincerity about the job. Being respectful of others' points of view can be a sign of your fairness, and being considerate of other people can be a sign of your kindness and friendliness. What can you say about yourself that will show your trustworthiness?

Dynamism

The third aspect of credibility is **dynamism**—the extent to which an audience perceives the speaker as bold, energetic, and assertive. Audiences value behavior described by these adjectives. Perhaps when we consider their opposites—timid, tired, and meek— we can see why dynamism is attractive. People who exude energy and show the spirit of their convictions impress others. Watch the evangelists and ministers on Sunday-morning television and note how dynamic they look and sound. You can learn to do the same. Evidence indicates the audience's perception of your dynamic qualities will enhance your credibility.

Dynamism is exhibited mainly by voice, movement, facial expression, and gesture. The person who speaks forcefully, rapidly, and with considerable vocal variety; the speaker who moves toward the audience, back behind the lectern, and over to the visual aid; and the speaker who employs facial expression and gestures to make a point are all exhibiting dynamism. What can you do with your voice, movement, facial expressions, and gestures to show the audience you are a dynamic speaker?

Co-orientation

Co-orientation refers to the sharing of values, beliefs, attitudes, and interests.[10] It is not a mask of agreement worn to fool the audience. Instead, co-orientation is telling the audience explicitly how you agree with them. This kind of information sharing is not just demographic—sharing similarities about hometowns, family sizes, and so on—but is also ideological. That is, the speaker tells the audience which ideas he or she has in common with the audience. An informative speech may require less co-orientation; a persuasive speech requires the speaker go beyond areas of complete agreement into areas where the speaker is trying to make a case for acceptance of his or her point of view on the issue.

Examples of student speeches the authors have heard in which the speaker employed co-orientation include speeches about student housing, dormitory food, and honors societies. The student who spoke about student housing was complaining about the use of three-person rooms in the dormitories. He knew the majority of the students in the class had suffered through a year or two of these same living conditions, and he established co-orientation by simply recounting some of his experiences in trying to study, entertain, and sleep in a three-person room. The student who spoke about the low quality of dormitory food knew most of the audience members had tasted it. She brought in a tray of dormitory food to remind them and to establish co-orientation. The student who spoke about honors societies was in an honors section full of students who had received invitations to join various honors societies. Unfortunately, most of them met only once, and each honorary cost a high fee to join. The speaker established co-orientation by recounting a common experience of receiving such letters and of being uncertain whether to join. What can you do to establish co-orientation with your audience?

A student reading the long list of adjectives describing the four aspects of credibility might feel establishing credibility is beyond the capability of the beginning speaker. You do not have to fit all of the adjectives or even to score well on all of the aspects. Many highly credible speakers are not dynamic; in fact, all they may possess is their specialized knowledge. Some speakers may be thought to be credible simply because they exude sincerity, even though they lack knowledge and expertise and are not dynamic.

You do not have to excel in all four aspects of source credibility to be an effective speaker, but competence, trustworthiness, dynamism, and co-orientation are the grounds on which your audience is likely to evaluate your credibility so you should take whatever steps you can to ensure you come across as a credible source.

To continue our examination of source credibility, we turn next to some research about increasing credibility.

Research Findings about Increasing Credibility

Credibility can be achieved before, during, or after a public speech. A speaker can have a reputation before arriving at a hall; that judgment can be altered during the presentation; and the evaluation can change again, long after the speech has ended. You might think that some speakers are great before you hear them. Their dull presentation reduces their credibility. Then, in the weeks after the speech, your evaluation of such speakers might rise again because you discover their message has given you new hope. In other words, credibility is not static—it is always in flux, always changing, always alterable.

Nor is credibility, we should remind you, something a speaker always possesses. It depends on topics, audiences, and situations. That makes the concept of source credibility a challenging one to public speakers. We intend these comments about the changing nature of credibility as a caution in interpreting the research findings that follow.

Reminding the Audience of Your Credibility

Most of the studies that try to measure the effect of a speaker's message on an audience indicate highly credible speakers change opinions more than speakers whose credibility is poor.[11] At least when the speech is delivered, a person perceived as credible can seek more changes of opinions and achieve more changes.[12]

However, as time passes, an interesting phenomenon occurs. Apparently, the source of the speech and the message become separated in the listener's mind— "I don't remember who said this, but. . . ." The result of this separation of source and message is that the message loses impact as audience members later forget they heard it from a highly credible speaker. The speaker with little credibility benefits from the opposite effect. As time passes, the audience forgets the source of the information, and the message gains impact. In one study, three or four weeks after a speech, a highly credible speaker and one with little credibility had pulled about even with respect to their ability to change opinions.

Gains made by the less credible speaker are due to the **sleeper effect.**[13] When we say a film or a television show is a "sleeper," we mean it did much better than anyone ever anticipated. The sleeper effect in source credibility is similar. You would not expect a speaker low in credibility to achieve much attitude change, but after time has passed, and after the listener has separated the speaker from the message, the message from the low credibility source may have as much impact as the message from the highly credible speaker.

The lesson for the public speaker is that the effect of credibility may be short-lived. In most speech classes, several weeks or more may elapse between your presentations. In between, your classmates are exposed to other speakers and speeches. They need reminders of your credibility. We like to think audiences remember us and our speeches, but, in fact, it is sometimes difficult for students to remember a speech they heard the day before yesterday. Intelligent speakers remind the audience of their credibility. Remind your audience about your major subject, your special interest in the topic, your special knowledge, or your special experience. Credibility decays over time and must be renewed if you want to have the maximum effect on your audience.

Establishing Common Ground with the Audience

To establish common ground with an audience is to emphasize what you share with the audience—in the present situation, in your experience, in your ideas, or in your behavior. You can establish common ground by sharing the situation you and your classmates have in common—you all have speeches to give and exams to take. You can share ideological common ground—values, beliefs, or ideas. One way to earn an audience's trust is to point out some of the important ways you are like the audience. Revealing shared attitudes, beliefs, and values establishes co-orientation. You can address members of your audience as fellow students (common ground) or as people who believe grades are destructive to learning or bookstore prices are too high (co-orientation). The use of the pronoun *we* tends to help audience members to see themselves as having commonality with the speaker.

Some studies indicate areas of agreement should be established early in a speech for maximum effect; others say *when* commonality is established is not important, as long as it is established sometime during the speech. All of the studies agree speakers can enhance their relationship with the audience by talking about something they have in common with the audience. Some degree of commonality with voluntary audiences may be assumed, but it is necessary to be explicit to captive audiences.

Other Research-Based Findings about Credibility

The following generalizations and conclusions are based on a summary of nearly thirty years of credibility studies:[14]

The introduction of a speaker by another person can increase the speaker's credibility. The credibility of the person making the introduction is as important to the speaker's credibility as what is said in that introduction. A close friend introducing you can reveal information that could enhance or harm your status. To be safe, the speaker should always provide the introducer with information that could potentially increase credibility by showing the speaker's competence, trustworthiness, dynamism, or co-orientation. Your introducer can make evaluative statements about you that might sound self-serving from your own mouth. Your credibility may also be enhanced if the audience believes your introducer is highly credible.

The way *you are identified by the person introducing you also can affect your credibility.* Students who are identified as graduate students are thought to be more competent than undergraduates. Graduate students are also seen as more fair-minded, likeable, and sincere.[15] It is possible, therefore, that your identification as a sophomore, junior, or senior might contribute to your credibility with a student audience.

The perceived status of a speaker can make a difference in credibility. Speakers of high status are consistently rated as more credible than speakers of low status. Even more striking was the finding that listeners judged credibility and status during the first ten or fifteen seconds of the speech.[16] The probable explanation of this finding is the audience receives a barrage of cues about the speaker at the very beginning of the speech: they see how the speaker is dressed; they see and make judgments about the speaker's appearance; they hear the speaker's voice; and they get an initial impression of the speaker's confidence, competence, trustworthiness, and dynamism.

The organization of your speech can affect your credibility. Students who listen to a disorganized speech think less of a speaker after the speech than they did before the speech.[17] This judgment by the audience may be based on its expectations—in the speech classroom, the students expect good organization, and when they perceive a speech as poorly organized, they lower their evaluation of the speaker. The lesson from this study is relatively clear. The classroom speaker should strive for sound organization, lest he or she lose credibility even while speaking.

Other interesting findings about credibility are related to delivery, fluency, and repetition. *A speaker whose delivery is considered effective, whose use of voice, movement, and gesture is effective, can become more credible during a speech.*[18] A payoff exists for the student who practices a speech and who learns to be comfortable enough in front of an audience to appear natural, confident, and competent. Nonfluencies—breaks in the smooth and fluid delivery of the speech—are judged negatively. Vocalized pauses, such as *mmh,* and *ahh* are nonfluencies. Another kind of nonfluency is the repetitive use of certain words and phrases, such as *well, like,* and *you know* at every transition. These nonfluencies decrease the audience's ratings of competence and dynamism but do not affect the speaker's trustworthiness.[19]

The effective speaker is constantly aware of his or her personal impact on the speech and on the audience. We have examined four aspects of credibility: competence, trustworthiness, dynamism, and co-orientation. We have reviewed the results of studies that indicate a highly credible speaker has an advantage at the time of the speech, establishing common ground can help your speech, the introduction of a speaker can help or harm credibility; the speaker's status, sincerity, and organization can influence credibility; and effective delivery can enhance credibility. The credibility of your sources, or the value of the materials you find to support what you say in a speech, also affects the success of your speeches, and we explore this area in detail in the next chapter.

Strategies for Improving Your Credibility: A Checklist

A checklist you can use to make sure you have considered the possible ways to improve your credibility follows. Place a check in the blank on the right to indicate you have considered the implications of the statement.

1. Have you selected a topic in which you are involved, so you can be perceived as sincere, responsible, reputable, and trustworthy? _____

2. Have you considered the relationship between your apparent competence and your credibility by building into your speech cues that indicate your experience, training, skill, and expertise in the subject? _____

3. Have you considered the relationship between your apparent trustworthiness and your credibility by building trust through concern for your audience's welfare, through objective consideration of your audience's needs, through friendly rapport, and through responsible and honest handling of the speech content? _____

4. Have you selected a means of delivery and content that will help the audience to see you as dynamic—energetic, strong, empathic, and assertive? _____

5. Are you indicating in your speech one or more ideas, beliefs, attitudes, or characteristics you hold in common with most of the people in your audience? _____

6. Can you ask your instructor or someone else who introduces you to say something praiseworthy about you or your qualifications? _____

7. Have you reminded your audience, descriptively, of your qualifications to speak on the subject? _____

8. Are you dressed appropriately for this audience? _____

9. Given the classroom situation, your class audience, and the topic you have selected, are you likely to be perceived as competent, trustworthy, dynamic, and interested in this audience's well-being? _____

10. Have you carefully pointed out how your topic is related to the audience, selected appropriate supporting materials, organized the content, and found a way to deliver your speech that will help your audience to learn and to retain what you say? _____

Summary

This chapter opened with a consideration of communication apprehension, the fear of communicating with others. The 10 to 20 percent of the population who suffer from high communication apprehension show their fear by avoiding communication with others. They tend to live away from other people, to sit away from other people, and to speak less and to disclose less than others. They also tend to be judged negatively by others. In the public speaking situation, people suffering from high communication apprehension exhibit the signs of fear that make them seem ineffective as speakers: they look at the floor, hesitate, pause unexpectedly, and appear powerless and slow. Remedies for high communication apprehension include professional help and systematic desensitization.

Fortunately, most people have only normal anxiety about public speaking and can overcome their fear through self-determination and by knowing their topic; knowing their audience; knowing themselves; knowing their speech; focusing on communication, not themselves; and recognizing their value and uniqueness.

This chapter also explored the concept of source credibility by examining what people seek in a speaker and how they judge a speaker's worthiness. The four dimensions of source credibility are competency, trustworthiness, dynamism, and co-orientation. High credibility speakers have an initial advantage in changing audience opinion. To be an effective speaker, you should establish common ground with the audience. As a speaker, your credibility can be influenced by who introduces you and how you are introduced. A speaker's status, organization, and delivery also can influence credibility.

Finding Information

*S*ome books are to be tasted, others to be
swallowed, and some few to be chewed
and digested . . .

Francis Bacon

*N*othing you cannot spell will ever work.

Will Rogers

*K*nowledge is the only instrument of
production that is not subject to
diminishing returns.

J. M. Clark

Objectives

1. Seek information for your speech in appropriate places.
2. Cite your information by crediting your source.
3. Interview another person for information on your topic.
4. Find appropriate supporting materials to support, substantiate, and clarify your position.
5. Use evidence as proof in your speech.

Key Terms

plagiarism
supporting
  materials
examples
surveys
testimonial
  evidence
statistics
mean or average
median

mode
percentage
range
raw numbers
analogies
explanations
definitions
evidence
proof

A college sophomore had agreed to teach medieval history to a summer class of high school ninth- and tenth-graders. The college student was smart enough to know these teenagers would be bored by his lectures on the subject. Instead of telling them about people in the Middle Ages, he gave them a task. They had to answer questions: What would one find in the home of a serf? Could a third daughter of a titled father marry the son of a wealthy but untitled merchant? What was it like in a monastery? If you owned a castle, how many people would it take to operate it? The college student who taught the class told his students a few things about medieval times, but mainly he supplied them with books that provided answers to their questions. The students learned more about history by answering their questions than they would have learned in a series of lectures. Why? Because they had interesting questions and a way to find answers to those questions.

In your public speaking class, you are in a similar situation. The students mentioned in the previous paragraph wanted to learn history in an interesting way. You want to learn public speaking, but you want to learn it in an interesting way. The important ingredients missing for you, but provided to the students described in the previous paragraph, are the interesting questions. You have to find some interesting questions to pursue. You have to find a topic that invites questions, the answers to which will be interesting to you and to your classmates.

A speech on dogs becomes, "Which breed is best for an apartment-dwelling college student on a limited income?" A speech on the economy becomes, "What is the difference between recession and depression?" And a speech on cars becomes, "What do you need to know about buying a used car?" In each case, the topic becomes an interesting question you can pursue by exploring your own experience; reading papers, magazines, and books; watching films, television, or videotapes; or talking to other people. The teacher in the earlier example made medieval history interesting to his students; you can make your own speech interesting to yourself and to your audience by picking a topic about which you can ask interesting questions.

This chapter is about how to answer your questions. How do you find information? Where do you look for it? To whom can you speak about your topic? Once found, how do you use information in your speech? In this chapter, we take you from your initial question to the places where the answers wait for your discovery. The task of finding information is exciting if you select something exciting to explore. Now we turn to the places where you should seek information for your speech.

Information Sources

Information sources for your speech include your personal experiences, written and visual resources, and other people. Let us look at each of these areas in turn.

Personal Experiences

The first place you should look for materials for the content of your speech is yourself. Your personal experience is something you can talk about with some authority. One student had been a "headhunter," a person who tries to find employees for employers

ANIMAL CRACKERS

Reprinted by permission: Tribune Media Services, Inc.

who are willing to pay a premium for specific kinds of employees. This student gave a speech from his personal experience concerning what employers particularly value in employees. Another student had a brother who was retarded and who died at age nine. She gave a speech about retarded individuals and the way they are treated in our society. Your special causes, your jobs, and even your family can provide you with firsthand information you can use in your speech.

You should not, however, use your personal experience uncritically. Important questions should be asked about personal experience before you employ it in your speech. Is your experience typical? If you are among the very few who had an unfortunate experience with a local bank, you should think carefully before you generalize and assume that many people have been treated similarly. You can ask some questions about your personal experience that will help you to evaluate it as evidence—data on which proof may be based—of what you plan to say in your speech:

1. Was your experience typical?
2. Was your experience so typical it will be boring?
3. Was your experience so atypical it was a chance occurrence?
4. Was your experience one this audience will appreciate or from which this audience can learn a lesson?
5. Does your experience really constitute proof or evidence of anything?

Not all personal experiences can be shared with an audience. Only a limited number of them can really be used as evidence or proof.

Another question about your experience is whether it was firsthand or the experience of someone else. If the information is not firsthand, it is usually questionable. It may have been distorted in transmission. The old game of passing a message down a line of people illustrates the problem of getting a message intact from person to person. You might find yourself passing along a falsehood to your audience unless the experience is your own.

Written and visual resources aid in
preparing a speech.

Written and Visual Resources

A second place you can look for substance for your speech is in written and visual resources. Perhaps the quickest and most efficient way to find information in written sources is to go to the *Reader's Guide to Periodical Literature*. This multivolume work lists articles that have appeared in magazines. You can look up a topic like *cocaine* and find a listing of all the articles that recently have appeared in popular magazines on the subject. If you want to explore the topic further, you can look up "key words" in the *Reader's Guide* that will lead you to still other sources. For example, you could explore the subject of cocaine further by looking up key words like *drugs, law enforcement, international regulation, medicine,* and *crime.* It would be difficult to think of a topic not covered in the popular literature. As a student of public speaking, you should learn how to use the *Reader's Guide* to help you learn more about your topic.

The following are some additional sources frequently used by speech students for finding information:

1. Frequently used yearbooks include the *World Almanac,* the *Book of Facts, Facts on File,* and the *Statistical Abstract of the United States.* These compendia contain facts and figures about a wide variety of subjects, from population to yearly coal production. The encyclopedias contain short bibliographies and background material about many topics. Among the popular encyclopedias are the *Encyclopedia Americana* and the *Encyclopedia Britannica.*

2. Sourcebooks for examples, literary allusions, and quotations include Bartlett's *Familiar Quotations,* George Seldes' *The Great Quotations,* and Arthur Richmond's *Modern Quotations for Ready Reference.*

3. Biographies of famous persons can be found in *Who's Who in America, Current Biography,* and the *Dictionary of American Biography* (deceased Americans).

4. Newspaper files are helpful, especially if your college has the *New York Times,* one of the few newspapers that has an index. Newspapers tend to be most useful for recent information.

5. Professional journals, which are also indexed, are collected by many libraries. You can find articles about speech, communication, psychology, sociology, economics, chemistry, mathematics, and many other subjects.

6. Many modern libraries own volumes of material on microfilm. Media resource centers on campuses have lists of slides, films, and other visual materials.

7. The reference librarian is an expert at helping others to locate materials.

You can also use information from television news and documentaries, films, and records. An effective public speaker becomes like a skilled debater—he or she learns rapidly where to find good supporting materials.

Still another resource important to the public speaker is the *card catalog.* The card catalog lists every book in the library by author, title, and subject. The books are usually cross-indexed so you can find them by simply looking at the cards collected under a particular subject heading. If you pick a subject in which you are involved and to which you are committed, you should not have to read a large number of books on the subject. On the other hand, if the subject is truly of interest to you, you may *want* to read some of the books. Usually, it is sufficient to check out several of the best books on the topic and to read them selectively for information most usable to you in your speech. The kind of information selected is usually quotations and evidence or proof that supports your position on the issue. As in interviewing, it is important to take good notes, to record the information accurately and precisely, and to credit the author of the book in your speech when you deliver it. An entry like the one in figure 14.1 on an index card or a separate sheet of paper usually helps. Be sure to include author, title, publisher, place of publication, date of publication, and page reference, as well as the information.

In your search for information you can use in your speech, you might also want to examine the written resources listed in figure 14.2. The indices will lead you to other sources, the dictionaries and encyclopedias will provide definitions and explanations, and the yearbooks will provide facts and statistics.

The Importance of Citing Sources

When you write an outline, compose a manuscript speech, or deliver a speech, you are expected to indicate where you got your information. Two reasons for this expectation are a rule of scholarship dictates any ideas that are not your own must be credited to the person whose ideas they are and writers and speakers must be able to verify what they say. What if a speaker claims chocolate contains an addictive drug. Your first

Figure 14.1
Index card: A speaker's notes from a book.

```
        Alcoholism: Its Effect on Women and Children


Ann Kramer, ed., Woman's Body: An Owner's Manual (New York:

Simon & Schuster, 1981), p. 98.

According to this source, 17 percent of babies born to

alcoholic mothers die within a week; only 2 percent of

babies born to nonalcoholic mothers die during the first

week after birth. P. 98.

This source also says: "At the age of seven, 44 percent of

the children born to alcoholic mothers had an IQ of seventy

or under." P. 98.
```

response might be, "Who says?" The speaker might reveal a source. You might come up with ten other sources who disagree. The notion of citing sources, of crediting others with ideas that originated with them, and of challenging sources and the credibility of authors is an important aspect of speech composition, delivery, and criticism.

Lest we appear to understate the importance of citing sources in written and spoken discourse, we should point out neglecting to cite sources is an offense called **plagiarism,** a crime is punishable in many colleges and universities by measures as serious as expulsion. Outside the classroom, plagiarism can result in disgrace, fines, and even jail. Do not forget to reveal where you got your information: There is a moral and a legal obligation to do so.

Formats for Citing Sources

A number of different forms are used in citing sources, including the *Publication Manual of the American Psychological Association* and the *MLA Handbook for Writers of Research Papers.* Some, including MLA, use the footnote form in manuscripts and outlines when you want to reveal where you found the information. The footnote typically follows the information cited and is signaled by an elevated number in the manuscript.

Bettinghaus argues "the study of *proof* is vital to the student of communication."[1]

Figure 14.2
Written resources for the public speaker.

General Indexes to Periodicals
Book Review Digest. 1905–. (Author, title, subject)
New York Times Index. 1913–. (Author, subject)
Reader's Guide to Periodical Literature. 1900–. (Author, title, subject)
Social Sciences and Humanities Index. 1965–. (Author, subject)

Special Indexes to Periodicals
Art Index. 1929–. (Author, subject)
Bibliographic Index. 1937–. (Subject)
Biography Index. 1946–. (Subject)
Biological and Agricultural Index. 1964–. (Subject)
Book Review Index. 1965–.
Business Periodicals Index. 1958–. (Subject)
Catholic Periodical Index. 1930–. (Subject)
Communication Abstracts. 1978–. (Subject)
Education Index. 1929–. (Author, subject)
Engineering Index. 1884–. (Subject)
Index to Book Reviews in the Humanities. 1960–.
Index to Legal Periodicals. 1908–. (Author, subject)
Music Index. 1949–. (Author, subject)
Psychological Abstracts. 1927–. (Author, subject)
Public Affairs Information Service. 1915–. (Subject)
Quarterly Cumulative Index Medicus. 1927–. (Author, subject)
Sociological Abstracts. 1952–. (Subject)

Specialized Dictionaries
Partridge, Eric. *A Dictionary of Catch Phrases.* 1979.
Partridge, Eric. *A Dictionary of Cliches* 5th ed., 1978.

Roget, Peter M. *Roget's University Thesaurus.* 1981.
Webster's New World Bible Dictionary. 1986.
Webster's New World Dictionary of Business Terms. 1985.
Webster's New World Dictionary of Synonyms. 1984.

Specialized Encyclopedias
Adams, J. T. *Dictionary of American History.* 6 vols. 1942.
Encyclopedia of the Social Sciences. 15 vols. 1930–35.
Encyclopedia of World Art. 1959–.
Grove's Dictionary of Music and Musicians. 9 vols. 1954. (Supplement, 1961.)
Harris, Chester W. *Encyclopedia of Educational Research.* 1960.
Hastings, James. *Interpreter's Dictionary of the Bible.* 4 vols. 1962.
McGraw-Hill. *Encyclopedia of Science and Technology.* 15 vols. 1966.
Munn, Glenn G. *Encyclopedia of Banking and Finance.* 7th ed., 1973.
Van Nostrand's *Scientific Encyclopedia.* 4th ed., 1968.
Worldmark Encyclopedia of the Nations. 5 vols. 1963.

Yearbooks
Americana Annual. 1923–.
The Annual Register of World Events. 1958–.
Economic Almanac. 1940–.
Facts on File. 1940–.
Information Please Almanac. 1947–.
New International Year Book. 1907–.
Statesman's Year-Book. 1864–.
Statistical Abstract of the United States. 1878–.
World Almanac and Book of Facts. 1868–.

Knowing Your Library

You are more likely to use reference works if you know where they are in the library and if you know what kind of information is in them. The exercise that follows will help to better acquaint you with the library and its reference works.

1. From the card catalog, find the author and title of one book that deals with your topic.

Author _____

Title _____

2. From the *Reader's Guide to Periodical Literature,* find the title and author of one article on your topic.

Author _____

Title _____

3. Using a specialized index to periodicals, give the author, title, and the name of the publication for an article on the topic you have selected.

Author _____

Title _____

Publication _____

4. Using an encyclopedia or a yearbook, find specific information about your topic. In one sentence, explain what kind of information you found.

_____

_____

Source _____

In this case, the footnote follows a direct quotation, a statement set apart with quotation marks that states the exact words used in the source. A *paraphrased* statement, a statement recast in your own words, is also footnoted:

Bettinghaus argues students of communication should study the nature of proof.[2]

If a direct quote is longer than three sentences, it should be indented on both the right and the left margins, stated exactly as the source states it, typed single-spaced, and followed by a footnote.

As Bettinghaus says in his book *The Nature of Proof:*

Modes of proof have changed greatly over the centuries, but the concept of proof is recognizable over a span of two thousand years. Ancient Greeks recognized confessions obtained from the torture of witnesses as valid evidence—and perfectly good proof—in their courts. During the Roman era, a defendant was allowed to parade his weeping wife and children before the judges as proof of his innocence. During the Middle Ages, the "water test" could establish the proof of a man's guilt. The accused was thrown into a lake or pond. If he swam, he was judged guilty; if he drowned, he was believed to have been innocent.[3]

Similarly, when you paraphrase a number of sentences based on somebody else's idea or information, you so indicate by following it with an elevated number but without indenting.

As you might suspect, you have to do more than simply place an elevated number after a direct quotation or a paraphrased statement. The elevated number indicates the source is cited or listed either at the bottom of the page (thus the name "foot" note) or at the end of the paper in endnotes. The footnotes or endnotes in which you indicate your sources should be in a consistent form.

If the footnote cites an article from a magazine or journal, you should indicate the author, the title of the article (in quotation marks), the name of the magazine or journal (underlined), the volume number, the date (in parentheses), and the page on which you found the information. For a single-authored magazine article, the footnote would look like this:

[1]Margaret Carlson, "The Fight of the Decade," *Savvy* 8 (January 1987):43–48.

Notice the first line is indented three spaces; the second line (if one exists) moves out to the left margin. Notice also when you include a volume number, you do not write "p." or "pp." before the page reference.

If the footnote cites a newspaper, you use the same basic format:

[1]Carol Parker, "Naples Youngster Battles Against Disorder in Blood," *Naples Daily News,* 14 December 1986, p. 1G.

A footnote for a book looks like this:

[1]Erwin P. Bettinghaus, *The Nature of Proof* (New York: Bobbs-Merrill Company, 1972), pp. 1–2.

In a footnote for a book, the publication information is placed in parentheses, and the pages are indicated either with a "p." for a reference from a single page or with a "pp." for material from more than one page. The name of the book, like the names of magazines, journals, and newspapers, is underlined when you type, or set in italics when it appears in print.

A quotation or paraphrased material from an interview, lecture, or television program follows the same basic form except that the footnote contains slightly different information, including the person's qualifications when the reader is unlikely to know them.

[1]Dr. George Kirk, Associate Professor of Anthropology, in an interview on 23 September 1987.

[2]Ronald Reagan, "Meet the Press," Sunday, 21 December 1986.

With pamphlets, the amount and type of information you can provide may be quite different:

[1]"Controlling Garden Pests," U.S. Department of Agriculture pamphlet, available through State University's agricultural extension office, p. 3.

Remember the purpose of citing sources and writing footnotes is to provide sufficient information to lead the reader to the source for verification or for further reading. The basic footnote format suggested here is just one of a number of acceptable forms that you can find in stylebooks.

Footnotes might be fine in written manuscripts or outlines, but what are you to do about indicating your sources in a speech? The answer is oral footnotes. An oral footnote is simply an abbreviated manuscript or outline footnote that tells the audience

Citing sources provides verification and
invites further **reading**.

where you **found your information. In a speech, the footnotes illustrated previously**
would sound like this:

> "A recent article by Margaret Carlson in *Savvy* pointed out how difficult it is for voters
> to . . ."
>
> "The *Naples Daily News* revealed a story about a child's courage in his fight against a
> rare anemia."
>
> "Professor Erwin Bettinghaus of Michigan State says in his book *The Nature of Proof*
> that . . ."
>
> "When I interviewed Dr. Kirk, an anthropology professor, last week, he said . . ."
>
> "Ronald Reagan was on 'Meet the Press' last Sunday. In that interview, he said . . ."

In other words, in a speech, the speaker indicates the information or idea came from
a magazine, newspaper, book, or interview by providing some signal to the audience
the material came from some other source.

We have already discussed the moral and legal obligation to reveal your sources of
information, and now you know how to indicate where you got your information, both
in written compositions like outlines and manuscripts and in oral performances. Another reason for citing sources of information should not be overlooked: Sometimes,
quotations from a credible source can improve your own credibility. Audience members
who may not be impressed with your statements on a topic might be more influenced
if you demonstrate that people important to them support your ideas.

People Sources

One student wanted to do his speech on a topic in which he was involved, but almost
every source he located through the library's reference works had been vandalized:
Most of the written sources in newspapers, magazines, and journals had been cut out
by someone who had researched the topic earlier. The student was so angry he stormed

into his speech professor's office, ready to quit the course. "What is the point in trying to write well-prepared speeches if the information isn't even available in the library?" he asked.

The student was asked to do one thing before dropping the course: to go to see the director of libraries about his complaint. The director of libraries not only made an appointment with the student, she also showed considerable interest in the student's complaint. The director was chairing a task force for sixteen colleges and universities who were delving into the problem of mutilation, the destruction of library holdings by students who thought it was all right to destroy sources for everyone who came after them. The director spoke to the student for an hour. She gave him facts, figures, arguments, and ideas about the mutilation of library holdings. The student ended up delivering an excellent speech—not on the topic he had originally planned—but on the problem of library mutilation and what to do about it.

The point of this actual account is speakers often overlook the most obvious sources of information—the people around us. You can get information for your speech from personal experience, written and visual resources, *and* from other people. The easiest way to secure information from other people is to ask them through an information interview.

Finding People to Interview

As a person who needs information about a particular topic, your first step is to find the person or persons who can help you to discover more about your topic. Your instructor might have some suggestions about whom to approach. Among the easier and best sources of information are professors and administrators who are available on campus. They can be contacted during office hours or by appointment. Government officials, too, have a certain obligation to be responsive to your questions. Even big business and industrial concerns have public relations offices that can answer your questions. Your object is to find someone, or a few people, who can provide you with the best information in the limited time in which you have to prepare your speech.

Conducting the Interview

Once you have carefully selected the person or persons you wish to interview, you need to observe some proprieties:

1. On first contact with your interviewee or the interviewee's secretary, you should be honest about your purpose. For example, you might say, "I want to interview Dr. Schwartz for ten minutes about the plans for student aid for next year so I can share that information with the twenty students in my public speaking class." In other words, it is good to reveal why you want to talk to the person. It is also good to reveal how much of the interviewee's time you need to take, and it is smart to keep time short. If your interviewee wants to give you more time than you requested, that should be the interviewee's choice. Finally, it is unwise to be deceptive about why you want to talk to the person, or not to reveal why you want to talk, because you want the interviewee to trust you.

2. You should prepare specific questions for the interview. Think ahead of time of exactly what kinds of information you need to satisfy yourself and your audience. Keep your list of questions short enough to fit the time limit you have suggested to the interviewee.

3. Be respectful toward the person you interview. Remember the person is doing you a favor. You do not need to act like Mike Wallace on "60 Minutes." Instead, you should dress appropriately for the person's status, you should ask your questions with politeness and concern, and you should thank your interviewee for granting you an interview.

4. You should tell the interviewee you are going to take notes on his or her answers so you can use the information in your speech. If you are going to record the interview on a tape recorder, you need to ask the interviewee's permission, and you should be prepared to take written notes in case the interviewee does not wish to be recorded.

5. When you quote the interviewee or paraphrase the person's ideas in your speech, you should use oral footnotes to indicate where you got the information: "According to Dr. Fred Schwartz, the Director of Financial Aids, the amount of student financial aid for next year will be slightly less than it was this year."

Sometimes, the person you interview will be a good resource for still other information. For example, if the interviewee is an expert on your topic, he or she may be able to lead you to other people or additional written resources for your speech. Remember, too, how you behave before, during, and after the interview is a reflection on you, the class you are taking, and even the college or university. For more information on interviewing, return to chapter 9, where the skill is discussed in more detail.

Finding Appropriate Supporting Materials

You already know that indices, card catalogs, and interviews will lead you to new ideas and information about your topic, but what exactly are you supposed to be seeking when you find the magazine articles, journals, and books or interview the expert on the topic? You might find additional materials that help to clarify information or arguments you can use to persuade. But the most useful material that you can find is the abundant **supporting materials,** those materials you can employ to support your ideas, to substantiate your arguments, and to clarify your position. The supporting materials we examine most closely are examples, surveys, testimonial evidence, statistics, analogies, explanations, and definitions. Some of these supporting materials are used as evidence or proof, others are used mainly for clarification or amplification, but all are found in researching your topic.

Examples

Examples are among the most common supporting materials found in speeches. Sometimes, a single example helps to convince an audience; at other times, a relatively large number of examples may be necessary to achieve your purpose. For instance, if you are arguing in your speech that television commercials are sexist, you can support your claim with the example that men are rarely shown drinking tea on television commercials and women are rarely shown drinking beer in magazine advertisements, even though we all know both men and women drink tea and beer. Similarly, in your informative speech on cell division, you can use the cell division of an amoeba to demonstrate your point through a single example. When you find articles or when you interview an expert, consider if they will be appealing to your audience.

You should also be careful of examples or specific instances. Sometimes, an example may be so unusual an audience will not accept it as evidence or proof of anything. The student who refers to crime in his hometown as an example of the increasing crime problem is unconvincing if his hometown has considerably less crime than the audience is accustomed to. A good example must be plausible, typical, and related to the main point before it will be effective in a speech.

Surveys

Surveys are a source of supporting materials commonly used in speeches. Surveys are found most often in magazines or journals and are usually seen as more credible than one person's experience or an example or two because they synthesize the experience of hundreds or thousands of people. Public opinion polls fall into this category. One person's experience with alcohol can have an impact on an audience, but a survey indicating one third of Americans are abstainers, one third are occasional drinkers, and one third are regular drinkers provides better support for an argument.

As with personal experience, there are some important questions you should ask about the evidence found in surveys:

1. *How reliable is the source you used?* A report in a professional journal of sociology, psychology, or speech communication is likely to be more thorough and more valid than one found in a local newspaper.

2. *How broad was the sample used in the survey?* Was it a survey of the entire nation, the region, the state, the city, the campus, or the class?

3. *Who was included in the survey?* Did everyone in the sample have an equally good chance of being selected, or were volunteers asked to respond to the questions?

4. *How representative was the survey sample? Playboy's* readers may not be typical of the population in your state.

5. *Who performed the survey?* Was it a nationally recognized survey firm like Lou Harris or Gallup, or was it the local newspaper editor? Was it performed by professionals like professors, researchers, or management consultants?

6. *Why was the survey done?* Was it performed for any self-serving purpose—for example, to attract more readers—or did the government make it to help establish policy or legislation?

Testimonial Evidence

Testimonial evidence, a third kind of supporting material, can be obtained from interviews, television or radio, and printed sources. Testimonial evidence is the use of "testimony," or the words of others, to support or clarify your points. When using testimonial evidence, you should either select persons or sources the audience respects, or choose quotations that state the ideas in a new, original, or better way.

Testimonial evidence can be very convincing. Christian fundamentalists often use testimonies of believers to help reinforce the beliefs of the group. Similarly, Alcoholics Anonymous members give testimonials about why they gave up drinking. Expert testimony is also a potent source of influence. We tend to believe an expert on cancer, politics, religion, drugs, or law. Remember to tell audience members about an expert's qualifications if the expert is unfamiliar to them.

Some questions you should ask about the sources of your testimonial evidence include:

1. Is the person you quote an expert whose opinions or conclusions are worthier than most other people's opinions?
2. Is the quotation about a subject in the person's area of expertise?
3. Is the person's statement based on extensive personal experience, professional study or research, or another form of firsthand proof?
4. Will your classmates find the statement more believable because you got it from this outside source?

Statistics

A fourth kind of evidence useful for clarification or persuasion is **statistics.** Statistics is a kind of numerical shorthand that can summarize large quantities of data for easy consumption by an audience. This type of data must be used with care, however, because the data can be deceiving.

To assist you in your use of statistics, both as a speaker and as a critical listener, you should have a brief vocabulary relating to statistics and numbers, and you should know some of the questions that can be asked about them.

The terms that follow are only a partial list of words that are commonly used in statistics. Along with each term is a brief explanation and some appropriate questions to ask about it.

Mean or Average

Mean or average refers to the total of a list of numbers divided by the number of items. For example, given these six scores—4, 7, 7, 11, 13, and 15—the mean would be 9.5, or the sum of the scores (57) divided by the number of scores (6). Sometimes, the mean is not a good indicator of central tendency. For example, if the scores were 1, 2, 2, 1, 14, 15, the mean would be 5.8. But all the scores actually fell on the extremes, and nobody received a score even close to the mean. The average grade in a class could be *C* if the class were given an equal number of *A*s and *F*s. Two good questions to ask about the mean or average are: (1) does the mean tell us where most of the numbers or scores are clustered? and (2) what was the range of the numbers?

Median

The **median** is the midpoint in a series of numbers—the middle score. Knowing a median runs down the middle of a road helps some students to remember the median is the middle score. The median is not the mean or average, although sometimes they are the same. In the series of numbers 1, 3, 5, 9, and 15, the median or middle score is 5, but the mean or average is 6.6.

Supporting material is limited only by your imagination in the communication age.

Mode

The **mode** is the most frequently recurring number in a list of numbers or a distribution. If the mode on an examination were 7, it would mean more people earned a 7 than any other score. However, the mode is not necessarily where most of the other numbers are clustered. The critical listener should ask for several measures of central tendency: What was the mean? Was the mode near the average?

Percentage

The term **percentage** literally means "by the hundred" because it refers to the ratio or fraction of one hundred. Percentage can be expressed as a decimal: .56 means 56 percent or 56/100. Among the questions to be asked about percentages are: What is the basis for the whole? That is, what is 100 percent? A 500 percent increase in sales, for example, can mean the person sold one car last year and five cars this year. One hundred percent, then, represented one car.

Percentages can be difficult for an audience to comprehend unless you make them palatable. It is easier for an audience to understand percentages stated as percentages rather than as decimals, although they mean the same thing. It is also easier for an audience to comprehend percentages rounded off rather than percentages stated too specifically. A number like 49.67 percent is easier to understand if it is rounded off to 50 percent.

Range

The difference between the highest and lowest numbers in a distribution is the **range** of that distribution. For example, examination scores may have a range of 25 since the highest score was 45 and the lowest score was 20. The range does not reveal where most of the numbers are clustered; it simply tells the length of a distribution of numbers. Two questions that give a better idea of where the numbers cluster are: Where was the mean or average? Where was the mode?

Raw Numbers

Raw numbers are specific numbers often cited in population, production, and other measures of quantity. If the number of teenagers in a state increased by 325,465 this year, this raw number is difficult to absorb because it is so specific. It would be easier for an audience to understand if the number was rounded off (over 325,000) or stated as a percentage of increase (a 15 percent increase).

Good questions to ask about a raw number are: What percentage of increase or decrease does raw number represent? What was the original number, and what is the new total? Raw numbers are hard to interpret if you have no basis for comparison. If the speaker does not provide that basis, the critical listener must ask for additional information before the number can be understood. Listeners should not feel embarrassed about inquiring about statistics and numbers in speeches. They are often difficult to understand and interpret. As a speaker, you should strive to provide all of the information necessary for interpreting numbers and statistics. For example, you can make numbers meaningful by comparing them to familiar things, by showing them visually, and by converting them into bar graphs, line graphs, and pie charts. As a listener, you should ask for additional information when you need it.

Analogies

Another kind of supporting material used in public speeches is the analogy. An **analogy** is a comparison of things in some respects, especially in position or function, that are otherwise dissimilar. For instance, human beings and bees are different, but one could draw a comparison of these two different groups by pointing out that, in many ways, human beings are like bees—we have people who are like the queen bees, who are pampered and cared for by others; we have the drones, who do nothing and yet are cared for; and we have the workers, who seem to do all of the labor without any pampering care. Similarly, analogies can be used to show the Roman society is analogous to American society, that a law applied in one state will work the same way in another, and that if animals get cancer from drinking too much diet soda, so will human beings.

An analogy often provides clarification, but it is a risky means of arguing because somewhere along the line the comparison inevitably breaks down. Therefore, the speaker who argues the American society will fail just as Roman society did can carry the comparison only so far because the two societies exist in a very different time frame, because the form of government and the institutions in the two societies are quite different, and so on. Likewise, you can question the bee/human being analogy by pointing out the vast differences between the two things being compared. Nonetheless, the analogy can be quite successful as a way to illustrate or clarify.

Explanations

Explanations are another important means of clarification and persuasion you can find in written and visual sources and in interviews. An explanation clarifies what something is or how it works to the audience. How does the stock market work? What is a Dow Jones Industrial average? What does "buying on the margin" mean? What is a "bull market" and a "bear market"? All of these questions can be answered by explanations, by stating in ways the audience can understand what these terms mean and how they work in the stock market.

A good explanation usually simplifies a concept or idea for an audience by explaining it from their point of view. William Safire, once a presidential speech writer and now a syndicated columnist, provided an explanation in one of his columns about how the spelling of a word gets changed. In his explanation, he pointed out experts who write dictionaries observe how writers and editors use the language. "When enough citations come in from cultivated writers, passed by trained copy editors," he quotes a lexicographer as saying, "the 'mistake' becomes the spelling."[4] You may find, too, much of your informative speaking is explanation, explaining what an idea means or how something works.

Definitions

Definitions are still another kind of clarifying information you can garner from written and visual sources or interviews. Often, the jargon of your field of interest will be unfamiliar to your audience, and you will have to explain through definitions what different terms mean. Sometimes, definitions are brief explanations—telling an audience *hydroponics* is a system of growing plants in a chemical culture instead of in soil. Other times, your best definition may be an operational definition, that is, a definition telling what operations need to be performed. An angel food cake can be defined by the recipe that must be followed to make it; a secretary can be defined by his or her job description; and a dash and a cross-country run can be differentiated by stating the distance and the speed needed to be employed in the two kinds of running.

Definitions, like explanations, simplify; they state what something is in terms the audience can understand. If they try to clarify by using terms that the audience does not understand, they fail as definitions. Some of the most complete definitions of words can be found in the *Oxford English Dictionary,* common words can be found in a college desk dictionary, and unusual words can be found in the specialized dictionaries and encyclopedias listed earlier in this chapter.

Using Evidence as Proof

Supporting material in your speech can be nearly anything that lends support to your argument. It can be as simple as, "I know this works because I did it myself," or as complex as a fifty-page report by a government body about a topic. *Evidence* is both a stronger and a narrower term than the term *supporting material*. **Evidence** refers to data or information from which you can draw a conclusion, make a judgment, or establish the probability of something occurring. In the legal system, strict rules govern what may or may not be used as evidence. In public speaking, the rules are considerably looser, but common sense still applies. For instance, a single example is supporting material and it is probably even evidence, but a single example is usually insufficient evidence on which to base a claim. So evidence is often described as being strong or weak. The statement, "This works for me," is weak evidence compared to, "This has worked for millions of people."

If supporting material can be considered an umbrella term for nearly anything that supports a contention, and if evidence is a stronger term on which a conclusion or judgment can be based, then the term *proof* is the strongest. **Proof** is sufficient evidence to convince your audience what you say is true. Sufficient evidence could be a single example or hundreds of experiments. What makes the evidence proof is its acceptability to the audience.

Norman Cousins, the long-time editor of *Saturday Review* magazine, was the subject of a network television video about his fight against a supposedly incurable disease of the spine and nervous system. Cousins and his physician worked out an untried experimental program to help Cousins's body fight the disease. The program consisted of megadoses of vitamin C and healthy doses of laughter. Cousins even had humorous records and films hauled to his room to make him feel happy. After considerable time and several serious setbacks, Cousins managed to conquer a disease diagnosed as progressive and crippling.

The point of this story in a section on using evidence as proof is that Cousins's case raises interesting questions about how much and what kind of evidence constitutes proof. The physicians who diagnosed his disease were recognized authorities. Yet, Cousins thought up a prescription for his own incurable illness, a prescription for which there was no proof or evidence that it would work. His own doctor who reluctantly went along with the strange plan did not personally believe in the therapy because it was inconsistent with the scientific method. Now Cousins stands as a single instance of a person who survived a supposedly incurable illness. Many persons grounded in the scientific method would contend Cousins's case does not prove much. Others would say his case proves the "doctor within us" is more powerful than the physician who would treat us. You should recognize from the Cousins case that proof is in the eye of the beholder. The relevance of perception from chapter 2 should be apparent to the public speaker.

How can you handle evidence in a speech so it will be regarded as proof? The central concern is in knowing what kind and how much evidence will convince an audience your assertions are true. Some audiences—students grounded in math, business, and economics come to mind—are partial to statistics and numerical treatments of a topic.

Other audiences are actually repelled by numbers and respond more favorably to long, dramatic stories or examples. How much evidence to use is also an important consideration. Sometimes, one example proves the point for most of the people in your audience. At other times, all the examples in the world would be insufficient to prove a point to an audience.

Actually, no rules govern how much or what kind of evidence should be used in your speech. Instead, you have to apply your intelligence to the problem: Given your skills and the nature of this audience, what can you say about your topic that will convince the audience of the truth in your statements?

One last bit of advice concerning evidence: Standard ways of presenting evidence in a speech exist. First, you need to be highly selective about which of the many possible claims you intend to make in your speech. Literally hundreds of claims can be made about any given issue. You need to choose the ones most important to you and your audience.

Second, you need to be highly selective about which evidence you use in your speech to support your claims. Literally hundreds of pieces of evidence can be used to support a claim. You need to choose the evidence most important to you and to your audience.

Finally, you need to arrange your argument with a statement either before, after, or both before and after the evidence that reveals what you are trying to prove. Many names for this kind of statement exist—argument, assertion, proposition, claim, and main point. Whatever the name, the content of the statement is a claim that invites evidence, that needs to be proved. It might be a statement of policy: "The United States should approve a single six-year term for our president." It might be a statement of value: "Ohio University has the strongest College of Communication in the country." Or it might be a statement of fact: "The School of Telecommunications is the largest school of radio-television east of the Mississippi." Statements of fact are evaluated for truth and accuracy because there is a "right answer" to a question of fact. Statements of value and policy are endlessly debatable because the answer ultimately comes down to what the audience is willing to believe and what the audience will consider as proof.

For example, you may decide that, given your audience and the particular occasion on which you intend to speak, your best approach might be to state first the position you want to prove and then provide what you think is sufficient evidence to prove it:

Claim: Central States University (CSU) has the best general education requirements in the region.

Evidence: CSU requires every student to master English composition by passing a first- and third-year course.

Evidence: CSU requires every student to pass at least one quantitative course in mathematics, statistics, computer science, or logic.

Evidence: CSU requires every student to take thirty credits in three of five broad areas like science, the arts, third-world cultures, literature, and applied engineering.

Evidence: CSU requires every student to take a capstone course in the senior year that synthesizes a body of knowledge.

In another situation with a different audience, you may decide to begin with the evidence that leads to your claim:

Evidence: One female student was assaulted by an unidentified male just outside the library last Tuesday.

Evidence: A male student was robbed of his watch and billfold near the student union last Thursday just after dark.

Evidence: In the last year, the number of assaults, robberies, and rapes has tripled over the number the year before.

Claim: This school needs to establish a student-sponsored crime watch to reduce crime on campus.

The important point to remember about proof is it is perceived differently by different people. The speaker is responsible for demonstrating the truth or probability of a claim. Intelligent analysis of the audience helps the speaker to discover which claims and which evidence will be perceived as proof.

Summary

This chapter focused on how to find information for the content of your speech and how to use that information once you have found it. Sources to consider when gathering information for a speech include your personal experiences, written and visual resources, and other people. Personal experiences are something you can discuss with authority, but care must be taken to evaluate personal experiences as evidence.

Written and visual resources can lead you to important information on a wide variety of topics, but it is important to know and understand how to use a variety of sources, such as the *Reader's Guide,* yearbooks, encyclopedias, sourcebooks, newspaper files, journals, and the card catalog, to find your information. Explaining where you found your information through written and oral footnotes helps you to avoid charges of plagiarism and enhances your credibility.

Interviewing other people is another way to obtain information for your speech. The interviewee can provide expert information, quotations, and examples, and sometimes also can lead you to other experts or additional written resources.

Supporting material is information you can employ to support your ideas, to substantiate your arguments, and to clarify your position. The supporting materials discussed in this chapter are examples, surveys, testimonial evidence, statistics, analogies, explanations, and definitions.

Evidence refers to data or information from which you can draw a conclusion, make a judgment, or establish the probability of something occurring. Proof is sufficient evidence to convince your audience what you say is true. Knowing what kind and how much evidence will be regarded as proof is an important consideration for a speaker. Knowing how to select and organize a claim and its evidence so the audience will accept it as proof is also important.

Organizing Your Speech

*O*rder and simplification are the first
steps toward mastery of a subject.

Thomas Mann

*W*ithout discipline, there is no life at all.

Katharine Hepburn

*D*on't agonize. Organize.

Florynce R. Kennedy

Objectives

1. Describe the five functions of an introduction to a speech.
2. Explain the functions of the body of a speech.
3. Compose an outline for your speech.
4. Provide examples of transitions and signposts.
5. Explain the functions of a conclusion to a speech.

Key Terms

introduction
body
outlining
main points
subpoints
sub-subpoints
parallel form
rough draft
sentence outline
key-word outline
organizational
  patterns
time-sequence
  pattern
topical-sequence
  pattern

problem-and-
  solution pattern
Monroe motivated
  sequence
spatial
  organization
cause-effect
  organization
bibliography
transitions
signposts
conclusion
brakelight
  function

In this chapter, we examine the three main parts of a speech: the introduction, the body, and the conclusion. First, we discuss the five functions of an introduction along with many ways that you can fulfill those functions. Then we turn to the body of the speech, with special emphasis on the functions of the body and the many kinds of organizational patterns that can be used to organize the content of the speech. Finally, we examine the functions of a conclusion.

The Introduction

The **introduction** in a public speech is important because audiences use the introduction to "size up" a speaker. In the first few sentences and certainly in the first few minutes of a speech, audience members decide whether to listen to you or not. They also decide whether your topic is important enough to warrant their consideration. In those crucial minutes early in the speech, you can capture your audience's attention and keep it, or you can lose it—perhaps for the remainder of the speech. This section of the chapter is devoted to helping you compose the best possible introduction—an introduction that will grab your audience's attention and keep their minds on your topic.

The five functions of an introduction are:

1. To gain and maintain audience attention
2. To arouse audience interest in the topic being presented
3. To reveal the purpose of your speech
4. To establish your qualifications for speaking on the topic
5. To forecast the development and organization of the speech

These five functions are not necessarily fulfilled in the order indicated. Gaining audience attention often comes at the very beginning, but it is an important function throughout the speech. You cannot afford to lose your audience at any point in your speech. Forecasting organization often comes toward the end of an introduction, but it does not have to be the last item.

Several of the functions of the introduction can be fulfilled by the same words. For example, you could start your speech with words that both gain attention and establish your credibility to speak on a certain topic: "I have been a steelworker for twelve years. That is why I am interested in telling you today about what imported steel is doing to one of our biggest industries."

To assist you in composing an introduction for your public speech, we move systematically through the five functions, explain each, and provide examples.

Gaining and Maintaining Audience Attention

We begin by presenting twelve ways to gain and maintain audience attention. Perhaps these twelve suggestions will inspire you to think of even better ideas for your own particular speech. Remember the twelve suggestions that follow are not just a bag of tricks you perform for their own sake. Instead, you gain and maintain the audience's attention by relating your audience to your topic.

The introduction of a public speech gains
and maintains audience attention.

1. *Bring the object or person about which you are going to speak.* Examples: A student
   speaking on health foods brings a small table full of health foods, which he shares with
   the audience after the speech; a student speaking on weight lifting brings her 250-pound
   friend to demonstrate the moves during the speech; or the student demonstrating the fine
   points of choreography employs the dancing talents of ten friends.
2. *Invite your audience to participate.* Examples: Ask questions and ask audience members
   to raise their hands and answer; teach the audience first-aid techniques by having them
   do some of the techniques with you; or have audience members move their chairs closer
   together for your speech about overcrowded housing.
3. *Let your attire relate to your speech.* Examples: A nurse talking about the dangers of
   acute hepatitis wears a nurse's uniform; the construction worker dons a hard hat; or the
   private security person wears a uniform and badge.
4. *Exercise your audience's imagination.* Examples: Have the audience members close their
   eyes and imagine they are standing on a ski slope, standing before a judge on an
   operating-while-intoxicated charge, or entering the warm waters of Hawaii when it is
   freezing in Cleveland.
5. *Start with sight or sound.* Examples: One minute of classical music from a speaker
   encouraging others to listen to classical music stations; a large poster-size picture
   showing the horrors of war; or the sounds of forest birds chirping in the cool dawn. One
   student gave a powerful speech on motorcycle safety. He showed slides as he talked
   about the importance of wearing a helmet while driving or riding on a motorcycle. Only
   one item appeared in color on each slide: a crushed, smashed, or battered helmet that
   was worn by someone who lived through a motorcycle accident.

6. *Arouse audience curiosity.* Example: One student began his speech by saying, "A new sport has hit this state, yet it is a national tradition. Held in the spring of the year in some of our most beautiful timbered areas, this sport is open to men and women alike. It is for responsible adults only and requires common sense and patience. This sport of our grandparents is . . ." Naturally, by this time, the audience was very curious about the student's topic and anxious to hear more about it.

7. *Role-play.* Example: A student invites an audience member to pretend to be a choking victim. The speaker then "saves" the victim by using the maneuver she is teaching the audience. Speakers themselves can play the role, for example, of a mechanic fixing a small engine, a nurse showing how to take vital signs, or an architect selling a proposal. Audiences can be asked to play the role of people whose cars will not start, of paramedics learning what to do in the first few minutes with an accident victim, or of a board of directors considering a new building.

8. *Show a few slides or a very short film.* Examples: A football player speaking on violence in that sport shows a short film of a punt return while he points out which players were deliberately trying to maim their opponents with faceguards—as they had been taught to do; an international student shows a few slides of her native land; or a student speaking on city slums presents a mind-grabbing sequence of twelve slides showing winos in doorways, rats in a child's room, and a family portrait of ten people living in three rooms.

9. *Present a brief quotation or have the audience read something provided by you.* Example: Sometimes, reading a few lines by T. S. Eliot, Wordsworth, or Faulkner can prepare the audience for your message. One enterprising student wrote a letter to every student in his class. When class members opened their letters, they read a personalized invitation to report to their local draft board for induction into the armed services of the United States.

10. *State striking facts or statistics.* Examples: "Scientists have discovered the bones of a seventeen-million-year-old apelike creature, a creature that could be the common ancestor of the great apes and human beings";[1] or "Women under fifty years of age could reduce their heart attacks by 65 percent by simply quitting smoking, according to a study in the *Journal of the American Medical Association.*"[2]

11. *Self-disclosure.* Tell audience members something about yourself—related to the topic— they would not otherwise know. Examples: "I took hard drugs for six years"; "I was an eagle scout"; or "I earn over fifty thousand dollars a year—legally."

12. *Tell a story, a narration.* Example: "I want to tell you about Lonnie Frank, a friend of mine. Lonnie was a big success at South High: he lettered in track and football, and he was second highest for grades in our senior year. Lonnie was just as good in college: he had a 3.5 GPA, drove a Corvette, and was selected for a student internship with IBM. But you read about my friend Lonnie in last week's newspaper. Maybe you didn't know who he was, but he was the one who died in a car wreck with his girlfriend out on Route 340. They were killed by a drunken driver." If you choose to use a narration, you should indicate to your audience whether the story is hypothetical, fiction, or an actual account.

The preceding twelve suggestions for gaining and maintaining audience attention certainly are not the only possibilities. Indeed, you could begin your speech by stating a problem for which your speech proposes a solution; you could depict dramatic conflict between labor and management, teachers and students, conservatives and liberals; or you could simply inform the audience about everyday items we only partially understand: stock market reports, barometric pressure readings, and sales tax. Your introduction should not simply imitate something you read in this book; you should think of ideas of your own that work best for you and for your audience.

This section on gaining and maintaining audience attention concludes with a warning. The warning is you should always make sure your attention-getting strategy is related to your topic. Some speakers think every public speech must start with a joke. Starting with a joke is a big mistake if you are not good at telling jokes or if your audience is disinterested in hearing them. Jokes can be used in the introduction of a speech if they are topically relevant, but they are just one of hundreds of ways a speaker can gain attention. Another overused device is writing some word like S-E-X on the chalkboard and then announcing your speech has nothing to do with sex but that you wanted to get the audience's attention. Again, the problem with this approach is that the attention-getting strategy had nothing to do with the topic.

Avoid being overly dramatic. One of our colleagues had a harrowing experience in class. She was still writing down some comments about the previous speech when the next student rose to deliver his speech. She heard a horrifying groan and looked up to see the student on the floor with his whole leg laid open and bleeding. The students in the class leaped up and surrounded the injured student while she ran to the office to call for emergency assistance. The student planned to give a speech on first aid. He had gotten a plastic leg wound in living color from the student health center. He had a bag of simulated blood on his stomach which he squeezed rhythmically so it would spurt like a severed artery. Unfortunately for the student, his attention-getting action introduction was too realistic. Instead of capturing the audience's attention, he managed to get so much adrenalin into their bloodstreams they were in no mood to listen to any more speeches that day.

Arousing Audience Interest

A second function of an introduction is to arouse audience interest in the subject matter. The best way to arouse audience interest is to show clearly how the topic is related to the audience. A highly skilled speaker can determine how to adapt almost any topic to a particular audience. Do you want to talk about collecting coins? Thousands of coins pass through each person's hands every year. Can you tell your audience how to spot a rare one? If you can arouse the audience's interest in currency, you will find it easier to encourage them to listen to your speech about the rare coins you have collected. Similarly, speeches about your life as a mother of four, a camp counselor, or the manager of a business can be linked to audience interests.

Stating the Purpose

A third function of the introduction is to state, like the thesis sentence in composition, the purpose of your speech. Generally, an audience is more likely to learn from your informative speech if you are quite specific about what you expect them to learn. Stating

Creative introductions arouse audience interest.

the exact purpose of your persuasive speech can be a mistake, but most speeches benefit from revealing the purpose very explicitly, as in the examples that follow:

Today I will show you the basic construction of a simple electric motor.
There are three main causes of the inflation that reduces the value of your money.
I will provide you with a new way of looking at welfare.

In speaking, as in teaching, the members of an audience are more likely to learn and to understand if they know what is expected of them.

Establishing Your Qualifications

A fourth function of an introduction is to describe any special qualifications you have. You can talk about your experience, your research, the experts you interviewed, and your own education and training in the subject. You should be wary about self-praise, but you need not be reserved in stating why you can speak about the topic with authority. Chapter 13 provided considerably more information about what behaviors audiences look for in a speaker, along with some suggestions concerning what information should be included about the speaker.

Forecasting Development and Organization

A fifth function of an introduction is to forecast the organization and development of the speech. The forecast provides a brief outline of your organization, a preview of the main points you plan to cover. Audience members feel more comfortable when they know what to expect. You can help by revealing your plan for the speech. Are you going to discuss a problem and its solution? Are you going to make three main arguments with supporting materials? Are you going to talk for five minutes or for twenty? Let your audience know what you plan to do early in your speech.

The Body

The organization of the introduction centers on the five functions the introduction should fulfill. The organization of the **body** of the speech is more complicated, but we approach it through a concept that should be familiar to you—**outlining.**

Outlining

One important reason for learning about outlining is some speakers write out their speeches. Some write them out entirely. Others write outlines from which they speak. In either case, outlining is the most commonly used method of organizing a speech. A second good reason for outlining is an outline is a blueprint for the speech. In the same way a blueprint shows the builder where the load-bearing walls will be, the outline indicates which ideas in the speech are most important. Finally, outlining helps to ensure you have fulfilled the functions of the speech body, which are:

1. To indicate to the audience the main ideas or arguments in your message
2. To develop and provide support for ideas and rationales for arguments in your message
3. To indicate where you found the ideas, arguments, and supporting materials in your message
4. To increase what an audience knows about your topic or to change people's minds with your message

Principles of Outlining

The first principle of outlining is that *all of the items of information in your outline should be directly related to your purpose.* In chapter 12, you learned a speech can have an immediate purpose and a long-range goal. The *immediate purpose* is what you expect to achieve by the end of your speech. You might want the audience to be able to state your three main arguments; you might want the audience to respond to your speech by reading an article, signing a petition, or by trying some synthetic food; or you might want audience members to start changing their minds about the topic by discussing it with others. The *long-range goal* is what you expect to achieve over a longer time period. Eventually, you may want the audience to vote for your candidate; to act more tolerantly toward persons of your race, sex, or religion; or to join an activist group for a cause you represent. The first principle of outlining is that the content of your outline should reflect your immediate purpose and your long-range goal.

The second principle of outlining is that *the outline should be an abstract of the speech you will deliver;* that is, it should be less than every word you speak but should include all important points and supporting materials. Some instructors say an outline should be about one-third the length of the actual speech if the speech were in manuscript form. However, you should ask what your instructor expects in an outline because some instructors like to see a very complete outline and others prefer a brief outline. Nonetheless, the outline is not a manuscript. Instead, it is an abstract of the speech you intend to deliver, a plan that includes the important arguments or information you intend to present.

The third principle of outlining is that *the outline should consist of single units of information,* usually in the form of complete sentences that express a single idea. The following example is incorrect because it expresses more than one idea in more than one sentence:

I. Gun control should be employed to reduce the number of deaths in the United States that result from the use of handguns. Half of the deaths from handguns are because criminals murder other people with them.

The same ideas can be outlined correctly by presenting a single idea in each sentence:

I. Government regulation of handguns should be implemented to reduce the number of murders in this country.
   A. Half of the murders in the United States are committed by criminals using handguns.
   B. Half of the murders in the United States are committed by relatives, friends, and acquaintances of the victim.

The fourth principle of outlining is that *the outline should indicate the importance of an item with an outlining symbol.* In the example, the **main points** or most important points are indicated with Roman numerals, such as I, II, III, IV, and V. The number of main points in a five-to-ten-minute speech or even a longer one should be limited to the number you can reasonably cover, explain, or prove in the time permitted. Most five-minute speeches have from one to three main points. Even hour-long speeches must have a limited number of main points because audiences seem unable to remember more than seven main points.

Subpoints, those supporting of the main points or those of less importance, are indicated with capital letters, such as A, B, C, D, and E. Ordinarily, two subpoints under a main point are regarded as the minimum if any subpoints are to be presented at all. As with the main points, the subpoints should be limited in number because the audience may otherwise lose sight of the main point you are trying to make. A good guideline is to present two or three of your best pieces of supporting material in support of each main point.

Sub-subpoints are even less important than the subpoints; they are introduced with Arabic numbers, such as 1, 2, 3, 4, and 5. Typically, the number of sub-subpoints is limited like the number of subpoints. Sub-subpoints usually do not exceed three in number. If you should have to present any additional ideas under a sub-subpoint, they are presented with lowercase alphabetical letters, such as a, b, c, d, and e.

The fifth principle of outlining is that *the outline should provide margins that indicate the relative importance of the items.* The larger the margin on the left, the less important is the item to your purpose. However, the margins are coordinated with the symbols explained previously so main points have the same left margin, the subpoints have a left margin with slightly more space on the left, the sub-subpoints have a left margin with slightly more space on the left, and so on. A correct outline with the appropriate symbols and margins looks like this:

I. The constitutional right to bear arms is being threatened by ineffective gun control.[3]
  A. Murders are being committed with handguns by psychopaths, criminals, and ordinary people.
    1. A psychopath killed John Lennon, a famous singer, with a .38-caliber handgun.[4]
    2. The same week, an ex-convict killed a famous physician, Dr. Michael Halberstam, with a .32-caliber handgun.[5]
    3. Of the twenty thousand persons killed by handguns each year, only two thousand are murdered by criminals engaged in crime.[6]
  B. The number of handguns in circulation is immense.
    1. Nationally, 55 million handguns are in circulation.[7]
    2. Every year, about 2.5 million handguns add to the total.[8]
    3. Handgun Control in Washington, D.C., estimates we will have 100 million handguns in circulation by the end of the century.[9]
II. The solution may be federal gun control or harsher punishment for handgun offenders.
  A. *New York Times* columnist Tom Wicker recommends gun control.[10]
  B. Columnist James J. Kilpatrick recommends the death sentence for persons who murder with handguns.[11]

The sixth principle of outlining is that *the content of an item in an outline should be less than or subordinate to the content of items with higher-order symbols or smaller left-hand margins.* Notice in the outline just illustrated that the items with the highest-order symbols (I, II) and the smallest margins are larger or more important ideas than the items that appear below them with lesser-order symbols (A, B) and larger left-hand margins. Similarly, those items beneath the subpoints—the sub-subpoints—are less than or subordinate to the items that appear above them. The sub-subpoints merely amplify or provide additional evidence. Hence, items in an outline are ranked in importance by symbols, by margins, and by content.

The seventh principle of outlining is that the items should appear in **parallel form.** *Parallel* in this instance means similar or same, and *form* means simple sentences, phrases, or words. So the principle of parallel form means that you should consistently use either sentences, phrases, or words in an outline.

An example of incorrect parallel form follows:

I. Three measures of educational quality are college entrance tests, teacher-pupil ratios, and expenditures per pupil.
  A. College entrance tests:
    1. Top SAT states—New Hampshire, Oregon, and Vermont
    2. Top ACT states—Wisconsin, Iowa, and Minnesota
  B. Teacher-pupil ratios:
    1. Connecticut and Wyoming tie for first.
    2. Others in top ten: New York, Washington, D.C., New Jersey, Oregon, Delaware, Maryland, Wyoming, Rhode Island, and Massachusetts

The Principles of Outlining: A Checklist

Check each of the following items while composing an outline and before submitting the outline for evaluation to ensure you have taken all of the principles of outlining into consideration.

_____ 1. All of the items of information in my outline are directly related to my purpose.

_____ 2. My outline is an abstract of the speech I intend to deliver.

_____ 3. My outline consists of single units of information.

_____ 4. My outline indicates the importance of an item with an outlining symbol that shows main points, subpoints, and sub-subpoints.

_____ 5. My outline provides margins that indicate the relative importance of the items.

_____ 6. The content of an item in my outline is less than or subordinate to the content of items with higher-order symbols or smaller left-hand margins.

_____ 7. The items in my outline appear in parallel form.

An example of correct parallel form follows:[12]

I. Three measures of educational quality are college entrance tests, teacher-pupil ratios, and expenditures per pupil.
   A. The two most often used college entrance tests are the ACT (American College Test) and the SAT (Scholastic Aptitude Test).
      1. The top-scoring states on the ACT are Wisconsin, Iowa, and Minnesota.
      2. The top-scoring states on the SAT are New Hampshire, Oregon, and Vermont.
   B. The teacher-pupil ratio is a second measure of educational quality.
      1. The top states in the nation in teacher-student ratio were Connecticut and Wyoming, who tied for first place.
      2. The other states in the top ten included New York, Washington, D.C., New Jersey, Oregon, Delaware, Maryland, Wyoming, Rhode Island, and Massachusetts.

The example of incorrect parallel form is incorrect because it mixes sentences, phrases, and words instead of consistently using one form, like complete sentences. The example of correct parallel form uses complete sentences throughout; it is parallel because it repeats same or similar forms.

Developing a Rough Draft

Before you begin composing your outline, you can save time and energy by (1) selecting a topic appropriate for you, for your audience, and for the situation; (2) finding arguments, examples, illustrations, quotations, and other supporting materials from your experience, from written and visual resources, and from other people; and (3) narrowing your immediate purpose so you have to select the best materials from a much larger supply of available items than you could include in your outline and your speech.

Once you have gathered materials consistent with your purpose, you can begin by developing a **rough draft** of your outline. The most efficient way to develop a rough draft is to find the main points important for your purpose and your audience. The number of main points should be limited, especially in a five-to-ten-minute speech. In the outline about gun control in the previous section, the speaker decided the best approach to talking about gun control was to explore the problem first (item I) and then to discuss the two possible solutions (item II).

Next, you should see what materials you have from your experience, written and visual resources, and from other people to support these main ideas. In the outline in the previous section, the speaker determined the number of murders and the number of handguns in circulation illustrated the lack of effective gun control. Similarly, you need to find out if you have any supporting materials that back up your subpoints. In the same outline, the speaker found two famous people murdered by handguns within a week and a statistic that illustrated the scope of the problem. In short, you assemble your main points, your subpoints, and your sub-subpoints for your speech always with your audience and purpose in mind. What arguments, illustrations, and supporting materials will be most likely to have an impact on the audience? Sometimes, speakers get so involved in a topic they select mainly those items that interest them. In public speaking, you should select the items likely to have the maximum impact on the audience, not on you.

Composing an outline for a speech is not easy. Even professional speech writers may have to make important changes on their first draft. Some of the questions you need to consider as you revise your rough draft are the following:

1. Are my main points consistent with my purpose?
2. Are my subpoints and sub-subpoints subordinate to my main points?
3. Are the items in my outline the best possible ones for this particular audience, for this topic, for me, and for the occasion?
4. Does my outline follow the principles of outlining?

Even after you have rewritten your rough draft, you would be wise to have another person—perhaps a classmate—examine your outline and provide an opinion about its content.

The Sentence Outline

One of the most useful forms of speech organization is the **sentence outline.** This kind of outline shows in sentence form your order of presentation and where and what kind of arguments, points, supporting materials, and evidence you plan to use in your speech. A look at your own outline might indicate, for example, you have insufficient information to back one of your points or, perhaps, a surplus of information for another.

In addition to the sentence outline itself, you may want to write in the functions being served by each part of your outline. For example, where are you trying to gain and maintain attention? Where are you trying to back up a major argument with supporting materials like statistics, testimony, or specific instances? The end result of a sentence outline along with sidenotes indicating functions is a blueprint, a plan for your speech that can strengthen your speech performance by aiding you in presenting evidence or supporting materials that will make sense to audience members and that will help inform or persuade them.

The outline that follows is based on a student's speech.[13] The immediate purpose of the speech was to challenge the belief in a materialistic society based on consumption by having audience members state at the conclusion of the speech some qualities of life besides wealth they should strive for in a life-style designed for permanence. As you read the outline, see if you think the main points are consistent with the immediate purpose and the long-range goal, which is to convince the audience to adopt a nonmaterialistic life-style after college. Notice the outline is a sentence outline because every entry, whether it is a main point, a subpoint, or a sub-subpoint, is a complete sentence. Also notice the student finished the outline with a bibliography of sources indicating where she found her information. (Forms for bibliographic style are presented later in the chapter.)

Functions	A Life-Style Designed for Permanence

Topic-relevant rhetorical questions to gain attention	Introduction
	I. I want to ask all of you three general questions.
	   A. Do you want to preserve the world's natural resources?
	   B. Do you want our country to be independent of other nations for energy supplies?
	   C. Do you want to ensure a good future for your children?

Questions to relate the topic to the audience	II. Next, I want to ask you three questions that pertain to us as college students.
	   A. Do you want to become wealthy?
	   B. Do you want to drive a big, prestigious Cadillac?
	   C. Do you want to live in a big house?

Qualifications of speaker on this topic	III. I have been listening to and reading about some very serious facts concerning the scarcity of natural resources in the world.
Forecast and statement of expectations	IV. I am going to show you that, if you answered "yes" to the first three questions, then you are going to have to answer "no" to the last three.

Paraphrase an authority to demonstrate the speaker has read about the topic and to make the first main point in the speech	Body
	I. E. F. Schumacher's book *Small Is Beautiful* says our most fateful error is in believing that the problems of production have been solved.
	   A. We have come to believe anything can be produced by technology and good old American ingenuity.
	   B. Unfortunately, our technology depends on fossil fuels, which are being rapidly depleted.

Speaker gives the audience credit for what they have done before, asks them to do more	II. We are trying to conserve our resources by decreasing energy consumption.
	  A. Statistics indicate mass transit systems are being utilized more and more.
	  B. The automobile industry has greatly increased the production of small cars.

Paraphrases an authority, presents second main point, and demonstrates again the speaker's interest in the topic	III. Kenneth Boulding, a world-renowned economist, gave a lecture last week on campus in which he promoted the idea of a new moral order within a new life-style.
	  A. The new moral order is based on being, living, and working together.
	  B. The new life-style is one in which we learn to get along with less and accept it.

Third subpoint with three sub-subpoints to clarify the idea	C. Boulding's "mature world" has implications for our careers, for production, and for our attitudes. 1. Instead of seeking jobs to give us wealth, we should strive for occupations that enable everyone to have a decent existence.
Advances the idea of smaller places of production Example of one change	2. Instead of large-scale, highly complex, and highly capital-intensive production, we should try smaller units of production. a. Instead of one big factory, we should have many smaller plants located closer to where resources are located.
Advances the idea of area instead of national companies	b. Instead of encouraging bigger and bigger megacorporations, we could encourage a wider assortment of smaller, locally or regionally owned companies.
Mentions an attitude that must be overcome	3. We have to overcome our "bigger is better" notion that has been encouraged during most of this century.

Challenge to the audience: two alternatives	Conclusion
	  I. A life-style designed for permanence is possible!
	  A. Do we want a world where quality means more than quantity?
	  B. Do we want a world that exhausts its resources on the way to self-destruction?
	  II. Americans need to learn how to "live small."

Bibliography

Boulding, Kenneth. "The Economic Implications of Living in a World of Limits." A lecture-seminar held at Iowa State University, 3 November 1980.

Satin, Mark. *New Age Politics*. New York: Delta Publishing, 1979.

Schumacher, E. F. *Small Is Beautiful*. London: Perennial, 1973.

Wood, Donald F., and James C. Johnson. *Contemporary Transportation*. Tulsa, Okla.: Petroleum Publishing, 1980.

The Key-Word Outline

Speakers who use a manuscript of their entire speech sometimes become too dependent on the manuscript. It reduces their eye contact and minimizes their attention to audience responses. Nonetheless, some speakers become very proficient at reading from a manuscript on which they have highlighted the important words, phrases, and quotations. A complete sentence outline may be superior to a manuscript in that it forces the speaker to extemporize, to maintain eye contact, and to respond to audience feedback. Key words and phrases can be underlined or highlighted on a sentence outline. An alternative method is to simply use a **key-word outline,** which includes only those items you would normally highlight on a complete sentence outline.

The key-word outline consists of important words and phrases that remind the speaker of the topic or main idea being addressed. However, it may contain statistics or quotations that are too long or complicated to memorize. The key-word outline abstracts the ideas in the speech considerably more than a sentence outline. The key-word outline that follows is based on the same speech upon which the sentence outline presented in the previous section was based. A comparison of the two types of outlines illustrates how much more the key-word outline abstracts or reduces the content to the bare essentials.

A Life-Style Designed for Permanence
Introduction
   I. Three questions
      A. Preserving resources?
      B. Energy independence?
      C. Good future?
  II. Three questions
      A. Wealth?
      B. Expensive car?
      C. Big house?
 III. Facts on scarcity
 IV. Yes to three; no to three

Body
   I. Production problems not solved—Schumacher
      A. Technology and ingenuity
      B. Fossil fuels
  II. Decreasing energy consumption
      A. Mass transit
      B. Small cars
 III. New moral order—Boulding
      A. Togetherness
      B. Getting along with less
      C. Boulding's "mature world"
         1. Occupations
         2. Smallness
            a. Small factories
            b. Small companies
         3. Bigness attitude

Conclusion
  I. Permanence
    A. Quality
    B. Resources
 II. "Live small"

The key-word outline fits easily on three-by-five inch or four-by-six-inch notecards or on 8½-by-11-inch paper. If you choose notecards on which you write or type a key-word outline, the following suggestions may be helpful:

1. Write down instructions to yourself on your notecards. For instance, if you are supposed to write the title of your speech and your name on the chalkboard before your speech begins, then you can write that instruction on the top of your first card.
2. Write on one side of the cards only. It is better to use more cards with your key-word outline on one side only than to write front and back because the latter method is more likely to result in confusion.
3. Number your notecards on the top so they will be unlikely to get out of order and so if they are dropped, they can be quickly reassembled.
4. Write out items that might be difficult to remember. Extended quotations, difficult names, unfamiliar terms, and statistics are examples of items you may want to include on your notecards to reduce the chances for error.
5. Practice delivering your speech at least two times using your notecards. Effective delivery may be difficult to achieve if you have to fumble with unfamiliar cards.
6. Write clearly and legibly.

Organizational Patterns

The body of a speech can be outlined using a number of **organizational patterns.** Exactly which pattern of organization is most appropriate for your speech depends in part on your purpose and on the nature of your material. For instance, if your purpose is to present a solution to a problem, your purpose lends itself well to the problem-and-solution organizational pattern. If the nature of your material is something that occurred over a period of time, then your material might be most easily outlined with a chronological or time-sequence pattern of organization.

In this section, we examine four organizational patterns—the time-sequence pattern, the topical-sequence pattern, the problem-and-solution pattern, and the Monroe motivated sequence—in detail, giving a description, an application, and an example for each. Two other organizational patterns are also briefly described. However, you should keep in mind these six patterns of organization are prototypes from which a skilled speaker can construct many additional patterns of organization. Also, a number of organizational patterns may appear in the same speech: an overall problem-and-solution organization may have within it a time-sequence pattern that explains the history of the problem.

The organizational pattern of your speech may depend upon your purpose and the nature of your information.

Time-Sequence Pattern

The **time-sequence pattern** is also known as chronological order because it is used to indicate what happens to something over time. This pattern of organization is applied in speeches that consider the past, present, and future of some idea, issue, group, plan, or project. It is most useful on topics like the following:

How the Salvation Army Began
The Origins of the Electoral College
The "Today" Show: A Brief History
The Naming of a Stadium
The Future for Space Exploration
The Steps in Making a Cedar Chest
The Formula for Foolproof Gravy

Any topic that requires attention to events, incidents, or steps that take place over time is appropriate for this pattern of organization. A brief outline of a speech organized in a time-sequence pattern follows:[14]

South Africa
  I. The Bushmen first came to South Africa seeking better land, only to be pushed aside and enslaved by others.
    A. The San or Bushmen were nomadic hunters.
    B. The Bushmen later worked the African gold mines.

II. Europeans (the Dutch) established an outpost at the Cape of Good Hope in 1652.
   A. The Dutch overcame the San and the Khoikhoi.
   B. The Dutch settlers and the black natives produced a repressed class of persons labeled "coloureds."
   C. The Dutch fought formidable black tribes like the Zulu and the Xhosa.
III. The nineteenth century brought armed conflict between the English settlers and the Dutch Boers.
   A. The British won a military victory in the Boer War (1899–1902).
   B. The Boers won a political victory by becoming Afrikaners with their own language, laws, and culture.
IV. In the twentieth century, the Afrikaners have established the concept of apartheid to control blacks, coloureds, and Asians.

Notice the emphasis in this brief outline is on the history of South Africa, on the events that took place over the centuries and resulted in the society there today. A simpler example of a time-sequence pattern of organization might be a recipe that depends on the combining of ingredients in the correct order.

Topical-Sequence Pattern

The **topical-sequence pattern** addresses the advantages, disadvantages, qualities, and types of persons, places, or things. The topical-sequence pattern can be used to explain to audience members why you want them to adopt a certain point of view. It is appropriate when you have three to five points to make: three reasons why people should buy used cars, four of the main benefits of studying speech, or five characteristics of a good football player. This pattern of organization is among the most versatile. In a speech encouraging audience members to adopt tarantulas as pets, a portion of the topical-sequence outline would look like the following:[15]

I. The name *tarantula* has an interesting history.
   A. The word *tarantula* is derived from the name of a small town in Italy.
      1. Taranto was a town in Italy where the people experienced a large number of spider bites.
      2. The people of Taranto were bitten so frequently they developed a dance to sweat the spider poison out of their blood.
   B. The name *tarantula* was applied originally to the European wolf spider, the one encountered in Taranto.
   C. The name was transferred to the tropical spider, which is now known as the tarantula.
II. The tarantula is characterized by five unusual characteristics.
   A. One unusual feature of the tarantula is its size.
      1. Tropical tarantulas are as large as three inches in body length and ten inches in leg span.
      2. Species in the United States range from one to three inches in body length and up to five inches in leg span.
   B. A second unusual feature of the tarantula is that it is nocturnal; that is, it hunts at night.
   C. A third interesting feature of the tarantula is that it can see only two inches and relies on leg hairs to sense the presence of other things.

D. A fourth characteristic of the tarantula is that the species is cannibalistic.

E. A fifth characteristic of the tarantula is that it moults.

    1. Moulting decreases with age.

    2. Moulting can be accompanied by regeneration of lost parts such as legs.

The outline could continue to develop main points on why tarantulas make interesting and economical pets and on the myths about their poison. However, the portion of the outline shown here illustrates the main advantage of the topical-sequence outline—it can be used to organize diverse ideas into a commonsense sequence that appeals to an audience.

Problem-and-Solution Pattern

The third pattern of organization we consider in detail is the **problem-and-solution pattern.** As the name of this pattern suggests, the pattern describes a problem and proposes a solution. A speech based on this pattern is divisible into two distinct parts, with an optional third part in which the speaker meets any anticipated objections to the proposed solution. The problem-and-solution pattern can have other patterns within it. For example, you might discuss the problem in time-sequence order, and you might discuss the solution using a topical-sequence pattern.

The problem-and-solution pattern of organization requires close audience analysis because you have to decide how much time and effort to spend on each portion of the speech. Is the audience already familiar with the problem? If so, you might be able to discuss the problem briefly with a few reminders to the audience of the problem's seriousness or importance. On the other hand, the problem may be so complex both the problem and the solution cannot be covered in a single speech. In that case, you may have found a topic that requires a problem speech and a solution speech or speeches. In any case, your audience analysis should be an important first step in determining the ratio of time devoted to the problem and to the solution in this pattern.

The problem-and-solution speech in outline form might look like this:

Physical Fitness for College Students

  I. Many college students are in poor physical condition.

    A. Fewer colleges are requiring physical education courses.

    B. Increasing numbers of college students are overweight.

    C. Increasing numbers of college students suffer from physical problems caused by poor physical conditioning.

  II. Jogging is good for social, psychological, and physical reasons.

    A. People who jog together get to know each other very well.

    B. Joggers can take out some of their frustrations, anxieties, and aggressions on the track.

    C. Joggers can gain and maintain good physical conditioning through regular workouts.

 III. The main objections to jogging are the time and the energy it takes.

    A. We should take the time to keep our bodies in good condition, just as we do our minds and spirits.

    B. The effort required in jogging is its main benefit—strengthening our cardiovascular system.

The problem-and-solution pattern has many applications in speeches on contemporary problems and issues. It can be used to discuss inflation, price-fixing, poverty, welfare, housing costs, the quality of goods, the quality of services, and the problems of being a student.

Monroe Motivated Sequence

The **Monroe motivated sequence,** developed originally by Professor Alan Monroe, has been widely acclaimed for its usefulness in organizing speeches.[16] The sequence has five steps:

1. *Attention.* You must gain and maintain audience attention, and you must determine a way to focus audience attention on the content of your speech. (Twelve ideas for gaining and maintaining audience attention were presented earlier in this chapter.)
2. *Need.* Once you have the audience's attention, you must show audience members how the speech is relevant to them. You must arouse a need for your information in an informative speech and for the change you suggest in a persuasive speech.
3. *Satisfaction.* Your speech presents the information the audience needs or is a solution to their needs. You satisfy the audience by meeting needs with your plan.
4. *Visualization.* You reinforce your idea in the audience's collective mind by getting audience members to *see* how your information or ideas will help them.
5. *Action.* Once the audience has visualized your idea, you plea for action. The audience might remember your main points in an informative speech and state them to others, or the audience may go out and do what you ask in a persuasive speech.

The Monroe motivated sequence is a kind of problem-solving format that encourages an audience to get concerned about an issue. It is an appropriate organizational pattern for persuasive speeches, especially when the audience is reluctant to change or to accept the proposed action. A speech designed to motivate audience members to reduce the sugar in their diet could use the Monroe motivated sequence as follows:[17]

Where Sugar Goes, Trouble Follows

Attention	I. Americans consume an average of 125 pounds of sugar per year, about 60 percent of which is hidden in foods.
Need	II. Myths abound about why Americans consume such large quantities of sugar.
	A. One myth about sugar is humans have a psychological need for it.
	B. A second myth is sugar is needed for quick energy.
	C. A third myth is all carbohydrates are the same.
Satisfaction	III. Reduced sugar consumption can result in better teeth, less body fat, and fewer diseases.
Visualization	IV. Reduced sugar consumption can help to eliminate the pain and expense of dental work and can make you look better and last longer.
Action	V. You should substitute fruits with their natural sugars for the refined sugars hidden in many foods: a two-ounce candy bar has the same calories as one pound of apples.

Other Organizational Patterns

Spatial Organization

A speech can have **spatial organization,** with emphasis on where the parts of a whole exist in space. Examples of speeches that could be organized spatially are descriptions of a control panel from center to periphery, the electrical transmission from an energy source to the home, and a dress design from top to bottom.

Cause-Effect Organization

With **cause-effect organization,** the speaker explains the cause or causes and the consequences, results, or effects. A speech on inflation that uses the cause-effect organization might review causes of inflation, such as low productivity and high wages, and review effects of inflation, such as high unemployment and high interest. Cause-effect organization is often used in informative speeches that seek to explain an issue. It differs from the problem-and-solution organization because the cause-effect organization does not necessarily reveal what to do about a problem; instead, the cause-effect organization allows for full explanation of an issue.

Organizing a Bibliography

When you have completed your outline, you may be asked to provide a **bibliography,** a list of the sources you used in your speech. In chapter 14, we examined footnote form; in this chapter, we look at the correct forms for the bibliography.

The most common source students use for their speeches is magazine articles, usually obtained by using the *Reader's Guide.* The following is the correct form for a bibliographic entry for a periodical or magazine article:

Card, Josefina J., and William S. Farrell, Jr. "Nontraditional Careers for Women: A Prototypical Example." *Sex Roles: A Journal of Research* 9(October 1983): 1005–22.

"Marketing Marijuana." *Psychology Today* 18(January 1984): 77.

Notice that in bibliography form the name of the first author appears in reverse order so the list can be alphabetized. Notice also that if there is no author, then the bibliographic entry begins with the next available information. In the case of the second entry, the first information is the title of the article. Your instructor may or may not require volume numbers for magazine articles, but if a volume number is included, you do not write "p." or "pp." in the entry. An example which does not include a volume number or author is:

"Marketing Marijuana." *Psychology Today,* January 1984, p. 77.

"How to Use Best-Selling Home Plans." *Best Selling Home Plans from Home Magazine,* Winter 1986, p. 16.

In this instance, because there is no volume number, you should include "p." for a single page or "pp." for more than one page. Notice also, unlike the footnote form, the name of the author or authors and the title of the article are followed by a period.

The following is the correct bibliographic form for a book in your list of sources:

Collins, Jackie. *Hollywood Husbands*. New York: Simon and Schuster, 1986.

The author's name is in reverse order for accurate alphabetization. The name of the author and the name of the book are followed by a period. The place of publication is followed by a colon, the name of the publisher is followed by a comma, and the date of publication is followed by a period. A bibliographic entry must include the pages of a book that were used if the entire book was not used.

If you use an interview for your source, the bibliographic entry would look like this:

Stempel, III, Guido. Distinguished Professor in the E.W. Scripps School of Journalism, Ohio University. Interviewed on 12 January 1987.

Pamphlets, handbooks, and manuals may not have complete information about who wrote them, who published them, or when they were published. In that case, you are expected to provide as much information as possible so that others can verify the source.

The main idea behind a bibliography is to inform others what sources you used for your speech and to permit others to check those sources for themselves. If you run across sources you do not know how to footnote or to place in bibliographic form, you can ask your bookstore or a librarian for *The Publication Manual of the American Psychological Association, The MLA Style Sheet*, or *The Chicago Manual of Style*. College composition texts also include the standard forms for footnote and bibliographic entries.

Transitions and Signposts

So far, we have examined the organization of a speech in its broadest sense. To look at the speech as a problem-and-solution or cause-effect organization is like looking at a house's first floor and basement. It is important we also look more closely at the design of the speech by examining whatever connects the parts of a speech together.

Transitions and signposts are two items that hold the speech together. A **transition** is a bridge from one idea to another. It is a link between whatever came before in a speech and whatever is coming next. A typical transition is a brief flashback and a brief forecast that tells your audience when you are moving from one main point to another.

The most important transitions are between the introduction and the body, between the main points of the body, and between the body and the conclusion of the speech. Other transitions can appear between the main heading and main points, between main points and subpoints, between subpoints and sub-subpoints, between examples, and between visual aids and the point being illustrated. The transitions can review, preview, or even be an internal summary, but they always explain the relationship between one idea and another. Transitions are the mortar between the building blocks of the speech. Without them, cracks appear, and the structure is less solid. Figure 15.1 gives examples of transitions.

Figure 15.1

Transitions.

Transition from One Main Point to Another
"Now that we have seen why computers are coming down in cost, let us look next at why software is so expensive."

Transition from Main Point to a Visual Aid
"I have explained that higher education is becoming more and more expensive. This bar graph will show exactly how expensive it has become over the last five years."

Transition That Includes a Review, Internal Summary, and Preview
"You have heard that suntanning ages the skin, and I have shown you the pictures of a Buddhist monk and a nighttime bartender who hardly ever exposed themselves to direct sunlight. Now I want to show you a picture of a thirty-five-year-old woman who spent most of her life working by day in direct sunlight."

Figure 15.2

Signposts.

First, I will illustrate . . .
A second idea is . . .
Another reason for . . .
Finally, we will . . .
Look at this bar graph . . .
See what you think of this evidence . . .
Furthermore, you should consider . . .

Signposts are a way a speaker signals to an audience where the speech is going. Signposts, as the name implies, are like road signs that tell a driver there is a curve, bump, or rough road ahead; they are a warning, a sign the speaker is making a move. Whereas transitions are often several to many sentences in length, signposts are usually no longer than a sentence or a few words in length. Whereas transitions review, state a relationship, and forecast, signposts just point.

Beginning speakers often are admonished by their instructors for using signposts that are too blatant: "This is my introduction," "This is my third main point," or "This is my conclusion." More experienced speakers choose more subtle but equally clear means of signposting: "Let me begin by showing you . . .," "A third reason for avoiding the sun is . . .," or "The best inference you can draw from what I have told you is . . .." Figure 15.2 gives examples of signposts.

Transitions and signposts help speakers to map a speech for the audience. Transitions explain the relationships in the speech by reflecting backward and forward. Signposts point more briefly to what the speaker is going to do at the moment. Both transitions and signposts help bind the speech into a unified whole.

The Conclusion

Like the introduction and the body of a speech, the **conclusion** has certain functions. Complex speeches frequently conclude with a summary of main points from the body of the speech. Persuasive speeches frequently end with an appeal to the audience to think or behave in some manner that is consistent with the persuader's purpose. The means of ending speeches are numerous. The speaker can terminate a speech with a rhetorical question ("Knowing what you now know, will you feel safe riding with a driver who drinks?") or with a quotation from some famous person ("As John F. Kennedy said, 'Forgive your enemies, but never forget their names.'") or with a literary passage ("We conclude with the words of Ralph Waldo Emerson, who said, 'It is one light which beams out of a thousand stars; it is one soul which animates all men.'") or perhaps with some action that demonstrates the point of the speech (the quickly assembled electric motor works for the class to see; the speaker twirls and does the splits in one graceful motion; the experiment is completed, and the mixture of soda and vinegar boils and smokes).

Introductions and conclusions—getting started and drawing to a close—are often a challenge for beginning speakers. Because of this, these two parts of the speech should be rehearsed so they can be presented as planned. The speaker who fails to plan a conclusion may approach the end with nothing more to say.

Audiences need to be warned by your words, your tone, or your actions the speech is nearly completed. Otherwise, you might end your speech with the audience dangling in the wind as you head for your seat. Audiences appreciate a sense of closure, a sense of completeness, and a sense of finality in the conclusion of a speech. Speakers who ignore this expectation risk offending the very people they seek to influence.

In conversations with friends, we indicate the conversation must stop by our words, facial expressions, gestures, and movements. Similarly, in public speaking, you indicate the end of your speech is near by signaling your audience with words and actions. Notice how the following ending signals the impending conclusion of the speech: "Now that you have heard my three arguments concerning why we should encourage the student newspaper to cover assaults on campus, I want to leave you with these words from the editor of the student newspaper . . ." You can also signal the conclusion of your speech with your movement—some speakers literally fade back and away from the audience as they draw to a conclusion because they want to show they are almost done; others end their speech with a challenge in which they approach the audience for their final words. Either may be appropriate depending on whether a tranquil or a challenging ending is invited by the topic. Finally, you can simply tell your audience you are finished by using the words that most often signal a conclusion: "Finally . . .," "To summarize . . .," "And my final words for you tonight are . . .," or "Wendell Johnson once summed up the main message I have tried to convey to you this afternoon when he said . . ."

Certain functions are fulfilled by a conclusion. Those functions are:

1. To forewarn the audience you are about to stop, which is the brakelight function
2. To remind the audience of your central idea or the main points in your message

3. To specify precisely what the audience should think or do in response to your speech
4. To end the speech in a manner that makes audience members want to think and do what you recommend

Let's examine each of these functions of a conclusion in greater detail.

The **brakelight function** warns the audience you are about to stop. Can you tell when a song is about to end? Do you know when someone in a conversation is about to complete a story? Can you tell in a television drama the narrative is drawing to a close? The answer to these questions is usually "yes" because we get verbal and nonverbal signals that songs, stories, and dramas are about to end. But, how do you use the brakelight function in a speech?

One student signaled the end of her speech by saying, "Five minutes is hardly time to consider all the complications of abortion . . ." By stating her time was up, she signaled her conclusion. Another said, "Thus, men have the potential for much greater role flexibility than our society encourages . . ." The word *thus*, like the word *therefore*, signals the conclusion for a logical argument and indicates the argument is drawing to a close.

The second function of a conclusion—reminding the audience of your central idea or the main points in your message—can be fulfilled by restating the main points, by summarizing them briefly, or by selecting the most important one for special treatment. A woman who was delivering a pro-choice speech on abortion ended it by reminding her audience of her main point. Her method was to use two contrasting quotations:[18]

> We need to protect ourselves from closed-minded opinions like that of Senator Jesse Helms who proposed the following amendment:
>
> "The paramount right to life is vested in each human being from the moment of fertilization without regard to age, health, or condition of dependency."
>
> Instead, let's consider the words of Rhonda Copelon, a staff lawyer with the Center for Constitutional Rights:
>
> "To use the Bill of Rights—which also and not incidently guarantees the separation of church and state—to establish laws as a religious belief on a matter of private moral conduct would be unprecedented. It would transform into a tool of oppression a document which guarantees rights by limiting the power of the state to invade people's lives."
>
> All I ask you to do is to look at the woman's side for a moment. Consider all the implications upon her life. The unborn is not the only one with a right to life. The woman has one too.

Whether you agree with the position stated in the conclusion or not, it was an insightful way to restate the main message and to reiterate the conflicting viewpoints on the issue.

The third function of a conclusion is to specify exactly what you expect audience members to do as a result of your speech. Do you want them to simply remember a few of your important points? Then tell them one last time the points you think are worth remembering. Do you want the audience members to write down the argument they found most convincing, sign a petition, talk to their friends? If so, you should specify what you would regard as an appropriate response to your speech. One student who gave her speech on unions concluded with the slogan: "Buy the union label." The ending statement specified exactly what the speaker expected of the audience.

The fourth function of a conclusion is to end the speech in a manner that makes audience members pleased they listened to you. Perhaps you taught the audience how to do something during the speech—how to help a choking victim, how to defend themselves, or how to find a better product. If you successfully teach audience members how to do something, they may already feel better because they know more than they did before they heard your speech.

In concluding a speech, as in beginning, it is possible to be overly dramatic. At one large midwestern college, the speech classes were taught on the third floor of a building. In one room, a student was delivering a speech about insanity. As the speech progressed, the class became increasingly aware the young man delivering the speech had a few problems. At first, it was difficult to understand what he was saying: words were run together, parts of sentences were incoherent, pauses were too long. Near the end of the speech, the young man's eyes were rolling, and his jaw had fallen slack. At the very end of the speech, he looked wildly at the audience, ran over to the open window, and jumped. The class was aghast. Instructor and students rushed to the window expecting to see his shattered remains. Far below, on the ground, were twenty fraternity brothers holding a large fire fighter's net with the speaker waving happily from the center.

A better idea is to conclude your speech with an inspirational statement, with words that make audience members glad they took the time and energy to listen to you. One student came up with a single line at the end of his speech on automobile accidents that summarized his speech and gave his audience a line to remember: "It is not who is right in a traffic accident that really counts," he said, "it is who is left." That conclusion was clever, provided a brief summary, and was an intelligent and safe way to end a speech.

Summary

In this chapter, we discuss the three basic parts of a speech—the introduction, the body, and the conclusion—and their functions.

The five functions of an introduction are: (1) to gain and maintain audience attention, (2) to arouse audience interest in the topic, (3) to reveal the purpose of the speech, (4) to describe the speaker's qualifications, and (5) to forecast the organization and development of the speech.

The body of a speech can be organized through outlining. The seven principles of outlining are: (1) relating all items in an outline to the immediate purpose and the long-range goal, (2) limiting the outline to an abstract of the speech itself, (3) expressing ideas in single units of information, (4) indicating the importance of items with rank-ordered symbols, (5) indicating the importance of items with margins that increase with decreasing importance, (6) coordinating less important content with less important symbols and larger margins, and (7) stating items in parallel form. Useful outline styles include the sentence outline and the key-word outline. Typical patterns of organization commonly used in public speaking are: the time-sequence pattern, the topical-sequence pattern, the problem-and-solution pattern, the Monroe motivated sequence, spatial organization, and cause-effect organization.

A completed outline should be accompanied by a bibliography that lists the sources used in your speech.

Transitions are bridges from one idea to another. Signposts are a way of signaling to an audience where the speech is going. Both transitions and signposts bind the speech into a unified whole.

The functions of a speech conclusion are: (1) to forewarn the audience the speech is about to end, (2) to remind the audience of the central idea or the main points of your message, (3) to specify the desired audience response, and (4) to end the speech in a manner that encourages your audience to think and do as you recommend.

chapter 16

Delivery and Visual Aids

I call him a master who can speak keenly
and clearly to an average audience from
an average point of view; but I call him
eloquent who more wondrously and largely
can enhance and adorn what he will, and
hold in mind and memory all the sources of
things that pertain to public speaking.

Cicero in De Oratore
(55 B.C.)

N othing great was ever achieved without
enthusiasm.

Ralph Waldo Emerson

C ourage is grace under pressure.

Ernest Hemingway

Objectives

1. Recognize four modes of speech delivery.
2. State seven vocal aspects of speech delivery.
3. Discuss the four bodily aspects of speech delivery.
4. Demonstrate effective vocal and bodily delivery.
5. Use visual aids effectively.

Key Terms

modes of delivery
pitch
rate
listenability
comprehension
pause
vocalized pauses
volume
projection
enunciation
pronunciation
articulation
fluency
vocal variety
gestures
eye contact
visual aids

The delivery of a speech is an important part of public speaking. The words of a speech are only part of the message; the remainder of the message may be carried by the speaker's vocal and bodily actions. For example, the speaker can deliver a speech with a tone of voice that expresses conviction, anger, or irony. Similarly, the speaker's smile, alert posture, and forceful gestures convey a message to the audience.

In this chapter, we examine four modes of delivery, explore the vocal and bodily aspects of delivery, survey the use of visual aids, and conclude with some suggestions on how to effectively deliver your speeches.

Four Modes of Speech Delivery

Four **modes of delivery** are possible for the public speaker: the speaker can read a manuscript, deliver an extemporaneous speech, make an impromptu speech, or memorize the speech. We look at each mode of delivery and point out the appropriate circumstances for selecting it.

Manuscript Mode

Speakers who have to be very careful about what they say and how they say it choose to present speeches delivered from manuscripts. In other words, the speaker has a script of the entire speech. The advantage of the manuscript mode of delivery is the speaker is never at a loss for words—they are all right there. The disadvantages of a manuscript speech are that it is often a mere reading of the words, it invites the speaker to watch the script instead of the audience, it lacks spontaneity, and it discourages the speaker from responding to listeners' feedback.

The best time to read a manuscript is when every word, phrase, and sentence must be exact, when an error can be serious, as when the president of the United States makes an important address. The president may appear to be speaking without any notes at all, but he is actually reading his speech off a teleprompter that permits him to read every word while looking directly at the television camera or his audience. Many ministers write out their sermons so their main points are correctly supported with Biblical verses. College teachers often lecture from a manuscript so they give the same lesson to each section they teach. Students may be asked to use a manuscript, but usually the emphasis for beginning speakers is on the next mode we consider—the extemporaneous mode of delivery.

Extemporaneous Mode

Extemporaneous speeches are the most common in the classroom where students are learning how to prepare and deliver speeches. The extemporaneous speech is carefully prepared and researched, but it appears to be conversational in its delivery. The extemporaneous mode of delivery does not have the disadvantages of the manuscript speech. While reading a manuscript invites reading of the script, reduces eye contact,

The speech occasion affects your mode of delivery.

and makes changes difficult, extemporaneous delivery invites freedom from notes, encourages eye contact, and makes adaptation easier. The speaker who employs the extemporaneous mode delivers the speech from key words, an outline, or a list of main points. Because much of the speech is composed in the speaker's head as the speech is being delivered, it appears to be done "on the spur of the moment," the literal Latin meaning of the term *extemporaneous*. One sign of the spontaneity in an extemporaneous speech is the speaker does not use the same word choices each time the speech is delivered.

Impromptu Mode

The impromptu mode is delivery of a speech without notes and without plans or preparation. The term *impromptu* comes from Latin and French roots meaning "in readiness." You have already given impromptu speeches. When you answer a question in class, you are giving an impromptu answer. When someone asks you to explain something at a meeting, your explanation is usually impromptu. When you are asked to introduce yourself, to say a few words about yourself, or to reveal what you know about some subject, you are making an impromptu speech. You may be prepared for the speech in that you do have something to say, but you did not prepare to give a speech the way you would prepare for an extemporaneous speech. Some speech instructors give students an opportunity to practice impromptu speaking by having students introduce themselves; others have students draw topics out of a hat for an impromptu speech. One of the advantages of this mode of delivery is you learn how to think on your feet without benefit of notes. A disadvantage is this mode of delivery does not encourage research, preparation, or practice.

Memorized Mode

The memorized mode of delivery is simply one in which the speaker has committed the speech to memory. The speaker learns the speech either by rote memory or by delivering it so many times it is not forgotten. This type of delivery is common in oratory contests, on the lecture circuit, and at banquets. Many politicians have a stock speech they have committed to memory so it can be used wherever the politically faithful might gather. The main advantage of a memorized address is it permits the speaker to concentrate on delivery. Eye contact can be continuous; searching for words is eliminated. The main disadvantage is the memorized address permits little or no adaptation during the speech. The speaker risks having a speech that sounds memorized. However, in some formal situations, there may be little need for adaptation—some speakers have delivered the same speech so many times they even know when the audience is going to applaud, and for how long.

Different speakers prefer different modes of delivery. Whereas the impromptu mode teaches students very little about preparing a speech, both the reading of manuscripts and the delivery of memorized speeches require a great deal of time. The extemporaneous mode is favored in the public speaking classroom because it is useful and efficient, because it allows for maximum adaptation to the audience before and during the speech, and because it helps students to learn how to prepare a speech.

Nonetheless, the mode of delivery does not determine the effectiveness of a speech. In a study to determine whether the extemporaneous or the manuscript mode of delivery was more effective, two researchers concluded the mode of delivery simply did not determine effectiveness. The ability of the speaker was more important—some speakers were more effective with extemporaneous speeches than with manuscripts, but others used both modes with equal effectiveness.[1]

Vocal and Bodily Aspects of Speech Delivery

Delivery, as we have already observed, is concerned with how the voice and body affect the meaning of your speech. They are important parts of the message you communicate to your audience.

Effective speech delivery has many advantages. Research indicates effective delivery—the appropriate use of voice and body in public speaking—contributes to the credibility of the speaker.[2] Indeed, student audiences characterize the poorest speakers by their voices and the physical aspects of delivery.[3] Poor speakers are judged to be fidgety, nervous, and monotonous. They also maintain little eye contact and show little animation or facial expression.[4] Good delivery increases the audience's capacity for handling complex information.[5] Thus, public speakers' credibility—the audience's evaluation of them as good or poor speakers—and their ability to convey complex information may all be affected by the vocal and bodily aspects of delivery.

Vocal Aspects of Speech Delivery

Studying the vocal aspects of speech delivery is like studying the music that comes from the notes. Musical notes are like the words of the speech. The music results in the sounds we hear when someone says the words. Just as different musicians can make the same notes sound quite different, public speakers can say words in different ways to get the audience to respond in various ways. The seven vocal aspects of delivery are pitch, rate, pauses, volume, enunciation, fluency, and vocal variety.

Pitch

Pitch is the highness or lowness of the speaker's voice, its upward and downward movement, the melody produced by the voice. Pitch is what makes the difference between the "ohhh" you utter when you earn a poor grade in a class and the "ohhh" you utter when you see something or someone really attractive. The "ohhh" looks the same in print, but when the notes turn to music, the difference between the two expressions is vast. The pitch of your voice can make you sound lively, or it can make you sound listless. As a speaker, you learn to avoid the two extremes: you avoid the lack of change in pitch that results in a monotone, and you avoid repeated changes in pitch that result in a singsong delivery. The best public speakers employ the full range of their normal pitch.

Control of pitch does more than make a speech sound pleasing. Changes in pitch can actually help an audience to remember information.[6] Voices perceived as "good" are characterized by a greater range of pitch, more upward inflections, more downward inflections, and more pitch shifts.[7] Certainly, one of the important features of pitch control is it can be employed to alter the way in which an audience will respond to the words. Many subtle changes in meaning are accomplished by changes in pitch. The speaker's pitch tells an audience whether the words are a statement or a question, whether the words mean what they say, and whether the speaker is expressing doubt, determination, or surprise.

Pitch control, whether in baseball or speech, is learned only by regular practice. An actor who is learning to utter a line has to practice it many times and in many ways before he or she can be sure that most people in the audience will understand the words as intended. The public speaker practices a speech before friends to discover whether the words are being understood as intended. Sometimes, we sound angry when we do not intend to; sometimes we sound opposed when we intend to sound doubtful; and sometimes we sound frightened when we are only surprised. We are not always the best judge of how we sound to others, so we have to place some trust in other people's evaluations.

Rate

Rate, the second vocal characteristic of speech delivery, is the speed of delivery. The normal rate for American speakers is between 125 and 190 words per minute. But our minds can understand many more words per minute than that. That is why some medical schools are recording professors' lectures in a compressed form. Mechanically speeding up the lecture allows students to hear a one-hour lecture in forty-five minutes.

An early study of students who won collegiate oratory contests indicated they spoke an average of 120 words per minute.[8] That rate is slightly below the average speaking rate for Americans. In oratorical contests, there may be some advantage to a slow delivery. There have also been studies of the relationship between rate and **listenability.** Can the audience understand the speaker when the rate varies? One researcher used recorded stories and found no differences in listenability when the stories were played back at 125, 150, 175, and 200 words per minute.[9] Notice that only the 200-word-per-minute rate exceeds the normal range of 125 to 190 words per minute and it exceeds the normal rate only slightly. We may safely conclude from this study that, with recorded stories at least, a rate within the normal range does not adversely affect listenability.

How does rate relate to **comprehension,** or understanding of the content of a speech? One study indicated that comprehension at 282 words per minute, well above the normal range, was only 10 percent less than it was at 141 words per minute, near the middle of the normal range.[10] Given the rather large increase in rate, the loss in comprehension was relatively small. Another study related to rate and comprehension showed, with just ten minutes of practice, students could learn to listen to double the amount without a loss of comprehension.[11]

These research findings suggest that speakers can talk faster than normal without affecting listening and without affecting the audience's understanding. Indeed, when students shortened their pauses and raised their speaking rate from 126 words to 172 words per minute, neither the audience members' understanding nor their rating of the speaker's delivery was affected.[12] The human mind can understand information delivered at a faster rate than we normally speak and that rapid delivery can increase the amount of material covered without negatively affecting the audience's rating of the speaker's delivery. Then why do winners of oratory contests speak even more slowly than most speakers? Perhaps because speech instructors tell their students more often to slow down than to speed up. Many speakers show their anxiety by speeding up, which is unpleasant to an audience. Then again, perhaps the studies are not conclusive. While increasing the speed of recorded stories did not reduce listenability, all but one speed was well within the normal range, and stories are among the easiest verbal material to understand. In another study, the speed was increased from 126 to 172 words per minute without reducing comprehension or the audience's evaluation of delivery. But both speeds are within the normal range. A rate well beyond normal resulted in a 10 percent loss of comprehension. Instead of reading the studies as an indication that faster is better, it turns out a speaker need only to stay within a normal range of rates.

The essential point, not revealed in the studies, is speaking rate needs to be adapted to the audience and the situation. A grade-school teacher does not rip through a fairy tale—the audience is just learning how to understand words. The public speaker addressing a large audience without a microphone speaks slowly and distinctly to enhance the audience's understanding of the words. If audience and situation need to be taken into account in determining appropriate rate, so does content. Stories delivered at a relatively fast rate may be easy to understand, but a string of statistics may have to be delivered slowly and be repeated to be fully understood. The rate also may depend

Do not underestimate the importance of the delivery of a message.

on what effect you are seeking. Telling a frightening story would be difficult at a high speed. Effective public speakers adjust their speed according to the audience, the situation, the content of the speech, and the effect they are trying to produce.

Pauses

A third vocal characteristic of speech delivery is the **pause.** Speeches seem to be meant for a steady stream of words, without silences. Yet pauses and silence can be used for dramatic effect and to get an audience to consider content. The speaker may begin a speech with rhetorical questions: "Have you had a cigarette today? Have you had two or three? Ten or eleven? Do you know what your habit is costing you in a year? A decade? A lifetime?" After each rhetorical question, a pause allows each member of the audience to answer the question in his or her own mind.

On the other hand, **vocalized pauses** are interruptions that negatively affect an audience's perception of the speaker's competence and dynamism. The "ahhhs," and "mmhhs," of the beginning speaker are disturbing to the public speaking instructor. Unfortunately, even some highly experienced speakers have the habit of filling silences with vocalized pauses. At least one group teaches public speaking to laypersons by having members of the audience drop a marble into a can every time a speaker uses a vocalized pause. The resulting punishment, the clanging of the cans, is intended to break the habit. A more humane method might be to rehearse your speech before a friend who signals you every time you vocalize a pause, so you do it less often when you deliver your speech to an audience. One speech instructor hit on the idea of rigging a light to the lectern so every time the student speaker used a vocalized pause, the light went on for a moment. Perhaps we should be less afraid of silence—many audiences would prefer a little silence to vocalized pauses.

One way to learn how to use pauses effectively in public speaking is to listen to how your classmates use them. You should also listen to professional speakers. Paul Harvey, the radio commentator, practically orchestrates his pauses. His delivery of the "Page Two" section of his news broadcast helps make him unique. Oral Roberts, Billy Graham, or any of a dozen radio and television evangelists also use pauses effectively.

Volume

A fourth vocal characteristic of speech delivery is **volume,** the relative loudness of your voice. We are accustomed to speaking to people at a close distance, about an arm's length in conversation. To speak effectively in front of a class, a meeting, or an auditorium full of people, we speak louder or project our voices so all may hear. Telling speech students to speak louder might sound like very elementary advice, but many beginning speakers see those people in the first few rows and speak only to them. We project our voices (**projection**) to ensure the most distant people in the room can hear what we say. Even when practicing in an empty room, it is a good idea to project your voice so someone sitting at the back of the room could hear with ease.

Volume is more than just projection. Variations in volume can convey emotion, importance, suspense, and changes in meaning. We whisper a secret, and we use a stage whisper in front of an audience. We may speak loudly and strongly on important points and let our voices carry our conviction. An orchestra never plays so quietly patrons cannot hear, but the musicians vary their volume. Similarly, a public speaker who considers the voice an instrument learns how to speak softly, loudly, and everywhere in-between to convey meaning.

Enunciation

Enunciation, the fifth vocal aspect of speech delivery, is the pronunciation and articulation of words. Because our reading vocabulary is larger than our speaking vocabulary, we may use, in our speeches, words we have rarely or never heard before. It is risky to deliver unfamiliar words. One student in a speech class gave a speech about the human reproductive system. During the speech, he managed to mispronounce nearly half the words used to describe the female anatomy. The speaker sounded incompetent to his audience. Rehearsing in front of friends, roommates, or family is a safer way to try out your vocabulary and pronunciation on an audience.

Your objective should be to practice words new to you until they are easy for you to pronounce, until you are comfortable with them. Also be alert to the names of people you quote, introduce, or cite in your speech. Audiences are almost overly impressed when a student speaker correctly pronounces names like Goethe, Monet, and de Chardin.

The best way to avoid **pronunciation** problems is to find unfamiliar words in a dictionary. Every dictionary has a pronunciation key. For instance, the entry for the word *belie* in the *Random House Dictionary of the English Language* looks like this:

be·lie (bi–lī′), v.t., -lied, -ly·ing. 1. to show to be false; contradict: His trembling hands belied his calm voice . . .[13]

The entry illustrates the word *belie* has two syllables. The pronunciation key states the first *e* should be pronounced like the *i* in *if,* the *u* in *busy,* or the *ee* in *been.* The *i,* according to the pronunciation key, should be pronounced like the *ye* in *lye,* the *i* in *ice,* or the *ais* in *aisle.* The accent mark (') indicates which syllable should receive heavier emphasis. You should learn how to use the pronunciation key in a dictionary, but if you still have some misgivings about how to pronounce a word, you should ask your speech instructor for assistance.

Another way to improve your pronunciation is to learn how to prolong syllables. Prolonging vowel sounds, for instance, gives your voice a resonance attractive to audiences. Prolonging syllables can also make you easier to understand, especially if you are addressing a large audience, an audience assembled outside, or an audience in an auditorium without a microphone. The drawing out of syllables can be overdone, however. Some radio and television newspersons hang onto the final syllable so long the practice draws attention to itself.

Pronunciation and articulation are the important parts of enunciation. Poor **articulation,** poor production of sounds, is so common there are popular jokes about it. One adult remembers hearing a song about Willie the cross-eyed bear in Sunday school. The actual song title was "Willing the Cross I Bear." Some children have heard the Lord's Prayer mumbled so many times they think that one of the lines is "hollow be thy name."

Articulation problems are less humorous when they occur in your own speech. They occur in part because so many English words are spelled differently and sound alike and because we often articulate carelessly (figure 16.1). Among the common articulation problems are the dropping of final consonants and "-ing" sounds ("goin'," "comin'," and "leavin' "), the substitution of "fer" for "for," and the substitution of "ta" for "to." An important objective in public speaking, as it should be in all communication, is to state words clearly for more accurate transmission.

Fluency

The sixth vocal characteristic of speech delivery is **fluency**—the smoothness of delivery, the flow of the words, and the absence of vocalized pauses. Fluency is difficult because it cannot be achieved by looking up words in a dictionary or by any other simple solution. Fluency is not even very noticeable. Listeners are more likely to notice errors than to notice the seemingly effortless flow of words in a well-delivered speech. Also, it is possible to be too fluent. A speaker who seems too glib sometimes is considered "slick," or "smooth." The importance of fluency was emphasized in a study in which audiences tended to perceive a speaker's fluency and smoothness of presentation as a main determinant of effectiveness.[14]

To achieve fluency, public speakers must be confident of the content of their speeches. If the speakers know what they are going to say and have said it over and over in practice, then disruptive repetition and vocalized pauses are reduced. If speakers master what they are going to say and focus on the overall rhythm of the speech, their fluency improves. Speakers must pace, build, and time the various parts of the speech so they all fit together in a coherent whole.

Figure 16.1

Homonyms: Alike in sound, different in meaning.

See		Sea	
Saw		Saw	
Eight		Ate	
Weight		Wait	
Cite		Sight	Site
Address		Address	
Sow		Sew	

Vocal Variety

The seventh vocal aspect of speech delivery—one that summarizes many of the others—is **vocal variety.** This term refers to voice quality, intonation patterns, inflections of pitch, and syllabic duration. Vocal variety is encouraged in public speaking because studies show it improves effectiveness. Charles Woolbert, in a very early study of public reading, found audiences retained more information when there were large variations in rate, force, pitch, and voice quality. More recently, George Glasgow studied an audience's comprehension of prose and poetry and found comprehension decreased 10 percent when the material was delivered in a monotone. A third study proved audience members understood more when listening to skilled speakers than when listening to unskilled speakers. They also recalled more information immediately after the speech and at a later date. The skilled speakers were more effective, whether or not the material was organized, disorganized, easy, or difficult. Good vocalization was also found to include fewer but longer pauses, greater ranges of pitch, and more upward and downward inflections.[15]

Bodily Aspects of Speech Delivery

The four bodily aspects of speech delivery are gestures, eye contact, facial expression, and movement. These nonverbal indicators of meaning show how speakers relate to audiences, just as they show how individuals relate to each other. When we observe two persons busily engaged in conversation, we can judge their interest in the conversation without hearing their words. Similarly, in public speaking, the nonverbal bodily aspects of delivery reinforce what the speaker is saying. Audience members who can see the speaker comprehend more of the speech than audience members who cannot see the speaker.[16] Apparently, the speaker's actions convey enough meaning to improve the audience's understanding of what is being said.

Gestures

Gestures are movements of the head, arms, and hands we use to describe what we are talking about, to emphasize certain points, and to signal a change to another part of the speech. We rarely worry about gestures in a conversation, but when we give a speech in front of an audience, arms and hands seem to be bothersome. Perhaps we feel unnatural because public speaking is an unfamiliar situation. Do you remember the first time you drove a car, the first time you tried to swim or dive, or the first time you tried to kiss your date? The first time you give a speech you might not feel any more natural than you did then. Nonetheless, physically or artistically skilled people make their actions look easy. A skilled golfer, a talented painter, and a graceful dancer all perform with seeming ease. The beginners are the ones who make a performance look difficult. Apparently, human beings have to work diligently to make physical or artistic feats look easy.

What can you do to help yourself gesture naturally when you deliver your speech? The answer lies in feelings and practice. Angry farmers and angry miners appear on television to protest low prices and poor working conditions. These speakers have not spent a lot of time practicing, but they deliver their speeches with gusto and a lot of strong gestures. They also look very natural. The main reason for their natural delivery may be their feelings about the issue they are discussing. They are upset, and they show it in their words and actions. They are mainly concerned with getting their message across. The student of public speaking can also deliver a speech more naturally by concentrating on getting the message across. Self-conscious attention to your gestures is often self-defeating—the gestures look studied, rehearsed, or slightly out of

Gestures are essential to clarifying your
message.

rhythm with your message. Selecting a topic you find involving can have the unexpected benefit of improving your delivery, especially if you concentrate on your audience and your message.

Another way of learning to make appropriate gestures is to practice a speech in
front of friends who are willing to make positive suggestions. Indeed, constructive criticism is also one of the benefits you can receive from your speech instructor and your
classmates. Actors spend hours rehearsing lines and gestures so they will look spontaneous and unrehearsed on stage. In time and after many practice sessions, public
speakers learn which arm, head, and hand movements seem to help and which seem
to hinder their message. You, too, can learn, through practice, to gesture naturally—
in a way that reinforces your message instead of detracting from it.

Five suggestions for gesturing effectively are:

1. Keep your hands out of your pockets and at your sides when not gesturing.
2. Gesture with the hand not holding your notes.
3. Make your gestures deliberate—big and broad enough so that they do not look
   accidental or timid.
4. Keep your gestures meaningful by using them sparingly and only when they reinforce
   something you are saying.
5. Practice your gestures just as you do the rest of your speech so you become comfortable
   with the words and the gestures.

Eye Contact

Another physical aspect of delivery important to the public speaker is **eye contact.** Eye contact refers to sustained and meaningful contact with the eyes and faces of persons in the audience. It is not looking slightly over the heads of audience members or quick glances.

Audiences prefer maintenance of good eye contact[17] and that good eye contact improves source credibility.[18] Such conclusions are particularly important since individuals in other cultures may view eye contact differently. The public speaker from another country may be viewed less positively by an American audience than she would be in her native country. Similarly, Americans need to recognize and appreciate cultural differences in eye contact as well as other nonverbal cues.

Eye contact is one of the ways we indicate to others how we feel about them. We are wary of persons who, in conversation, do not look us in the eye. Similarly, in public speaking, eye contact conveys our relationship with our audience. The public speaker who rarely or never looks at the audience may appear disinterested in the audience, and the audience may resent it. The public speaker who looks over the heads of audience members or scans audience members so quickly that eye contact is not established may appear to be afraid of the audience. The proper relationship between audience and speaker is one of purposeful communication. We signal that sense of purpose by treating audience members as individuals with whom we wish to communicate—by looking at them for responses to our message.

How can you learn to maintain eye contact with your audience? One way is to know your speech so well you have to make only occasional glances at your notes. The speaker who does not know the speech well is manuscript-bound. Delivering an extemporaneous speech from key words or an outline is a way of encouraging yourself to keep an eye on the audience. One of the purposes of extemporaneous delivery is to enable you to adapt to your audience. That adaptation is not possible unless you are continually observing the audience's behavior to see if the individuals understand your message.

Other ways of learning to use eye contact include scanning or continually looking over your entire audience and addressing various sections of the audience as you progress through your speech. Concentrating on the head nodders may also improve your eye contact. In almost every audience, some individuals overtly indicate whether your message is coming across. These individuals usually nod "yes" or "no" with their heads, thus the name *nodders*. Some speakers find it helps their delivery to find friendly faces and positive nodders who signal when the message is getting through.

Facial Expression

A third physical aspect of delivery is facial expression. Your face is the most expressive part of your body. It consists of eyebrows that rise and fall; eyes that twinkle, glare, and cry; lips that pout or smile; cheeks that can dimple or harden; and a chin that can jut out in anger or recede in yielding. Some people's faces are a barometer of their feelings; other people's faces seem to maintain the same appearance whether they are happy or in pain or sorrow. Because you do not ordinarily see your own face when you are in action, you may not be fully aware of how you appear when you give a speech. In general, speakers are trying to maintain a warm and positive relationship with the audience, and they signal that intent by smiling as they would in conversation with someone they like. However, the topic, the speaker's intent, the situation, and the audience all help to determine the appropriate facial expressions in a public speech. You can discover the appropriateness of your facial expressions by having friends, relatives, or classmates tell you how you look when practicing your speech.

Movement

A fourth physical aspect of delivery is movement—what the speaker does with the entire body during a speech presentation. Sometimes, the situation limits movement. The presence of a fixed microphone, a lectern, a pulpit, or some other physical feature of the environment may limit your activity. The length of the speech can also make a difference. A short speech without movement is less difficult for both speaker and audience than a very long speech.

Good movement for the public speaker is appropriate and purposeful movement. The "caged lion" who paces back and forth to work off anxiety is moving inappropriately and purposelessly in relation to the content of the speech. You should move for a reason, such as walking a few steps when delivering a transition, thereby literally helping your audience to "follow you" to the next idea. Some speakers move forward on the points they regard as most important.

Because of the importance of eye contact, the speaker should always strive to face the audience, even when moving. Some other suggestions on movement relate to the use of visual aids. Speakers who write on the chalkboard during a speech have to turn their backs on the audience. This can be avoided either by writing information on the board between classes or by using a poster instead.

The college classroom is a laboratory for the student who wants to learn effective movement. By watching professors, lecturers, and fellow students when they deliver public speeches, you can learn through observation and practice what works for others and what works for you.

Speech Delivery Versus Speech Content

After reading this information on speech delivery, you might have the impression what you say is less important than how you say it. You might believe delivery is so important that the person who is fluent, who pauses appropriately, who speaks at the best pitch and rate, and who gestures and moves well does not have to worry much about the substance of the speech. You should be wary about drawing this conclusion from the evidence presented here. Eye contact, gestures, and enunciation are important, but content may be even more important. The same researcher who found poor speakers are identified by their voices and by the physical aspects of their delivery also found the best speakers were identified on the basis of the content of their speeches.[19] More of an audience's evaluation of a speaker is based on the content of the speech than on vocal characteristics such as intonation, pitch, and rate, and still another pair of researchers found a well-composed speech can mask poor delivery.[20] Finally, a review of the studies on informative speaking showed the influence of delivery on comprehension is overrated.[21]

What is the student of speech to conclude in the face of these reports that good delivery influences audience comprehension positively, but the influence of delivery on comprehension is overrated? In addition, one study says that poor vocal characteristics result in evaluation as a poor speaker and another says that good content can mask poor delivery. Perhaps we all tend to oversimplify problems by not recognizing degrees of importance. If we recognize such degrees, then we may be able to resolve the apparent conflict—at least until more evidence comes in. The studies cited in this chapter emphasize the importance of delivery. The researchers who challenge those findings do not say that delivery is unimportant; instead, they say that, in evaluating the relative importance of delivery and content, there is reason to believe content may be more important than delivery. However, the jury is still out on this question. Additional studies may modify what we believe at this time. For the moment, the safest position for the speech student is to regard both delivery and content—what you say and how you say it—as important in public speaking.

Visual Aids

Do you learn best when you read something, when you see something, or when you do something? Certainly, some skills are best learned by doing. Reading about how to make a dress from a pattern or watching another person do it are no substitute for trying it yourself. However, many things we know do not lend themselves to doing. You cannot do economics in the same way you can change a tire. Because so much public speaking deals with issues and topics that cannot be performed, we must know the most effective methods of communicating for a public speech.

Researchers tried to determine if people remember best through telling alone, through showing alone, or through both showing and telling by measuring retention three hours and three days after the communication attempt. The results were as follows:[22]

Method	Retention three hours later	Retention three days later
Telling alone	70%	10%
Showing alone	72%	20%
Showing and telling	85%	65%

Apparently, people retain information longer when they receive it both through their eyes and through their ears. Audiences that remember a message because the visual aids helped their comprehension or understanding are more persuaded by the presentation.

Students sometimes gain the impression public speaking instructors like them to use visual aids but they will not use visual aids for public speaking outside of the classroom. In fact, the use of visual aids is big business. Can you imagine an architect trying to explain to a board of directors how the new building will look without using models, drawings, and large-scale paintings? Can you sell most products without showing them? A colleague of the authors stated the point best of all:

> Any of our students going to work for a large corporation will seldom speak without visual aids. I know for certain that Caterpillar Tractor Company employees do not make any presentations inside or outside the company without visual aids. In fact, they have a whole department devoted to the preparation of visual aids.

Apparently, the skillful use of visual aids is an expectation in the world of business and industry. The place to learn how to use visual aids is in the classroom.

What are **visual aids?** They can be anything from the way you dress, to writing on the chalkboard, to items brought in to show what you are talking about. The student who wears a white lab coat while talking about paramedical training, the student who lists her three main points on the chalkboard, and the student who brings in his pet malamute are all using visual aids.

Using Visual Aids

One of the main reasons for using visual aids has already been stated: people tend to learn more and to retain it better when they both see and listen. Also, some messages are more effectively communicated through sight, touch, smell, and taste, and the effective speaker knows when words will not be sufficient to carry the message. In other words, if you are trying to tell an audience about a particularly complex problem in calculus, you might have considerable difficulty communicating that problem with voice only. Complex math problems are more effectively communicated through writing so the problem can be seen. Can audience members compare ten items in their minds? No, but they can if you show the ten items on a bar graph. Can the audience visualize the Philippines? Perhaps, but some travel posters or slides would result in a more accurate visualization.

Visual aids are not appropriate for all speeches at all times. In fact, because they take preparation and planning, they may not be possible in many impromptu situations. Also, visual aids should not be used for their own sake. There is no virtue in having visual aids unless they aid the audience in understanding your message or contribute in some other way to your purpose. Use visual aids when the message is easier to understand visually than orally; use visual aids when they reduce complexity for easier understanding, as when you are explaining many or complex statistics or ideas; and use visual aids when they support your message in ways that cannot be accomplished with words, such as when you display a bar graph showing the increasing costs of home ownership. The use of visual aids demands you become sensitive to what an audience will be unable to understand only through your words. Finally, visual aids should be visible to the audience only while being referred to and should be out of sight during the rest of the speech. Otherwise, visual aids can become a distraction that steals the focus from you.

Visual aids, like the facts in your speech, may require documentation. You should either show on the visual aid itself or tell the audience directly where you got the visual aid or the information on it.

Some helpful hints for using visual aids are:

1. Do not talk to your visual aids. Keep your eyes on your audience. Maintain good eye contact—instead of looking at your visuals.
2. Display visual aids only when you are using them. Before or after they are discussed, they usually become a needless distraction to the audience.
3. Make sure everyone in the room can see your visual aids. Above all, make sure you are not standing in front of a visual aid.

4. Leave a visual aid in front of the audience long enough for complete assimilation. Few things are more irritating to an audience than to have a half-read visual aid whipped away by a speaker.

5. Use a pointer or your inside arm for pointing to a visual aid. The pointer keeps you from masking the visual, and using your inside arm helps you to avoid closing off your body from the audience.

Types of Visual Aids

What kind of visual aids can you choose from? They are too numerous to catalogue here, but some of the main visual aids used by public speakers and some hints about their use follow.

Chalkboards

Chalkboards are the most readily available visual aid. You can write your name and the title of your speech on the chalkboard. You can use the chalkboard to write down important or unusual words you employ in your speech. Or you can use the chalkboard to list the items from your speech you want your audience to remember. Any statistics, facts, or details difficult to convey orally may be written on the chalkboard. Some questions to ask yourself before using the chalkboard are:

1. When should the information go on the chalkboard? Some speech instructors prefer that you place the information on the chalkboard before class begins. They dislike the delay caused by writing information on the chalkboard between speeches. Other instructors feel just as strongly that having information on the chalkboard before a speech is distracting. Few instructors object to having the speaker's name and the title of the speech on the chalkboard.

2. How should you write on the chalkboard? You should print legibly and large enough so people in the last row can read the information with ease. Also, you can avoid that tooth-shattering squeal by using chalk that has already been used and by angling the chalk so that it makes no noise. As any instructor can tell you, you should practice writing on the chalkboard between classes or when no one else is using the room because it takes some skill. If you don't practice, you might find your words look as if they are misspelled, your letters are too small, and your lines tend to go up or down as you proceed through a sentence.

3. How should you deliver your speech when you are talking about items that you have written on the chalkboard? You should try to face your audience while you speak. A pointer, a yardstick, or even your hand can direct the audience's attention to statements or illustrations on the chalkboard.

A skillful speaker knows when to place the information on the chalkboard, how to write the information on the chalkboard, and how to deliver the speech when using the chalkboard. The effective speaker also knows what kinds of information should be placed on the chalkboard and whether telling or showing or doing both will help the audience the most. Effective speakers use the chalkboard for "point clinchers," as a way to indicate to the audience the most important points in the speech.[23]

Be creative in your selection of visual aids.

Figure 16.2
A poster with a written message.

Sport	Calories/Hour
Run at 10 miles per hour	900/hour
Jog at 5 miles per hour	500/hour
Swim at 1/4 mile per hour	300/hour
Cycle at 13 miles per hour	600/hour

Source: *Consumer Digest*, May/June 1984, page 59

Posters

Posters are another way to present your ideas visually. They are handier than using the chalkboard because they can be prepared ahead of time. The general directions for creating an effective poster are similar to those listed for the chalkboard: the information on the poster should be information that is difficult to convey or to understand through listening; the information should be drawn or written in large scale so that people in the back of the room are able to see every word or illustration; the speaker should face the audience while working with the information on the poster; and the visual message should highlight important points.

The message on a poster may be a written message showing the number of calories in hamburgers from fast-food restaurants, stating the three primary reasons why tuition should be raised, or listing the advantages of co-op bookstores. As shown in figure 16.2, posters also can show numbers—for example, percentages, averages, calories per

Figure 16.3

A poster with a bar graph.

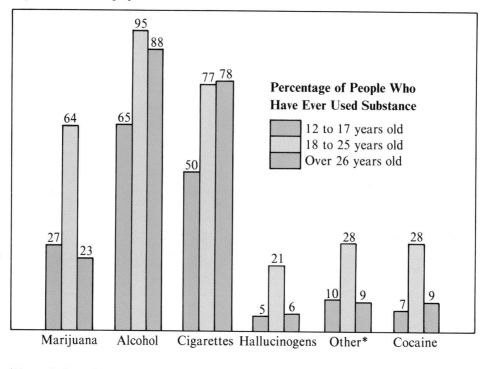

*Nonmedical use of stimulants, sedatives, tranquilizers, and analgesics

Source: Karen Karlsson.

hour, or miles per minute—that might otherwise be difficult to remember. When using numbers, you should remember to round off the numbers for easier understanding.

Three ways to illustrate information on posters are with bar graphs, pie charts, and line graphs. The *bar graph* helps you to show an audience how a number of different items compare. For example, the bar graph in figure 16.3 shows the percentages of persons in three different age groups who use six kinds of drugs. This information would be very difficult to communicate with words alone. With a bar graph, the differences among age groups and drugs become much simpler to explain. The *pie chart* shows how some whole is divided. The whole could be the federal budget with income figures showing how much of the federal "pie" comes from which sources. The pie chart in figure 16.4 shows what proportions of a family budget tend to go for various expenditures. A *line graph* is an effective way to show changes in quantity over time. The line graph in figure 16.5 shows how voluntary giving to colleges and universities has grown dramatically over the last thirty years.

Some suggestions for using posters for visual aids follow:

1. Keep the message simple. A common problem with visual aids is too much clutter. The audience should be able to grasp your point quickly.

Figure 16.4

A poster with a pie chart.

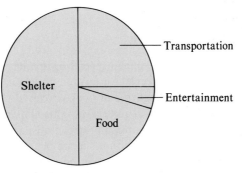

Figure 16.5

A poster with a line graph.

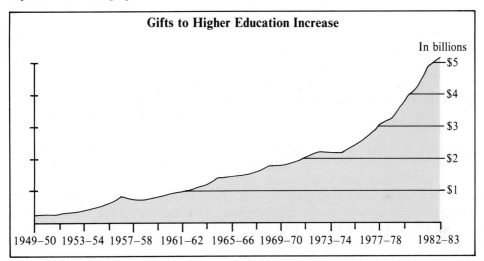

2. Use bar graphs rather than circle or pie charts whenever possible because people tend to underestimate the relative area of circles.[24]

3. Use color and artistic talents to make the poster attractive and to gain and maintain attention.

4. Be sure the poster is large enough for everyone to see.

5. Use ready-made posters or pictures such as travel posters or get hints for your own illustrations from those used on television commercials. Television advertisers tend to use outdoor, daytime shots, with one person, but not crowds, present.[25]

6. Learn to use flip charts—a series of posters. Uncover each item as you come to it for special effects.

Whatever kind of poster you use, keep the poster in front of the audience as long as you are talking about the subject portrayed. In some cases, it is appropriate to place the used poster on the chalk tray so you can refer to it again in your conclusion as you review the content of your speech.

Opaque and Overhead Projectors

Opaque and overhead projectors demand special equipment and practice, but they, too, have special advantages in a speech. An opaque projector is a machine that can project a picture or print from a magazine or book. It can also be used for relatively small, flat objects. Opaque projectors require dim lights and an empty wall or screen. An overhead projector is a machine that can project transparencies or sheets of clear plastic on which the speaker can write with a special pencil. Transparencies are best prepared ahead of time, but short messages can be printed on them as the speaker talks.

Movies and Slides

Movies and slides are good visual supplements to your speech as long as they do not become the speech. Both have the disadvantage of placing the audience and the speaker in the dark, where audience response is hidden. Even so, a one- or two-minute film showing violence on the basketball court or five or six slides showing alternative energy sources can add force to your speech. When you use slides and films, you should check out equipment and rehearse. An upside-down slide or a jittery film can ruin your speech. You should also arrange for a classmate to turn off the lights so you do not have to interrupt your speech by asking someone to turn off the lights or by doing it yourself.

Photographs

Another kind of visual aid is the photograph. The student who is speaking about Spanish architecture can use photographs of homes and public buildings; the student who is talking about identifying types of trees can have pictures of each type; and the student who is discussing how to do something—like assembling a bicycle—can have a series of photographs to illustrate and clarify. In figure 16.6, the student speaker used a photograph of a computer "painting" to show the capability of a computer to compose pictures.

Drawings

Drawings are another type of visual aid useful in public speaking. Most line drawings are simple and are used to clarify. When you draw a map to show your audience how to get to a specific place, when you draw the human foot and name the bones, or when you draw a cartoon character, you are using drawings as visual aids. Figure 16.7 shows a drawing used by a student speaker to illustrate a healthy life-style.

Figure 16.6

Today's graphics can be generated by a computer.

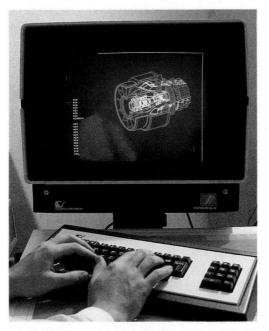

Figure 16.7

A drawing used as a visual aid.

Eat 3 ☐ meals
Sleep 8 hours
Work 8 hours
Exercise 3 times a week
Avoid

Avoid

Models and Physical Objects

Living models and physical objects can also be used as visual aids. For a speech on fashion design, you can have people model the clothes. For a speech on exercise machines, you can have another person demonstrate the machine.

Physical objects might be the best visual aid if your speech is about something small enough or controllable enough to show. Students have brought in polished rocks, model cars, chemistry sets, musical instruments, rappelling equipment, weights, and volcanic lava. Live pets, however, can pose special problems for the speaker. Snakes, dogs, cats, hamsters, and monkeys have a unique ability to make fools of their owners. Also, they are often highly distracting before and during the speech.

Handouts

Handouts are an especially effective way to communicate messages difficult to convey orally. One student passed out the American Cancer Society's list of cancer danger signs. Another distributed a handout with the names and call numbers of all of the country-western music stations because he knew the audience was unlikely to remember all the names and numbers. Still another student distributed the contract used when people will parts of their body to a medical center. Such handouts carry the impact of your speech beyond the classroom. They are usually kept, sometimes taken home where they are seen by others, and often discussed later by roommates and spouses.

Handouts have many advantages, but they also have some shortcomings. One shortcoming is they can be very distracting to the audience and disturbing to the speaker. When distributed during your speech, the handout gets the focus of attention instead of you. The problem is not entirely solved when you distribute handouts at the end of your speech because then they steal the focus from the next speaker. A second disadvantage is handouts sometimes carry too much of the content of the speech and may become a substitute for the speech. The audience does not have to listen to the speech because they already have it in print.

You as a Visual Aid

Finally, *you* might be the best visual aid for your speech. You can demonstrate karate, show some dance steps, or wear a lead apron. You can wear clothing appropriate for your speech: a suit when telling how to succeed in a job interview for a white-collar job, a lab coat when demonstrating chemical reactions, or a uniform when telling why other students should join the ROTC program. One student wore an old flannel shirt, tattered jeans, and a rag tied around his head. He carried a large lantern. His speech was about "steam tunneling," a sport in which students explored the university's steam tunnels. He was faulted for encouraging his audience to participate in an activity strongly discouraged by the university administration, but he certainly was appropriately dressed for his speech.

A friend can be a visual aid in a
demonstration speech.

Helpful Hints for Speech Delivery

This chapter discusses the vocal and bodily aspects of delivery and the use of visual aids. Perhaps how to deliver a speech effectively is obvious. However, the following hints should help you in delivering your speech and in using visual aids:

1. Practice your speech so you can deliver it with only occasional glances at your notes.
2. Keep your eyes on your audience so you can sense whether you are communicating your message.
3. Use facial expressions, gestures, and movements to help communicate your message.
4. Use your voice like a musical instrument to keep the sounds interesting and to affect the audience's response.
5. Speak loudly enough for audience members to hear, slowly enough so they can listen with understanding, and smoothly enough so they do not focus on your faults.
6. Use visual aids to communicate material not easily understood through listening.
7. Make your writing on the chalkboard or on posters large enough for all to see and simple enough for all to understand.
8. Consider using photographs, drawings, live models, objects, slides, films, handouts, and audiovisual equipment to help communicate your message.
9. Sound conversational, look natural, and strive to get your message across to your listeners.
10. Observe how your classmates, your professors, and other speakers deliver their speeches so you can learn from them.

Evaluating Your Delivery

Have a classmate, friend, or relative observe and evaluate your next speech for delivery skills. Have your critic use the following scale to fill in the blanks on the left:

1 = Excellent, 2 = Good,
3 = Average, 4 = Fair, 5 = Weak

Vocal Aspects of Delivery

_____ Pitch: Highness and lowness of voice; upward and downward inflections

_____ Rate: Words per minute; appropriate variation of rate for the difficulty of content

_____ Pauses: Intentional silence designed to aid understanding

_____ Volume: Loud enough to hear; variation with the content

_____ Enunciation: Correct pronunciation and articulation

_____ Fluency: Smoothness of delivery; appropriate pauses; good pacing, rhythm, and cadence without being so smooth as to sound artificial, contrived, or overly glib

_____ Vocal variety: Voice quality, intonation patterns, pitch inflections, and syllabic duration

Bodily Aspects of Delivery

_____ Gestures: Natural movement of the head, hands, arms, and torso consistent with the speaker, topic, and situation

_____ Eye contact: Natural, steady without staring, includes entire audience and is responsive to audience feedback

_____ Facial expression: Consistent with message; used to relate to the audience; appropriate for audience and situation

_____ Movement: Purposeful, natural, without anxiety; used to indicate organization

Use of Visual Aids

_____ Speaker uses smooth transitions into and away from visuals

_____ Visuals are easy to see with large print and/or pictures

_____ Visuals highlight message

_____ Any equipment is used without difficulty

_____ Visual aids are appropriate for the speaker, the audience, the topic, and the situation

Summary

Four modes of speech delivery are the manuscript mode, the extemporaneous mode, the impromptu mode, and the memorized mode. Each mode has advantages and disadvantages, and appropriate circumstances for its use.

An effective speech requires both vocal and bodily aspects of delivery. Vocal aspects of speech delivery include: (1) pitch—the highness or lowness of the speaker's voice; (2) rate—the speed of delivery; (3) pauses—for dramatic effect and for an audience to consider content; (4) volume—the relative loudness of a speaker's voice; (5) enunciation—the pronunciation and articulation of words; (6) fluency—the smoothness of delivery; and (7) vocal variety—voice quality, intonation patterns, inflections of speech, and syllabic duration.

Bodily aspects of speech delivery include: (1) gestures—movements of the head, arms, and hands; (2) eye contact—sustained and meaningful contact with the eyes and faces of audience members; (3) facial expression—the varieties of messages the face can convey; and (4) movement—what the speaker does with the entire body during a speech presentation.

Visual aids should be used in speeches when they contribute something to the message or when they help the audience understand the message or the purpose of the speech. Visual aids are broadly defined to include chalkboards, posters, opaque and overhead projectors, movies and slides, photographs, drawings, models and physical objects, handouts, and yourself. When appropriately and skillfully employed in a speech, visual aids can be a big asset. When used inappropriately or unskillfully, they can detract from the message.

The Informative Speech

*N*othing is so firmly believed as what we least know.

Michel de Montaigne

*E*verything has been thought of before; the challenge is to think of it again.

J. W. Goethe

A word to the wise is not sufficient if it doesn't make sense.

James Thurber

Objectives

1. State the behavioral purposes of your informative speech.
2. Explain the concepts of information hunger, information relevance, extrinsic motivation, informative content, and information overload.
3. Practice the skills of defining, describing, explaining, and narrating.
4. Deliver an effective informative speech.

Key Terms

informative speech
behavioral
  purposes
information
  hunger
information
  relevance
extrinsic
  motivation
informative
  content
information
  overload
comparison
contrast
synonym
antonym
etymology
operational
  definition
abstract words
concrete words
narration

As a student, you have already spent the better part of thirteen or fourteen years hearing informative speeches from your teachers. As an employee, you may have to tell others about products, sales goals, and service. As a religious person, you may want to explain scripture, morals, or ideals to others. As a citizen, you may have to speak to others about domestic politics, foreign affairs, or impending legislation. Teachers inform students, police officers inform citizens about protecting person and property, and supervisors inform workers. You, like all of these people, will likely find yourself informing others in verbal reports, instructions, and speeches. This chapter focuses on the primary vehicle for informing others—the **informative speech.**

Preparing an Informative Speech

To prepare an informative speech, you should know (1) the intent and the goal of informative speaking, (2) the kinds of topics that lend themselves best to informative speaking, and (3) the kinds of immediate behavioral purposes of informative speaking and how to determine if you have fulfilled them.

The Goal of Informative Speaking

Understanding the goal or intent of informative speaking requires you understand the "end product" you seek and how to reach that end in ways that enlighten the audience and clarify the topic. The "end product" of informative speaking is *to increase an audience's knowledge or understanding of a topic.* You accomplish that goal by clarifying your topic in ways that retain the interest of your audience. To *clarify* means

The informative speaker must arouse the interest of the audience and show the significance of the topic.

"to make clear," coming as it does from Latin, Middle English, and Old French roots denoting "to make clear" or "to make bright." To clarify some concept for an audience assumes the audience does not understand the topic clearly until the speaker has an opportunity to explain it. Typically, a majority of audience members have insufficient knowledge or understanding to master or comprehend the informative speech topic. For example, you might know that a set of stereophonic speakers has a "woofer" and a "tweeter," but you might need an informative speech to explain more clearly exactly what those two features mean.

Clarifying a topic for an audience is a primary goal of informative speaking, but a second concern is to make the topic of an informative speech interesting and significant to the audience. We arouse an audience's *interest* in a topic by showing how the subject can be of importance, by relating stories of our own experiences with the subject, and by demonstrating gaps in the audience's knowledge they will want to fill. In fact, if a bit of persuasion is likely to slip into an informative speech, the appropriate place is early in the speech, where you relate the topic to the audience. It is here you quite rightly may reveal why the audience should know more about Wagnerian opera, cross-country skiing, monetary inflation, or hamster breeding. How to make a topic palatable—literally digestible—to the audience is a continuing concern of the informative speaker.

Similarly, the informative speaker needs to demonstrate *significance*. If the relationship between your topic and your audience is not apparent, you need to explain to audience members why they need to know about your topic. The significance of your message is its importance and meaningfulness to, or its consequences for, the audience. A topic can be relevant to an audience without being particularly significant. Consider the student who gave a speech about the history of matches, information he found by looking in two encyclopedias. The student could have been faulted for selecting a topic about which he had no particular commitment or concern, but a more important shortcoming was the lack of significance. An informative speech on how to play tiddlywinks is not as significant as a speech on CPR training; a speech on understanding other people's race, religion, or fields of study; or a speech that clarifies concepts on our politics, philosophy, or technology. You, as an informative speaker, are expected to increase an audience's knowledge by clarifying concepts of significance.

Topics for Informative Speeches

Selecting a topic for an informative speech and narrowing the topic to the length restrictions of the speech are early concerns for the informative speaker. Chapter 12 provided some general information on topic selection: how to brainstorm for topics and how to conduct personal inventories of your reading and viewing habits to determine your interests. But even with that information, you may not know exactly what kinds of topics are most appropriate for informative speeches.

An informative speech is to be predominantly informative; that is, most of the content of the speech should focus on increasing audience knowledge and clarifying concepts for greater understanding. Many informative speeches reveal how to do something, what something is, or how something happens—speeches of exposition, definition, and description, respectively. A list of topics for a number of student-delivered informative speeches follows. The topics, not necessarily the titles of the speeches, are listed. Therefore, many of the topics look broader than they were when they were delivered as speeches. The speech topic "The Intoxicated Driver," for example, was limited to information about intoxicated drivers in the town around the campus. Nonetheless, this list of topics may give you some ideas for a topic for an informative speech.

Once you have selected and narrowed a topic in a manner appropriate for you, your audience, and the situation, you are ready to specify the behavioral purposes of your informative speech.

Sample Topics for Informative Speeches

The Intoxicated Driver	The Social Security System
What Is Agribusiness?	What Is a Pacifist?
Food Irradiation	Pewter
Etiquette	Saltwater Aquariums
Rappelling	Popcorn Poppers Compared
Genetic Cloning	Winterizing Your Car
Aerobic Conditioning	Unique Wood Products
First Aid	Clear-cutting in Forestry
Obesity	Ski Boots
What Coins Are Made Of	What Is an Engineer?

My Visit to Spain
Communicating with Dress
The Penalty for Possession
Underground Homes
College Alcoholics
Salt in Your Diet
Automobile Accidents
Divorce: The Facts
Chiropractors
The Basics of Interviewing
The Autistic Child
Eye Surgery
The Irish Universities
Unidentified Flying Objects
Exam Anxiety
The Dormitory System
Door-to-Door Sales
Personality Tests
Soft Drinks
What Is *Habeas Corpus?*
Who Are the Libertarians?
Substance Abuse Centers
Natural Childbirth
Grounds for Divorce
The Minimum Wage

Sleep and the College Student
Handling Handguns
Disc-Washers
The Concert Business
Inner-City Living
Adventures of a Bartender
My Tarantula
Generic Labeling
What Is Construction Management?
Writing Your Resumé
How Computer Science Makes Your Job
  Easier
What Is Active Listening?
Food Preservatives
What Is a Finance Major?
Motorcycle Safety
Radiation and Plutonium
Evolution and the Bible
What Is Political Philosophy?
More about Iran
Police Codes
Volcanoes
Cricket
Simple Automobile Repairs
Hairstyling Made Easy

Behavioral Purposes for Informative Speeches

Two important questions for the informative speaker are: (1) "What do I want my audience to know or do as a result of my speech?" and (2) "How will I know if I am successful?" A teacher can teach more effectively if the students know exactly what they are expected to know. Similarly, an audience learns more from an informative speech if the speaker states expectations early in the speech. The effects of an informative speech, however, are unknown unless you make the effects behavioral; that is, your speech should result in behavioral or observable change. A teacher discovers whether students learned from a lecture by giving a quiz or having the students answer questions in class. In the same way, the informative speaker seeks to discover whether or not a message was effectively communicated by seeking overt feedback from the audience. The overt feedback you seek concerns the immediate **behavioral purposes** you established for your informative speech.

The most common immediate behavioral purposes in an informative speech are to encourage audience members to:

1. *Recognize differences or similarities among objects, persons, or issues.* For example, after hearing a speech on the subject, audience members can recognize an English setter, a person suffering from Down's syndrome, or the Libertarian position on welfare.

How will you know if you achieve your behavioral purpose in the informative speech?

2. ***Distinguish*** *among different things.* For example, after hearing a speech on the subject, audience members can distinguish between fool's gold and real gold, between a counterfeit dollar and a real one, or between a conservative position and a liberal one.

3. ***Compare*** *items.* For example, after hearing a speech on the subject, audience members can compare prices on automobiles with the same features and options, can compare a poetic song and a sonnet, or can compare diamonds for cut, clarity, and carats.

4. ***Define*** *words, objects, or concepts.* For example, after hearing a speech on the subject, audience members can tell what kerogen is, can describe an English Tudor house, and can explain the concept of macroeconomics.

5. ***State*** *what they have learned.* After hearing a speech, audience members can tell you or write down your most important points or are able to tell others what you said.

Thus, the common behavioral purposes of an informative speech are to recognize, distinguish, compare, define, and state. But how does a speaker know whether or not these behavioral purposes were accomplished? One method of discovering whether audience members learned anything from your speech is to find out what they know both at the beginning and at the end of the speech. For example, you might ask early in your speech, "How many of you know the significance of kerogen embedded in marl?" If all you get is blank looks, then you know that you are going to inform audience members about something that they do not know. After explaining in your speech that kerogen is "shale oil," that it is embedded in marl or "limestone," and that this resource may be an important supply of fuel in the future, you can ask a few of your classmates at the end of your speech to tell you the significance of kerogen embedded in marl to demonstrate your message was received and understood.

Similarly, you may ask your classmates to write down something that indicates whether or not they understood your message. If you gave four reasons to buy food at a discount market, you might ask your classmates at the conclusion of your speech to restate two of those reasons to verify your message. Or if one of your purposes was to enable the audience to distinguish between edible mushrooms and toadstools, you might ask some people in your audience to point to the mushroom that provides nutrition or to the toadstool that will make them sick. In each case, the purpose is stated in such a way that the speaker can determine whether or not the purpose was accomplished.

Once you have decided on specific behavioral purposes for addressing an audience, you must select strategies for achieving those purposes. In other words, you must decide how to adapt your behavioral purposes and the materials of your speech to your particular audience.

Presenting Information to an Audience

If you, as an informative speaker, want to relate to an audience, you should first review the sections in chapter 12 on selecting and narrowing a topic and analyzing an audience. Then you will be ready to adapt your topic and purposes to your particular audience. Audience analysis should help you to determine how much audience members already know and how much you will have to tell them to engender understanding. Then you will have to decide how to generate information hunger, achieve information relevance, employ extrinsic motivation, select content, and avoid information overload in your speech.

Information Hunger

An informative speech is more effective if the speaker can generate **information hunger** in the audience; that is, if the speaker can create a need for information in the audience. Information hunger is easiest to create when a speaker has analyzed the audience and has reason to believe hunger for the information can be aroused. Interest in the subject matter of a speech before listening to it is not significantly related to comprehension, but arousal of interest during the speech is related to how much the audience will comprehend.[1] The following rhetorical questions, for example, could be used to introduce an informative speech and to arouse audience interest: "Do you know how to protect yourself from skin cancer?" "Can you repair your own stereo?" or "Can you tell a good used car from a bad one?" Depending on the audience, these rhetorical questions could be of interest.

Rhetorical questions are just one method of arousing information hunger. Another method is to arouse the audience's curiosity: "I have finally found a solution to our local problem of water purity," "The answer to the mysterious disappearance of our organizational funds has just been discovered in a most unlikely place," or "Every educated American should know the meaning of the word *cryogenics*." In addition, a brief quiz on your topic early in the speech arouses interest in finding the answers. Unusual clothing is likely to arouse interest in why you are so attired. And an object you created will likely inspire the audience to wonder how you made it. These are just some ways in which the public speaker can generate information hunger.

To an audience of prospective parents, an
informative speech about birth is relevant.

Information Relevance

A second factor in relating an informative speech to an audience is **information relevance.** When selecting a topic for an informative speech, the speaker should carefully consider the relevance of the topic. Skin cancer might be a better topic in the summer when students are sunbathing than in the winter when they are not. An audience might find a speech on tax laws dull; a speech on how present tax laws cost audience members more than they cost the rich might be more relevant; and a speech on three ways to reduce personal taxes might be even better. However, if your audience happens to be composed of eighteen- to twenty-one-year-olds who have never paid taxes, none of the three topics might be relevant. Similarly, a speech on raising racehorses, writing a textbook, or living on a pension might be informative but not relevant because of the financial status, occupation, or age of the listeners. The informative speaker, then, should exercise some care to select a topic that interests the audience.[2]

People expose themselves first to information that is supportive or that fits in with what they already believe or know. People reject less supportive information first. So an audience's predisposition toward a topic can determine whether an audience will show up to hear a speech and whether an audience will listen.[3]

Extrinsic Motivation

A third factor in relating an informative speech to an audience is **extrinsic motivation.** An audience is more likely to listen to and to comprehend a speech if there are reasons outside the speech itself for concentrating on the content of the speech.[4] A teacher who tells students to listen carefully because they will be tested at the end of the hour is using extrinsic motivation. A student can use extrinsic motivation at the beginning of a speech by telling an audience, "Careful attention to this informative speech will help you to improve your grades on objective tests," or "Listening to this speech today will save you money on gasoline," or, as one student said, "I will give each of you one dollar for listening to my speech today, and I will tell you how to turn that dollar into five dollars by the end of the week."

Extrinsic motivation is related to the concept of information relevance. The audience member who would ordinarily be disinterested in the topic of fashion might find that topic more relevant when it is linked to job interviews and the kinds of clothing, jewelry, and shoes that employers seem to prefer. The audience member's interest in getting a job makes the interviewer's preferences an extrinsic motivation for listening carefully to the speech.

Any external reasons for why audience members should listen need to be mentioned early in the speech, before the message you want audience members to remember. A statement like, "You will need this background material for the report due at the end of this week," provides extrinsic motivation for the managers who hear this message from their employer. Similarly, in an informative speech, you may be able to command more attention, comprehension, and action from audience members if they know some reasons outside the speech itself for why they should attend to your message.

Informative Content

A fourth factor in relating an informative speech to an audience is the selection of **informative content.** In chapter 14, we discussed information sources and how to find appropriate supporting materials for the content of your speech. Here, we briefly examine some principles of learning and some research findings that can guide you in selecting your speech content.

First, audiences tend to remember and comprehend generalizations and main ideas better than details and specific facts.[5] The usual advice to speakers—that content should be limited to a relatively small number of main points and generalizations—seems to be well grounded. Specifically, public speakers are well advised to limit themselves to two to five main points or contentions in a speech. Even if the speech is very long, audiences are unlikely to remember a larger number of main points.

Second, relatively simple words and concrete ideas are significantly easier to retain than more complex materials.[6] Long or abstruse words may dazzle an audience into thinking you are intellectually gifted or verbally skilled, but they may also reduce understanding of the speech content. The best advice is to keep the ideas and the words used to express those ideas at an appropriate level.

The informative speaker can increase audience comprehension through overt audience response.

Humor can make a dull speech more interesting to an audience, but it does not seem to increase information retention. The use of humor also improves the audience's perception of the character of the speaker, and it can increase a speaker's authoritativeness when a speech is dull, although not when the speech is interesting.[7]

Early remarks about how the speech will meet the audience's needs can create anticipation and increase the chances that the audience will listen and understand.[8] Whatever topic you select, you should tell audience members early in your speech how the topic is related to them. Unless you relate the topic to their needs, they may choose not to listen.

Calling for *overt audience response* increases comprehension more than repetition. In a study of this subject, the overt responses invited were specific, "programmed" questions to which the appropriate overt responses were anticipated.[9] The results were consistent with other studies that show the virtue of active participation by an audience.

An informative speaker can ask for overt responses from audience members by having them perform the task being demonstrated (for example, folding a paper airplane to demonstrate a principle of aerodynamics); by having them stand, raise hands, or move chairs to indicate affirmative understanding of the speaker's statements (for example, stand up if you are over twenty-five years old); or by having them write answers that will indicate understanding of the informative speech (for example, pictures of four

CROCK by Bill Rechin and Brant Parker. © Field Enterprises, Inc. 1978. Courtesy of Field Newspaper Syndicate.

plants are drawn on the chalkboard, and audience members are instructed to identify the plant they believe is marijuana). Having an audience go through some overt motion provides feedback to the speaker and can be rewarding and reinforcing for both speaker and listener.

Information Overload

The informative speaker needs to be wary about the amount of information included in a speech. The danger is **information overload.** Information overload comes in two forms. One is when the speaker tells us more than we ever wanted to know about a subject, even when we are interested in it. The speaker tries to cram as much information as possible into the time limits. Unfortunately, this cramming of information makes the information more difficult to understand.

A second form of information overload is when the speaker uses language or ideas that are beyond the capacity of the audience to understand. The engineer or mathematician who unloads his or her latest formulas on the audience or the philosopher who soars into the ethereal heights of high ideas may leave the audience feeling frustrated and less knowledgeable than before the speech. The solution to information overload is to select a limited number of main points with only the best supporting materials and to keep the message at a level the audience can understand.

Now that you have examined information hunger, information relevance, extrinsic motivation, findings about content, and information overload, you are ready to review some specific suggestions about organizing the informative speech.

Organizing Content

Chapter 15 contained detailed information about the overall organization of speeches. The additional suggestions that follow are based on studies that reveal specific ways in which the informative speaker can help an audience to understand the content of the speech. In general, the research supports the old saying you should tell audience members what you are going to tell them, tell them, and then tell them what you told them.

Petrie, in his studies of informative speaking, found the use of transitions can increase an audience's comprehension.[10] That finding underlines the importance of building into the organization of your informative speech transitions between your introduction and body and between your body and conclusion. Other places for transitions include the moves from one main point to another in your speech and into and out of visual aids.

In organizing your informative speech, you should determine which ideas, points, or supporting materials are of greatest importance. Apparently, an audience understands the important points better if the speaker signals their importance by saying, "Now get this," or "This is very important." Some redundancy, or planned repetition, also can help to increase comprehension.[11] Some of that planned repetition can be included in the previews and reviews in your informative speech.[12] *Advance organizers,* or previews in written work, aided retention by providing the reader with key points prior to their presentation in a meaningful, but unfamiliar, passage.[13] Perhaps it is true in speaking, as well as in writing, that listeners can more easily grasp information when they are invited to anticipate and to review both the organization and the content of a speech.

When you have completed a sentence outline or some other form of outline that includes everything you plan to say, you should check your speech for information overload. Overload is a special problem in the informative speech because speakers have a tendency to inundate listeners with information. Just as some writers believe a longer paper is a better paper, some speakers think the sheer quantity of information they present in a speech makes it better. The most effective public speakers know the quantity of material in a speech makes less difference than the quality of the material. They also know listeners pay more attention to carefully selected material that is well adapted to their needs. In a five-to-eight-minute informative speech, the speaker has only four to six minutes to actually present supporting materials; the remainder of the time is spent introducing the subject, making transitions, and making internal and final summaries. Your organizational plan should show you what material you intend to include in your speech. It can also be your final check on the quantity and quality of the information that you intend to present.

Special Skills for Informative Speaking

Public speakers who are highly effective at informative speaking demonstrate certain special skills that lead to their effectiveness. One of these skills is *defining.* Much of what an informative speaker does is revealing to an audience what certain terms, words, and concepts mean. Another skill is *describing,* for the informative speaker often tells an audience how something appears, what it looks like, sounds like, feels like, and even smells like. A third skill is *explaining,* or trying to say what something is in terms or words the audience can understand. A fourth skill is *narrating,* an oral interpretation of a story, event, or description.

Defining

A student who was a model gave a speech in which she talked about "parts modeling"; a student who made his own butter gave an informative speech in which he talked about the "dasher" and the "clabber," "bilky" milk, and butter that "gathered"; and an informative speech on aerobics included terms like "arteriosclerosis," "cardiovascular-pulmonary system," and "cardiorespiratory endurance." What were these students talking about? In each case, they were using words most persons in the audience did not understand. There is nothing particularly wrong with using terms audience members do not understand as long as you explain the terms in language they *can* understand. You do that by *defining* your terms. Among the most useful methods of defining are the use of comparison, contrast, synonyms, antonyms, etymology, and operational definitions.

The student who told about making butter defined through **comparison** by explaining that:

> The dasher consists of a stick similar to a broom handle. A cross made of two slats,
> four inches long and two inches wide, is nailed to the end of the handle. The dasher is
> inserted into the churn, and the churn's opening is covered by a tightly fitted wooden
> lid with a hole in the middle for the dasher.

The student defined a dasher by comparing it to the better-known broomstick and by revealing how it was constructed.

Another method of definition is through **contrast,** which means by telling what something is not. An informative speaker who is attempting to distinguish among drunkenness, diabetic comas, and epileptic fits may contrast the causes and characteristics of each.

A speaker also might define through a **synonym**—a word, term, or concept close or similar in meaning. For example, in an informative speech, the speaker might say depressive psychosis is characterized by loss of interest, dejection, stupor, and silence—a series of words similar to behaviors exhibited by the depressive psychotic patient.

An **antonym** defines by stating the opposite of the term being defined. A hyperactive child is not quiet, immobile, silent, patient, or unexpressive.

Sometimes, you may find it easier to explain a concept or term by revealing the term's **etymology** or history. A desk dictionary may give a very brief statement on the origin of a word. More complete origins can be located in specialized dictionaries like the *Oxford English Dictionary* or the *Etymological Dictionary of Modern English.* A speaker talking about sexual variations might use the term *lesbianism* and could define the term by explaining the Greek poet Sappho wrote poetry about sexual love between women about six hundred years before Christ. Because Sappho lived on the island of Lesbos, "followers of Sappho," or female homosexuals, became known as lesbians. The story about the origin of the word provides a memorable way for the audience to relate to the word.

Another means of defining is the **operational definition** (see chapter 6), or defining something by revealing how it is made or what it consists of. The earlier description of a "dasher" was an operational definition because it defined by revealing how a dasher is constructed. A student delivering an informative speech on rhinoplasty or "a nose job" did so through the following operational definition:

> Modern rhinoplasty is done for both cosmetic and health reasons. It consists of several minioperations. First, if the septum separating the nostrils has become deviated as the result of an injury or some other means, it is straightened with surgical pliers. Then, if the nose is to be remodeled, small incisions are made within each nostril, and working entirely within the nose, the surgeon is able to remove, reshape, or redistribute the bone and cartilage lying underneath the skin. Finally, if the nose is crooked, a chisel is taken to the bones of the upper nose, and they are broken so that they may be straightened and centered.[14]

An operational definition, then, defines by revealing the formula for the thing named: rhinoplasty is the surgery described in the previous sentences; a cake is its recipe; concrete is lime, cement, and water; a secretary is what a secretary does: typing, filing, answering phones, and so on.

Describing

A second special skill of the informative speaker is distinguishing between abstract and concrete words, and between general and specific words. One of the best ways to make an informative speech interesting is by using language forcefully and effectively to describe. You can do that best if you recognize certain differences in words.

For instance, some words refer generally to ideas, qualities, acts, or relationships: these are called **abstract words.** Examples might be existentialism (an idea), beauty (a quality), violence (an act), and marriage (a relationship). Other words are more specific or **concrete** because they refer to definite persons, places, objects, and acts: Dr. Linda Busby, Carver Hall, and my economics textbook. Abstract words are useful in theorizing, summarizing, and discussing and are more commonly used by educated persons discussing ideas. Concrete words are most useful in relating your personal experiences, direct observations, and feelings or attitudes. The important point about abstract and concrete or general and specific language is to use each where it is most appropriate. The most common error in informative speeches is the use of abstract terms where concrete words would be more forceful and clear. "I have really liked some courses of study here at Eastern College," says a student to his classmates and adds, "but others I have disliked." This abstract, general statement has minimal impact. If speaking in concrete and specific terms, the same student might say, "I most enjoyed English, speech, and political science courses, and I disliked Eastern College's courses in chemistry, mathematics, and physics." Descriptions in informative speeches should be specific, accurate, and detailed, rather than general and ambiguous.

Informative speakers should also attempt to use colorful imagery that appeals to the senses. A speaker describing a place might say "the sun sets in an orange sky against the purple mountain," a victim of shock "appears lifeless, pallid, and feels clammy," or a manufactured meat "tastes like top-grade sirloin."

A valuable exercise for the informative speaker is to carefully review the rough draft of the speech to discover abstract, general, ambiguous words that can be replaced by concrete, specific details.

Explaining

A third special skill for the informative speaker is explaining an idea in terms the audience can understand. An explanation is a means of idea development, an alternative way of stating an idea or concept. Often, an explanation simplifies or clarifies an idea while at the same time making it interesting to the audience.

An important step in explaining is dissecting, analyzing, or taking something apart so the audience can understand it. Unless you become skilled at disassembling a concept, your explanation may leave audience members more confused than they were before your speech. Thus, you have to determine what you can do to make the concept more palatable to the audience, what you can do to increase audience understanding. John Kenneth Galbraith, a retired professor of economics from Harvard University, wrote many books explaining economics to people who did not necessarily know very much about the subject. A close look at one of his explanations is instructive. Galbraith is trying to make the point that politicians and the public often take the voices of a few influential persons as a shift-of-opinion by the majority:

> On the need for tax relief, investment incentives, or a curb on welfare costs, the views of one articulate and affluent banker, businessman, lawyer, or acolyte economist are the equal of those of several thousand welfare mothers. In any recent year, the pleas by Walter Wriston of Citibank or David Rockefeller of Chase Manhattan for relief from oppressive taxation, regulation, or intrusive government have commanded at least as much attention as the expressions of discontent of all the deprived of the South Bronx.[15]

Galbraith is analyzing a situation: why do the persons of economic advantage have a bigger say in our economy than the millions who live with it? His language is specific and concrete. He is expanding on an idea with descriptive language, and he is doing so by dissecting the concept so we can understand its parts.

Narrating

A fourth special skill for informative speakers is **narration,** the oral presentation and interpretation of a story, description, or event. In a speech, narration includes the dramatic reading of some lines from a play, poem, or other piece of literature; the voice-over on a series of slides or a silent film to illustrate some point in a speech; and even the reading of such information as a letter, a quotation, or a selection from a newspaper or magazine. The person who does the play-by-play account of a ball game is narrating; so is the speaker who explains what a weaver is doing in an informative speech on home crafts.

Narration is an important skill for the informative speaker.

The person who uses narration in a speech moves just a little closer to oral interpretation of literature or even acting because the real cue to narrating is the narration is highlighted by being more dramatic than the words around it. Sections of your speech that require this kind of special reading also require special practice. If you want a few lines of poetry in your speech to have the desired impact, you will need to rehearse them.

An Example of an Informative Speech

So far in this chapter, you have learned additional information on how to select a topic for your informative speech, how to determine behavioral purposes and goals for the informative speech, how to present information to an audience, how to organize the informative speech, and how to define, describe, explain, and provide narration for the concepts in your speech. Now we look at an actual informative speech delivered by a student.[16]

Notice in this speech how the speaker gains and maintains the audience's attention, relates the topic to himself and to the audience, and forecasts the organization and development of the topic. Notice also how the speaker attempts to clarify the idea with examples high in audience interest, how ideas are translated into language the audience can understand, and how the speaker employs definitions, descriptions, and explanations. The sidenotes will help to identify how the speaker is fulfilling the important functions of the introduction, the body, and the conclusion of an informative speech. The speech that follows is also an example of a speech manuscript.

The Trouble with Codes

Speaker gains attention with a very brief tape recording of the opening for a television police show.

I would like you to listen to a very important type of communication (at this point, the speaker plays a few seconds of tape-recorded sound, the introduction to the televised police show called "Adam-12"):

> Adam-12, Adam-12. 211 in progress at 1443 52nd. Handle Code 3.

Speaker identifies with the audience's lack of knowledge by raising rhetorical questions most cannot answer.

What you just heard was the beginning of the television show "Adam-12." The voice you heard was the radio dispatcher giving a call to a patrol car. The first time that I heard those words and numbers I could only wonder what in the world she was saying. Who's Adam-12? What's a 211 "in progress," and how do you handle something "code 3"?

Speaker relates topic to himself and describes his credibility on the topic.
Speaker announces the topic.
Speaker relates topic to the audience.
Speaker forecasts the development of the speech.

Well, you could say that I found out the meaning of the message the hard way. After graduating at the top of my class from the state law enforcement academy and after spending two years on our own city police department, I can tell you what the dispatcher just said. But there are some problems with coding systems like the one you just heard because coding systems are used these days by police, computer scientists, physicians, lawyers, and everyday people. So today I'd like to explain to you troubles that can arise from the use of coding systems by telling you of some of my personal experiences with them.

Speaker reminds audience of his credibility.
Speaker raises his first question about the code system.

At the law enforcement academy, the instructors who taught us the police communication system told us how easy and efficient the system is. At the academy, the system sounded good, but the thought kept running through my mind: how will the system work when the officer is under pressure?

Speaker defines the police code system.
Speaker raises second issue concerning code.

The code system we use is based on numbers. The code contains one hundred entries: 10–1 to 10–100. We learned the codes at the academy, but like things we learn in college, if we don't practice, we forget them.

Speaker relates personal experience to arouse audience interest and attention.

As I started my career in police work, I found that, at times, the system worked very well. The times I'm talking about are the routine calls we'd receive every day—things like prowler calls and accidents.

Speaker uses hypothetical example to make his point more specific and concrete.
Speaker employs specific instance.

For example, if a woman called in and said someone was trying to get into her house, the dispatcher would key the microphone and call the police car designated to be patroling in that area. It would sound something like this:

> Ames 124, 10–14, 1004 West Street, Code 2.

Speaker compares coded message with its translation.

Speaker employs second specific example.

Speaker compares coded message with its translation.

Speaker uses specific, concrete language in his description.

Speaker contrasts routine code use with emergency code use.

Speaker uses personal experience to relate stories illustrating the problems with codes.

Speaker uses specific, concrete example.

Speaker's story arouses human interest in the topic.

Speaker employs humor to communicate his message about codes.

Speaker uses descriptive language to depict the situation in his story.

Speaker uses a second narrative to illustrate the problems with the code in actual use.

Speaker uses specific example.

Translated, it would sound like this:

> Ames Radio to West Area patrol car number 124; 10–14: there is a prowler there now at 1004 West Street; Code 2: get there as soon as possible.

Or another routine call would sound like this:

> Ames 124, 10–50 P. I. L-Way and State, Code 3.

Translated, the message would sound like this:

> West area patrol car, there is an accident with personal injury involved at the intersection of Lincoln Way and State Avenue; because this is an emergency, use your red light and siren.

From these examples, you can see that the code system does cut down time and makes the message easier to say. But what about the calls that aren't routine? What about situations in which the adrenaline is flowing?

I discovered how easy it is to forget these codes in a couple of scary ways. I received the following radio transmission from my dispatcher late one night toward the end of a hectic day:

> Ames 124 & 126, 10–94, Happy Chef west, Code 2.

Well, this is what I'd been afraid of! What the heck is a 10–94? So I reached for my handy codebook that I hadn't used for ages—but it wasn't there. I hoped that the backup officer in car 126 would have the answer I needed. As we pulled up to the restaurant, we both got out of our cars and said at the same time to each other: "What the heck is a 10–94?"

We figured the only way to save our pride was to walk in and find out what was wrong. As we walked calmly in, we were met by a very frantic and excited waitress who said that a man had just called to say that he had planted a bomb in the building. Now we knew! A 10–94 was a bomb threat, and we had just walked into the middle of it. So much for the code system.

Another confusing situation happened one night at the scene of a very bad accident. I arrived at the scene of the accident to see a very bloody man running toward my car. Immediately, I picked up my mike and shouted into it:

> 124 Ames, 10–23, 10–50 P. I., 10–56 several injured.

It wasn't until I saw the dispatcher the next day that I realized my mistake. The message I had transmitted was:

> West area car to Ames Radio: I have arrived at the scene of a personal injury accident; send a wrecker to pick up the several injured.

Checklist for an Informative Speech

As you prepare your informative speech, check off each item in the blank on the left to indicate you have taken that item under careful consideration.

Topic

_____ 1. Have you selected a topic about which your content can be predominantly informative?

_____ 2. Have you selected a topic in which you are interested?

_____ 3. Have you selected a topic the majority of your audience members do not know or understand?

_____ 4. Have you narrowed the topic to fit time limitations?

_____ 5. Have you considered the significance and relevance of your topic to your audience?

_____ 6. Have you reviewed the information in chapter 10 on topic selection?

Purpose

_____ 1. Have you determined immediate behavioral purposes for your speech?

_____ 2. Have you included methods of discovering whether or not your immediate behavioral purposes have been achieved?

Content

_____ 1. Have you included ways to arouse information hunger—a need for information in the audience?

_____ 2. Can you use extrinsic motivation to encourage your audience to listen carefully?

_____ 3. Have you selected information that will meet audience needs, reduce complexity, and increase understanding?

_____ 4. Have you used personal experiences, stories, and comparisons to increase audience interest in your information?

_____ 5. Have you reviewed chapter 12 so you know how to find the most effective supporting materials for your informative speech?

Speaker uses humor to maintain audience interest in the topic.

Speaker signals an impending ending—breaklight function. Speaker uses an oral footnote to indicate interview.

In my excited state, instead of saying 10–57—send an ambulance—I said 10–56—send a wrecker. Fortunately, the dispatcher caught my error and corrected it herself.

You can see the problems that can result with the system. Not understanding messages sent out by dispatchers who use the codes everyday and have them posted by their radios, many police officers have to call back and ask them to repeat the message in English. Last week, I went in to talk with Ann Benson, the head dispatcher and a twelve-year veteran of the Ames Police

Organization

_____ 1. Have you highlighted your main points by forecasting, by repetition, by summarizing, and by including transitions?

_____ 2. Have you limited your main points and illustrative materials to improve clarity and to avoid information overload?

_____ 3. Have you reviewed chapter 13 on speech organization to help you determine which patterns of organization are most appropriate for you, your topic, your situation, and your audience?

Special Skills

_____ 1. Have you employed your skills in defining, describing, explaining, and narrating?

_____ 2. Have you tried defining through comparisons, contrasts, synonyms, antonyms, etymologies, or operational definitions?

_____ 3. Have you used specific, concrete detail and abstract language where they are appropriate?

_____ 4. Have you tried to be as descriptive as possible by using precise, accurate, and detailed descriptors?

_____ 5. Have you explained by analyzing or dissecting your concept in ways that invite audience understanding?

_____ 6. Have you rehearsed any narration in your speech?

Special Features

_____ 1. Have you reviewed the information in chapter 10 on audience analysis so you know what the audience knows and needs to know?

_____ 2. Have you reviewed the information in chapter 14 on visual aids so you can employ them where appropriate in your speech?

_____ 3. Have you reviewed chapter 11 so you know how to indicate your credibility on the topic you select?

_____ 4. Have you reviewed the information in chapter 14 on delivery so that you know how to effectively deliver your informative speech?

Speaker uses an outside authoritative source to summarize his information on the police code system.

Department. I confronted her with these problems; this was her reply:

> The code system is designed for speed and efficiency. One problem is that police calls are monitored by everybody from housewives to the press, and there are things that we do not want them to know. So until something better is figured out, we're stuck with it. It's the best we've got, and we'll have to learn to live with it.

Well, that didn't solve my problem—the problem of confusion from forgetfulness or nonuse. I also do not know a better way for an officer to communicate when he or she is under pressure.

An Informative Speech Assignment

Deliver a five-to-eight-minute predominantly informative speech with immediate behavioral purposes that can be checked during or after the speech, employ visual aids if and where appropriate, is delivered extemporaneously, includes oral footnotes, and signals the important points in ways that will help the audience to remember them. The speech should include an introduction that gains and maintains attention, describes the origins of your credibility on the topic, relates the topic to the audience, reveals what you want the audience to learn from your speech, and indicates the organization and development of your speech. The speech should include a conclusion that indicates the end is near, summarizes the main point or points of the speech, and that makes the audience pleased that they listened to you.

A Written Assignment for the Informative Speech

Put the title of your speech and your name at the top of a sheet of paper. Then state the immediate behavioral purposes of your speech and how you will know if your behavioral purposes are fulfilled. Compose a sentence outline of the content of your speech, including the introduction, the body, the conclusion, and a bibliography of your sources—both written and oral.

Speaker is reviewing by repetition.	I learned the codes the hard way, and I won't forget them, but under pressure I can still slip up. I don't know the answers to the problems of code communication, but I do know what the dispatcher said on the tape that introduced this speech:
Speaker uses circular organization to bring us back to his initial attention-getter.	Adam-12 is a police patrol car; the 211 in progress is an armed robbery taking place; and code 3 is an emergency. So now I thank you for your attention and say:
Speaker uses clever ending.	10–8, 12–24, 10–42.

The immediate purpose of this informative speech was to demonstrate to the audience some problems with the police code system. The primary information the audience should have been able to write down after the speech was two causes of code failure: namely, the inability to use a code when much of it is not routinely used and the chances for error in an emergency situation. The speaker taught the audience parts of the police code by translating specific examples; he demonstrated the problems with the code by citing personal experiences in which he, as a police officer, had made mistakes with the code; and he clarified the code by defining what certain code numbers meant and by explaining how police utilize the code system. The speaker included a bibliography that cited his term of instruction at the police academy, his interview with the dispatcher, and his use of the police codebook.

Summary

The primary vehicle for informing others is the informative speech. To prepare an informative speech, you should know (1) the intent and the goal of informative speaking, (2) the kinds of topics that lend themselves best to informative speaking, and (3) the kinds of immediate behavioral purposes of informative speaking and how to determine if you have fulfilled them.

In presenting information to an audience, you should strive to generate information hunger (an audience need for the information), to achieve information relevance (providing information that is not simply informative), to employ extrinsic motivation (reasons outside the speech itself for concentrating on the content of the speech), to select informative content (a limited number of main points, generalizations, relatively simple words and concrete ideas, humor, statements about how the speech will meet audience needs), and to avoid information overload (too much information in a speech or information beyond the capacity of the audience to understand).

The Persuasive Speech

*Y*ou cannot convince a man against his will.

Samuel Johnson

A woman convinced against her will is of the same opinion still.

Leona Hughes

*W*e are more easily persuaded, in general, by the reasons that we ourselves discover than by those which are given to us by others.

Pascal

Objectives

1. State the four ultimate action goals of a persuasive speech.
2. Recognize some methods of persuading an audience.
3. Observe the rules of ethics in your persuasive speech.
4. Practice your skills in developing arguments, selecting evidence, and refuting arguments.
5. Deliver an effective persuasive speech.

Key Terms

persuasive speech
adoption
discontinuance
deterrence
continuance
boomerang effect
motivation
logical appeals
emotional appeals
arguments
counterarguments
proposition
justification
inference

deductive
  arguments
evidence
tests of evidence
believability
refutation
turning the tables
reducto ad
  absurdum
post hoc, ergo
  propter hoc
special pleading
red herring

Presenting an effective **persuasive speech** is one of the most practical skills you learn in your speech communication class. You use persuasion every day in your interpersonal relations: you may try to convince someone to lend you money, you may try to explain to your professor why you missed a class or an examination, or you may try to persuade someone to give you a job. But public persuasion is equally common: coaches try to persuade team members that they can win, managers persuade employees to try a new approach, ministers persuade congregations to obey scripture, lawyers persuade juries, and people persuade legislators. Public persuasion pervades the mass media through advertising and public relations, and people learn to respond to, and to resist, the appeals.

This chapter explores persuasive speaking by showing how to prepare a persuasive speech, by examining some methods of persuasion, and by reviewing some special skills useful to the persuader. An example of a persuasive speech is provided at the end of the chapter.

Preparing a Persuasive Speech

To assist you in delivering an effective persuasive speech, we discuss what persuasion is, what the goals of persuasive speaking are, what kinds of topics are appropriate for a persuasive speech, and what kinds of behavioral purposes are most appropriate in persuasive speaking.

Persuasion Defined

Persuasion is an ongoing process in which verbal and nonverbal messages are employed to shape, reinforce, or change people's responses.[1] Persuasion is called an "ongoing process" because our behavior is always undergoing modification based on alterations in our attitudes, beliefs, and values. Many people changed their attitude toward smoking cigarettes when scientific reports demonstrated a correlation between smoking and lung cancer. Their change in attitude may or may not have resulted in a behavioral change, which would have been stopping or reducing their cigarette smoking.

The definition of persuasion also refers to "verbal and nonverbal messages" that influence people's attitudes, beliefs, values, and their resulting behavior. Your friend's words or her frown may be sufficient to persuade you to stop moving her books. Our use of symbols in the form of language and nonverbal signals is the medium we use to convey our persuasive messages.

According to the definition, sometimes, we use our persuasive messages to "shape" responses. For example, after hearing a number of your friends talk about a particular movie, your usually negative attitude toward horror movies is reduced enough so you decide to see just this one. Your friends were *shaping* your response with a number of messages over time.

Sometimes, we use our persuasive messages to "reinforce" responses. We need constant nourishment for our attitudes, beliefs, and values if we are to continue holding them. So you might keep going to church to reinforce your religious beliefs, keep going to meetings of the conservation club to reinforce your value of natural resources, and keep going on coffee breaks with your co-workers to maintain your positive attitude toward them.

Sometimes, we use our persuasive messages to "change" people's responses, to replace one attitude, belief, value, or the resulting behavior with another. The mother nags the children to pick up their clothing, to change their uncaring attitude toward their clothing, and to change their belief in orderliness. The persuasive speaker works on audience attitudes, beliefs, and values with persuasive messages so the audience will start, stop, continue, or discontinue behavior.

The Goals of Persuasive Speaking

The *ultimate persuasive goal* is always behavioral; that is, its effectiveness can be evaluated by audience behavior, by some action on the part of the audience. The persuasive speaker tries to increase or change what audience members know; their attitudes, beliefs, or values; or the way in which they perceive something. But, ultimately, the goal of persuasion is some *action* by the audience.

A single example might illustrate the importance of behavior in evaluating persuasive effects. The evangelist can give sermon after sermon on the concept of human love in an effort to change the audience members' attitudes toward loved ones, neighbors, and other human beings. All of this attitude change comes to naught, however, unless it is borne out in the behavior of audience members—unless they really do *behave* differently toward others. The attitude change is something that occurs inside people's heads; it is only measurable when people *act* in accord with the attitude. The evangelist should not be satisfied until the behavioral change occurs.

There are four action goals in persuasion: adoption, discontinuance, deterrence, and continuance.[2] **Adoption** means acceptance of a new idea, attitude, or belief as indicated by behavior. The advertiser wants you to try a new soap, coffee maker, or perfume. The advertiser is not content with a change in attitude toward the product unless it is evidenced in behavioral change—that is, you buy the product. Your action goal is achieved if you convince audience members to carpool, ride a bicycle, or take the bus instead of filling the roads with gas-guzzling automobiles.

The second action goal of persuasion—**discontinuance**—means convincing audience members to stop doing something they do now—drinking, taking dope, or ignoring their studies. Your action goal is achieved when audience members stop doing those things.

The third action goal of persuasion—**deterrence**—means getting audience members to avoid some activity ("If you don't drink now, don't start"; "If you believe in special creation, don't listen to the evolutionists"; or "If you believe in hunting, don't vote for gun control"). Your action goal is achieved when audience members demonstrate they are avoiding such activities.

The fourth action goal of persuasion—**continuance**—means convincing audience members to continue to behave as they do now ("Don't falter in your religious beliefs"; "Keep studying"; or "Keep buying Avon"). Your action goal requires audience members continue their current behavior.

As you can see, the first two action goals—adoption and discontinuance—require the audience to change behaviors, while the last two—deterrence and continuance—ask the audience not to change behaviors. In general, it is easier to persuade people to continue their present behaviors and to avoid new behaviors than it is to persuade them to quit their present behaviors and to start new ones.

Topics for Persuasive Speeches

Some topics are more appropriate for persuasive speeches than others. For instance, current and controversial topics lend themselves to persuasion better than topics that are outdated and accepted by nearly everyone. Some speech instructors believe the best topics for persuasive speeches are those that place the speaker at odds with the majority of audience members. However, that position disregards speeches with a continuance or deterrence goal.

Chapter 12 focused on selecting a speech topic through brainstorming and personal inventories. Another method is to look through newspapers and magazines and to listen to radio talk shows to discover what issues people are currently concerned about. Even letters to the editor in your campus, local, or regional paper can provide ideas for a persuasive speech.

You may also find it helpful to survey topics used previously in persuasive speeches, like the persuasive speech topics in the list that follows. As you read over the list of topics for persuasive speeches, you should recognize what is current and controversial at one college may be bland at another, many topics and titles are broader than their treatment in the speech, and other excellent topics emerge every day.

Topics for Persuasive Speeches

Register to Vote	Drugs Are Dangerous
Should News Be Entertaining?	Advantages of ROTC
The Folly of Dieting	Why You Shouldn't Vote
Parking	Celibacy
In Favor of Nuclear Power	Male Chauvinism
The Megavitamin Myth	Against Football
The Trouble with Christianity	The Campus Food Service
Child Abuse	Hiring the Handicapped
Equal Pay for Women	Legalizing Drugs
Vegetarianism	Buying Real Estate
Political Apathy	Inexpensive Travel
Selecting Wines	Try Effective Listening
Bilingualism	The Facts about Hunting
Advantages of a Home Computer	Watch Less Television
Youth Gangs	Student Drinking
Affirmative Action	Cohabitation
Adopting a Child	Stop Sexual Assaults
Buying Used Cars	Appreciating Modern Art

Cured Meats and Cancer
The Truth about Pesticides
Less Money for Defense
Improve Your Nutrition
Should You Be a Parent?
The Power of Nonviolence
Add Fiber to Your Diet
Getting Involved in Government
Do We Need Trade Unions?
Sex Bias on the Job
Selling Automobiles
Against the Minimum Wage
Hauling Nuclear Waste
Strengthening Our Defense
Vacationing in Florida
Buy American

X Rays Are Dangerous
Legalize Gambling
Cocaine
Television Violence
Misbehavior at Games
Be Assertive
Volunteer Your Time
Generic Drugs
Child Discipline
Against Jogging
Motorcycle Safety
"Crack"
Racism
AIDS

Behavioral Purposes for Persuasive Speeches

Your action goal for your persuasive speech, whether it be adoption, discontinuance, deterrence, or continuance, is an *ultimate* goal. It is something you might achieve if you had time enough to work on the audience. With your ultimate goal in mind, you need to select more immediate behavioral purposes for your persuasive speech so you can estimate your effectiveness. You may wish to review the behavioral purposes for an informative speech in chapter 17 because many of them are applicable to the persuasive speech as well. On the way to your ultimate goal, you may want the audience to be able to recognize, distinguish, or state something just as you would in an informative speech. After all, part of persuasion is informing audience members, just as part of informing audience members is convincing them that they ought to listen to your information. Persuasion and information are interrelated.

In a persuasive speech, you may include immediate behavioral purposes consistent with your ultimate goal but that go beyond those you would expect in an informative speech. For example, persuasive speeches often call for audience members *to do* something: sign a petition, join a group, buy a product, or eat a particular food.

In selecting your immediate behavioral purposes for your persuasive speech, you must be careful to pick actions that are possible after a very short persuasive speech. If you ask audience members to do too much as a result of your speech, you may experience a **boomerang effect;** that is, audience members may be even less likely to do what you ask than they were before they heard your appeal. Imagine, for instance, a speaker asks you in a persuasive speech to change your religion, quit school, or start taking hard drugs. Chances are the speaker is asking too much of you and you will respond by disliking the speaker and the topic even more than you did before.

On the other hand, you can move audience members toward an ultimate goal they would not have accepted before by selecting immediate behavioral purposes that are more acceptable or reasonable. For example, your ultimate goal may be to have audience members vote for a candidate who is unknown to them. You are unlikely to enlist the group to work in campaign headquarters, but you might be able to get many of them to read a brief handout about the candidate or even to pass that handout to others who may be even more interested. You may not be able to get audience members to join your religious group, but you probably can persuade them to write down three of the group's central beliefs.

You can improve your chances of persuading an audience if you write out your ultimate goal and your immediate behavioral purposes. For example, a student delivering a persuasive speech against jogging might state the following for an ultimate goal:

> The ultimate goal of my persuasive speech is to convince people who jog that they should quit (discontinuance) and to convince people who do not jog that they should never start (deterrence).

The same speaker also might state the following immediate behavioral purposes:

> One of my immediate behavioral purposes is to have the audience write down at the conclusion of my speech the three harmful effects that jogging has on the body: shin splints, bone bruises, and knee problems. A second immediate behavioral purpose of my speech is to have the joggers in the audience start reducing their workout times to avoid problems encouraged by fatigue.

The persuasive speaker need not reveal the ultimate purpose of the speech itself but ordinarily should reveal the immediate behavioral purposes of the speech. Audience members are more likely to write down the harmful effects of jogging if they are told early in the speech of that expectation. They may resist the persuasive speaker, however, if they know the ultimate goal of the speech.

Persuading an Audience

Audiences may be persuaded in a variety of ways. Researchers Karlins and Abelson observed, "Information by itself almost never changes attitudes."[3] You can persuade an audience, however, by using motivational appeals, employing source credibility, using logical or emotional appeals, organizing your materials effectively, and observing ethical guidelines for persuasion. We will discuss each of these methods in this section.

Motivational Appeals

The word **motivation** is based on a Latin term that means "to move," and that is how we use the term in everyday conversations: "What was his motive in buying that expensive car?" "She had plenty of motivation for getting a job outside of the home"; or "His motive was to act just like the other firefighters." If we boil motivation down to its essential ingredients, three forces motivate or move people to behave in one way or another.[4]

Effective persuasive speakers analyze their
audiences to increase their success.

One motivating force is what our body tells us to do. This physical basis of motivation explains our need for air, water, and food. We can get along without air for less than three minutes, without water for a couple of days, and without food for a week. Having unpolluted air to breathe, clean water to drink, and desirable food to eat takes much human energy, but our basic bodily needs motivate us to do what is necessary to preserve these resources.

The second motivating force is what our minds tell us to do. This psychological basis of motivation is based on our sense of rationality, as well as on our emotions, feelings, and perceptions. We are moved to do some things because it is reasonable in our minds to do so. We do other things because we feel good about doing them. We avoid still other activities because they make us feel bad about ourselves. The human mind motivates us to act in ways that comfort it.

The third motivating force is what other people want us to do. This third force is a powerful one that encourages us to conform to roles and norms. You may act like a student because your fellow students reinforce you when you do and punish you when you do not. You may attend classes because that is what students are to do. You might find yourself doing any number of things because family, friends, and co-workers expect and reward them.

Human behavior is very complicated. No explanation of why human beings behave the way they do is entirely satisfactory. Knowing the three kinds of motivational forces will not permit you to pull strings with an audience to elicit the behavior that you seek. Nonetheless, the most effective persuasive speakers—advertisers, politicians, and lawyers—have learned how to analyze their audiences—consumers, voters, and juries—so they are more often successful than unsuccessful in reaching their objectives.

Speaker Credibility

Who and what you are can make a powerful difference in persuasion. In chapter 13, we explored the concept of speaker credibility and what audiences look for in a speaker: competence, trustworthiness, dynamism, and co-orientation. A highly credible speaker has more impact on an audience than a speaker with low credibility. A persuasive speaker who is seen as similar to the audience is more likely to be effective than one who is seen as quite dissimilar. Sometimes, a highly credible speaker can attain more attitude change when he or she asks for more.[5]

An example of how speaker credibility works occurred when Harvard University sent a recruiter to a large midwestern university in an effort to secure more first-rate students from that part of the country. The pre-law students gathered in a room to meet the recruiter, who turned out to be a second-year law student from Harvard. The all-white audience of pre-law students seemed quite surprised when the recruiter turned out to be black. They showed their skepticism with their initial questions. "What was your grade point average as an undergraduate?" asked one member of the audience. "3.9 on a 4.0 scale," answered the recruiter. "Well," inquired another student, who apparently was not suitably impressed with the grade point average, "what did you earn on the LSAT?" "Seven hundred seventy," replied the recruiter. The pre-law students asked no more questions. The speaker was of a different race and from a different part of the country, but his grade point average and his LSAT score (800 was top) were higher than anyone's in the room. The audience listened with respect to his speech on how to get into one of the best law schools in the country.

You can signal the origins of your credibility to your audience by describing how you earned the right to speak on the topic. Perhaps your major will help: a nuclear engineer has the authority to speak on nuclear energy; a business major is a credible source on buying stocks and bonds; and a physical education major can speak with authority on exercise programs. Maybe your experience is the key to your credibility: your years in the military may have given you some insights into military waste; your years as a mother and homemaker may have given you authority to speak on time efficiency, raising children, or relating to a spouse; or your part-time job at a fast-food establishment may permit you to speak with some authority on management-labor relations.

Whatever the origins of your credibility, remember to reveal them early in the speech. Your authority may very well provide a reason for the audience to listen. If you reveal your credibility late in the speech, audience members may have paid little attention because they did not know you spoke with authority on the topic.

Logical Appeals

Motivational appeals and speaker credibility are just two ways to persuade an audience; a third important method is the use of reasoning or logic to convince an audience. The main ingredients of **logical appeals** are propositions and proofs.

A *proposition* is a statement that asserts or proposes something: "The United States should have uniform regulations for child support"; "The city should reduce the fines for traffic offenses"; or "The college should change its definition of 'a student in good standing.' " Notice a proposition always recommends a change in the status quo, the way things are right now. The primary method of persuading an audience a current policy should be changed and another policy should be adopted is through the use of proof or evidence.

The persuasive speaker can use a wide array of evidence to demonstrate the wisdom of retaining present practice or of changing current policies: quotations from authoritative persons, conclusions from studies and reports, or experiences of individuals injured or helped by current policies. The underlying principle in logical appeals is the audience should accept the side that presents the most convincing or the "best" evidence to support that side. In other words, our behavior should be based on the best evidence; it should be consistent with the persuasive speaker who provides the most effective "proof" a position is the best position to adopt.

Logical appeals can also be refuted; that is, they can be attacked. Another persuasive speaker can analyze the situation suggested in the proposition and find the analysis faulty. The opposing persuasive speaker may find the authorities who were quoted were biased, the reports and studies were flawed, or better evidence would invite a different conclusion.

Finally, it is important to recognize the world does not run by logic or evidence alone, sometimes beliefs are irrational or not based on evidence. A persuasive speaker might come up with considerable evidence on why you should eat legumes and cheese instead of meat without changing your behavior or your beliefs on that subject. The persuasive speaker is always faced with the disconcerting fact that even the best evidence or proof in support of a persuasive proposition might not alter audience behavior.

Emotional Appeals

Although logical and **emotional appeals** are often seen as diametrically opposed concepts, most of our behavior is based on a mixture of emotional and rational "reasons." A speaker may persuade an audience to accept his or her immediate behavioral purposes for emotional rather than logical reasons. A story about one person's bad experience with the campus bookstore may inspire many persons in the audience to take their business to another store. It matters little that the experience may have been a one-in-a-thousand situation, that it may have been as much the customer's fault as the

A speaker may persuade an audience through emotional rather than logical means.

manager's, or that it never happened before. Such is the power of our emotions that they can persuade us to defy the law, fight another nation, or ignore evidence. As one writer put it:

> The creature man is best persuaded
> When heart, not mind, is inundated;
> Affect is what drives the will;
> Rationality keeps it still.[6]

The most studied emotional appeal is the *fear appeal*. Janis and Feshbach examined three levels of fear appeals in communication on dental hygiene and found the weak threat worked better than the moderate threat, which worked better than the strong threat.[7] Fredric Powell used strong and weak fear appeals in a civil defense communication that threatened loved ones. He found more change of opinion when the fear appeal was strong.[8] In other words, the research findings on fear appeals are mixed and do not provide a formula for using them.

One research result, however, is well established. If you use fear appeals to persuade your audience, you should include in your speech some way the audience can avoid or escape the fear. A fear appeal can make an audience aware of danger; the reassurance can tell them how to contend with the danger. Omitting such reassurance does not influence the audience's ability to recall the facts in a speech, but a speech with reassurance results in greater shifts of opinion than one without reassurance. Also, the speaker who includes reassurance is regarded as a better speaker than one who does not.[9]

Organizational Plans

Chapter 15 provided considerable information on how to organize a speech. After reviewing that information, you should note some organizational patterns lend themselves best to persuasive speaking. The problem-and-solution pattern, for example, is common in persuasive speaking. Sometimes, an entire speech is devoted to analyzing a problem unrecognized by the audience. At other times, the problem is recognized by all, so the focus of the speech falls heavily on solutions. Similarly, the cause-effect pattern is often utilized in persuasive speaking. These broad patterns of organization should be considered along with the more specific information that follows.

The introduction to your persuasive speech should fulfill the same functions as the introduction for an informative speech, with one exception. The introduction should relate the topic to the audience, relate the topic to the speaker (speaker credibility), gain and maintain audience attention, and forecast the organization and development of the speech, as explained in chapter 15. The one aspect of the introduction that may differ in a persuasive speech is introducing the topic. In an informative speech, where clarity is one of the most important considerations, you should reveal your expectations early in the speech. You tell audience members exactly what you expect them to know, understand, and do as a result of the speech. In persuasive speaking, your expectations for the audience may have to be delayed until late in the speech because either audience members will be unprepared for your persuasive proposition or they may be hostile to the idea at first.

Persuasion is a kind of seduction in which you may have to convince an audience to accept your position. Most people do not begin a relationship with another by announcing, "I want to marry you." The idea may be too early or too much. Similarly, an effective persuasive speaker knows how much to ask for and that some convincing may have to take place before the immediate purpose or ultimate goal is announced. So the persuasive speaker may not reveal in the introduction exactly what he or she wants from the audience unless audience members are in a state of readiness to accept the persuasive proposition.

Other considerations for the persuasive speaker include:

1. *Should my best arguments come first, in the middle, or last in my persuasive speech?* **Arguments** are information that supports your stated proposition. Arguments presented first or early in the body of the speech seem to have more impact in speeches on controversial issues, on topics with which the audience is uninvolved, on topics the audience perceives as interesting, and on topics highly familiar to the audience. On the other hand, arguments seem to have more impact on an audience later in the persuasive speech when audience members are involved in the issue, when the topic is likely to be

less interesting, and when the issue is moderately unfamiliar to the audience.[10] No research to date indicates the most important arguments should be presented in the middle of the speech. The middle is the place where attention is likely to wane, so the effective speaker usually builds in human interest stories and interesting supporting materials to maintain audience attention.

2. *Should I present one side of the issue, or both, or many?* A persuasive speaker should present one side of an issue when the audience is friendly, when the speaker's position is the only one the audience is likely to hear, and when the speaker is seeking immediate but temporary change of opinion. A persuasive speaker should present both sides or many sides of an issue when the audience initially disagrees with the speaker or when it is likely the audience will hear other sides from other people.[11] Presenting both sides or multiple sides to a hostile audience may make the speaker seem more open-minded or less rigid to the audience. Also, presenting the other sides of the issue reduces the impact of counterarguments.

3. *Should I refute counterarguments?* When you deliver your persuasive speech, you are likely to employ a number of arguments with supporting materials to encourage your audience to accept your persuasive proposition. The arguments against your stated position are called **counterarguments.** In a both- or multi-sided persuasive speech, you reveal arguments that might be against your position. The best advice based on current research is to refute counterarguments before proceeding to your own position on the issue, especially when the audience is likely to already know the counterarguments.[12] If you favor freedom of choice on the abortion issue and your audience is familiar with the pro-life (anti-abortion) side of the issue, then you should refute those known counterarguments—point out their relative weaknesses or flaws—before you reveal your own position on the issue.

4. *Should I use familiar or novel arguments in my persuasive speech?* On most topics, you will have to recognize familiar arguments even if it is for the purpose of refuting them. However, research indicates *novel* arguments, or new arguments the audience has not heard before, have more impact than familiar ones.[13] A student who delivered a persuasive speech in favor of gun control pointed out a common counterargument from anticontrol forces was that gun registration would provide national enemies with a ready-made list of gun owners. The student who favored gun control pointed out the membership list of the National Rifle Association already provided an extensive list of gun owners that could be used by national enemies. The argument was novel and served to nullify the claim made by the anticontrol side on the issue. You, too, should seek new, novel, or original arguments in support of your own case and against the positions of others. Old and familiar arguments may be useful in your persuasive speech, but the ones the audience has not heard before have greater impact.

Ethical Considerations

Ethics or standards of moral conduct are written and unwritten rules of conduct. Many of our standards for ethical behavior are codified into law: we may not slander in speech or in writing someone who is not a public figure; we may not start a panic that can endanger the lives of others; we may not advocate the overthrow of our form of government.

Many of the ethics of persuasion are not matters of law, but violations of these unwritten or uncodified rules do have consequences. There is no law against showing a picture of a fetus at the bottom of a wastebasket in your speech against abortion, pointing out acne sufferers in your speech on dermatology, or having your audience unknowingly eat cooked rat meat, but audience members may find your methods so distasteful that, as a consequence, they reject you and your persuasive message.

The following are some of the generally accepted rules that govern the preparation and delivery of persuasive speeches:

1. *Accurate citation of sources.* When you are preparing and delivering your speech, you should be very careful to gather your information and to state it accurately. Specifically, you should reveal where or from whom you received information if it was not your own idea or information. Oral footnotes, written footnotes, and bibliographies should be a continuing reminder to speakers that who said something or where the information was found is important. Making up quotations, attributing an idea to someone who never said it, omitting important qualifiers, quoting out of context, and distorting the information from others are all examples of ethical violations that spring from this rule.

2. *Respect for sources of information.* Have you ever gone to the library to do research for a paper or speech only to find that some inconsiderate individual has already cut out the information you seek? Removing or defacing information meant for everyone is a serious violation of ethics punishable in most colleges and universities. Unfortunately, few of the offenders are caught, but the idea of "doing unto others as you would have them do unto you" is in operation here. Unless all students respect public sources of information, everyone suffers. This rule extends to respect for persons whom you interview. These people are willing to share information with you, so it behooves you to treat them and their information with respect in person and in your speech.

3. *Respect for your audience.* Persuasion is a process that works most effectively when there is mutual respect between speaker and audience. Attempts to trick the audience into believing something, lying to the audience, distorting the views of your opposition, or exaggerating claims for your own position are all ethically questionable acts. It helps if you already accept the idea a speaker should speak truthfully and accurately, that the persuasive speaker is best if he or she can accurately portray the opposing arguments and still win with arguments and evidence. If you do not believe the truth works better than the alternatives, then perhaps the fact audiences can be very hostile to a person who has tricked them or who has lied, distorted, or exaggerated simply to meet an immediate behavioral purpose or an ultimate goal may sway you.

4. *Respect for your opponent.* Persuasive speeches invite rebuttal. Nearly always there is someone inside or outside your audience who thinks your ideas or positions are wrong. A good rule of thumb is to respect your opponent, not only because he or she may be right, but also because an effective persuasive speaker can take the best the opposition has to offer and still convince the audience he or she should be believed. The idea that you should respect your opponent means you should not indulge in name-calling or in bringing up past behaviors are irrelevant to the issue. It means you should attack the other person's evidence, sources, or logic—not the person. Practical reasons for observing this rule of ethics are few of the issues about which we persuade are settled yet, you may find in time that your opponent's position is better in many respects than your own, and you will have to live with many issues not resolved in the manner you most desire.

You may get the impression from these four ethical guidelines that every persuasive speaker must be part angel. Not quite. The ethical rules for persuasive speaking allow for considerable verbal combat, for devastating the arguments of others with better or more persuasive evidence, for finding new supporting materials your opposition has not found, and for majority acceptance of your ideas. Persuasive speaking is not for the fainthearted, but it is much cleaner verbal combat if you obey the ethical guidelines that call for accurate citation of sources, respect for written and human sources of information, respect for your audience, and respect for your opponent.

Special Skills for Persuasive Speaking

Just as the informative speaker must learn special skills in defining, describing, explaining, and narrating, the persuasive speaker must learn special skills in arguing, providing evidence, and rebutting the arguments of others. In this section, you discover what an argument is, what tests of evidence are, and how to counter the arguments of others.

Argumentation

An argument consists of a proposition and its justification.[14] In persuasive speaking, the **proposition** embodies what you want the audience to believe or do: communication classes should be required, physicians' fees should be competitive, or federal money for human services should be returned to the state for distribution. Because persuasive propositions often suggest change from present practice, they are usually controversial and state something "should" or "ought to" be changed. The **justification** is all of the evidence that can be gathered in support of the proposition: facts, statistics, quotations, reports, studies, stories, pictures, objects, illustrations, and demonstrations.

The proposition is a conclusion that can be inferred from the justification or evidence. The pattern in a persuasive speech often looks like this:

Proposition		Evidence
↓		↓
Evidence	or	Evidence
↓		↓
Evidence		Evidence
↓		↓
Evidence		Proposition

The speech might begin with the proposition, which is then followed by the evidence, or it might start with evidence that leads to the proposition. In either case, the argument hinges on an **inference;** a conclusion consistent with, but beyond or larger than, the evidence used to support it. A lawyer might argue the suspect was at the scene of the murder and was holding a smoking gun, the bullets in the weapon matched the slugs in the body, that the suspect had just publicly threatened the victim, and that,

The presentation of evidence, both verbal and visual, can help persuade an audience.

therefore, the suspect was the murderer. The lawyer could just as well argue the suspect was a murderer and then cite the evidence. In either case, the conclusion—the suspect was the murderer—follows from, but is beyond, the evidence itself. Even given the evidence of the case, it is possible the suspect was framed—someone else did the shooting and stuck the smoking gun in the hapless suspect's hand just before the police arrived.

Another kind of argument reaches a conclusion deductively. **Deductive arguments** are based on premises rather than on evidence, and the conclusion drawn from the premises includes the premises themselves:

Major premise: All rats are undesirable pests.

Minor premise: This animal is a rat.

Conclusion: Therefore, this animal is an undesirable pest.

The conclusion is not an inference that goes beyond evidence, but a deduction that includes two of the three terms (rats, undesirable pests, animal) already included in the two premises.

Deductive arguments follow certain rules. If they follow the rules, they are called *valid,* even if the terms are arranged in premises that are false. For instance, the deductive argument stated previously is valid, but we might question the major premise—are all rats undesirable pests? Are laboratory rats undesirable? Or, in the minor premise, are we sure the animal is actually a rat and not a hamster?

The effective persuasive speaker makes sure evidence is consistent with, and leads to, the conclusion. The effective persuasive speaker insures the premises in the deductive argument are valid (correctly arranged) and true. The most common kind of argument to emerge in persuasive speaking is the deductive argument.

Evidence

Evidence is data or information intended to get the audience to accept the persuasive proposition the evidence purportedly supports.[15] Evidence usually consists of examples or of statements from authorities. A speaker supporting the idea colleges should supply child-care services for students with children might use as evidence a statement from an authority: "Dr. Jeffrey Ringer, Director of the Counseling Bureau, says colleges should provide child-care facilities and personnel for students." Perhaps, the speaker could use himself or herself as an example of why the service is needed.

The best evidence has to meet two criteria: tests of evidence and believability. Let us say one of your classmates argues students should establish their own co-operative bookstore (proposition) because other schools have done so successfully (evidence), because students could get better value for used books (evidence), and because the vice president for student affairs favors the idea (evidence). Let us assume also the speaker expands on the evidence to provide specific examples of schools where student co-op bookstores have been successfully initiated, the speaker is able to demonstrate that used books bring a better price at student co-ops, and the speaker has a quotation from the vice president for student affairs.

How would you evaluate this evidence? What questions would you ask about it? What are the **tests of evidence** applicable in this case? The following are some of the questions that test this evidence:

1. Is the evidence consistent with other known facts? Did the speaker look at a relatively large number of student co-ops to determine student co-ops are successful? Have any student co-op stores failed?

2. Would another observer draw the same conclusions? Has anyone other than the speaker determined that other student co-ops are successful? What does the speaker mean by "success"?

3. Does the evidence come from unbiased sources? Does the vice president for student affairs have anything to gain by favoring student co-op bookstores? Who made the claim students will get better value for their used books? Who said other schools have established successful student co-ops?

4. Is the source of the information qualified by education and/or experience to make a statement about the issue? The vice president may be well educated, but what does he or she know about co-op bookstores? What about the qualifications of the sources for the information on used books or successful co-ops?

5. If the evidence is based on personal experience, how typical was that personal experience? Unless the personal experience was typical, generalizable, realistic, and relevant, it is questionable as evidence.

6. If statistics were used as evidence, were they from a reliable source, comparable with other known information, current, applicable, and interpreted so the audience could understand them?

7. If studies and surveys were employed, were they authoritative, valid, reliable, objective, and generalizable? A study done by persons who favor student co-op bookstores, for instance, would be questionable because the source of the study is biased.

8. Were the speaker's inferences appropriate to the data presented? Did the speaker go too far beyond the evidence in reaching the conclusion students should establish their own co-op bookstore?

9. Was important counterevidence overlooked? Often, in our haste to make a positive case, counterevidence is ignored or omitted. What evidence against student co-ops was left out?

10. What is the speaker's credibility on the topic? Did the speaker "earn the right to speak" on the topic through research, interviews, and a thorough examination of the issue? Has the speaker had experience related to the issue?

The answers to these ten questions are important. Evidence that meets these tests has met the first requirement of good evidence.

The second requirement of good evidence is the audience believe in the evidence, trust it, and accept it—**believability.** Finding evidence that meets the tests of evidence is difficult enough, but at least the speaker has some guidelines. Why an audience will not believe evidence is more mysterious. The effective persuasive speaker knows all of the major arguments for, and against, the persuasive proposition. The evidence selected to be used in the speech is chosen from a multitude of arguments both because the evidence meets the tests of evidence and because the speaker's audience analysis indicates this evidence is most likely to be believed. A speaker addressing a group of fundamentalist Christians may know supporting materials from scripture will fall on friendly ears; that same evidence may not be believed by groups who do not accept the authority of the Bible. The effective persuasive speaker chooses evidence both because it meets the tests of evidence and because it meets audience requirements for believability.

Refutation

Refutation is the art of opposing the arguments presented by someone else. You can oppose the arguments of another speaker by showing how the evidence does not meet the tests of evidence and by demonstrating that, for this particular audience, the evidence is not believable. Other methods of refutation are more subtle.

Turning the tables is one refutational strategy in which the same evidence one speaker used in support of a proposition is used by the opposition to attack the proposition. The speaker mentioned earlier who argued the membership list of the National Rifle Association already provides a national enemy with a ready-made list of ardent gun owners was using that strategy. Another speaker arguing against gun control said North Dakota, South Dakota, Wyoming, and Montana did not have gun control, yet their murder rate was very low. An opposing speaker turned the tables by arguing the reason these areas had few murders was that all of the states mentioned were devoid of large metropolitan areas, not the lack of gun control laws.

Another refutational strategy is *reducto ad absurdum,* or reducing the issue to absurdity. One speaker argued there should be no laws against gun possession because "people, not guns, kill other people." An opposing speaker reduced the argument to absurdity by pointing out such reasoning would justify the ownership of submachine guns, flamethrowers, and hand grenades. Listen carefully to the arguments presented by others. Are there any ways the principle they advocate can be applied in ways undesirable to the audience?

A common fault in public speeches is the fallacy called *post hoc, ergo propter hoc;* that is, the assumption that just because one thing occurred after another is reason to believe one thing caused the other.[16] The Latin statement means "after this; therefore, because of this." Most superstitions are based on this fallacy—"I saw a black cat on the way into the office, and I slipped and broke my wrist going into the building." When listening to the speeches of others make sure that events are really causally linked and not simply two events that happened to occur close together in time.

Special pleading is still another kind of arguing susceptible to refutation.[17] Special pleading means the speaker blissfully ignores contrary evidence. Often, an otherwise strong case can be critically weakened when one audience member or an opposing speaker brings up a convincing piece of evidence to the contrary. A student argued hearty eaters need not despair because the National Academy of Sciences had declared that no specific link existed between eating habits and heart disease. The argument was shot down in rebuttal by an opposing speaker who produced a current study of 1,900 men over a nineteen-year period. The study demonstrated men who ate more fat and cholesterol had more heart attacks than those who restricted their diets. The latter student found the study in the highly prestigious *New England Journal of Medicine.* The first speaker had been special pleading; the second produced a single piece of good evidence that destroyed the first speaker's case.

Still another characteristic for the refutational speaker to watch for is the **red herring**, an irrelevancy that is introduced to draw attention away from the main issue.[18] In a recent court case, a lawyer argued his clients, a respected couple in the community, had been faithful church members who enhanced community life by sponsoring garage sales and by giving the money to the church. This glowing report was presented in an attempt to get the jury to overlook the fact the goods sold at the garage sale had been stolen from the firm where the couple worked. Another type of red herring is found in cases where the persuader presents a mountain of largely irrelevant evidence in an attempt to make quantity look like quality. Both types of red herring are readily attackable by the public speaker who can distinguish between relevant and irrelevant evidence.

There are other kinds of refutation, but turning the tables; *reducto ad absurdum; post hoc, ergo propter hoc;* special pleading; and the red herring give the beginning public speaker a sufficient arsenal with which to attack the evidence in a persuasive speech.

Two Examples of Persuasive Speeches

The following persuasive speeches are provided by a student enrolled in a speech communication course and by a faculty member who both teaches and serves as a communication consultant to major organizations.[19] While they may not be perfect speeches, they provide you with examples of how two people composed persuasive messages. The first example is of a manuscript speech and the second is an outline from which an extemporaneous speech was delivered. The first speech is on a topic appropriate for the classroom while the second speech was specifically designed to sell a communication consulting program to a particular organization.

Where Sugar Goes, Trouble Follows

Speaker gains audience attention.

Appeal to physical motive—the learned preference for sugar.

Are you closing your eyes to a situation you do not wish to acknowledge? Are you aware of the dangers in your diet? Yes, my friends, you are in trouble, and that trouble is sugar. You may think that you consume reasonable amounts of sugar, but today I am going to demonstrate that you may be consuming considerably more than you think.

Speaker states immediate purpose, a discontinuance goal: Stop eating so much sugar.

Source credibility: Did research and reduced consumption (experience).

Forecast.

Specific statement of purpose and expectations.

This habitual consumption of large amounts of sugar is truly undesirable so all of us should cut down immediately. We are all sugar addicts. After reviewing the evidence, I tried to consciously reduce my sugar consumption. That made me more fully aware of how much sugar I really do consume and how dependent I am on it. As a result of my speech, in which I will dispel a few myths and talk of the adverse effects of sugar, you, too, may make a conscious effort to reduce your sugar consumption.

Evidence that Americans consume large quantities of sugar.

Statistical evidence.

Visual aid: List of foods containing hidden sugar as a main ingredient.

Immediate behavioral purpose: Check the label before buying.

The average American consumes about 125 pounds of sugar annually. Even with the increasing price of sugar, the figure remains relatively constant. Of this sugar consumption, 70 percent is hidden, is contained in foods and beverages prepared outside the home.[1] Here is a list of the common foods that contain a lot of hidden sugar. (Speaker refers to visual aid.) Go to a supermarket, glance at the labels, and if sugar is listed among the first ingredients, then it is a major component.

*Organization: Reviews
first myth and moves to
second.*

*Argument: Bodily needs
can be met with
nutritious foods.*

*Organization: Signals
third point in speech.*

*Counterarguments:
Each myth is an
argument the speaker
refutes, thereby
reviewing the arguments
that could be leveled
against her case.*

*A main point with three
subpoints: Tooth
problems, weight
problems, and diabetes.*

*Organization: First
subpoint.*

Explanation.

Statistical evidence.

Oral footnote.

*Organization: Second
subpoint.*

Oral footnote.

Statistical evidence.

*Relates statistics to
audience with
alternative explanation.*

*Argument from
comparison.*

*Immediate behavioral
purpose.*

A second myth, besides the one that we don't think that we consume much sugar, is that the body needs sugar for energy. The body has no physiological need for sugar that cannot be satisfied by other, more nutritious foods. Your body can convert starches to sugar or use the sugar in fruits and vegetables for energy. The alleged need for sugar as "quick energy" is a myth—except in such rare situations as insulin shock.

A third myth is that all carbohydrates are the same, that it is the number of calories that really matters. On the contrary, sugar is essentially a pure chemical species that is broken down in one step and quickly absorbed into the bloodstream. Other carbohydrates are complex and are digested relatively slowly. Eventually, these complex carbohydrates become blood sugar, the primary fuel for your body. This metabolic difference may have different effects on your health.

One adverse effect that sugar can have on your health is tooth decay. Bacteria in the mouth digest the sugar on tooth surfaces. This bacterial action produces an acid that etches the protective tooth enamel and fosters gum disease. Interestingly, it is the amount of time that sugar remains on the teeth—not the quantity eaten—that makes the difference. In the United States today, it has been estimated in a recent *New York Times Magazine* article that 98 percent of American children have some tooth decay; by age fifty-five, approximately half the population have no teeth.[2]

A second metabolic difference that sugar can make besides tooth decay is excessive weight. According to Jean Mayer in an article entitled "The Bitter Truth about Sugar," 10 to 20 percent of all U.S. children and 35 to 50 percent of all middle-aged Americans are overweight.[3] Each person, on the average, consumes five hundred calories worth of sugar per day. This is the energy equivalent of more than fifty pounds of fat per year for each one of us.[4] The basic cause of obesity is not sugar; it is excess calories. But since calories can be highly concentrated in sugar-sweetened foods, you may eat more calories than you need of such foods before you feel full or even realize how much you have consumed. Compare the satiety value of a pound of apples with that of a two-ounce candy bar: both have the same caloric content. I'm not trying to say that everyone should cut down on calories, but instead of having one-fourth of your daily calories being supplied by sugar, which is essentially devoid of nutrients, eat foods that make a significant contribution to your nutrition.

Organization: Third subpoint and repetition of first two subpoints.	A third metabolic problem related to sugar—besides tooth decay and obesity—is diabetes in adults who have a genetic predisposition for the disease. Diabetes is a major cause of death in the United States, and between five and twelve million Americans are classified as diabetics. About one thousand new cases are reported every day.[5] There is a strong suspicion that a large sugar consumption may be causally related to diabetes, both indirectly by promoting obesity, and directly as a source of repeated stress on the insulin-producing mechanism of the body.

Statistical evidence.

Suggested causal link.

Conclusion: Breaklight function.

Summary of main arguments and subpoints.

Relates arguments, evidence with speaker and audience.

Immediate behavioral purpose repeated.

I have suggested today that we Americans consume more sugar than we think we do, that we do not really need refined sugar to gain energy for our bodies, and that all carbohydrates are not the same. To demonstrate that all carbohydrates are not the same, I showed that refined sugar is related to tooth decay, that sugar encourages excess weight, and that sugar is bad for adults who are predisposed to diabetes. With these arguments and evidence in mind, I urge you to join me in reducing the sugar in your diet. Be an intelligent consumer who reads the labels, who eats healthy, nutritious foods instead of sugar-laden foods and drinks. Remember, sugar is a villain in disguise: where sugar goes, trouble follows.

Endnotes or Footnotes

1. J. E. Brody, "Sugar: Villain in Disguise," *Reader's Digest,* October 1977, p. 164.
2. Jean Mayer, "The Bitter Truth about Sugar," *New York Times Magazine,* 20 June 1976, p. 31.
3. Mayer, p. 31.
4. Mayer, p. 31.
5. Mayer, p. 31.

Bibliography

Brody, J. E. "Sugar: Villain in Disguise." *Reader's Digest,* October 1977, pp. 163–65.
Mayer, Jean. "The Bitter Truth about Sugar." *New York Times Magazine,* 20 June 1976, pp. 26–34.

Outline of a Persuasive Sales Presentation

Product/service being sold—"Supervisory Skills for Women" training program marketed by Management Development Associates, (MDA, Inc.) Inc.
Thesis statement—The purchase of "Supervisory Skills for Women" will meet the training needs of XPQ Corporation to more effectively prepare its women supervisors for their job responsibilities.

I. Women are an integral part of contemporary organizations.
  A. Women are placed in disadvantageous positions within organizations.
    1. They are compensated at a lower wage level than men.
      a. Presently, women earn only $.59 for each $1.00 earned by men.
      b. The trend for compensation levels reflects an overall loss in buying power since the 1950's.

2. The majority of part-time employment positions are filled by women.
   a. The pay is usually lower.
   b. It is not necessary to provide health and welfare benefits to part-time employees in many states and organizations.
B. Women are promoted less often than men.
C. Women are inadequately represented at the upper levels of management in most organizations.
   1. Women hold fewer than 10 percent of the executive positions in Fortune 500 companies.
   2. Women have a shorter tenure than men in executive positions.
II. The women in XPQ Corporation need training in supervisory skills.
   A. The 132 women supervisors in this corporation collectively supervise 1,543 employees.
      1. XPQ's own research reports that only 15 percent of the women received formal training in supervision.
         a. The comparative figure for the males is 48 percent.
         b. Male supervisors had the advantage of a network of support they could draw on for their training.
      2. There are more female supervisors than male supervisors.
   B. The female supervisors perceive they need more training.
      1. The corporate training needs survey reports that there are significant differences between male and female supervisors on the topics on which training is needed.
         a. In fact, of the five top-ranked areas for training, women reported the highest level of perceived need across all five.
         b. The differences between the males and females was statistically significant for all topics.
      2. Furthermore, the survey revealed that female supervisors perceive they need training in the most fundamental of supervisory skills.
         a. They are concerned about crisis management, team building, motivation, decision making, and group leadership.
         b. Corresponding male responses indicate these are less important items to them.
   C. The perceived need for training is present in all companies but appears particularly acute in the XPQ Corporation.
      1. Women supervisors reported high levels of need.
         a. Inadequate training is holding them back.
         b. In addition, 70 percent of the women said they preferred supervisory training over technical skills training.
      2. Women supervisors want to do well in their jobs.
III. XPQ Corporation can take the first step in solving its training problems by entering into a contract with Management Development Associates, Inc. for its "Supervisory Skills for Women" training package.
   A. The "Supervisory Skills for Women" package offers several advantages over similar skills-based training programs.
      1. The package is designed exclusively for women.
         a. Training modules were designed after testing and feedback with women supervisors.
         b. Training modules address the special concerns of women.
         c. The situations and examples are common to women in organizations.

Checklist for a Persuasive Speech

Topic

_____ 1. Have you selected a topic about which your content can be predominantly persuasive?

_____ 2. Have you selected a topic about which your audience is not already persuaded?

_____ 3. Is your topic current?

_____ 4. Is your topic of any importance to this audience?

Purpose

_____ 1. Have you determined an ultimate persuasive goal for your speech?

_____ 2. Is your speech purpose aimed at adoption, discontinuance, deterrence, or continuance?

_____ 3. Have you determined immediate behavioral purposes for your speech?

_____ 4. How are you going to be able to tell the degree to which you have achieved your purposes?

Content

_____ 1. Have you found physical, psychological, or social motives to which you can appeal?

_____ 2. Have you included information about yourself that can improve your speaker credibility?

_____ 3. Have you used logical appeals that allow reasoning to persuade?

_____ 4. Have you used emotional appeals that might persuade your audience?

---

    2. The package is taught exclusively by women when it is presented on-site.
      a. Women trainers bring credibility and empathy to the training setting.
      b. Women training women permits a more open exchange of ideas.
  B. The "Supervisory Skills for Women" training package most closely meet XPQ's needs.
    1. The format is flexible and varied.
      a. The package includes all of the materials necessary to continue the reinforcement after the initial training.
        i. Videotapes.
        ii. Workbooks.
        iii. Pocket cards.
        iv. Reinforcement sessions.
      b. After the initial on-site presentation, MDA, Inc. will provide training for an on-site, corporate coordinator.
        i. Ensures continuity for the training.
        ii. Increases the probable level of long-term success of the training.

Organization

_____ 1. Where have you placed your best information or argument and why?

_____ 2. Are you presenting one side of the issue or more and why?

_____ 3. Can you refute potential counterarguments?

_____ 4. Have you thought of any new or novel arguments?

Ethics

_____ 1. Have you cited sources accurately throughout your speech?

_____ 2. Have you avoided misrepresentation, distortion, exaggeration, and deception by sticking to a high standard of truthfulness?

_____ 3. Have you planned anything in your speech you would not want others to do to you in a persuasive speech?

Special Skills

_____ 1. Have you employed inferences or deductive arguments in your speech?

_____ 2. Have you used tests of evidence and believability to ensure you have the best evidence?

_____ 3. Can you refute opposing arguments in a way that avoids fallacies or highlights the fallacies used by an opponent?

2. The program is tailored to reflect the job requirements of XPQ and its industrial group.
   a. It's not a "canned, mass marketed" program to which one simply "adds local water and watches it happen."
      i. Attention is given to "getting it right" for the purchasing organization.
      ii. No two packages are exactly alike, even within the same industry.
   b. Individual modules can be designed to meet special needs as defined by XPQ.
IV. The XPQ Corporation will derive significant benefits from the purchase and use of the "Supervisory Skills for Women" training package.
   A. Your women supervisors will experience a renewal of their energy and commitment to the organization.
      1. Perceptions of self-confidence will increase.
         a. Fewer negative concerns will be perceived.
         b. A more positive spirit will be present throughout the company.
      2. With increased self-confidence will come increased work commitment and job performance.

B. Your women supervisors will report increased levels of satisfaction with corporate policies, opportunities, and similar issues.
   1. The high quality and intensive nature of the "Supervisory Skills for Women" package positions the XPQ Corporation favorably with the women supervisors.
      a. The impression is made of concern for employees.
      b. There is an apparent willingness to invest significant amounts of resources in adequately training the women supervisors.
   2. The long-term supportive design of the training package is reinforcement to the women that the corporation is looking for continued excellence from its supervisory personnel.
C. There will be less turnover among supervisory staff.
   1. Replacement of supervisory personnel is an expensive and time consuming process.
      a. The loss of "organizational intelligence" cannot be erased simply because a person is replaced.
      b. Each replacement of a supervisor results in a cumulative loss of momentum for that supervisor's area.
   2. Stability among the supervisory personnel is reflected in more stability within the ranks of the employees.
V. The way is clear for the XPQ Corporation—*sign the contract for the "Supervisory Skills for Women" training package.*
   A. The advantages are obvious.
      1. Enhance the effectiveness of your women supervisors.
      2. Reduce the costs associated with replacing personnel.
      3. Free the women supervisors from feeling inadequate.
      4. Provide the company with long-term support for the training.
   B. No other option provides XPQ with so much of such quality! Sign now!

The ultimate goal of the persuasive speech on sugar in the diet was discontinuance, to persuade the audience to reduce consumption of refined sugar. The speech also had an explicit ultimate goal of adoption—to get the audience to start eating more nutritious foods instead of sugar-laden foods and drinks. The immediate behavioral purposes were stated intermittently through the speech: check labels to determine the amount of hidden sugar in food and drink products and eat natural sugars in fruits and vegetables instead of refined sugars in candy and other junk foods. The main motivational appeal was physical: alter your learned preference for sugar and avoid tooth decay, obesity, and diabetes. Much of the evidence was in the form of statistics from authoritative sources.

The ultimate goal of the sales presentation was to persuade the management of the XPQ Corporation to adopt the training program marketed by Management Development Associates. The main motivational appeal was psychological: adopt our training program and a large portion of your supervisors will perform more effectively within your corporation. To a great extent, the speaker relied upon logical appeals.

Persuasive Speech Performance

Deliver an eight-to-ten-minute persuasive speech in which you try to achieve immediate behavioral purposes consistent with an ultimate action goal like adoption or discontinuance. The speech should fulfill the functions of an introduction (see chapter 15), with special emphasis on establishing your credibility (see chapter 13). The speech should also fulfill the functions of a conclusion (see chapter 15). The body of the speech should consist of at least three major arguments with supporting materials (evidence) selected because of their appropriateness for your audience. Include oral footnotes and, if appropriate, visual aids (see chapter 16). Deliver the speech extemporaneously with as much eye contact and as little attention to notes as possible.

Persuasive Speech Document

Put the title of your persuasive speech and your name at the top of a sheet of paper. State your ultimate action goal and your immediate behavioral purposes. Then compose a manuscript of your persuasive speech, with sidenotes to indicate what functions you are fulfilling in the introduction and conclusion, what your main and subpoints are, and what kinds of evidence you are using. Conclude with endnotes or footnotes and a bibliography in proper form.

Summary

Preparing a persuasive speech requires we classify our ultimate purpose in behavioral terms as a speech of adoption, discontinuance, deterrence, or continuance; we find an appropriate topic; and we write an ultimate goal and immediate behavioral purposes for persuasion.

Audience members may be persuaded through motivational appeals (physical, psychological, and social), speaker credibility, logical appeals, and emotional appeals. The organization of a persuasive speech takes into account the placement of arguments and evidence, the number of sides presented to different kinds of audiences, the use of refutation, and the use of familiar and novel arguments.

answers
to chapter activities

notes

Chapter 1

1. See, for example, Paul T. Rankin, "Measurements of the Ability to Understand the Spoken Language" (Ph.D. diss., University of Michigan, 1926); Paul T. Rankin, "Listening Ability: Its Importance, Measurement, and Development," *Chicago Schools Journal* 12 (1930): 177; and J. Donald Weinrauch and John R. Swanda, Jr., "Examining the Significance of Listening: An Exploratory Study of Contemporary Management," *Journal of Business Communication* 13 (Fall 1975): 25–32.

2. See, for example, Ritch L. Sorenson and Judy C. Pearson, "Alumni Perspectives on Speech Communication Training: Implications for Communication Faculty," *Communication Education* 30 (1981): 299–307; Vincent Di Salvo, David C. Larsen, and William J. Seiler, "Communication Skills Needed by Persons in Business Organizations," *Communication Education* 25 (1976): 69–75; and Dan H. Swensen, "Relative Importance of Business Communication Skills for the Next Ten Years," *Journal of Business Communication* 17 (Winter 1980): 41–49.

3. David K. Berlo, *The Process of Communication* (New York: Holt, Rinehart and Winston, 1960).

4. Carl R. Rogers, *On Becoming A Person* (Boston: Houghton Mifflin, 1961), p. 18.

5. Students who wish to learn more about non-human communication systems are directed to Jane Goodall, *The Chimpanzees of Gombe* (Cambridge, Mass.: Belknap-Harvard, 1986).

6. Carl R. Rogers, *Client-Centered Therapy* (Boston: Houghton Mifflin, 1951), p. 483.

7. Dean C. Barnlund, "A Transactional Model of Communication," in *Foundations of Communication Theory,* eds. Kenneth K. Sereno and C. David Mortensen (New York: Harper & Row, 1970), pp. 98–101.

8. George Herbert Mead, quoted in *Sociology: Human Society* by Melvin De Fleur et al. (Glenview, Ill.: Scott, Foresman, 1977), p. 138.

9. Oliver Wendell Holmes, *The Autocrat of the Breakfast-Table* (Boston: Phillips, Simpson and Co., 1858), p. 59.

10. John Stewart, "An Interpersonal Approach to the Basic Course," *The Speech Teacher* 21 (1972): 7–14.

11. Blaine Goss, *Processing Communication* (Belmont, Calif.: Wadsworth, 1982).

12. Judy C. Pearson, *Communication in the Family* (New York: Harper & Row, in press), p. 15.

13. Arthur P. Bochner, "Conceptual Frontiers in the Study of Communication in Families: An Introduction to the Literature," *Human Communication Research* 2 (1976): 381–97.

14. Ronald B. Adler, *Communicating at Work: Principles and Practices for Business and the Professions* (New York: Random House, 1983), p. 12.

15. G. Kreps and B. Thornton, *Health Communication* (New York: Longman, Inc., 1984), p. 2.

16. For a review of literature in this area, see, for example, Teresa Thompson, The Invisible Helping Hand: The Role of Communication in Health and Social Service Professions. *Communication Quarterly* 32 (1984): 148–63.

Chapter 2

1. See, for example, C. R. Berger and R. J. Calabrese, "Some Explorations in Initial Interaction and Beyond: Toward a Developmental Theory of Interpersonal Communication," *Human Communication Research* 1 (1975): 99–112.

2. Richard Restak, *The Brain* (New York: Bantam Books, 1984), p. 244.

3. Marshall R. Singer, "Culture: A Perceptual Approach." In *Intercultural Communication: A Reader,* 4th ed., edited by Larry A. Samovar and Richard E. Porter (Belmont, Calif.: Wadsworth, 1985), p. 63.

4. V. P. Richmond and D. Robertson, "Communication Apprehension as a Function of Being Raised in an Urban or Rural Environment" (Monograph, West Virginia Northern Community College, 1976).

5. Judy C. Pearson, *Gender and Communication* (Dubuque, Iowa: Wm. C. Brown Publishers, 1985).

6. Alistair B. Fraser, "Fata Morgana—The Grand Illusion," *Psychology Today* 9 (January 1976): 22.

7. Clifton Fadiman, *The Little, Brown Book of Anecdotes* (Boston: Little, Brown and Company, 1985), p.105.

8. Fadiman, *The Little, Brown Book of Anecdotes,* p. 281.

9. Fadiman, *The Little, Brown Book of Anecdotes,* p. 341.

10. Fadiman, *The Little, Brown Book of Anecdotes,* p. 127.

11. Fadiman, *The Little, Brown Book of Anecdotes,* p. 242.

12. From Laing, R. D., "Differences in Perception," *Knots.* © 1970 R. D. Laing. Reprinted by permission of Pantheon Books, Div. of Random House, Inc.

13. Fadiman, *The Little, Brown Book of Anecdotes,* p. 223.

Chapter 3

1. Abraham H. Maslow, "Hierarchy of Needs," in *Motivation and Personality,* 2d ed. (New York: Harper & Row, 1970), pp. 35–72. Copyright © 1970 by Abraham H. Maslow.

2. From Schultz, Wm., *Here Comes Everybody.* © 1971 The Sterling Lord Agency, Inc. All Rights Reserved.

3. Jane Anderson, "Discover Yourself: Go Hiking Alone," Fort Wayne *Journal Gazette,* 21 March 1976.

4. George Herbert Mead, *Mind, Self, and Society* (Chicago: University of Chicago Press, 1934). Early theorists include Harry Stack Sullivan, William James, Charles Cooley, John Dewey, and I. A. Thomas.

5. From *Group Processes: An Introduction to Group Dynamics* by Joseph Luft, by permission of Mayfield Publishing Company. Copyright © 1984, 1970 and 1969 by Joseph Luft.

6. Paul Watzlawick, Janet Helmick Beavin, and Don D. Jackson, *Pragmatics of Human Communication: A Study of Interactional Patterns, Pathologies, and Paradoxes* (New York: W. W. Norton, 1967).

7. Michael Argyle, *Social Interaction* (New York: Atherton, 1969), p. 133.

8. Robert Rosenthal and Lenore Jacobson, *Pygmalion in the Classroom: Teacher Expectation and Pupils' Intellectual Development* (New York: Holt, Rinehart and Winston, 1968), p. vii.

9. Walker Percy, *Lost in the Cosmos: The Last Self-Help Book* (New York: Farrar, Straus and Giroux, 1983), pp. 39–40.

10. Nancy J. Bell and William Carver, "A Reevaluation of Gender Label Effects: Expectant Mothers' Responses to Infants," *Child Development* 51 (1980): 925–27.

11. J. Condry and S. Condry, "Sex Differences: A Study of the Eye of the Beholder," *Child Development* 47 (1976): 812–19.

12. Bonni R. Seegmiller, "Sex-Typed Behavior is Pre-Schoolers: Sex, Age, and Social Class Effects," *Journal of Psychology* 104 (1980): 31–33.

13. S. Tibbits, "Sex-Role Stereotyping in the Lower Grades: Part of a Solution," *Journal of Vocational Behavior* 6 (1975): 255–61.

14. A. B. Heilbrun, "Measurement of Masculine and Feminine Sex Role Identities as Independent Dimensions," *Journal of Consulting and Clinical Psychology* 44 (1976): 183–90.

15. Sandra L. Bem, "The Measurement of Psychological Androgyny," *Journal of Consulting and Clinical Psychology* 42 (1974): 155–62.

16. See, for example, Diana M. Zuckerman, "Self-Esteem, Self-Concept and the Life Goals and Sex-Role Attitudes of College Students," *Journal of Personality* 48 (1980): 149–62.

17. See, for example, Alice Ross Gold, Lorelei R. Brush, and Eve R. Sprotzer, "Developmental Changes in Self-Perceptions of Intelligence and Self-Confidence," *Psychology of Women Quarterly* 5 (1980): 231–39.

18. Susan Pomerantz and Robert C. House, "Liberated versus Traditional Women's Performance Satisfaction and Perceptions of Ability," *The Journal of Psychology* 95 (1977): 205–11.

19. Lynn L. Gigy, "Self-Concept of Single Women," *Psychology of Women Quarterly* 5 (1980): 321–40.

20. Mason Williams, "Here I Am Again," liner notes from *Sharepickers*. Copyright by Mason Williams. Used by permission. All rights reserved.

21. Constance J. Seidner, "Interaction of Sex and Locus of Control in Predicting Self-Esteem," *Psychological Reports* (1978), 895–98.

22. Judy C. Pearson, "Academic Women: How to Succeed in the University" (Paper presented to the Speech Communication Association, Chicago, Illinois, 1986).

Chapter 4

1. Robert N. Bostrom and Carol L. Bryant, "Factors in the Retention of Information Presented Orally: The Role of Short-Term Listening," *Western Journal of Speech Communication* 44 (1980): 137–45.

2. Ralph G. Nichols and Leonard A. Stevens, "Listening to People," *Harvard Business Review* 35 (1957): 85–92.

3. P. T. Rankin, "The Measurement of the Ability to Understand Spoken Language," *Dissertation Abstracts* 12 (1926): 847.

4. J. Donald Weinrauch and John R. Swanda, Jr., "Examining the Significance of Listening: An Exploratory Study of Contemporary Management," *Journal of Business Communication* 13 (February 1975): 25–32.

5. Elyse K. Werner, "A Study of Communication Time" (Master's thesis, University of Maryland, 1975).

6. See, for example, Miriam E. Wilt, "A Study of Teacher Awareness of Listening as a Factor in Elementary Education," *Journal of Educational Research* 43 (1950): 626; D. Bird, "Have You Tried Listening?" *Journal of the American Dietetic Association* 30 (1954): 225–30; and B. Markgraf, "An Observational Study Determining the Amount of Time That Students in the Tenth and Twelfth Grades Are Expected to Listen in the Classroom" (Master's thesis, University of Wisconsin, 1957).

7. Andrew D. Wolvin and Carolyn G. Coakley, *Listening* (Dubuque, Iowa: Wm. C. Brown Publishers, 1982); and Florence I. Wolff, Nadine C. Marsnik, William S. Tacey, and Ralph G. Nichols, *Perceptive Listening* (New York: Holt, Rinehart and Winston, 1983).

8. Larry L. Barker, *Listening Behavior* (Englewood Cliffs, N.J.: Prentice-Hall, 1971), p. 10.

9. D. Barbara, "On Listening—the Role of the Ear in Psychic Life," *Today's Speech* 5 (1957): 12.

10. John Stewart, "Interpretive Listening: An Alternative to Empathy," *Communication Education* 32 (1983): 379–91. Stewart includes four major themes: openness, linguisticality, play, and fusion of horizons. This section on interpretive listening is drawn from Stewart's excellent article and the reader is encouraged to read the original article for a more thorough treatment of the topic.

11. Clifton Fadiman, ed., *The Little, Brown Book of Anecdotes* (Boston: Little, Brown and Company, 1985), p. 79.

12. Hans-Georg Gadamer, *Truth and Method*, p. 269 cited in Stewart, p. 391.

13. Gadamer, *Truth and Method*, p. 272.

14. Stewart, "Interpretive Listening," p. 388.

Chapter 5

1. Ray L. Birdwhistell, *Kinesics and Context* (Philadelphia: University of Pennsylvania Press, 1970), pp. 128–43; Albert Mehrabian and Susan R. Kerris, "Inference of Attitude from Nonverbal Communication in Two Channels," *Journal of Consulting Psychology* 31 (1967): 248–52; and Timothy G. Hegstrom, "Message Impact: What Percentage Is Nonverbal?" *Western Journal of Speech Communication* 43 (1979): 134–42.

2. Paul Ekman and Wallace V. Friesen, "Head and Body Cues in the Judgment of Emotion: A Reformulation," *Perceptual and Motor Skills* 24 (1967): 711–24.

3. Albert Mehrabian, *Silent Messages* (Belmont, Calif.: Wadsworth, 1971), pp. 113–18.

4. Paul Ekman and Wallace V. Friesen, "The Repertoire of Nonverbal Behavior: Categories, Origins, Usage, and Coding," *Semiotica* 1 (1969): 49–98.

5. Ross Buck, Robert E. Miller, and William F. Caul, "Sex, Personality, and Physiological Variables in the Communication of Affect Via Facial Expression," *Journal of Personality and Social Psychology* 30 (1974): 587–96.

6. Edward J. J. Kramer and Thomas R. Lewis, "Comparison of Visual and Nonvisual Listening," *Journal of Communication* 1 (1951): 16–20.

7. Edward T. Hall, *The Hidden Dimension* (New York: Doubleday, 1966).

8. "Feeling Sad Tonight," words and music by Carole King and Toni Stern. Copyright © 1972 by Colgems Music Corp., 711 Fifth Avenue, New York, N.Y. 10022.

9. James R. Graves and John D. Robinson, II, "Proxemic Behavior as a Function of Inconsistent Verbal and Nonverbal Messages," *Journal of Counseling Psychology* 23 (1976): 333–38; and Judee K. Burgoon, "A Communication Model of Personal Space Violations: Explication and an Initial Test," *Human Communication Research* 4 (1978): 129–42.

10. Michael Argyle and Janet Dean, "Eye-Contact, Distance, and Affiliation," *Sociometry* 28 (1965): 289–304.

11. B. R. Addis, "The Relationship of Physical Interpersonal Distance to Sex, Race, and Age" (Master's thesis, University of Oklahoma, 1966); Gloria Leventhal and Michelle Matturro, "Differential Effects of Spatial Crowding and Sex on Behavior," *Perceptual and Motor Skills* 51 (1980): 111–19; and C. R. Snyder and Janet R. Endelman, "Effects of Degree of Interpersonal Similarity on Physical Distance and Self-Reinforcement Theory Predictions," *Journal of Personality* 47 (1979): 492–505.

12. Carol J. Guardo, "Personal Space in Children," *Child Development* 40 (1969): 143–51.

13. Robert Sommer, "The Distance for Comfortable Conversation: A Further Study," *Sociometry* 25 (1962): 111–16.

14. Edward T. Hall, "Proxemics: The Study of Man's Spatial Relations and Boundaries," *Man's Image in Medicine and Anthropology* (New York: International Universities Press, 1963), pp. 422–45.

15. Ashley Montagu, *Touching: The Human Significance of the Skin* (New York: Harper & Row, 1971), p. 82; J. L. Desper, "Emotional Aspects of Speech and Language Development," *International Journal of Psychiatry and Neurology* 105 (1941): 193–222; John Bowlby, *Maternal Care and Mental Health* (Geneva: World Health Organization, 1951), pp. 15–29; and Ronald Adler and Neil Towne, *Looking Out/Looking In* (San Francisco: Rinehart Press, 1975), pp. 225–26.

16. William C. Schutz, *Here Comes Everybody* (New York: Harper & Row, 1971), p. 16.

17. S. M. Jourard, *Disclosing Man to Himself* (Princeton, N.J.: Van Nostrand, 1968).

18. D. C. Barnlund, "Communicative Styles of Two Cultures: Public and Private Self in Japan and the United States," in *Organization of Behavior in Face-to-Face Interaction,* eds. A. Kendon, R. M. Harris, and M. R. Key (The Hague: Mouton, 1975).

19. J. D. Fisher, M. Rytting, and R. Heslin, "Hands Touching Hands: Affective and Evaluative Effects of Interpersonal Touch," *Sociometry* 3 (1976): 416–21.

20. V. S. Clay, "The Effect of Culture on Mother-Child Tactile Communication," *Family Coordinator* 17 (1968): 204–10; and S. Goldberg and M. Lewis, "Play Behavior in the Year-Old Infant: Early Sex Differences," *Child Development* 40 (1969): 21–31.

21. Sidney Jourard, "An Exploratory Study of Body Accessibility," *British Journal of Social and Clinical Psychology* 5 (1966): 221–31.

22. Sidney Jourard and J. E. Rubin, "Self-Disclosure and Touching: A Study of Two Modes of Interpersonal Encounter and Their Inter-Relation," *Journal of Humanistic Psychology* 8 (1968): 39–48.

23. Nancy Henley, "Power, Sex, and Nonverbal Communication," *Berkeley Journal of Sociology* 18 (1973–1974): 10–11.

24. Ernest Kramer, "The Judgment of Personal Characteristics and Emotions from Nonverbal Properties of Speech," *Psychological Bulletin* 60 (1963): 408–20.

25. James C. McCroskey, Carl E. Larson, and Mark L. Knapp, *An Introduction to Interpersonal Communication* (Englewood Cliffs, N.J.: Prentice-Hall, 1971), pp. 116–18.

26. Kramer, "Judgement of Personal Characteristics," pp. 408–20.

27. Gregory Bateson, D. D. Jackson, J. Haley, and J. H. Weakland, "Toward a Theory of Schizophrenia," *Behavioral Science* 1 (1956): 251–64.

28. Barbara Westbrook Eakins and R. Gene Eakins, *Sex Differences in Human Communication* (Boston: Houghton Mifflin, 1978), pp. 99–103; and Teresa J. Rosegrant and James C. McCroskey, "The Effect of Race and Sex on Proxemic Behavior in an Interview Setting," *Southern Speech Communication Journal* 40 (1975): 408–20.

29. Reprinted from "Every Human Being Is a Separate Language" by Pat Hardman in *The Salt Lake Tribune* 3 September 1971.

30. Seymour Fisher, "Body Decoration and Camouflage," in *Dimensions of Dress and Adornment: A Book of Readings,* eds. Lois M. Gurel and Marianne S. Beeson (Dubuque, Iowa: Kendall/Hunt, 1975).

31. Lynn Procter, *Fashion and Anti-Fashion* (London: Cox and Wyman, 1978).

32. Marilyn J. Horn, "Carrying It Off in Style," in *Dimensions of Dress and Adornment: A Book of Readings,* eds. Lois M. Gurel and Marianne S. Beeson (Dubuque, Iowa: Kendall/Hunt, 1975).

33. M. O. Perry, H. G. Schutz, and M. H. Rucker, "Clothing Interest, Self-Actualization and Demographic Variables," *Home Economics Research Journal* 11 (1983): 280–88.

34. L. R. Aiken, "The Relationship of Dress to Selected Measures of Personality in Undergraduate Women," *Journal of Social Psychology* 59 (1963): 119–28.

35. L. C. Taylor and N. H. Compton, "Personality Correlates of Dress Conformity," *Journal of Home Economics* 60 (1968): 653–56.

36. S. H. Hendricks, E. A. Kelley, and J. B. Eicher, "Senior Girls' Appearance and Social Acceptance," *Journal of Home Economics* 60 (1968): 167–72.

37. H. I. Douty, "Influence of Clothing on Perception of Persons," *Journal of Home Economics* 55 (1963): 197–202.

38. M. C. Williams and J. B. Eicher, "Teenagers' Appearance and Social Acceptance," *Journal of Home Economics* 58 (1966): 457–61.

39. P. N. Hamid, "Some Effects of Dress Cues on Observational Accuracy, Perceptual Estimate and Impression Formation," *Journal of Social Psychology* 86 (1972): 279–89.

Chapter 6

1. Benjamin Lee Whorf, "Science and Linguistics," in *Language, Thought and Reality,* ed. John B. Carroll (Cambridge, Mass.: M.I.T. Press, 1956), pp. 207–19.

2. John Barbour, "Edwin Newman Talks to Himself, But for a Good Reason," *Des Moines Sunday Register,* 5 June 1977.

3. Lewis Carroll, *Alice's Adventures in Wonderland* (New York: Random House, 1965), pp. 27–28.

Chapter 7

1. C. Berger and R. Calabrese, "Some Explorations in Initial Interactions and Beyond: Toward a Developmental Theory of Interpersonal Communication," *Human Communication Research* 1 (1975): 98–112.

2. William Schutz, *The Interpersonal Underworld* (Palo Alto, Calif.: Science and Behavior Books, 1976).

3. J. W. Thibaut and H. H. Kelley, *The Social Psychology of Groups* (New York: Wiley, 1959); and G. C. Homans, *Social Behavior: Its Elementary Forms* (New York: Harcourt Brace Jovanovich, 1961).

4. Morton Deusch and Robert M. Kraus, "Studies of Interpersonal Bargaining," *Journal of Conflict Resolution* 6 (1962): 52.

5. See the Thibaut and Kelley citation in note 3 above.

6. Gerald R. Miller, *Explorations in Interpersonal Communication* (Beverly Hills, Calif.: Sage Publications, 1976).

7. I. Altman and D. A. Taylor, *Social Penetration: The Development of Interpersonal Relationships* (New York: Holt, Rinehart & Winston, 1973).

8. See, for example, Leslie Baxter, "Self-Disclosure as a Relationship Disengagement Strategy: An Exploratory Investigation," *Human Communication Research* 5 (1979): 212–22; Leslie Baxter, "Strategies for Ending Relationships: Two Studies," *Western Journal of Speech Communication* 46 (1982): 223–41; Leslie Baxter,

"Relationship Disengagement: An Examination of the Reversal Hypothesis," *Western Journal of Speech Communication* 47 (1983): 85–98; and Leslie Baxter, "Trajectories of Relationship Disengagement," *Journal of Social* and *Personal Relationships* 1 (1984): 29–48.

9. Mark L. Knapp, *Social Intercourse: From Greeting to Goodbye* (Boston: Allyn & Bacon, 1978).

10. William W. Wilmot, *Dyadic Communication,* 2d ed. (Reading, Mass.: Addison-Wesley, 1980).

11. Malcolm R. Parks, "Ideology in interpersonal communication: Off the couch and into the world." In *Communication Yearbook 5.* M. Burgoon, ed. (New Brunswick, N.J.: Transaction Books, 1982).

12. See, for example, Joe Ayres, "Strategies to maintain relationships: Their identification and perceived usage," *Communication Quarterly* 31 (1983): 62–67; J. G. Delia, "Some Tentative Thoughts Concerning the Study of Interpersonal Relationships and Their Development," *Western Journal of Speech Communication* 44 (1980): 97–103; and Julia T. Wood, "Communication and Relational Culture: Bases for the Study of Human Relationships," *Communication Quarterly* 30 (1982): 75–83.

13. Melvin Lee, Philip G. Zimbardo, and Minerva Bertholf, "Shy Murderers," *Psychology Today* 11 (November 1977): 148.

14. Reprinted by permission of William Morrow & Company, Inc. from *The Shoes of the Fisherman* by Morris L. West. Copyright © 1963 by Morris L. West.

15. John Powell, *Why Am I Afraid to Tell You Who I Am?* (Niles, Ill.: Argus, 1969), p. 12.

16. L. B. Rosenfeld, "Self-Disclosure Avoidance: Why I Am Afraid to Tell You Who I Am," *Communication Monographs* 46 (1979): 63–74.

17. Joseph Stokes, Ann Fuehrer, and Lawrence Childs, "Gender Differences in Self-Disclosure to Various Target Persons," *Journal of Counseling Psychology* 27 (1980): 192–98.

18. Jack R. Gibb, "Defensive Communication," *The Journal of Communication* 11 (1961): 141–48.

19. Joyce L. Hocker and William W. Wilmot, *Interpersonal Conflict,* 2d ed. (Dubuque, Iowa: Wm. C. Brown, 1985), p. 23.

20. Judy C. Pearson, *Interpersonal Communication: Clarity, Confidence, Concern* (Glenview, Ill.: Scott, Foresman, 1983).

21. Gail Sheehy, *Passages: Predictable Crises of Adult Life,* pp. 24–25, E. P. Dutton, Inc. © 1974, 1976 by Gail Sheehy.

Chapter 8

1. Joseph A. DeVito, *The Interpersonal Communication Book,* 3d ed. (New York: Harper & Row, Publishers, 1983), p. 373.

2. Muriel James and Louis M. Savary, *The Heart of Friendship* (New York: Harper & Row, Publishers, 1976).

3. "You've Got a Friend," by Carole King. Copyright © 1971 by Colgems-EM1 Music Inc. All rights reserved.

4. Carol Werner and Pat Parmelee, "Similarity of Activity, Preferences Among Friends: Those Who Play Together Stay Together," *Social Psychology Quarterly* 42 (1979): 62–66.

5. Zick Rubin and Stephen Shenker, "Friendship, Proximity, and Self-Disclosure," *Journal of Personality* 46 (1978): 1–22.

6. Jane Howard, *Families* (New York: Simon and Schuster, 1978), p. 175.

7. Howard, *Families,* p. 260.

8. Sven Wahlroos, *Family Communication: A Guide to Emotional Health* (New York: New American Library, 1974), p. xi.

9. Jules Henry, *Pathways to Madness* (New York: Vintage Books, 1973).

10. R. D. Hess and G. Handel, *Family Worlds: A Psychological Approach to Family Life* (Chicago: University of Chicago Press, 1959).

11. Howard, *Families,* p. 13.

12. Arthur A. Bochner, "Conceptual Frontiers in the Study of Communication in Families: An Introduction to the Literature," *Human Communication Research* 2 (1976): 381–97.

13. S. L. Silverman and M. G. Silverman, *Theory of Relationships* (New York: Philosophical Library, 1963), p. xi.

14. George Herbert Mead, *Mind, Self, and Society* (Chicago: University of Chicago Press, 1934).

15. John Naisbitt, *Megatrends: Ten New Directions Transforming Our Lives* (New York: Warner Books, 1982), p. 259.

16. Naisbitt, *Megatrends,* p. 260.

17. Daniel Yankelovich, *New Rules: Searching for Self-Fulfillment in a World Turned Upside Down* (New York: Random House, 1981).

18. E. A. McGee, *Too Little, Too Late: Services for Teenage Parents* (New York: Ford Foundation, 1982).

19. Yankelovich, *New Rules.*

20. S. R. H. Beach and I. Arias, "Assessment of Perceptual Discrepancy: Utility of the Primary Communication Inventory," *Family Process* 22 (1983): 309–16.

21. See, for example, G. R. Birchler and L. J. Webb, "Discriminating Interaction Behaviors in Happy and Unhappy Marriages," *Journal of Consulting and Clinical Psychology* 45 (1977): 494–95; and L. Boyd and A. Roach, "Interpersonal Communicating Skills Differentiating More Satisfying from Less Satisfying Marital Relationships," *Journal of Counseling Psychology* 24 (1977): 540–42.

22. L. Snyder, "The Deserting, Nonsupporting Father: Scapegoat of Family Nonpolicy," *Family Coordinator* 28 (1979): 594–98.

23. Carla R. Dersch and Judy C. Pearson, "Interpersonal Communication Competence and Marital Adjustment among Dual Career and Dual Worker Women" (Paper presented to the annual meeting of the Central States Speech Association Convention, Cincinnati, Ohio, 1986).

24. E. Walster, G. W. Walster, and E. Berscheid, *Equity: Theory and Research* (Boston: Allyn & Bacon, 1978).

25. D. Reiss, R. Costell, H. Berkman, and C. Jones, "How One Family Perceives Another: The Relationship Between Social Constructions and Problem-Solving Competence," *Family Process* 19 (1980): 239–56.

26. See, for example, J. Gottman, *Marital Interaction: Experimental Investigations* (New York: Academic Press, 1979); P. Noller, "Channel Consistency and Inconsistency in the Communication of Married Couples," *Journal of Personality and Social Psychology* 39 (1980): 732–41; and G. R. Pike and A. L. Sillars, "Reciprocity of Marital Communication," *Journal of Social and Personal Relationships* 2 (1985): 303–24.

27. J. P. Vincent, L. Friedman, J. Nugent, and L. Messerly, "Demand Characteristics in the Observation of Marital Interaction," *Journal of Consulting and Clinical Psychology* 47 (1979): 557–67.

28. See, for example, J. Riskin and E. E. Faunce, "Family Interaction Scales: Discussion of Methodology and Substantive Findings," *Archives of General Psychiatry* 22 (1970): 527–37.

29. Risken and Faunce, "Family Interaction Scales," p. 402.

30. Risken and Faunce, "Family Interaction Scales," p. 402.

31. E. J. Thomas, *Marital Communication and Decision Making* (New York: The Free Press, 1977).

32. J. P. Vincent, R. L. Weiss, and G. Birchler, "A Behavioral Analysis of Problem Solving in Distressed and Nondistressed Married and Stranger Dyads," *Behavior Therapy* 6 (1975): 475–87.

33. A. Billings, "Conflict Resolution in Distressed and Nondistressed Married Couples," *Journal of Consulting and Clinical Psychology* 47 (1979): 368–76.

34. N. S. Jacobson, "Behavioral Marital Therapy." In *Handbook of Family Therapy,* A. S. Gurman and D. P. Kniskern, eds. (New York: Brunner/Mazel, 1981).

35. J. F. Alexander, "Defensive and Supportive Communications in Family Systems," *Journal of Marriage and the Family* 35 (1973): 613–17.

36. R. B. Stuart, "Operant-Interpersonal Treatment for Marital Discord," *Journal of Consulting and Clinical Psychology* 33 (1971): 675–82.

37. M. A. Fitzpatrick and P. G. Best, "Dyadic Adjustment in Traditional, Independent, and Separate Relationships: A Validation Study," *Communication Monographs* 46 (1979): 167–78.

38. J. M. Gottman, *Marital Interaction: Experimental Investigations* (New York: Academic Press, 1979), pp. 9–10.

39. J. Scanzoni and K. Polonko, "A Conceptual Approach to Explicit Marital Negotiation," *Journal of Marriage and the Family* 42 (1980): 45–56.

Chapter 9

1. Felix M. Lopez, *Personnel Interviewing* (New York: McGraw-Hill, 1975), p. 1.

2. See, for example, John T. Hopkins, "The Top Twelve Questions for Employment Agency Interviews," *Personnel Journal* 59 (May 1980): 209–13; and Jack Bucalo, "The Balanced Approach to Successful Screening Interviews," *Personnel Journal* 57 (August 1978): 420–28.

3. Two recent articles that clarify the EEOC guidelines are William A. Simon, Jr., "A Practical Approach to the Uniform Selection Guidelines," *Personnel Administrator* 24 (November 1979): 75–79; and Robert D. Gatewood and James Ledvinka, "Selection Interviewing and the EEOC: Mandate for Objectivity," *Personnel Administrator* 24 (December 1979): 51–54.

4. Richard M. Coffina, "Management Recruitment Is a Two-Way Street," *Personnel Journal* 58 (February 1979): 86.

5. John P. Galassi and Merna Dee Galassi, "Preparing Individuals for Job Interviews," *Personnel and Guidance Journal* 57 (December 1958): 188–91.

6. Robert E. Kraut, "Verbal and Nonverbal Cues in the Perception of Lying," *Journal of Personality and Social Psychology* 36 (1978): 380–91.

7. Hopkins, "Top Twelve Questions," 209–13.

8. Revised from suggestions made by Michael S. Hanna and Gerald L. Wilson, *Communicating in Business and Professional Settings* (New York: Random House, 1984), p. 207; Cal W. Downs, Wil Linkugel, and David M. Berg, *The Organizational Communicator* (New York: Harper & Row, 1977), p. 104; and Felix M. Lopez, Jr., *Personnel Interviewing* (New York: McGraw-Hill, 1965), p. 148.

9. Norman R. F. Maier, *The Appraisal Interview* (New York: John Wiley and Sons, 1958), p. 22; and Charles J. Stewart and William B. Cash, *Interviewing: Principles and Practices* (Dubuque, Iowa: Wm. C. Brown Publishers, 1978), pp. 172–73.

10. Alva F. Kindall and James Gatza, "Positive Program of Performance Appraisal," *Harvard Business Review* 41 (November–December, 1963), pp. 153–60.

Chapter 10

1. Louis Cassels, "You Can Be a Better Leader," *Nation's Business,* June 1960.

2. Judy C. Pearson, Ritch L. Sorenson, and Paul E. Nelson, "How Students and Alumni Perceive the Basic Course," *Communication Education* 30 (1981): 299–307.

3. Gerald M. Goldhaber, *Organizational Communication,* 2d ed. (Dubuque, Iowa: Wm. C. Brown Publishers, 1979), p. 236.

4. Gary L. Kreps and Barbara C. Thornton, *Health Communication: Theory and Practice* (New York: Longman, 1984), pp. 126–28.

5. John K. Brilhart, *Effective Group Discussion,* 3d ed. (Dubuque, Iowa: Wm. C. Brown Publishers, 1978), pp. 20–21.

6. Marvin E. Shaw, "Communication Networks," in *Advances in Experimental Social Psychology,* ed. Leonard Berkowitz, vol. 1 (New York: Academic Press, 1964), pp. 111–47.

7. The information that follows is based on Judy C. Pearson, *Gender and Communication* (Dubuque, Iowa: Wm. C. Brown Publishers, 1985), pp. 316–19. The reader is encouraged to consult that source or a summary provided by John E. Baird, "Sex Differences in Group Communication: A Review of Relevant Research," *Quarterly Journal of Speech* 62 (1976): 179–92.

8. Dennis S. Gouran, "Variables Related to Consensus in Group Discussions of Questions of Policy," *Speech Monographs* 36 (1968): 387–91.

9. Jerold W. Young, "Willingness to Disclose Symptoms to a Male Physician: Effects of the Physician's Physical Attractiveness, Body Area of Symptom and the Patient's Self-Esteem, Locus of Control and Sex" (Paper presented to the International Communication Association Convention, Acapulco, Mexico, May, 1980).

10. Earl Bennett South, "Some Psychological Aspects of Committee Work," *Journal of Applied Psychology* 11 (1927): 348–68.

11. Richard L. Hoffman & Norman K. V. Maier, "Quality and Acceptance of Problem Solutions by Members of Homogeneous and Heterogeneous Groups," *Journal of Abnormal and Social Psychology* 62 (1961): 401–7.

12. B. F. Meeker & P. A. Weitzel-O'Neill, "Sex Roles and Interpersonal Behavior in Task-Oriented Groups," *American Sociological Review* 42 (1977): 91–105.

13. Patricia Hayes Bradley, "Sex, Competence and Opinion Deviation: An Expectation States Approach," *Communication Monographs* 47 (1980): 105–10.

14. See, for example, Richard Bauer and James H. Turner, "Betting Behavior in Sexually Homogeneous and Heterogeneous Groups," *Psychological Reports* 34 (1974): 251–58.

15. R. Harper, "The Effects of Sex and Levels of Acquaintance on Risk-Taking in Groups" (Ph.D. diss., University of North Dakota, 1970).

16. See, for example, Alan H. Benton, "Reactions to Demands to Win from an Opposite Sex Opponent," *Journal of Personality* 41 (1973): 430–42.

17. See, for example, Joseph H. Hattes and Arnold Kahn, "Sex Differences in a Mixed-Motive Conflict Situation," *Journal of Personality* 42 (1974): 260–75.

18. See, for example, Monroe M. Lefkowitz, Leonard D. Eron, Leopold O. Walder, and L. Rowell Huesmann, *Growing up to Be Violent: A Longitudinal Study of the Development of Aggression* (New York: Pergamon Press, Inc., 1977).

19. See, for example, H. L. Kaplowitz, "Machiavellianism and Forming Impressions of Others," in *Contemporary Social Psychology: Representative Readings,* ed. Thomas Blass (Itasca, Ill.: F. E. Peacock, 1976).

20. Michael E. Roloff, "The Impact of Socialization on Sex Differences in Conflict Resolution" (Paper presented at the Annual Convention of the International Communication Association, Acapulco, Mexico, May, 1980).

21. Sidney M. Jourard, *Self-Disclosure: An Experimental Analysis of the Transparent Self* (New York: John Wiley, 1971).

22. J. Bond and W. Vinacke, "Coalition in Mixed Sex Triads," *Sociometry* 24 (1961): 61–75.

23. Thomas K. Uesugi and W. Edgar Vinacke, "Strategy in a Feminine Game," *Sociometry* 26 (1963): 75–88.

24. I. Mat Amidjaja and W. Edgar Vinacke, "Achievement, Nurturance, and Competition in Male and Female Triads," *Journal of Personality and Social Psychology* 2 (1965): 447–51.

25. *Ibid.*

26. Joan E. Marshall and Richard Heslin, "Boys and Girls Together: Sexual Composition and the Effect of Density and Group Size on Cohesiveness," *Journal of Personality and Social Psychology* 31 (1975): 952–61.

27. B. Aubrey Fisher, "Differential Effects of Sexual Composition and Interactional Context on Interaction Patterns in Dyads," *Human Communication Research* 9 (1983): 225–38; Elaine M. Yamada, Dean Tjosvold, and Juris G. Draguns, "Effects of Sex-Linked Situations and Sex Composition on Cooperation and Style of Interaction," *Sex Roles* 9 (1983): 541–54.

28. Donald G. Ellis and Linda McCallister, "Relational Control in Sex-Typed and Androgynous Groups," *Western Journal of Speech Communication* 44 (1980): 35–49.

29. Alex F. Osborn, *Applied Imagination: Principles and Procedures of Creative Thinking* (New York: Scribner's, 1953), pp. 300–301.

Chapter 11

1. Cecil A. Gibb, "The Principles and Traits of Leadership," in *Small Groups: Studies in Social Interaction,* ed. A. Paul Hare, E. F. Borgatta, and R. F. Bales, rev. ed. (New York: Alfred A. Knopf, 1965), pp. 87–95.

2. Paul Hersey and Kenneth Blanchard, *Management of Organizational Behavior: Utilizing Human Resources,* 4th ed. (Englewood Cliffs, N.J.: Prentice-Hall, 1982).

3. Connie S. Hellman, "An Investigation of the Communication Behavior of Emergent and Appointed Leaders in Small Group Discussion" (Ph.D. diss., Indiana University, 1974).

4. Adapted from Robert Terry, "The Leading Edge," *Minnesota: University of Minnesota Alumni Association* (January/February, 1987), p. 17.

5. J. H. Tindall, L. Boyler, P. Cline, P. Emberger, S. Powell, and J. Wions, "Perceived Leadership Rankings of Males and Females in Small Task Groups," *Journal of Psychology* 100 (1978): 13–20.

6. Walter A. Kaess, Sam L. Witryol, and Richard E. Nolan, "Reliability, Sex Differences and Validity in the Leaderless Group Discussion Technique," *Journal of Applied Psychology* 45 (1961): 345–50; and

K. Hall, "Sex Differences in Initiation and Influence in Decision-Making Among Prospective Teachers" (Ph.D. Diss., Stanford University, 1972).

7. Edwin E. Megargee, "Influence of Sex Roles on the Manifestation of Leadership," *Journal of Applied Psychology* 53 (1969): 377–82.

8. Libby O. Ruch and Rae R. Newton, "Sex Characteristics, Task Clarity, and Authority," *Sex Roles* 3 (1977): 479–94.

9. See, for example, Christopher Stitt, Stuart Schmidt, Kari Price, and David Kipnis, "Sex of Leader, Leader Behavior, and Subordinate Satisfaction," *Sex Roles* 9 (1983): 31–42.

10. Marsha B. Jacobson and Joan Effertz, "Sex Roles and Leadership: Perceptions of the Leaders and the Led," *Organizational Behavior and Performance* 12 (1974): 383–96.

11. Joy Carter, "Creativity and Leadership," *Journal of Creative Behavior* 12 (1978): 217–18.

12. Morris Aderman and Carol A. Johnson, "Leadership Style and Personal History Information," *Journal of Psychology* 102 (1979): 243–50.

13. R. White and R. Lippit, "Leader Behavior and Member Reaction in Three 'Social Climates'," in *Group Dynamics: Research and Theory,* ed. Dorwin Cartwright and Alvin Zander, 2d ed. (New York: Harper & Row, 1960), pp. 527–53; L. P. Bradford and R. Lippit, "Building a Democratic Work Group," *Personnel* 22 (1945): 142–52; and William M. Fox, "Group Reaction to Two Types of Conference Leadership," *Human Relations* 10 (1957): 279–89.

14. See, for example, L. L. Rosenbaum and W. B. Rosenbaum, "Morale and Productivity Consequences of Group Leadership Styles, Stress, and Type of Task," *Journal of Applied Psychology* 55 (1971): 343–58; and Paul Hersey and Kenneth Blanchard, *Management of Organizational Behavior: Utilizing Human Resources,* 4th ed. (Englewood Cliffs, N.J.: Prentice-Hall, 1982).

15. Dorothy M. Haccoun, Robert R. Haccoun, and George Sallay, "Sex Differences in the Appropriateness of Supervisory Styles: A Nonmanagement View," *Journal of Applied Psychology* 63 (1978): 124–27.

16. Paul Hersey and Kenneth H. Blanchard, *Management of Organizational Behavior: Utilizing Human Resources,* 3d ed. (Englewood Cliffs, N.J.: Prentice-Hall, 1977).

17. George Homans. *The Human Group* (New York: Harcourt Brace Jovanovich, 1950), p. 423.

18. See, for example, John E. Baird and Patricia Hayes Bradley, "Styles of Management and Communication: A Comparative Study of Men and Women," *Communication Monographs* 46 (1979): 101–11.

19. See, for example, Denise Serafini and Judy C. Pearson, "Leadership Behavior and Sex Role Socialization: Two Sides of the Same Coin," *Southern Speech Communication Journal* 49 (1984): 396–405.

20. See A. Paul Hare, *Handbook of Small Group Research* (New York: Free Press, 1962), pp. 293–94.

21. Ralph M. Stogdill, *Handbook of Leadership: A Survey of Theory and Research* (New York: Free Press, 1974), p. 30.

22. Terry, p. 18.

23. Wally D. Jacobson, *Power and Interpersonal Relations* (Belmont, Calif.: Wadsworth, 1972).

24. Terry, p. 20.

25. Warren Bennis and Burt Nanus, *Leaders: The Strategies for Taking Charge* (New York: Harper & Row, 1985), p. 27.

26. *Ibid.,* p. 28.

27. Terry, p. 22.

28. *Ibid.*

29. John K. Brilhart, *Effective Group Discussion,* 3d ed. (Dubuque, Iowa: Wm. C. Brown Publishers, 1978), pp. 170–82.

Chapter 12

1. From Heath, Robert L., "Variability in value system priorities as decision-making adaptation to situational differences," *Communication Monographs,* 43, pp. 325–33. © 1976 Speech Communication Association. Reprinted by permission.

Chapter 13

1. "What Are Americans Afraid Of?" *Bruskin Report* 53 (1973).

2. Much of the following information concerning communication apprehension comes from "The Nature and Effects of Communication Apprehension" in James C. McCroskey and Lawrence R. Wheeless, *Introduction to Human Communication* (Boston: Allyn and Bacon, 1976), pp. 81–90.

3. Judy C. Pearson and Donald D. Yoder, "Public Speaking or Interpersonal Communication: The Perspective of the High Communication Apprehensive Student," Educational Resources Information Center (ERIC), ED 173 870, May 1979.

4. G. D. Hemsley and A. M. Doob, "The Effect of Looking Behavior on Perceptions of a Communicator's Credibility," *Journal of Applied Social Psychology* 8 (1978): 136–44.

5. E. A. Lind and W. M. O'Barr, "The Social Significance of Speech in the Courtroom," in *Language and Social Psychology,* ed. H. Giles and R. St. Clair (Oxford, England: Blackwells, 1979).

6. N. Miller, G. Maruyama, R. J. Beaber, and K. Valone, "Speed of Speech and Persuasion," *Journal of Personality and Social Psychology* 34 (1976): 615–25.

7. Aristotle, *Rhetoric,* in *The Basic Works of Aristotle,* trans. W. Rhys Roberts and ed. by Richard McKeon (New York: Random House, 1941), 1, 1356a, LL. 12–14.

8. Ralph L. Rosnow and Edward J. Robinson, eds., *Experiments in Persuasion* (New York: Academic Press, 1967), p. 18.

9. Derived from a study by Christopher J. S. Tuppen, "Dimensions of Communicator Credibility: An Oblique Solution," *Speech Monographs* 41 (1974): 253–60.

10. *Ibid.*

11. Rosnow and Robinson, p. 8. *See also,* Kenneth Andersen and Theodore Clevenger, Jr., "A Summary of Experimental Research in Ethos," *Speech Monographs* 30 (1963): 59–78.

12. Marvin Karlins and Herbert I. Abelson, *Persuasion* (New York: Springer, 1970), pp. 113–14.

13. Carl I. Hovland and Walter Weiss, "The Influence of Source Credibility on Communicator Effectiveness," in Rosnow and Robinson, p. 21.

14. Wayne N. Thompson, *Quantitative Research in Public Address and Communication* (New York: Random House, 1967), p. 54.

15. Andersen and Clevenger, pp. 59–78.

16. L. S. Harms, "Listener Judgments of Status Cues in Speech," *Quarterly Journal of Speech* 47 (1961): 168.

17. Harry Sharp, Jr. and Thomas McClung, "Effects of Organization on the Speaker's Ethos," *Speech Monographs* 33 (1966): 182–83.

18. Thompson, p. 56.

19. *Ibid.*

Chapter 14

1. Erwin P. Bettinghaus, *The Nature of Proof* (New York: Bobbs-Merrill, 1972), p. v.

2. *Ibid.*

3. *Ibid.*

4. William Safire, "When a Mistake Becomes Correct, and Vice Versa," *Des Moines Sunday Register,* 30 November 1980, p. 3C.

Chapter 15

1. "Bones Found in Kenya May Be from Apes' Progenitor," *Chronicle of Higher Education,* 7 December 1983, 1.

2. "Research Notes," *Chronicle of Higher Education,* 7 December 1983, 1–2.

3. James J. Kilpatrick, "Death Sentence as Gun Control?" *Des Moines Tribune,* 12 December 1980, p. 18.

4. "The Killing Goes On," *Des Moines Tribune,* 11 December 1980, p. 18.

5. See note 4.

6. See note 3.

7. Tom Wicker, "You, Me and Handguns," *Ames Daily Tribune,* 18 December 1980, p. A4.

8. *Ibid.*

9. *Ibid.*

10. *Ibid.*

11. See note 3.

12. The examples of incorrect and correct parallel form are derived from U.S. Education Secretary T. H. Bell's announcement in 1984 concerning figures from 1982 and before, "State School Official Pleased by Ohio's Grade," *Athens Messenger,* 6 January 1984, p. 13.

13. Based on a speech manuscript composed by Jane Wolf in Speech 211H, Iowa State University.

14. From a fictional account based on historical facts: James A. Michener, *The Covenant,* 2 vols. (New York: Random House, 1980).

15. Based on an outline composed by Terry Hermiston in Speech 211, Iowa State University.

16. Douglas Ehninger, Bruce E. Gronbeck, and Alan H. Monroe, *Principles of Speech Communication,* 9th brief ed. (Glenview, Ill.: Scott, Foresman, 1984), p. 249.

17. Based on a manuscript composed by Melanie Comito in Speech 211H, Iowa State University.

18. From a speech delivered by Nancy Stuss in Speech 211H, Iowa State University.

Chapter 16

1. Herbert W. Hildebrandt and Walter Stevens, "Manuscript and Extemporaneous Delivery in Communicating Information," *Speech Monographs* 30 (1963): 369–72.

2. Erwin Bettinghaus, "The Operation of Congruity in an Oral Communication Situation," *Speech Monographs* 28 (1961): 131–42.

3. Ernest H. Henrikson, "An Analysis of the Characteristics of Some 'Good' and 'Poor' Speakers," *Speech Monographs* 11 (1944): 120–24.

4. Howard Gilkinson and Franklin H. Knower, "Individual Differences among Students of Speech as Revealed by Psychological Tests— I," *Journal of Educational Psychology* 32 (1941): 161–75.

5. John L. Vohs, "An Empirical Approach to the Concept of Attention," *Speech Monographs* 31 (1964): 355–60.

6. Charles Woolbert, "The Effects of Various Modes of Public Reading," *Journal of Applied Psychology* 4 (1920): 162–85.

7. John W. Black, "A Study of Voice Merit," *Quarterly Journal of Speech* 28 (1942): 67–74.

8. William N. Brigance, "How Fast Do We Talk?" *Quarterly Journal of Speech* 12 (1926): 337–42.

9. Kenneth A. Harwood, "Listenability and Rate of Presentation," *Speech Monographs* 22 (1955): 57–59.

10. Grant Fairbanks, Newman Guttman, and Miron S. Murray, "Effects of Time Compression upon the Comprehension of Connected Speech," *Journal of Speech and Hearing Disorders* 22 (1957): 10–19.

11. John B. Voor and Joseph M. Miller, "The Effect of Practice upon the Comprehension of Time-Compressed Speech," *Speech Monographs* 32 (1965): 452–54.

12. Charles F. Diehl, Richard C. White, and Kenneth W. Burk, "Rate and Communication," *Speech Monographs* 26 (1959): 229–32.

13. From *The Random House Dictionary of the English Language.* Copyright © Random House, Inc. Reprinted by permission of Random House, Inc.

14. Donald Hayworth, "A Search for Facts on the Teaching of Public Speaking," *Quarterly Journal of Speech* 28 (1942): 247–54.

15. Charles Woolbert, "The Effects of Various Modes of Public Reading," *Journal of Applied Psychology* 4 (1920): 162–85; George M. Glasgow, "A Semantic Index of Vocal Pitch," *Speech Monographs* 19 (1952): 64–68; Kenneth C. Beighley, "An Experimental Study of the Effect of Four Speech Variables on Listener Comprehension," *Speech Monographs* 19 (1952): 249–58 and 21 (1954): 248–53; and see also note 7.

16. Edward J. J. Kramer and Thomas R. Lewis, "Comparison of Visual and Nonvisual Listening," *Journal of Communication* I (1931): 16–20.

17. Martin Cobin, "Response to Eye Contact," *Quarterly Journal of Speech* 48 (1962): 415–18.

18. Steven A. Beebe, "Eye Contact: A Nonverbal Determinant of Speaker Credibility," *Speech Teacher* 23 (1974): 21–25.

19. See note 3.

20. Roland J. Hard and Bruce L. Brown, "Interpersonal Information Conveyed by the Content and Vocal Aspects of Speech," *Speech Monographs* 41 (1974): 371–80; and D. F. Gundersen and Robert Hopper, "Relationships between Speech Delivery and Speech Effectiveness," *Speech Monographs* 43 (1976): 158–65.

21. Charles R. Petrie, Jr., "Informative Speaking: A Summary and Bibliography of Related Research," *Speech Monographs* 30 (1963): 81.

22. Elena P. Zayas-Baya, "Instructional Media in the Total Language Picture," *International Journal of Instructional Media* 5 (1977–78): 145–50.

23. Kenneth B. Haas and Harry Q. Packer, *Preparation and Use of Audiovisual Aids* (New York: Prentice-Hall, 1955), pp. 163–68.

24. Michael MacDonald-Ross, "How Numbers Are Shown: A Review of Research on the Presentation of Quantitative Data in Texts," *AV Communication Review* 25 (Winter 1977): 359–409.

25. Isbrabim M. Hebyallah and W. Paul Maloney, "Content Analysis of T.V. Commercials," *International Journal of Instructional Media* 5 (1977–78): 9–16.

Chapter 17

1. Charles R. Petrie, Jr., "Informative Speaking: A Summary and Bibliography of Related Research," *Speech Monographs* 30 (1963): 79–91.

2. See N. C. Cofer, *Verbal Learning and Verbal Behavior* (New York: McGraw-Hill, 1961).

3. Lawrence R. Wheeless, "The Effects of Attitude, Credibility, and Homophily on Selective Exposure to Information," *Speech Monographs* 41 (1974): 329–38.

4. Charles R. Petrie, Jr. and Susan D. Carrel, "The Relationship of Motivation, Listening Capability, Initial Information, and Verbal Organization Ability to Lecture Comprehension and Retention," *Speech Monographs* 43 (1976): 187–94.

5. Petrie, "Informative Speaking," p. 80.

6. Carole Ernest, "Listening Comprehension as a Function of Type of Material and Rate of Presentation," *Speech Monographs* 35 (1968): 154–58. See also, John A. Baird, "The Effects of Speech Summaries upon Audience Comprehension of Expository Speeches of Varying Quality and Complexity," *Central States Speech Journal* 25 (1974): 119–27.

7. Charles R. Gruner, "The Effect of Humor in Dull and Interesting Informative Speeches," *Central States Speech Journal* 21 (1970): 160–66.

8. Petrie, "Informative Speaking," p. 84.

9. Charles O. Tucker, "An Application of Programmed Learning to Informative Speech," *Speech Monographs* 31 (1964): 142–52.

10. Petrie, "Informative Speaking," p. 81.

11. See O. L. Pence, "Emotionally Loaded Argument: Its Effectiveness in Stimulating Recall," *Quarterly Journal of Speech* 40 (1954): 272–76.

12. Baird, pp. 119–27 (see note 6).

13. David Ausubel, "The Use of Advance Organizers in the Learning and Retention of Meaningful Material," *Journal of Educational Psychology* 51 (1960): 267–72.

14. From a speech delivered by Mark Dupont in the honors section of Fundamentals of Public Speaking, Iowa State University. Used with permission.

15. John Kenneth Galbraith, "The Three Attacks on Social and Economic Consensus," *Des Moines Sunday Register,* 4 January 1981. Reprinted from an article in the *New York Review of Books.* Reprinted with permission.

16. From a speech manuscript submitted by Steven D. Shupp in Speech 312, Business and Professional Speaking, Iowa State University.

Chapter 18

1. Marvin Karlins and Herbert I. Abelson, *Persuasion: How Opinions and Attitudes Are Changed,* 2d ed. (New York: Springer, 1970).

2. Based on Gerald R. Miller, "On Being Persuaded: Some Basic Distinctions," in *Persuasion: New Directions in Theory and Research,* edited by Michael E. Roloff and Gerald R. Miller (Beverly Hills, Calif.: Sage, 1980).

3. Adapted from Wallace Fotheringham, *Perspectives on Persuasion* (Boston: Allyn and Bacon, 1966), p. 33.

4. Based on James V. McConnell, *Understanding Human Behavior: An Introduction to Psychology* (New York: Holt, Rinehart and Winston, 1977), pp. 243–51.

5. C. Hovland and H. Pritzker, "Extent of Opinion Change as a Function of Amount of Change Advocated," *Journal of Abnormal and Social Psychology* 54 (1957): 257–61.

6. Reprinted from Marvin Karlins and Herbert I. Abelson, *Persuasion: How Opinions and Attitudes Are Changed,* 2d ed., p. 35. Copyright 1970 by Springer Publishing Company, New York. Used by permission.

7. I. S. Janis and S. Feshbach, "Effects of Fear-Arousing Communications," *Journal of Abnormal and Social Psychology* 48 (1953): 78–92.

8. Fredric A. Powell, "The Effects of Anxiety-Arousing Messages When Related to Personal, Familial, and Impersonal Referents," *Speech Monographs* 32 (1965): 102–6.

9. Frances Cope and Don Richardson, "The Effects of Measuring Recommendations in a Fear-Arousing Speech," *Speech Monographs* 39 (1972): 148–50.

10. R. L. Rosnow and E. Robinson, *Experiments in Persuasion* (New York: Academic Press, 1967), pp. 99–104.

11. Karlins and Abelson, pp. 22–26.

12. Karlins and Abelson, pp. 22–26.

13. D. Sears and J. Freedman, "Effects of Expected Familiarity with Arguments upon Opinion Change and Selective Exposure," *Journal of Personality and Social Psychology* 2 (1965): 420–26.

14. For additional information on the uses and limits of argument, see Douglas Ehninger, "Argument as Method: Its Nature, Its Limitations, and Its Uses," *Speech Monographs* 37 (1970): 101–10.

15. Gerald R. Miller, "Evidence and Argument," in *Perspectives on Argument,* edited by Gerald R. Miller and Thomas R. Nilsen (Chicago: Scott, Foresman, 1966), p. 25. See also Robert P. Newman and Dale R. Newman, *Evidence* (Boston: Houghton Mifflin, 1969).

16. Erwin P. Bettinghaus, *The Nature of Proof,* 2d ed. (New York: Bobbs-Merrill, 1972), p. 135.

17. *Ibid,* pp. 137–38.

18. *Ibid,* p. 138.

19. From a persuasive speech delivered by Melanie Comito in the honors section of Fundamentals of Public Speaking, Iowa State University.

abstract Words or phrases not rooted in physical reality; less than a complete manuscript but includes all important points and supporting materials, for example, an outline.

active listening Involved listening with a purpose.

active participation Asking the audience to write, reply, or act in a certain way during the speech to demonstrate ideas, ascertain audience attitudes, or involve the audience in the topic.

active perception The view that people select the stimuli they receive.

adaptors Almost habitual nonverbal movements we use to help make ourselves feel more comfortable in communication interactions; examples include twisting a ring, stroking our face, or playing with cigarettes, cigars, or matches.

adoption Inducing an audience to accept a new idea, attitude, belief, or product and to demonstrate that acceptance by behavioral change; an action goal of the persuasive speech.

advance organizers Previews of the organization and idea development in a speech or written composition; a forewarning of what is to appear.

affect displays Movements of the face and body that hold emotional meaning; examples are banging our fist on the table to show anger or jumping up and down to show excitement.

affection The need to be cared for by others; one of the three basic interpersonal needs satisfied through interaction with others.

analogy A kind of supporting material in which the speaker compares or points out similarities between two things that are basically unalike, such as comparing the British and the American medical systems.

androgynous The term used to describe an individual who possesses both female and male traits.

antonym A word that means the opposite of another.

appointed leadership Leaders who are selected by someone outside the group, elected by the group members, or selected in some formal way.

arguments Propositions and proof or evidence used to persuade.

arousal Initiating and maintaining audience interest, focusing attention on the speaker, stating the specific purpose of the speech, and describing the speaker's qualifications; a function of the introduction.

articulation The production of sounds; a component of enunciation.

artifacts Ornaments or adornments we display and hold communicative potential; examples include jewelry, hairstyles, cosmetics, glasses, and automobiles.

assertiveness The ability to communicate our feelings, attitudes, and beliefs honestly and directly; a communication skill associated with positive self-concept.

attitude A predisposition to respond favorably or unfavorably to some person, object, idea, or event.

audience adaptation Adjusting the verbal and nonverbal elements of the speech on the basis of data derived from audience analysis.

audience analysis The collection and interpretation of data on the demographics, attitudes, values, and beliefs of the audience obtained by observation, inferences, questionnaires, or interviews.

audience interest The relevance and importance of the topic to an audience; sometimes related to the uniqueness of the topic.

audience knowledge The amount of information the audience already has about the topic.

autocratic leadership Leadership that exerts complete control over a group.

availability The access one has to one's friends.

avoiding The ninth stage of Knapp's relationship development model that is characterized by a reluctance to interact.

bargaining That which occurs when two parties attempt to reach an agreement as to what each should give and receive in a transaction between them; may be explicit and formal, or implicit and informal.

behavioral flexibility The ability to alter behavior in order to adapt to new situations and to relate in new ways when necessary.

behavioral purposes Actions a speaker seeks in an audience.

belief A conviction; often thought to be more enduring than an attitude and less enduring than a value.

believability The idea an argument has to go beyond logic and common sense; it must also be acceptable to an audience before it will be effective in a speech.

bibliography A list of written sources used in a speech.

blended family A family that consists of two adults with step-, adoptive, or foster children.

blind self The quadrant of the Johari Window that illustrates the proportion of information about ourselves known to others but not to us.

body The part of the speech that contains the arguments, evidence, and main content.

body of the interview The central part of the interview; comprises the most time of the three major interview divisions; during the body, the purpose of the interview is either achieved or not achieved.

bonding The fifth stage of Knapp's relationship development model where partners commit to each other.

boomerang effect Occurs when the audience's attitudes toward the speaker's position on a topic become more negative during the speech.

brainstorming Listing or naming as many ideas as a group or an individual can within a limited period of time.

brakelight function A function of a conclusion fulfilled by forewarning the audience the end of the speech is near; can be a word, phrase, sentence, gesture, or movement.

captive audience An audience that did not choose to hear a particular speaker or speech.

caring The attentive, thoughtful, and watchful quality of friendship.

cause-effect organization A method of organization in which the speaker first explains the causes of an event, problem, or issue, and then discusses its consequences.

channel The mode by which a message moves from the source of the message to the receiver of the message; both light waves and sound waves are major channels when we interact and can see and hear the other communicators.

circumscribing The seventh stage of Knapp's relationship development model marked by a decrease in interaction duration and depth.

clarify To make a message clearly understood by an audience.

classification The process of ordering stimuli into meaningful groups or classes by using language to identify similarities and ignore differences; abstraction.

clichés Words or phrases that have lost their effectiveness because of overuse; examples include, "Don't lose any sleep over it," "Give them an inch and they'll take a mile," "Watch him like a hawk," and "You can't take it with you."

closed questions Questions framed so the possible answers are specified or restricted.

closing of the interview The conclusion of the interview; its purpose is to create goodwill, to establish a positive atmosphere, and to clarify for the interviewee what will occur next.

closure The organization of stimuli so missing information in the original is filled in by the perceiver to provide the appearance of a complete unit or whole.

code Any systematic arrangement or comprehensive collection of symbols, letters, or words given arbitrary meanings and used for communication.

cohabiting couples Two unrelated adults who share living quarters, with or without children.

cohesiveness The sense of belonging or groupness.

colloquialisms Words and phrases used informally but not formally, such as, "Have a happy day," "Good to see you," "Take care now," "How you doin'?" and "See you."

commitment Individual dedication to a group because of interpersonal attraction, commonality, fulfillment, or reinforcement.

common ground The experience, ideas, or behavior the speaker shares with the audience.

communication Making common; the process of understanding and sharing meaning.

communication apprehension The generalized fear of communication, regardless of context.

communication networks The patterns of communication among members of a small group.

comparison A behavioral goal of the informative speech in which the audience weighs the relative values and characteristics of the speech or its uses of objects, events, or issues.

competence The degree to which the speaker is perceived as skilled, experienced, qualified, authoritative, and informed; an aspect of credibility.

complementary relationships Relationships in which each person supplies something the other person or persons lack; relationships based on differences rather than on similarities.

comprehension The understanding of the meaning of a message; sometimes tested by retention.

conclusion The last part of the speech; a summary of the major ideas designed to induce some mental or behavioral change in an audience.

concreteness Specificity of expression; using words that are not ambiguous or abstract.

confidentiality The quality of friendship that implies we can trust our friends with intimate information. They will not disclose information to others.

confirmation The feeling that occurs when others treat us in the manner that is consistent with our own notion of who we are.

connotative meaning Individualized or personalized meaning for a term; the emotional content of words.

consensus Complete agreement among group members and their support of group decisions.

content The evidence, illustrations, proof, arguments, and examples used to develop a speech topic.

continuance Persuading an audience to continue present behavior; an action goal of the persuasive speech.

contrast The comparison of unlike things.

control The need to influence others, our environment, and ourselves; one of the three basic interpersonal needs satisfied through interaction with others.

co-orientation The degree to which the speaker's values, beliefs, attitudes, and interests are shared with the audience; an aspect of credibility.

cost-benefit theory A theory of interpersonal relationships which suggests we alter our relationships with others on the basis of a consideration of the costs and benefits involved.

counterarguments Rebuttals to an argument.

couples with no children A family that consists of two adults with no children.

creative perception The view that meaning is imparted to stimuli by the perceiver, rather than being an inherent property of the thing perceived.

credibility The audience's perception of a speaker's competence, dynamism, trustworthiness, and co-orientation.

cultural differences The influence on perception of stimuli by the environments and situations imposed by the culture.

cultural role The pattern of behavior imposed upon a person who serves a particular function by the culture of which the person is part.

culture Groups or classes of people defined in terms of their heritage, traditions, social structure, and value systems.

dating A component skill of concreteness; identifying and stating when we made an inference or observation.

decoding To assign meaning to a verbal code we receive.

deductive arguments Arguments based on a major premise, a minor premise, and a conclusion, rather than on evidence.

defensiveness Protecting and supporting our ideas and attitudes against attack by others; induced by the feeling that the self and the validity of self-expression are threatened.

definition Revealing what something is through description, comparison, explanation, or illustration.

delivery of a speech Use of voice and body to communicate a message.

democratic leadership Leadership that exerts a balance of control and freedom over a group.

demographic analysis The collection and interpretation of data about the characteristics of people, excluding their attitudes, values, and beliefs.

denotative meaning An agreed-upon meaning of a word or phrase; a formal meaning determined by agreement within a society or culture.

descriptive feedback Describing to another person his or her nonverbal and verbal behavior; telling the other person our objective understanding of messages we are receiving.

descriptiveness The describing of observed behavior or phenomena instead of offering personal reactions or judgments.

deterrence Persuading an audience to avoid some activity; an action goal of the persuasive speech.

Dewey's method of reflective thinking A sequence of steps for organizing, defining, researching, and solving problems in groups.

diamond approach A method of organizing an interview that involves closed questions that become increasingly open and then become restrictive again.

differentiation The sixth stage of Knapp's relationship development model where partners emphasize their individual differences rather than their similarities.

disconfirmation The feeling that occurs when others fail to respond to our notion of self or when others respond in a neutral way.

discontinuance Inducing an audience to stop doing something; an action goal of the persuasive speech.

distinguish The ability of an audience to differentiate the characteristics of events or objects; a behavioral goal of the informative speech.

dual worker family A family that consists of two working adults.

dyadic communication Communication between two persons.

dynamism The degree to which the speaker is perceived as bold, active, energetic, strong, empathic, and assertive; an aspect of credibility.

eclectic approach An approach to leadership that combines all other approaches. Leadership is viewed as being based on traits, styles, situations, functions, power, organizational position, vision, and ethical assessment.

egocentrism The tendency to view ourselves as the center of any exchange or activity; an overconcern with the presentation of ourselves to others.

emblems Nonverbal behaviors that directly suggest words or phrases; frequently substitute for words, rather than accompany them.

emergent leadership A leader who is not officially elected or chosen, but whom the group identifies as a leader.

emotional appeals Persuading audience members to change an attitude or behavior through an appeal—usually in a narrative form—to their emotions.

empathy The ability to perceive another person's view of the world as though the view were our own.

employment interview An interview for the purpose of screening job applicants or hiring a person.

encoding To put an idea or thought into a code.

enunciation The pronunciation and articulation of sounds and words; an aspect of vocal delivery.

ethical approach An approach to leadership that builds upon the visionary approach. Leaders are ethical human beings who behave in accordance with the acceptable principles of right and wrong. Leadership involves ethical assessment, reflection, and action.

etymology The historical origins of a word.

euphemisms Inoffensive words or phrases that are substituted for words that are considered vulgar or that have unacceptable connotations; for example, *washroom* as a substitute for *toilet*.

evidence Anything that constitutes proof of a proposition.

examples Evidence consisting of illustrating by using specific instances.

experiential superiority The attitude our experiences are more important and valid than the experiences of others.

experimenting The second stage of Knapp's relationship development model where partners attempt to discover information about the other.

explanations Means of clarification by simplifying, amplifying, or restating.

extemporaneous mode A delivery style; the speech is carefully prepared and researched, but it appears to be spontaneous in its delivery.

extended family A family that includes not only parents and children but also grandparents, aunts, uncles, cousins, and/or others.

extrinsic motivation A method of making information relevant by providing the audience with reasons outside the speech itself for attending to the content of the speech.

eye contact The extent to which a speaker looks directly at the audience; an aspect of bodily delivery.

facial expression Use of the face to reinforce a message; an aspect of bodily delivery.

factual distractions The tendency to listen to facts rather than to main ideas; a barrier to listening.

family An organized, relational transactional group, usually occupying a common living space over an extended time period, and possessing a confluence of interpersonal images which evolve through the exchange of meaning over time.

family communication Communication within the family.

family satisfaction One's positive or negative assessment of one's family life.

fear appeals A strategy of the rhetoric of emotions that attempts to create anxiety in the audience and then offers reassurance the speaker's ideas will reduce the anxiety.

feedback The receiver's verbal and nonverbal responses to the source's messages; the responses must be received and understood by the source.

figure and ground The organization of perception so some stimuli are brought into focus while other stimuli form the background.

fluency The smoothness of delivery, the flow of words, and the absence of vocalized pauses; an aspect of vocal delivery.

forecast An overview of the speech's organization; occurs during the introduction or early in the body of the speech.

forum The forum occurs when audience members participate in a public discussion; a forum may follow a speech, a symposium, or a panel discussion.

friendship An interpersonal relationship between two persons that is mutually productive, established, and maintained through perceived mutual free choice, and characterized by mutual positive regard.

functional approach An approach to leadership that suggests leaders are made, rather than born, and views leadership as a composite of certain behaviors groups need to achieve their goals.

funnel approach A method of organizing an interview that involves broad, open questions at first, then becomes restrictive as more closed questions are asked, and finally concludes with very closed questions.

general semantics A field of study proposed by Alfred Korzybski that emphasizes improving human behavior through a more critical use of words and symbols.

gestures The movements of head, arms, and hands to illustrate, emphasize, or signal ideas in the speech; an aspect of bodily delivery.

Health communication Communication that occurs within the health care process.

hearing The physiological process by which sound is received by the ear.

heterogeneity The amount and variety of differences that exist between individual audience members.

hidden agenda When the underlying goal of the communication is different than the stated goal, the underlying goal is the hidden agenda.

hidden self The quadrant of the Johari Window that illustrates the proportion of information about ourselves that is known to us but not to others.

high communication apprehension The fear of communicating that is extreme for 10 to 20 percent of the population.

homogeneity The similarity between individual audience members.

honesty The truthful and open quality of friendship.

hourglass approach A method of organizing an interview that involves open questions that become increasingly restrictive and then become increasingly open.

illustrators Nonverbal behaviors that accompany verbal messages and reinforce them.

immediate purpose The short-range immediate goal the speaker wishes to achieve.

implications When we make an implication, we suggest or hint at a thought, rather than directly express an idea.

impromptu mode A delivery style; the speech is delivered without notes and without preparation.

inclusion The need to become involved with others; one of the three basic interpersonal needs satisfied through interaction with others.

indexing A component skill of concreteness; identifying the uniqueness of objects, events, and people and stating our observations and inferences are specific rather than generalizable.

inferences Conclusions drawn from observation.

inflection The patterns of alteration, or lack of alteration, in the pitch of a person's voice.

informational interview An interview for the purpose of collecting information, opinions, or data about a specific topic.

informational overload Occurs when the quantity or difficulty of the information presented is greater than the audience can assimilate within the given time.

information hunger The audience's need for the information contained in the speech.

information relevance The importance, novelty, and usefulness of the topic and the information; a factor in adapting an informative speech to an audience.

informative content The use of generalizations, simple and concrete words, humor, and statements about how the speech will meet audience needs; the propositions and evidence in a speech.

informative speech A speech whose purpose is to get audience members to understand, learn, or change their behavior.

inherent meaning The view that meaning is inherent in stimuli; hence, that perception is passive.

initiating The short beginning period of an interaction. This is the first stage of Knapp's model of relationship development.

integrating The fourth stage of Knapp's relationship development model where partners begin to mirror each other's behavior.

intensifying The third stage of Knapp's relationship development model where partners become more aware of each other and actively participate in the relationship.

interest A function of an introduction that enhances the audience's concentration on the subject matter.

interpersonal communication The process of sharing and understanding between ourselves and at least one other person.

interpersonal conflict An expressed struggle between at least two interdependent parties who perceive incompatible goals, scarce rewards, and interference from the other parties in achieving their goals.

interpersonal relationship The association of two or more people who are interdependent, who use some consistent patterns of interaction, and who have interacted for some period of time.

interpretation The assignment of meaning to stimuli.

interpretive listening Listening in which we attempt to perceive the other person's view of the world.

interpretive perception The view that perception is a blend of internal states and external stimuli.

interview Planned communication between two parties which has a predetermined purpose and involves the asking and answering of questions arranged in some order.

intimate distance The distance used with persons to whom we are emotionally close; extends from touch to eighteen inches.

intrapersonal communication The process of sharing and understanding within ourselves.

introduction The first part of the speech; its function is to arouse the audience and to lead into the main ideas presented in the body.

involvement The importance of the topic to the speaker; determined by the strength of the feelings the speaker has about the topic and the time and energy the speaker devotes to that subject area or topic.

jargon The technical language reserved by a special group or profession, such as physicians, educators, electricians, economists, and computer operators; examples of jargon include "angina," "duodenal," "dyadic interaction," "bytes," and "CPU."

Johari Window A model of self-disclosure that indicates the proportion of information about ourselves that is known and/or unknown to ourselves, others, and both.

justification All of the evidence that can be gathered in support of a proposition.

key-word outline An outline consisting of important words or phrases to remind the speaker of the content of the speech.

kinesics The study of bodily movements, including posture, gestures, and facial expressions.

laissez-faire **leadership** Leadership that exerts only minimal control on a group.

language distortion The use of ambiguous or misleading language for the purpose of confusing others.

leadership Verbal and nonverbal communication behavior that helps to clarify or achieve a group's goals; influence.

leading questions Questions that suggest the answer; a question worded so there is only one acceptable answer.

limiting the topic The process of reducing a general topic to a less abstract and more concrete topic.

listenability The degree to which sounds and meaning can be easily ascertained by listeners; closely related to comprehension.

listening The process of receiving and interpreting aural stimuli.

logical appeals Use of propositions and proofs to persuade an audience.

long-range goal The long-range effect the speaker hopes to have on the audience.

loyalty The faithful quality of a friendship.

main points The most important points in a speech; indicated by Roman numerals.

manipulation A controlled, planned communication for the purpose of influencing or controlling the behavior of others.

manuscript mode A delivery style; the speech is written and is read word for word.

marital satisfaction One's positive or negative assessment of one's marriage.

Maslow's hierarchy of needs A ranking order of physical, safety and security, social, esteem, and self-actualization needs; Maslow states lower-order needs must be satisfied before higher-order needs.

mean, or average The arithmetic sum of a series of numbers divided by the total number of items in the series.

meaning What we share and understand in the process of communication; that which is felt to be the significance of something; a more accurate and useful descriptor of the object of communication than the words *message* or *thought.*

median The midpoint in a series of numbers; the middle score.

member satisfaction The positive or negative evaluation of a group by its members.

memorized mode A delivery style; the speech is committed to memory either by rote or repeated delivery.

mental distractions Occur when we communicate with ourselves while we are engaged in communication with others; a barrier to listening.

message A unit containing verbal and nonverbal symbols, but in which meaning is not inherent.

mode The most frequently recurring number in a series of numbers.

modes of delivery Four styles of delivery that vary in the amount of preparation required and their degree of spontaneity; includes memorized, impromptu, manuscript, and extemporaneous modes.

Monroe motivated sequence An organizational pattern that includes five steps: attention, need, satisfaction, visualization, and action.

motivation Physical, psychological, and social reasons for why people behave the way they do.

movement The speaker's use of the entire body; an aspect of bodily delivery.

narration The oral presentation and interpretation of a story, description, or event; includes dramatic reading of prose or poetry.

negative self-disclosure Disclosure of information about ourselves that tends to decrease our esteem in the eyes of others.

neutrality Indifference to another person.

neutral questions Questions that do not suggest any particular or preferred response or direction.

noise Any interference in the encoding and decoding processes that lessens the fidelity of the message.

nonfluency Delivery characteristics, usually vocal, that break the smooth and fluid delivery of the speech and are judged negatively by the audience.

nonverbal code A code that consists of any symbols that are not words, including nonword vocalizations.

norms Unwritten rules of acceptable and unacceptable behavior in a group.

novel arguments New and original evidence or reasoning audience members have seldom or never heard; often has more impact than the repetition of familiar arguments.

nuclear families A family that consists of a breadwinning father, homemaking mother, and resident children.

objectics The study of the human use of clothing and other artifacts as nonverbal codes; object language.

objective perception The view of the perceiver as a nonevaluative recorder of stimuli.

observation Active observation of the behavior and characteristics of an audience.

obstacles The characteristics of the speaker, audience, topic, situation, or content of a speech that are likely to hamper the effectiveness of the presentation.

one-sided message Presentation of the arguments and evidence that support only the speaker's position on a persuasive topic; used when the audience is generally friendly, when the audience will hear only the speaker's position, or when the speaker is seeking immediate but temporary opinion change.

opening of the interview The introduction of the interview that sets the tone for the rest of the interview; the purposes of the opening are to introduce the two parties and to establish a cordial and warm atmosphere.

open questions Questions are broad in nature and generally unstructured in form that require a rather lengthy response.

open self The quadrant of the Johari Window that illustrates the proportion of information about ourselves that is known to ourselves and others.

operational definition A definition that consists of stating the process that results in the thing being defined; hence, a cake can be operationally defined by a recipe, a particular house by its blueprints, and a job by its job description.

organization The structuring of stimuli into meaningful units or wholes; as a form, the outline, structure, or design of a speech; as a function, the functions of the parts of the speech, how organization governs content.

organizational approach An approach to leadership that views leaders as those who hold leadership positions or roles in organizations.

organizational communication Communication that occurs within an organization.

organizational patterns Methods of arranging the contents of the speech, for example, problem-and-solution pattern.

outlining The most commonly used method of organizing a speech; a blueprint for the speech.

outlining symbols Roman numerals and Arabic capital letters and numerals to indicate subordination.

overt audience response The involvement of an audience with a topic through signalling or actual performance of a task.

panel A discussion among people who attempt to solve a problem or to make a policy decision; a panel generally includes one person whose job is to moderate the discussion.

paralanguage The vocal or physical aspects of delivery that accompany the language used.

parallel form The consistent use of complete sentences, clauses, phrases, or words in an outline.

paraphrasing Restating the other person's message by rephrasing the content or intent of the message.

passive participation The nonbehavioral involvement of the audience in a persuasive speech; cognitive change.

passive perception The view perceivers are mere recorders of stimuli.

pauses The absence of vocal sound used for dramatic effect, transition, or emphasis of ideas; an aspect of vocal delivery.

percentage The ratio or fraction of one hundred represented by a specific number; obtained by dividing the number by one hundred.

perception What a person sees, hears, smells, feels, or tastes; the process by which we come to understand the phenomena in the world.

perceptual constancy The invariable nature of the perception of a stimulus once it has been selected, organized, and interpreted by the perceiver.

performance appraisal interview An interview where one person evaluates the work of another.

personal distance The distance used most often in ordinary conversation; extends from eighteen inches to four feet.

personal inventories A speaker's surveys of his or her reading and viewing habits and behavior to discover what topics and subjects are of personal interest.

personal language The language of the individual, which varies slightly from the agreed-upon meanings because of past experiences and present conditions.

personal space The space between one person and another; the space a person controls that moves with the person.

persuasive speech A form of communication in which the speaker attempts to modify audience members' behavior by changing their perceptions, attitudes, beliefs, or values.

physical distractions Environmental stimuli that interfere with our focus on another person's message; a barrier to listening.

pitch The highness or lowness of a speaker's voice; technically, the frequency of sound made by the vocal cords; an aspect of vocal delivery.

plagiarism The use of someone else's ideas or words without permission.

positive self-disclosure The expression of information about ourselves that tends to increase our esteem in the eyes of others.

post hoc, ergo proptor hoc Confusing causation with correlation; "after this; therefore, because of this."

power approach An approach to leadership that views one's ability to influence as the determinant of leadership.

primary questions Questions asked in an interview to introduce a new topic or a new area of a topic under discussion.

primary research Firsthand research; the acquisition of information from personal experiences, interviews, surveys, questionnaires, or experiments.

problem-and-solution pattern A method of organization in which the speaker describes a problem and proposes a solution to that problem.

problem-solving discussion A discussion in which the nature and solution of a problem are determined.

process Action, change, exchange, and movement.

productivity The relative success the group has in completing a specific task.

projection The body's support of the voice that ensures that the most distant people in the room can hear what is said.

pronunciation The conformance of the speaker's production of words with agreed-upon rules about the sounds of vowels and consonants, and for syllabic emphasis.

proof Evidence offered in support of a proposition.

proposition A statement that asserts or proposes something.

proxemics The study of the human use of space and distance.

proximity The organization of stimuli into meaningful units or wholes according to their perceived physical or psychological distance from each other.

public communication The process of sharing and understanding between ourselves and a large number of other people.

public distance The distance used in public speaking situations; exceeds twelve feet.

pyramid approach A method of organizing an interview that involves tightly closed questions at first, gradually becomes more open, and concludes with broad, open questions.

quality The pleasant or unpleasant characteristics of a person's voice, including nasality, raspiness, and whininess; the timbre of the sounds produced by the vocal cords.

questionnaire A method of obtaining information about an audience by asking written questions about audience members' demographic characteristics or attitudes.

questions of fact Discussion questions that deal with truth and falsity; concern the occurrence, existence, or particular properties of something.

questions of policy Discussion questions that concern future action.

questions of value Discussion questions that require a judgment of good and bad.

range The highest and lowest numbers in a distribution.

rate The speed at which a speech is delivered, normally between 125 and 190 words per minute; an aspect of vocal delivery.

raw numbers Exact numbers cited in measures of population, production, and other measures of quantity.

reassurance Permitting an audience a means of avoiding the consequences of a fear appeal.

receiver The component of the communication process that receives the message.

recognition The ability of an audience to identify the presence or absence of characteristics, properties, or elements of objects and events; a behavioral goal of the informative speech.

red herring An irrelevancy introduced to distract from the main issue.

reducto ad absurdum Reducing an argument to a ridiculous extreme by demonstrating how the argument could be carried beyond the intention originally proposed.

redundancy Planned repetition of words, phrases, or ideas.

refutation The use of counterarguments, evidence, and proof to dispute the arguments of another person.

regionalisms Words or phrases specific to a particular region or part of the country; for example, the word *coke* in Texas is similar to the word *soda* in New York and is the same as the word *pop* in Indiana.

regulators Nonverbal behaviors that monitor or control the communication of another individual.

rejection The feeling that occurs when others treat us in a manner that is inconsistent with our self-definition.

relational deterioration The process by which relationships de-escalate.

relational development The process by which relationships grow. Many researchers believe this process is marked by information exchange.

relational maintenance The process by which couples attempt to keep their relationship at an acceptable level of intimacy.

reliability The credibility of the source of specific information or evidence.

rhetorical questions Questions asked by the speaker to stimulate an audience's thinking but to which no overt response is expected.

role Behavior expected by others because of the social category in which a person is placed.

roles in groups Patterns of behavior demonstrated by individual members of small groups.

rough draft The preliminary organization of the outline of a speech.

sample The people who received a questionnaire or were interviewed; a large sample is usually more useful, generalizable, and valid than a small sample.

Sapir-Whorf hypothesis The theory our perception of reality is determined by our thought processes and our thought processes are limited by our language; therefore, language shapes our perception of reality.

secondary questions Questions asked in an interview to follow up or develop a primary question.

secondary research Secondhand research; the acquisition of information from published sources.

selection Neglecting some stimuli in our environment to focus on other stimuli.

selective attention A focus on particular stimuli such that other stimuli are ignored.

selective retention The recollection of information after selection, organization, and interpretation have occurred; the mental categorization, storage, and retrieval of selected information.

self-awareness The ability to consciously distinguish between our self-image and our self-esteem.

self-concept Our consciousness of our total, essential, and particular being; composed of self-image and self-esteem.

self-consciousness An excessive concern about self-esteem.

self-control Our manipulative, strategic, and analytical responses to the demands and expectations of others and situations; unspontaneous self-expression.

self-disclosure Verbal and nonverbal statements we make about ourselves that are intentional and that the other person or persons are unlikely to know.

self-esteem Our attitudes and feelings toward our self-image; how well we like ourselves.

self-expression Our open, genuine, and spontaneous response to people and situations.

self-focus Developing a view of ourselves from our own perspective, rather than through the eyes of others; a preoccupation with thoughts about ourselves.

self-fulfilling prophecy The self-image and self-esteem expected of us by others; the tendency to become what others expect us to become.

self-image The sort of person we think we are; our own description of who we are and what we do.

self-improvement The strengthening of the awareness of self; the development of clear goals for ourselves; the development of self-esteem and self-expression.

semantic distractions Bits or units of information in the message that interfere with understanding the main ideas or the total meaning of the entire message; a barrier to listening.

semantics The study or science of meaning in language forms, especially with regard to historical change; the examination of the relationship between words and meaning.

sentence outline An outline consisting entirely of complete sentences.

shared activities The common events we engage in with friends.

sharing Interaction between ourselves and others, with the purpose of exchanging meaning.

significance The importance and meaningfulness of a speech to an audience.

signposts Ways in which a speaker signals to an audience where the speech is going.

similarity A basis for organizing stimuli into meaningful units by perceiving the similarities among them.

single-parent family A family that consists of one adult with adopted, natural, step-, or foster children.

situational approach An approach to leadership that suggests the interrelationship of the demands of the situation allows or disallows people success in leadership.

slang A specialized language of a group of people who share a common interest or belong to a similar subculture, such as teenagers, blacks, women, and members of the drug culture.

sleeper effect An increase in changes of opinion created by a speaker with little credibility; caused by the separation of the message content from its source over a period of time.

small group communication Communication that consists of a relatively small number of persons who have a mutually interdependent purpose and a sense of belonging, demonstrate behavior based on norms and values, use procedures accepted by the group, and interact orally.

social distance The distance used by people conducting business; extends from four feet to twelve feet.

social penetration theory A theory that explains how relationships develop and deteriorate through the exchange of intimate information.

source The component of the communication process that initiates a message.

spatial organization A method of organization in which the speaker explains by location in space; for example, the student who describes the instrument panel of a small airplane by moving from left to right across the instrument panel.

special pleading Making an argument while ignoring contrary evidence.

speech delivery The behavior of the speaker; the manner in which the verbal content of a message is enhanced or diminished by nonverbal vocal and physical behavior.

stagnating The eighth stage of Knapp's relationship development model that is marked by a lack of activity. Interaction during this stage is awkward and difficult.

statement The ability of an audience to verbally list the major ideas, reasons, or propositions of the speech; a behavioral goal of the informative speech.

statement of purpose A statement in which the speaker tells the audience what he or she wants the audience to do, learn, or understand.

statistics Numbers that summarize numerical information or compare quantities.

status The relative social position, reputation, or importance of another person.

status quo The way things currently are.

stereotypes Conventional, oversimplified generalizations about a group, event, or issue.

stereotyping The process of placing people and things into established categories, or of basing judgments about people or things on the categories into which they fit, rather than on their individual characteristics.

street language Words or phrases specific to one section of one city used by a group to demonstrate their unity.

strength of belief The stability and importance of a belief held by the audience; can be inferred from the responses of audience members to an attitudinal scale.

styles of leadership approach An approach to leadership that suggests if we examine the influential communication of an individual, patterns of behavior emerge that typify a particular leadership style, such as *laissez-faire,* democratic, or autocratic.

subculture Cultural subgroups differentiated by status, ethnic background, religion, or other factors.

subjective perception The view that perception is based on the physiological and psychological characteristics of the perceiver.

subordinate A point that is less important than another point in an outline.

subpoints Those points in a speech that support the main points; indicated by capital letters.

sub-subpoints Those points in a speech that support the subpoints; indicated by Arabic numbers.

supervisory leadership Leaders who exert considerable control with minimal freedom.

supporting materials Any information used to support an argument or idea.

surveys Studies in which a limited number of questions are answered by a sample of the population to discover opinions on issues.

symbol Something that stands for, or represents, something else by association, resemblance, or convention.

symbolic interactionism A theory that suggests the self develops through interplay or interaction with others.

symmetrical relationships Relationships between people who mirror each other or who are highly similar.

symposium A form of small group communication that does not allow for equal give-and-take among members, but does include a number of speeches oriented around a topic.

synonym A word that means approximately the same as another.

syntactics The study of how we put words together to form phrases and sentences.

systematic desensitization A therapy for reducing high communication apprehension by repeated exposure to small doses of whatever makes one apprehensive in a situation that is designed to reduce or eradicate the fear.

tactile communication Communicating by touch.

terminating The tenth and final stage of Knapp's relationship development model. At this stage the couple demonstrates both distance and disassociation. It's over.

territoriality The need to establish and maintain certain spaces of our own; the control of space that is typically immovable and separate from the person.

testimonial evidence Written or oral statements of the experience of people other than the speaker.

tests of evidence The methods for evaluating information based on the qualifications of the source, the recency of the information, the completeness and accuracy of the information, and the generalizability of the evidence.

thought The cognitive process by which meaning is assigned to our perceptions.

time-sequence pattern A method of organization in which the speaker explains a sequence of events.

topical-sequence pattern A method of organization in which the speaker emphasizes the major reasons why an audience should accept a certain point of view.

trait approach An approach to leadership that suggests leaders have certain personality traits or characteristics that allow them positions of leadership.

transactional view The view of communication that describes communicators as continually and unavoidably sending and receiving messages at the same time.

transitions Linkages between sections of the speech that help the speaker to move smoothly from one idea to another; principal transitions are forecasts, internal summaries, and statements of relationship.

trustworthiness The degree to which the speaker is perceived as honest, fair, sincere, honorable, friendly, and kind; an aspect of credibility.

tube approach A method of organizing an interview that involves questions that are generally either all closed or all open.

turning the tables Using the same evidence but with a different interpretation so it works against the original proposition.

uncertainty principle The principle that suggests that, when we initially meet others, we know little about them, and we rid ourselves of this uncertainty by drawing inferences from the physical data with which we are presented.

understanding The perception and comprehension of the meaning of incoming stimuli, usually the verbal and nonverbal behavior of others. The quality of friendship that shows our friends comprehend us.

unknown self The quadrant of the Johari Window that illustrates the proportion of information about ourselves that is unknown to ourselves and others.

valid Deductive argument that follows the rules for arranging the terms.

value A deeply rooted belief that governs our attitude about something; a goal rather than the means of reaching that goal.

verbal Anything associated with or pertaining to words.

verbal code A code that consists of words and their grammatical arrangement.

visionary approach An approach to leadership that views leaders as those who have imaginary insight or foresight into the future.

visual aids Any item that can be seen by an audience, for the purpose of reinforcing a message.

vocal cues All the oral aspects of sound except words themselves; part of paralanguage.

vocalized pauses Breaks in fluency; the use of meaningless words or sounds to fill in silences.

vocal variety Vocal quality, intonation patterns, inflections of pitch, and syllabic duration; a lack of sameness or repetitious patterns in vocal delivery; an aspect of vocal delivery.

volume The loudness or softness of a person's voice; an aspect of vocal delivery.

voluntary audience A collection of people who choose to listen to a particular speaker or speech.

words Verbal symbols by which we codify and share our perceptions of reality.

c r e d i t s

Chapter 13

Page 251: © Rich Rosenkoetter; **page 255 left:** © Janice Rogovii/The Picture Cube, Inc., **right:** © Patricia Fisher/Folio, Inc.

Chapter 14

Pages 265, 271: © David Strickler; **page 276:** © Alan Carey/The Image Works.

Chapter 15

Page 284: © Steve Takatsuno; **page 287:** © Mark Antman/The Image Works; **page 297:** © Paul Buddle.

Chapter 16

Page 310: © Gans/The Image Works; **page 314:** © Michael A. DiSpezio; **page 319:** © Alan Carey; **page 325:** © Michael A. DiSpezio; **page 329:** © Bryce Flynn/Picture Group, Inc.; **page 331:** © G. Cloyd/Taurus Photos, Inc.

Chapter 17

Pages 336, 339: © Mary Messenger; **page 341:** © William Hopkins; **page 343:** © Bob Coyle; **page 349:** © Michael A. DiSpezio.

Chapter 18

Page 362: © Art Stein/Photo Researchers, Inc.; **page 365:** © James L. Shaffer; **page 370:** © Howard Dratch/The Image Works.

index